Lecture Notes
in Business Information Processing   538

Series Editors

Wil van der Aalst ⓘ, *RWTH Aachen University, Aachen, Germany*
Sudha Ram ⓘ, *University of Arizona, Tucson, AZ, USA*
Michael Rosemann ⓘ, *Queensland University of Technology, Brisbane, QLD, Australia*
Clemens Szyperski, *Microsoft Research, Redmond, WA, USA*
Giancarlo Guizzardi ⓘ, *University of Twente, Enschede, The Netherlands*

LNBIP reports state-of-the-art results in areas related to business information systems and industrial application software development – timely, at a high level, and in both printed and electronic form.

The type of material published includes

- Proceedings (published in time for the respective event)
- Postproceedings (consisting of thoroughly revised and/or extended final papers)
- Other edited monographs (such as, for example, project reports or invited volumes)
- Tutorials (coherently integrated collections of lectures given at advanced courses, seminars, schools, etc.)
- Award-winning or exceptional theses

LNBIP is abstracted/indexed in DBLP, EI and Scopus. LNBIP volumes are also submitted for the inclusion in ISI Proceedings.

Elda Paja · Jelena Zdravkovic ·
Evangelia Kavakli · Janis Stirna
Editors

The Practice of Enterprise Modeling

17th IFIP Working Conference, PoEM 2024
Stockholm, Sweden, December 3–5, 2024
Proceedings

 Springer

Editors
Elda Paja
IT University of Copenhagen
Copenhagen, Denmark

Evangelia Kavakli
University of the Aegean
Mitilini, Greece

Jelena Zdravkovic
Stockholm University
Kista, Sweden

Janis Stirna
Stockholm University
Kista, Sweden

ISSN 1865-1348 ISSN 1865-1356 (electronic)
Lecture Notes in Business Information Processing
ISBN 978-3-031-77907-7 ISBN 978-3-031-77908-4 (eBook)
https://doi.org/10.1007/978-3-031-77908-4

© IFIP International Federation for Information Processing 2025, corrected publication 2025

This work is subject to copyright. All rights are solely and exclusively licensed by the Publisher, whether the whole or part of the material is concerned, specifically the rights of translation, reprinting, reuse of illustrations, recitation, broadcasting, reproduction on microfilms or in any other physical way, and transmission or information storage and retrieval, electronic adaptation, computer software, or by similar or dissimilar methodology now known or hereafter developed.
The use of general descriptive names, registered names, trademarks, service marks, etc. in this publication does not imply, even in the absence of a specific statement, that such names are exempt from the relevant protective laws and regulations and therefore free for general use.
The publisher, the authors and the editors are safe to assume that the advice and information in this book are believed to be true and accurate at the date of publication. Neither the publisher nor the authors or the editors give a warranty, expressed or implied, with respect to the material contained herein or for any errors or omissions that may have been made. The publisher remains neutral with regard to jurisdictional claims in published maps and institutional affiliations.

This Springer imprint is published by the registered company Springer Nature Switzerland AG
The registered company address is: Gewerbestrasse 11, 6330 Cham, Switzerland

If disposing of this product, please recycle the paper.

Preface

This volume of the Lecture Notes in Business Information Processing series contains the proceedings of the 17th IFIP 8.1 Working Conference on the Practice of Enterprise Modeling (PoEM), held in Stockholm, Sweden, during December 3rd to December 5th, 2024. The PoEM conference aims to improve understanding of topics related to the practice of *Enterprise Modeling* by offering a forum for sharing knowledge and future challenges between the academic community and practitioners from industry and the public sector.

This year, the theme of the conference was the use of *Enterprise Modeling* for system analysis and design to support Industry 5.0 and Society 5.0. At the core of fulfilling these visions are the adoption of a human-centric approach for digital technologies, alongside efforts in up-skilling and reskilling European workers, fostering modern, resource-efficient and sustainable industries, transitioning to a circular economy, as well as a globally competitive and world-leading industry, accelerating investment in research and innovation. All of these challenges require support for ensuring alignment between business and information technology. This congruence is essential for driving innovation, improving operational efficiency, and enabling businesses to adapt to evolving technological demands while maintaining competitiveness.

Enterprise Modeling with its related topics spanning from Conceptual Modeling and Ontologies to Enterprise Architecture, Requirements Engineering, and Enterprise Engineering is well positioned to support this effort by providing methods and tools for system development, as well as investigating and reporting both on the current state of research and the state of practice.

PoEM 2024 received 48 full paper submissions, with all submissions being in the scope of the conference and reviewed independently by at least three Program Committee (PC) members, in the single-blind form. The recommendations were discussed further by the program co-chairs, before final decisions were made. Following this process, 17 submissions were accepted in the end, resulting in a 35.4% acceptance rate. In addition, 6 submissions were invited for acceptance to the PoEM Forum.

As a tradition at PoEM, the conference program started with the Workshops, PoEM Forum, and Tool Demonstrations. We would like to thank all the Chairs of these events for their great effort and enrichment of the overall conference program. The main conference included sessions on research papers, keynotes, and a panel.

The accepted papers were grouped into the following topical sessions: *Enterprise Modeling for Digital Transformation and Industry Applications, Advances in Enterprise Modelling Techniques, Process Mining and Business Process Analysis*, and *Security, Compliance, and Configuration in Enterprise Modeling*.

The three invited keynote presentations were: (1) *"Accelerating Innovation: AstraZeneca's Digital Transformation Towards Industry 5.0"* by Anders Bergman, Digital Business Transformation Lead at AstraZeneca, Sweden; (2) *"Navigating the seas of Society 5.0"* by Dragoljub Nesic, CTO at Skippo, Sweden; and (3) *"Data Analytics in*

Industry 5.0 for Sustainable Business Practices" by Maribel Yasmina Santos, Professor in Information Systems at the University of Minho, Portugal. Speaking on behalf of our community, we are grateful to the keynote speakers for showcasing the significant impact of enterprise modeling research on our society yesterday, today, and tomorrow.

As the editors of this volume, we want to express our heartfelt thanks to all authors who submited their novel research results to the conference, and to the members of the Program Committee for their dedication and expertise in reviewing and discussing paper submissions. We are grateful to the Organizing Committee for arranging all aspects of preparing and running the conference, including its promotion, attracting submissions, administering conference information, designing the portal, communicating, and actioning any progress towards and throughout the conference. Finally, we warmly thank Stockholm University and the Department of Computer and Systems Sciences for hosting PoEM 2024.

December 2024

Elda Paja
Jelena Zdravkovic
Evangelia Kavakli
Janis Stirna

Organization

General Chairs

Evangelia Kavakli   University of the Aegean, Greece
Janis Stirna   Stockholm University, Sweden

Program Committee Chairs

Elda Paja   IT University of Copenhagen, Denmark
Jelena Zdravkovic   Stockholm University, Sweden

Steering Committee Chairs

Jolita Ralyté   University of Geneva, Switzerland
Kurt Sandkuhl   University of Rostock, Germany
Janis Stirna   Stockholm University, Sweden

Program Committee

Judith Albornoz   University of the Andes, Venezuela
Saïd Assar   Institut Mines-Télécom BS, France
João Paulo Almeida   Federal University of Espírito Santo, Brazil
Souvik Barat   Tata Consultancy Services Research, UK
Balbir Barn   Middlesex University London, UK
Dominik Bork   TU Wien, Austria
Robert Andrei Buchmann   Babeş-Bolyai University, Romania
Evellin Cardoso   Free University of Bozen-Bolzano, Italy
Tony Clark   Aston University, UK
Sybren De Kinderen   Eindhoven University of Technology, Netherlands
Michael Fellmann   University of Rostock, Germany
Hans-Georg Fill   University of Fribourg, Germany
Xavier Franch   Universitat Politècnica de Catalunya, Spain
Mohamad Gharib   University of Tartu, Estonia
Ana-Maria Ghiran   Babes-Bolyai University, Romania
Jaap Gordijn   Vrije Universiteit Amsterdam, Netherlands

Jānis Grabis	Riga Technical University, Latvia
Giancarlo Guizzardi	University of Twente, Netherlands
Simon Hacks	Stockholm University, Sweden
Martin Henkel	Stockholm University, Sweden
Stijn Hoppenbrouwers	HAN University of Applied Sciences, Netherlands
Jennifer Horkoff	Chalmers University of Technology, Sweden
Manfred Jeusfeld	University of Skövde, Sweden
Monika Kaczmarek-Heß	University of Duisburg-Essen, Germany
Kristos Kalloniatis	University of the Aegean, Greece
Konstantinos Kotis	University of the Aegean, Greece
Georgios Koutsopoulos	Stockholm University, Sweden
John Krogstie	NTNU, Norway
Ulrike Lechner	Universität der Bundeswehr München, Germany
Ginta Majore	Vidzeme University of Applied Sciences, Latvia
Beatriz Marin	Universidad Politécnica de Valencia, Spain
Raimundas Matulevicius	University of Tartu, Estonia
Andreas L. Opdahl	University of Bergen, Norway
Jose Ignacio Panach Navarrete	Universitat de València, Spain
Oscar Pastor	Universidad Politécnica de Valencia, Spain
Luca Piras	Middlesex University London, UK
Rūta Pirta	Riga Technical University, Latvia
Geert Poels	Ghent University, Belgium
Henderik A. Proper	TU Wien, Austria
Jolita Ralyté	University of Geneva, Switzerland
Iris Reinhartz-Berger	University of Haifa, Israel
Ben Roelens	Open University, UK
Marcela Ruiz	Zurich University of Applied Sciences, Switzerland
Irina Rychkova	Paris 1 Panthéon-Sorbonne University, France
Mattia Salnitri	Politecnico di Milano, Italy
Kurt Sandkuhl	University of Rostock, Germany
Maribel Y. Santos	University of Minho, Portugal
Estefanía Serral	KU Leuven, Belgium
Monique Snoeck	KU Leuven, Belgium
Pnina Soffer	University of Haifa, Israel
Stefan Strecker	University of Hagen, Germany
Yves Wautelet	KU Leuven, Belgium
Hans Weigand	Tilburg University, Germany
Robert Woitsch	BOC Products and Services, Austria

Additional Reviewers

Zahra Ahmadi — KU Leuven, Belgium
Vjatšeslav Antipenko — University of Tartu, Estonia
Sven Christ — University of Twente, Netherlands
Simon Curty — University of Fribourg, Switzerland
Diana Malakhova — Stockholm University, Sweden
Argyri Pattakou — University of the Aegean, Greece
Philip Winkler — Fern Universität in Hagen, Germany

Contents

Enterprise Modelling for Digital Transformation and Industry Applications

Enterprise Modelling Support for the Transition of Manufacturing Enterprises Towards Circular Economy 3
    Kurt Sandkuhl, Ulf Seigerroth, Dan Lennartsson, and Dag Raudberget

The Challenge of Digitally Improving a Nonprofit Associative Enterprise for the Occupational Risk Prevention of Healthcare Professionals 19
    Xavier Portell, Xavier Franch, and Joan Antoni Pastor

Fostering Digital Progression of Society: Exploratory Case Studies of Third Place for Services 35
    Jolita Ralyté and Michel Léonard

Using Enterprise Modeling for Dealing with Complexity of Elderly Care in Sweden 52
    Erik Perjons, Ilia Bider, and Martin Henkel

Evaluation of Categorization Patterns for Conceptual Modeling of IoT Applications 67
    Mathis Wyffels, Zahra Ahmadi, Estefanía Serral, Irene Vanderfeesten, and Monique Snoeck

Advances in Enterprise Modelling Techniques

SmartCML: A Visual Modeling Language to Enhance the Comprehensibility of Smart Contract Implementations 87
    Simon Curty and Hans-Georg Fill

Assessing Model Quality Using Large Language Models 105
    Anne Gutschmidt and Benjamin Nast

Grass-Root Enterprise Modelling: How Large Language Models Can Help 123
    Peter-Alexander Kolev, Hauke Hansen Pruss, Jim Robert Wilken, and Kurt Sandkuhl

Investigating the Effectiveness of Feedback-Driven Exercises on Deadlock Detection Skills in Conceptual Modelling 140
    Vlada Mekhryukova, Felix Cammaerts, and Monique Snoeck

Knowledge Graphs as a Scholarly Data Fabric: A Data Silo Transformation
Pipeline with Visualization Semantics 157
   Robert Andrei Buchmann and Ana-Maria Ghiran

Process Mining and Business Process Analysis

Enriching Business Process Event Logs with Multimodal Evidence 175
   Aleksandar Gavric, Dominik Bork, and Henderik A. Proper

Towards Timeline-Based Layout for Process Mining 192
   *Harleen Kaur, Jan Mendling, Timotheus Kampik,
   and Christoffer Rubensson*

Conceptualisation and (Meta)modelling of Problem-Solution Chains
in Early Business-IT Alignment and System Design 207
   Stijn Hoppenbrouwers, Mark A. T. Mulder, and Joris Sunnotel

Security, Compliance, and Configuration in Enterprise Modeling

SYMBOLEOAC: An Access Control Model for Legal Contracts 227
   *Sofana Alfuhaid, Amal Ahmed Anda, Daniel Amyot, Marco Roveri,
   and John Mylopoulos*

Functional Security in Automation: The FAST Approach 244
   Vjatšeslav Antipenko and Raimundas Matulevičius

Configuration of Software Product Lines Driven by the Softgoals:
The TEAEM Approach 262
   *Eddy Kiomba Kambilo, Nicolas Herbaut, Irina Rychkova,
   and Carine Souveyet*

The Dual Nature of Organizational Policies 279
   Hans Weigand, Paul Johannesson, and Giancarlo Guizzardi

Correction to: Towards Timeline-Based Layout for Process Mining C1
   *Harleen Kaur, Jan Mendling, Timotheus Kampik,
   and Christoffer Rubensson*

Author Index 295

Enterprise Modelling for Digital Transformation and Industry Applications

Enterprise Modelling Support for the Transition of Manufacturing Enterprises Towards Circular Economy

Kurt Sandkuhl[1,2(✉)], Ulf Seigerroth[1], Dan Lennartsson[1], and Dag Raudberget[1]

[1] Jönköping University, 55111 Jönköping, Sweden
{ulf.seigerroth,dan.lennartsson,dag.raudberget}@ju.se
[2] Rostock University, 18051 Rostock, Germany
kurt.sandkuhl@uni-rostock.de

Abstract. The circular economy (CE) is an economic philosophy aimed at eliminating waste and the continual use of resources. It emphasises designing products for longevity, reuse, and recycling to create a closed-loop system. One of the goals of enterprise modelling (EM) is to support enterprises in change processes from the current situation into a desired future state. In the context of the transition to the CE, the question arises if and how EM methods and languages must be adapted for the CE. The main contributions of this work are a better understanding of the challenges manufacturing enterprises face when preparing their product architectures for the circular economy, a meta-model preparing the product perspective in EM methods for CE, and an investigation of what changes are required in EM methods. The aim is also to identify necessary methodical and technological adaptations of EM for supporting the transition of enterprises to CE.

Keywords: Modularization · Enterprise Modelling · Circular Economy

1 Introduction

International initiatives to establish sustainability, like the European Union's "Green Deal[1]" and the United Nation's sustainability goals[2], and the related regulations have firmly positioned the circular economy on the strategic agenda of manufacturing enterprises as a concept to reach sustainability [2]. The circular economy (CE) is an economic philosophy aimed at eliminating waste and the continual use of resources [19]. It emphasises designing products for longevity, reuse, and recycling to create a closed-loop system. This contrasts with the traditional linear economy, which follows a "take, make, dispose" model. By focusing on resource efficiency, reducing environmental impact, and enhancing sustainability, the circular economy promotes the continuous use of materials and a reduction in resource extraction.

---

[1] https://commission.europa.eu/strategy-and-policy/priorities-2019-2024/european-green-deal_en.
[2] https://sdgs.un.org/goals.

Strategic considerations and economic opportunities motivate enterprises to explore CE-based value propositions and develop business models exploiting circularity. Such circular business models [4] align an enterprise's value proposition with the creation, delivery, and capturing of value by a focus on high-value and high-quality material cycles. In the development of circular business models, product design plays a fundamental role. If the fundamental approach for value creation and value capture changes, also the product design must change substantially. Products, services, and product-service systems (PSS) not designed for resource efficiency and reuse cannot stand as the basis for creating value in a circular business model [10].

One of the goals of enterprise modelling (EM) as a research discipline is to support enterprises in change processes by offering methods, tools and best practices to systematically support a transition from the current situation into a desired future state. In the context of the transition to the circular economy, the question arises if and how EM methods and languages must be adapted to support enterprises in the transition towards the circular economy. Most EM approaches are general purpose approaches that do not have a specific focus on a certain application case and, thus, can also be applied for preparing the transition to the circular economy. However, the specific importance of changing product designs motivates a more detailed analysis of product modelling as part of EM, which is of particular importance for manufacturing enterprises. The paper investigates how to adapt EM to support the transition to CE, specifically focusing on product modelling.

Starting from a case study, we aim to better understand what adaptations are required in EM for CE-focused projects. The case study shows an increased need for supporting product modularisation, which must encompass products, services and product-service systems. We argue that it is essential to treat this modularisation as an integral part of enterprise models, to understand what modules motivate certain CE-related goals, what product-service packages depend on certain business processes, what product parts have to be designed for easy replacement or refurbishment, and other dependencies to perspectives of the enterprise model. To implement the increased modularisation support, we propose a meta-model and its integration with other perspectives for enterprise models. The main contributions of this work are a better understanding of the challenges manufacturing enterprises face when preparing their product architectures for the circular economy, a meta-model preparing the product perspective in EM methods for CE, and an investigation what changes are required in EM methods. The aim is also to identify necessary methodical and technological adaptations of EM for supporting the transition of these enterprises to CE.

The remainder of this paper is structured as follows: Sect. 2 presents relevant background from product development for the circular economy and EM. Section 3 summarises the research methods applied in our work. Section 4 presents a case study to explore challenges in industrial practice when transforming products for the CE. Observations from the case study motivate the development of a meta-model for product/service modelling in Sect. 5. Section 6 investigates the required changes in EM methods to support the transition to the CE.

2 Theoretical Background

This section briefly summarises the theoretical background for our work from product development for the circular economy (Sect. 2.1) and product modelling as part of EM (Sect. 2.2).

2.1 Product Development for the Circular Economy

The circular economy is an economic philosophy aimed at the continual use of resources that motivates designing products for longevity, reuse, and recycling to create a closed-loop system. To prepare for the circular economy, manufacturing enterprises need to adopt several key changes in their products with the objective of promoting sustainability and resource efficiency [10]:

- Modular product design: products should be designed to last longer, using robust materials and construction techniques to reduce the need for frequent replacements. Modular product design with interchangeable and easily replaceable parts to facilitate repairs and upgrades can support this goal of durability and longevity. In this context, design for disassembly is important, i.e., to ensure products can be easily taken apart to separate different materials for recycling and repurposing.
- Product-as-a-Service Models: Shift from selling products to offering them as services, where the manufacturer retains ownership and responsibility for maintenance, repair, and eventual recycling.
- Eco-friendly and recyclable materials: Utilization of sustainable, non-toxic materials that have a lower environmental impact during production and disposal. In this context, materials should be prioritised that can be easily recycled at the end of the product's life cycle, reducing waste and resource extraction. Furthermore, waste minimisation in manufacturing processes by optimising resource use has to be achieved.
- Closed-Loop Supply Chains: Establish systems to take back used products, refurbish them, and reintroduce them into the market, creating a closed-loop system.

From a product development perspective, sustainable and modular product architectures and product-service-systems contribute to the above key changes.

Developing a sustainable product architecture requires the identification of modules, the design of individual modules and combining modules into a specific product variant. From a lifecycle perspective, modularisation facilitates a rapid creation of new product variants [8] which significantly reduces the time and resources required to develop new products as well as their corresponding manufacturing systems [9]. A critical step in modularisation is the specification of interfaces between interacting modules [20]. The importance of interfaces throughout the entire product lifecycle is further emphasised by Blees et al. [1]. Here, the interfaces are considered as enablers for ensuring that manufacturing, recycling, and supplier interaction are consistent within a product family. Moreover, interfaces must be purposely designed and managed considering the complete product life cycle [13].

Interfaces are also necessary for integrating products with the services that accompany them or are enabled by the product in a product-service system. Various techniques and technologies have been identified to implement this. Development methods for cyber-physical systems (CPS) are particularly relevant for integrating physical products with IT components and services. An overview of methodologies in this area is provided in [6]. The primary conclusion of this overview paper is the necessity to distinguish between the conceptual design phase and the system design phase. In both phases, the modelling of physical processes, computation, and the integration of physical processes with computation is essential, requiring modelling approaches from the participating disciplines. From an information system (IS) perspective, the IT component can be viewed as a specific category of information systems. Consequently, methods for IS development can be regarded as contributing to the development of product-service systems.

2.2 Product Modelling in Enterprise Modelling

EM addresses the "systematic analysis and modelling of processes, organisation structures, product structures, IT systems or any other perspective relevant for the modelling purpose" [21]. EM is meant to support organisations in coping with a broad range of challenges, including managing organisational change in dynamic market environments. Many EM approaches use multiple perspectives when analysing an organisation's current situation or designing the future situation [3]. The motivation for multiple perspectives, in general, is to reduce the complexity of the modelling process and to improve the manageability of the resulting enterprise model.

From an economic viewpoint, the purpose of an enterprise is commonly the creation of value for its customers and profits for its owners by providing defined products or services. Given the importance of products and services for an enterprise, EM languages can be expected to offer modelling constructs for representing the product/service information relevant to a given modelling purpose. However, only a few EM languages offer explicit concepts for product and service modelling or a product perspective, such as AKM [14] and 4EM [18]. A detailed analysis of product modelling as part of EM is provided in [15].

Much of the product information captured in enterprise models is relevant for strategic or operational activities in an enterprise. An example is product innovation: enterprises usually assign the responsibility for certain products, their components or variants to organizational roles. When new products or variants are introduced, the responsibility may have to change, which can also impact accountability or responsibilities for the product-related processes.

3 Research Method

The main objective of this research is to contribute to a better understanding of the challenges manufacturing enterprises face when preparing their product architectures for the circular economy. The long-term aim is to adapt the methodical and technological EM to support the transition of these enterprises to CE. The project follows the paradigm of design science research (DSR). The overall research question (RQ) for this paper is: *How do enterprise modelling languages have to be adapted to support product development in manufacturing enterprises in the transition towards the circular economy?*

DSR is a research paradigm aiming at problem-solving in organisational settings, focusing on developing valid and reliable knowledge for designing the required solutions [7]. DSR research projects typically consist of several phases and require the use of different research methods depending on the DSR phase and intended design solution. Table 1 provides an overview of the different DSR phases and their results. The table is organised along the phases of the DSR process and contains the research methods applied or envisioned and the results achieved or planned. This paper concerns the first phases of a DSR project: problem investigation, requirements definition, and initial design of the envisioned artefact, which in our project is methodical and technological support for CE-centric EM.

Table 1. Research activities performed in DSR phases and their results

DSR Phase	Research method	Result
Problem Investigation	Literature analysis to identify relevant scientific work	Lack of work on effects of CE on EM methods (Sect. 2.2 and [12])
	Case study on adaptation of product modularization to CE	Confirmed business relevance (Sect. 4)
Define Requirements	Argumentative-deductive work to derive requirements from results of problem investigation	Requirements to adaptation of EM methods (Sect. 4.3) and [12]
Design and evaluate Artefact	Conceptual-deductive work on meta-model for CE-centric EM	Initial version (Sect. 5)
	More iterations and case studies on method and tool design & eval	Future work
Demonstrate	Case studies: application of the CE-centric EM	Future work
Evaluate Artefact	Evaluation of CE-centric EM method and tools by CE and EM experts	Future work

Among the basic principles of DSR is the need to consider the relevance of the research that is expressed in business needs and rigorous evaluation of the research results against the existing scientific knowledge base. In problem investigation, we acknowledge the regulatory demand to advance the product manufacturing industries towards CE. In this context and with a focus on product development it is evident that the traditional EM methods need to be extended. The relevance of this need has been proven through several case studies; one of them is presented in Sect. 4. This industrial case is analysed to demonstrate business relevance and extract initial requirements for the envisioned method and tool support. Existing work on product modelling in the scientific knowledge base is summarised in Sect. 2.2. In this context, the state of research in product modularisation is also relevant and was analysed in previous work [12]. Furthermore, we use the case study for a feasibility study on the possibility of designing a CE-prepared modular product architecture. This feasibility study is based on conceptual-deductive work.

Case Study Research
Yin differentiates various kinds of case studies [22]: explanatory, exploratory and descriptive. The case study presented in Sect. 4 has to be considered descriptive, as it describes the phenomenon of adaptation of product design and modularisation to CE and the real-life context in which it occurs. Based on the case study results, we conclude that there is a need to adapt EM methods to support the transition to CE better. The research question for the case study is RQ-CS "What challenges do enterprises experience in preparing the transition of their product modularisation to CE in industrial practice?".

Conceptual-Deductive Research
The basic principle of conceptual-deductive research is applying theoretical concepts to empirical data in order to gain new insights in the research field. In this paper, we apply concepts from product modularisation to the structures of enterprise models in order to incorporate the required concepts for cross-domain modularisation that supports CE. The motivation is to enable product architectures with different kinds of modules and even product-service module compositions. The result can be considered as input to the first design & evaluate phase for the envisioned DSR artefact, the methodical and technological support for CE-centric EM.

4 Case Study: Modular Product Design

The subject of the case study is a company from Sweden offering technical solutions for trains. The product in focus of the case study is a redesign of a train coupler for the CE due to changes in customer and market requirements. Two of the authors of this paper actively participated in redesign projects that aimed at introducing a new manufacturing strategy in the enterprise, preparing for easy interchangeability of product parts and components. In this project, the product architecture was redesigned, which is the focus of this case description. The case study resulted in material sufficiently rich to be analysed in a scientific paper: we collected documents, minutes of meetings and interviews with company representatives, field notes taken when working with the companies, models of processes, information structures and business models, and other relevant information. This material concerns the situation before starting the modularisation process, the intermediate steps taken and the situation at the end of the project. The section starts with a description of the modularisation process (Sect. 4.1), followed by the current modularisation and interface design (Sect. 4.2) and observations (Sect. 4.3).

4.1 Modularisation Process of Train Coupler

The first phase of the modularisation process was scoping and business case development. This phase aimed to develop an understanding of the financial potential of modularisation and to find a suitable strategy based on the three aspects of operational excellence, customer intimacy and product leadership. The potential of a modularization initiative was calculated by proposing initial modularisation metrics and project goals based on reviewing the current product offering, market challenges and development towards CE. Conventional economic metrics, such as the return on investment, were derived from a value map [11]. Modularization-specific goals were used as input to the value map based on company-specific requirements. These requirements were manifested through costs for the current product structure, such as cost per part number, number of parts currently in use, number of new parts introduced, production volumes, number of customers and markets, etc. Important goals are shown in Table 2.

Table 2. Business goals and results from modularization

Aspect	Business Goal	Train Coupler
Operational excellence	Shorter Time to Customer	From 40 weeks to 12 weeks
	Increased reuse of development resources	70% reduction of development hours
Product leadership	New technologies	Double acting damper, Internet in cables, Green buffer
	More interchangeable parts	50% increase
	Increased reuse of components	50% reduction of article numbers
Customer intimacy	More product variants	4000 New products
	Increased customer satisfaction	No problems in the field

The second phase was the module concept development executed according to the Module Function Deployment Framework (MFD), which consists of several methods aligned with the company's specific needs. The starting point was to define customer segments and their needs through a simplified Quality Function Deployment (QFD). Using QFD, the desired product properties were defined for the product architecture and connected to the customer requirements in a matrix. This cross-functional approach involved different roles: product management, R&D, purchasing, production and quality departments.

The next activity was to create a Design Property Matrix that connected components and functions to product properties. When new technologies were introduced, the required functions were identified through a function-driven decomposition, and for mature technologies, the component functions were already known. At this stage, previous problems from the field were also addressed to increase product quality.

The modules were then integrated into a product architecture by combining technical solutions into modules in the Module Indicator Matrix and the dendrogram. In this phase, it was important to consider the characteristics of each module, e.g. to identify the interaction relations between modules. For example, it was important to avoid combining module characteristics that pull in opposite directions, such as combining a common unit in a module that requires high variability. A common unit was reused as a carry-over to new projects.

Finally, we moved on to the Design Property Matrix and Module Indicator Matrix to continue the modularisation. The result of the Design Property Matrix and the Module Indicator Matrix was a proposed modular concept for architecture that was iteratively refined with detailed design and interface design. Now, the number of articles, modules and product variants could be calculated together with the corresponding inventory level to compare this with the current situation and the project goals. Moreover, the properties for all modules, including new technologies, were quantified in order to be measurable and possible to use in the detailed design. For example, the goal of "no problems in the field" was solved by a major re-design. In this case, the project risks were handled by keeping the same/compatible interfaces and keeping the old solution as a backup.

4.2 Module and Interface Design

Part of the modular concept, the centre section, with goal values and interfaces, is presented in the figure below.

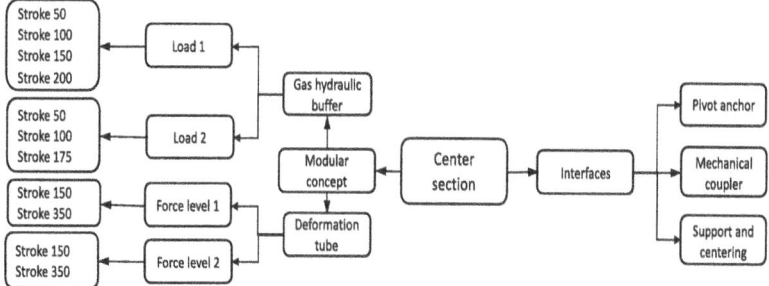

Fig. 1. Module concept and interface concept for center section

In a modular design, creating both a detailed design of the artefact (i.e., a module or component) and an interface design is mandatory. The attachment, interface, and module design were done in parallel for the module center section. The interfaces were documented separately, which was important to facilitate sufficient reuse of modules to reach the modularization goals. In the analysis of all interfaces, it had to be clear what modules that were reused and what modules that were new. Here, it was important to consider if a new module presented any risks and if an old solution had to be kept as a backup. In this case, interfaces had to be compatible between both designs.

A separate interface requirement specification was used to describe geometric interface design, tolerances and non-geometric properties, such as the required tension in the fasteners and the properties used for detailed design. In this case, the interface must handle the torque, bending moment, and buff load. The center section is modularized in two performance levels that handle different force levels.

Metrics such as, the number of products, number of module variants and number of articles were carried over from the module concept taking into consideration the result from the detailed design. A redesign may have to be done to achieve the modularization goals. Thereby, most modules are configurable, combined with the design of new modules to fit each customer.

4.3 Observations

When participating in the case study, we made several observations indicating challenges in the modularisation project when preparing for CE:

- Enterprise-level goals concerning the circular economy exist. Their implementation is planned via changes in the QFD. Effects on the current module structure are evaluated by the product owners based on their experiences but are not visualised.
- The established product architectures, including their modularisation and interfaces, must be modified to prepare for the circular economy. Products must be designed in a way that allows easy refurbishment, replacement and exchange of parts.
- The visualisation of the module structure does not follow defined modelling language; rather, it is a drawing. To use this modularisation for knowledge management, export of interface definitions to requirements management systems, etc., is not possible
- Many module variants and product variants exist. However, what exactly the differences are, and their reciprocal dependencies are only visible in the QFD (Excel file)
- Relationships between product architectures and processes and roles are not documented at all. Processes are captured in the quality management documentation, but in this documentation, there is no explicit relation to product modularisation.
- Services accompanying the product use gain importance for ensuring circularity. Such services include various potential offerings, from traditional (predictive or preventive) maintenance to continuous monitoring, tracking and operating the product.
- The case study enterprise faces the challenge of including various professions and engineering disciplines in the product lifecycle to develop a viable modularisation

5 Circular Economy-Aware Product Modelling in EM

The observations in the case study expose several shortcomings that can be addressed by using techniques from EM. The most obvious ones are the missing connection between goals, processes, and product/service structures, as well as the missing visualization of dependencies and interrelations between products, modules, components, and their variants. The possibility of EM to capture multiple perspectives in one model, to capture mutual dependencies between the perspectives and to prepare process and product innovations can support remedying these shortcomings. The transition to CE does not cause these shortcomings but amplifies the importance to be able to handle them. The transition to CE increases the complexity of product architectures to facilitate the interchangeability of modules/components and leads to the need for services accompanying the products. This is visible in the decision of the case study company to integrate "green buffers" in the train coupler as one step towards CE, which is briefly introduced in Sect. 5.1.

To address the above shortcomings, we propose to extend the product/services perspective of enterprise models to capture the variability and dependencies between products, modules, and components and integrate this extended product/service architecture into EM methods. As a starting point, Sect. 5.2 presents the meta-model for an extended product/service model, and Sect. 5.3 validates this meta-model based on the CE extension of the train coupler discussed in Sect. 5.1. The integration of the extended product/service perspective into EM methods is tackled in Sect. 6.

5.1 Circular Economy-Related Changes in Product Design

While preparing the product design for the CE, the case study company decided to modify the module structure (see Fig. 1) for better interchangeability of components and, at the same time, integrate new product features that allow for monitoring the product status and protecting the coaches. The latter is achieved by integrating the "green buffer" solution.

Green Buffer is an add-on system for train couplers. It is designed to absorb the energy between train carriages in the case of a collision. It solves the problem with coupling links between carriages that cannot manage the dynamic energy where the front and the first following coaches absorb almost all the energy. This commonly leads to derailing and unnecessary structural damage. From a circular perspective, the life cycle of the couplers and the train increases when the absorbers are consumed to prevent damage. They, therefore, need to be replaced, and the interfaces are designed for disassembly through interchangeable and easily replaceable modules. The products are supported by an IT infrastructure that can monitor the damages and support the repair process.

All components are adapted to the specific train coupler specifications and are also part of a Cyber-Physical system with a unique identity that facilitates traceability and replacement of correct spare parts and correct recycling of the high-strength steel.

Starting with the QFD, the definition of customer requirements is based on the train coupler requirements given in [12], with added requirements for energy absorption. One class of requirements that emerged was the ability to assess the deformation of the energy absorbers and transmit this data to evaluate the crash severity. This required new modules and IT support to be developed, starting with the interface strategy and development. Here, the starting point is to identify the technical solutions in the interface between the modules, which is challenging when working with different suppliers having different interfaces in their existing train couplers. The interface properties and interface drivers will determine how many interfaces are needed for the specific module. It is vital to create as few interfaces as possible [13].

The module system consists of mechanical, electronic and data modules in different module variants that enable the configuration of different product variants to suit different train weights and customers, in this case, Wabtec Faiveley, Dellner Couplers, etc. The product variants include the Green Buffer Energy Dissipation system and may also include the Green Buffer Data Service or the Green Buffer Predictive Maintenance Service. Specific module variants are classified into product families that are adapted to the specifications given by different manufacturers of train couplers and the requirements of the train builders.

5.2 Meta-model for Extended Product/Service Modelling

As already explained in the introduction to this section, we propose to extend the product perspective in EM to include more details of the product architecture. In particular, the connection to the enterprise goals, the module, and product variants offering CE-relevant features and services that enhance the product offering must be represented. The starting point for this extension is a meta-model defining and integrating the required concepts and their relationships. The proposed meta-model shown in Fig. 2 extends earlier work on product modelling [17] and is modelled as a UML class diagram. It consists of four core sections:

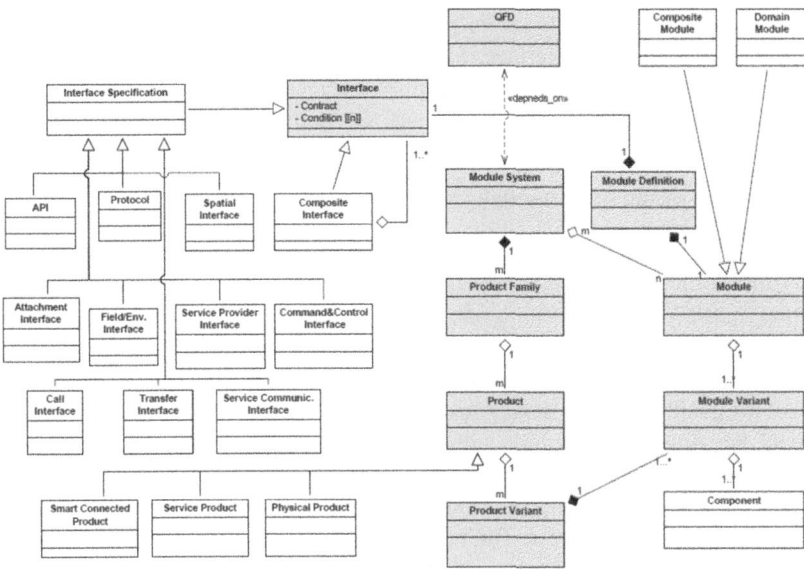

Fig. 2. Meta-model for representing CE related product and service composition

- The enterprise goals, the customer requirements, and how they are related to product features, variants, and modules are represented by the QFD class, which represents the results of the quality function deployment (see Sect. 4.1).
- The product architecture is visible as product family, including different products and their variants. Physical products, service products and smart connected products are distinguished.
- The modules used for the product family form a module system consisting of different modules and their variants. Each module also has a module definition that captures the dependencies between the interfaces. Modules can be defined for a single application domain or combined into composite modules.
- Interfaces of modules are represented as separate classes to represent the different kinds of interfaces (e.g., spatial, attachment or field environment interfaces of physical products) that different modules need to have.

It should be noted that – for the application in product modularization of industrial enterprises – the core terms of the meta-model are product, module and interface. Conceptually, a product consists of modules. As the same product can have different configurations (for example, for different customer groups), the concept of product variant is included. Product variants are composed of module variants; module variants represent the configuration of modules in a product variant. Module is represented as a concept that includes a module definition and can be specialized into module types. Thus, specific module types for domains (physical products, services or information systems) and composite modules can be defined. In the meta-model, interface is an abstract concept that needs specialization via interface specification to define different interface types such as API, call, and protocol for IT modules; command & control, field/environment, spatial, transfer and use interfaces for physical product modules; and service provider and service communication interfaces for service modules. Interface is related to module types via the concept of module definition.

The meta-model classes coloured grey are the focus of the next section.

5.3 Validation of the Meta-model

The case study's extension of the train coupler described in Sect. 5.1 offers the opportunity to validate the meta-model by instantiating it for the case study. Figure 3 shows this instantiation as a UML model for a selected part of the train coupler, the centre section (see also Fig. 1). We added small round labels to ease explanation of the model. The *QFD CE Version* (label: a) is the adapted QFD for the CE extension and captures the results of the quality function deployment process described in the case study section. In the model, we show only one product of the *train coupler family*, the actual *train coupler* (b) with its two specialisations, the physical product *"train coupler"* (1) and the smart connected product *"connected train coupler"* (2). Both have variants which are required by different train manufacturers. The module system *TC modules* consists of different modules, but Fig. 3 only shows on the *Center Section module* (c). This module consists of four modules ((A), (B), (C) and (D)) that have different variants. As compared to the module structure before preparing for CE, this extended one includes two new modules ((C) and (D)) that represent the *physical green buffer* and the *condition monitor*. Figure 3 also shows the four components of the two module variants for the *condition monitor*. What module variant is required for which product variant is captured by the relationships between the different instances.

The green buffer improves the longevity of the train coupler by indicating (via the condition monitor) when to do maintenance for the centre part and by improving the possibilities of how to exchange it, i.e., interchangeability of components is improved, and new features are added. It also improves the longevity of the train by protecting the coaches in case of collisions by reducing damages.

In the instantiation of the meta-model, it becomes quite clear that to move towards a more CE-friendly product lifecycle, it will be important to have capabilities to manage the modularisation of smart connected products (Green Buffer) and where the smart products have the capabilities for condition monitoring, both as modules and interfaces between modules. In the context of enterprise modeling methods this means that there is a need for a method component that can handle this extended product perspective.

6 Implications of Meta-model Use for Enterprise Modelling Methods

Although we put much emphasis on the product model in Sect. 5, the case study made clear that a transition towards CE does not only have effects on the product architecture but substantial parts of the enterprise. When changing the product composition towards better interchangeability of components or introducing new services, the business and production processes have to be adapted, changes in the organisation structure made (e.g., responsible roles and organisation units for the new services), new suppliers are

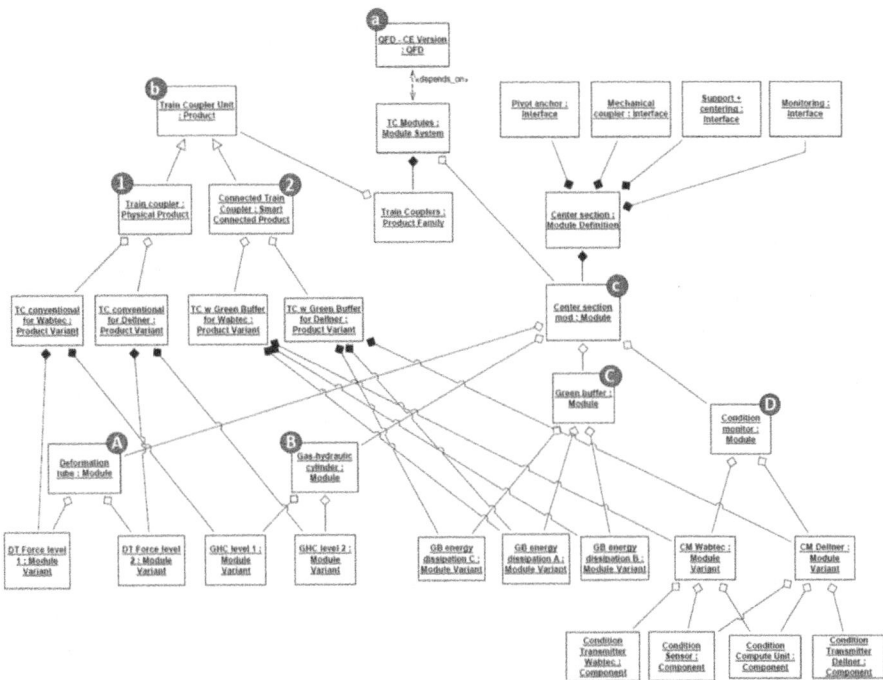

Fig. 3. Instantiation of the meta-model for the train coupler including green buffer (excerpt)

required, and the integration of company and product strategy has to be made explicit. Thus, integration into EM methods to support this transition is recommendable. In the case study, an important activity in this transition is the QFD process that leads to adaptation of product architecture. QFD, as such, is also a methodical procedure that could be considered an additional step in EM, such as a method extension.

In our view of methods, we rely on [5], that methods are supposed to give explicitly formulated guidance for actions that can be followed to achieve certain results; in our case, results for CE-centred product and service composition. Goldkuhl et al. [5] state that a method is composed of the following constituents:

Method components include n*otation* (rules for documentation and representation), *procedural guidelines* (guidelines for how to model a certain domain or focal area), and *concepts (*bridging glue between procedural guidelines and notation). In this case, the concepts for product modelling are represented in the meta-model in Fig. 2. Method components are supposed to give focus to an engineering activity by addressing a focal area, CE related product and service composition. A compound of method components together forms a structure that Goldkuhl et al. [5] refer to as a *framework*. A framework is a phase structure that gives instructions for what to do, in what order to do things and what results to produce, but not *how* to do things [16]. All methods are based on some foundations or *perspectives* that define the essence of the method. The perspective includes values, principles and categories manifested in the method and its method components, in this case, an extended product theory that covers CE-related product and service composition. The constituents of an extended product theory are manifested through the meta-model in Fig. 2 above. Different people interact and cooperate when performing method-guided work when a method component is used. This is what is referred to as *collection and cooperation principles* [5].

From the observations in the case study and the experiences in applying the meta-model, it is possible to derive implications for EM methods that we structure along the above-discussed method conceptualisation:

- To capture changes in the product architecture is essential for supporting the transition to CE. Thus, EM methods to be used for this purpose have to include the possibility to model products and services, which is not the case in all EM methods (see [15] for an overview). Methods without a product perspective would need a new method component; methods with a product perspective might benefit from the possibility of modelling variants and interfaces, as proposed in our meta-model.
- EM methods should allow for the definition of method components cross-cutting the traditional EM perspectives, for example, to enable the definition of QFD method components as a combination of business process, goal and product modelling.
- For the modelling procedure expressed in the framework, our impression is that flexibility has to be a key feature of methods supporting CE transition. In some enterprises, the target-setting process for the CE requires goal modelling and product modelling in several cycles for checking feasibility; in other enterprises, product models are well-elaborated, which eases target setting and puts more emphasis on activities for production optimisation – to name only two examples. EM methods must allow for situational adaptation to individual needs.
- The general composition of modelling teams with domain experts and method experts as main elements can be seen as suitable, but the need for CE and QFD experts has to be observed when selecting the domain experts.

7 Conclusion and Future Work

The view on methods that we have presented above and the presented case require that to handle CE-related product and service composition, we need to address several dimensions of a method: perspective, framework, method component, and collection and cooperation principles. In this work, we have adopted a bottom-up approach where we started on the method component level where we, with UML (notational rules), have modelled and defined what concepts are needed to handle CE-related product and service composition, the meta-model in Fig. 2. This gives us a foundation for the development of the other dimensions of the method, such as work procedures in the method component, the framework, the perspective, and collection and cooperation principles.

In future work we will further develop the dimensions of this EM-modelling method that is supposed to serve as a support for the transition of manufacturing enterprises towards a circular economy. An important part will be to develop a method support that covers all the way from capturing different business demands and how these are translated all the way into a QFD (Quality Function Deployment). This will require the development of a coherent framework that describes *what* to do, in what *order* to do things and what *results* to produce. The activities that will be defined in the framework will give the foundation to decide what, and how many method components that will be needed to manage *how* to support this transition process.

Future work must also include a more comprehensive validation of the meta-model than the initial one performed in Sect. 5. The applicability in the industrial case does mean that all required domain concepts and relations for product modularization in the large and CE-centric aspects of EM are already present. Furthermore, multiplicities and constraints require a more detailed investigation. The use of the meta-model in more industrial cases is required. Furthermore, product and service composition probably has to be complemented by other organisational changes to prepare for CE, such as waste minimization strategies and sustainable material sourcing. When adopting EM methods for CE, these changes might require specific method components, which has to be taken into account in future work.

References

1. Blees, C., Jonas, H., Krause, D.: Development of modular product families (2010)
2. Ferasso, M., Beliaeva, T., Kraus, S., Clauss, T., Ribeiro-Soriano, D.: Circular economy business models: the state of research and avenues ahead. Bus. Strateg. Environ. **29**(8), 3006–3024 (2020)
3. Frank, U.: Multi-perspective enterprise modeling: foundational concepts, prospects and future research challenges. Softw. Syst. Model. **13**(3), 941–962 (2014)
4. Geissdoerfer, M., Pieroni, M.P.P., Pigosso, D.C.A., Soufani, K.: Circular business models: a review. J. Clean. Prod. **277**, 123741 (2020)
5. Goldkuhl, G., Lind, M., Seigerroth, U.: Method integration: the need for a learning perspective. IEE Proc.-Softw. **145**(4), 113–118 (1998)
6. Hehenberger, P., Vogel-Heuser, B., Bradley, D., Eynard, B., Tomiyama, T., Achiche, S.: Design, modelling, simulation and integration of cyber physical systems: Methods and applications. Comput. Ind. **82**, 273–289 (2016)
7. Bichler, M.: Design science in information systems research. Wirtschaftsinformatik **48**(2), 133–135 (2006). https://doi.org/10.1007/s11576-006-0028-8
8. Im Halman, J., Hofer, A.P., van Vuuren, W.: Platform-driven development of product families. In: Simpson, T.W., Siddique, Z., Jiao, J.R. (eds.) Product Platform and Product Family Design: Methods and Applications, pp. 27–47 (2006)
9. Jose, A., Tollenaere, M.: Modular and platform methods for product family design: literature analysis. J. Intell. Manuf. **16**(3), 371–390 (2005)
10. de Kwant, C., Rahi, A.F., Laurenti, R.: The role of product design in circular business models: an analysis of challenges and opportunities for electric vehicles and white goods. Sustain. Prod. Consumption **27**, 1728–1742 (2021)
11. Larsson, T., Åslund, J.: ValueMap™-a Method for Understanding the Economical Potential of Product Modularisation and Cost of Variety, pp. 215–222 (2001)
12. Lennartsson, D., Raudberget, D., Sandkuhl, K., Seigerroth, U.: Modularisation metrics-contrasting industrial practice and state-of-research. Proc. Des. Soc. **2**, 2483–2492 (2022)
13. Lennartsson, D., Raudberget, D., Seigerroth, U., Sandkuhl, K.: An Approach Towards Operationalization of Modularization Interfaces for Industrial Product Development (2022)
14. Lillehagen, F., Krogstie, J.: Active Knowledge Modeling of Enterprises. Springer, Cham (2008)
15. Sandkuhl, K.: The product perspective in multi-perspective enterprise modelling. In: Strecker, S., Jung, J. (eds.) Informing Possible Future Worlds: Essays in Honour of Ulrich Frank, pp. 187–196. Logos, Berlin (2024)

16. Sandkuhl, K., Seigerroth, U.: Method engineering in information systems analysis and design: a balanced scorecard approach for method improvement. Softw. Syst. Model. **18**, 1833–1857 (2019)
17. Sandkuhl, K., Seigerroth, U., Lennartsson, D., Raudberget, D.: Module and interface: towards a cross-disciplinary understanding based on quantified product design. In: PoEM 2023 Companion Proceedings. CEUR Online Proceedings, vol. 3645 (2023)
18. Sandkuhl, K., Stirna, J., Persson, A., Wißotzki, M.: Enterprise Modeling. Springer, Cham (2014)
19. Stahel, W.R.: The circular economy. Nature **531**(7595), 435–438 (2016)
20. Ulrich, K.: The role of product architecture in the manufacturing firm. Res. Policy **24**(3), 419–440 (1995)
21. Vernadat, F.: Enterprise modelling: research review and outlook. Comput. Ind. **122**, 103265 (2020)
22. Yin, R.K.: The abridged version of case study research. Handb. Appl. Soc. Res. Methods **2**, 229–259 (1998)

The Challenge of Digitally Improving a Nonprofit Associative Enterprise for the Occupational Risk Prevention of Healthcare Professionals

Xavier Portell[1], Xavier Franch[2], and Joan Antoni Pastor[2]

[1] aMSP, Esteve Terrades 30, 08023 Barcelona, Spain
xportell@amsp.cat
[2] Universitat Politècnica de Catalunya, 08034 Barcelona, Spain
{xavier.franch,joan.antoni.pastor}@upc.edu

Abstract. Nothing is more human-centric than healthcare: humans caring for humans. Thus, ensuring the safety and well-being of healthcare workers is crucial for improving the quality of care. This is the mission of any institution dedicated to occupational risk prevention in healthcare. In this paper we present an ongoing study conducted at aMSP, a nonprofit associative enterprise, with a rich history and ambitious goals. Their strategic opportunities lie in transforming into a more data-intensive and process-oriented enterprise. Digital transformation can significantly improve its services, but it may also involve a profound shift in its operations, processes and culture. Here we present the challenge of digitally improving aMSP through an applied action-research project involving enterprise modeling and architectures, and IS strategic planning. From our literature review, this could be the first reported case in occupational risk prevention where these tools are used, an experience surely useful for other similar enterprises.

Keywords: Digital enterprise transformation · Enterprise modeling · Enterprise architectures · IS strategic planning · Action-research · Occupational risk prevention in healthcare

1 Introduction

According to the World Health Organization (WHO) [1], health workers include a broad range of professionals dedicated to improving health, such as doctors, nurses, technicians, community health workers, and support staff like cleaners and administrators. They are essential to any health system and should have safe and healthy working conditions to maintain their well-being.

Health workers face numerous occupational risks such as infections, hazardous chemicals, psychosocial hazards, and inadequate sanitation. Ensuring their safety is crucial to prevent work-related diseases and injuries, enhance job satisfaction, and improve the quality of care. Unsafe conditions can lead to significant financial costs due to illnesses, injuries, and absenteeism.

Traditional methods of managing these risks, while essential, often fall short in addressing the dynamic and complex nature of healthcare settings. This is where digital transformation comes into play. Technologies offer such organizations a unique opportunity to improve their services, by helping to become more data-intensive and process-oriented. This article describes this transformation challenge in one such organization, considering not only the technology itself, but also other key specific factors on healthcare sector such as organizational structure, work culture and political dynamics.

2 Context: The 'associació Mancomunitat Sanitària de Prevenció' (aMSP)

The Commonwealth Health Prevention association (aMSP, after its Catalan name, associació Mancomunitat Sanitària de Prevenció) is a nonprofit organization established in 1998. It aims to provide occupational risk prevention services for healthcare and social healthcare centers in the Catalan public sector, within a context of innovation and change both in the healthcare field and in the field of occupational health and safety. The association currently covers a total of more than 23,900 professionals from 35 healthcare and social healthcare public sector entities.

aMSP is the result of an alliance between healthcare and social healthcare entities. Its strategy is based on consolidating a skilled and versatile human team, deploying occupational health and prevention units in each associated entity. Thus, aMSP provides direct and exclusive services to its associates, who contribute their part of the common expenses through a proportional fee system based on the number of employees they have.

A prior business strategic plan (2012–2016) aimed to improve the risk prevention service by making decisions based on the data obtained from the wide healthcare population, and sharing knowledge bidirectionally with the associated entities. The implementation yielded several positive results but also some areas for improvement. On the positive side, synergies were created internally within the group of technicians, resulting in a pioneering service with all specialties working together in the same room for all areas to facilitate multidisciplinary data sharing. New measurement devices and technology enabled the collection and exploitation of additional data, both for the technical side and for health monitoring. Also, aMSP adhered to ISO 9001 and ISO 45001 certifications.

As for areas of improvement, the outcome at a transversal level incorporating the different entities was less optimal. The improvement of knowledge and data sharing from associated entities was not achieved. A key factor in this was the failure of the implementation of the new (at that moment; now discontinued) Prevenet software application for health surveillance and monitoring. Most entities decided not to use it because they found it excessively rigid and lacking flexibility.

The plan was finally updated in 2021 after the COVID pandemic. Goals related to the digital transformation were added to the initial objective of improving service delivery, quality, and efficiency. It was decided to launch a new tender to replace the core software application and to create a new position of head of information systems.

The management of aMSP sought assistance from the Universitat Politècnica de Catalunya (UPC) to both finding someone to lead their digital transformation and provide counselling advice on their future possibilities. Concretely, UPC mission was agreed to assist aMSP in:

- Assisting aMSP in their future digital transformation based on their current situation, which included implementing a newly acquired core application and analyzing additional software tools, using state-of-the-art academic methods developed in their research areas: services engineering, information systems, and software engineering.
- Helping aMSP address their future digital transformation to become a more data-intensive organization with better-modelled and controlled key business processes, while protecting themselves from excessive dependence on one or several software vendors.

3 Background

The two aMSP needs highlighted above can be translated into two main academic research streams, namely digital transformation and digital business strategy, for which we provide next basic background in the next sections.

3.1 Digital Transformation Definition and Description

There is a lack of common understanding of what Digital Transformation (DT) is [2]. The existing literature identifies attributes as digital capabilities and maturity, digital technologies, business models and strategies as factors that drive the DT agenda inside an organization [2]. Digital technologies play a vital role in the DT process. Their capabilities, when combined with factors like culture and strategy, enable the transformation process. However, "simply using digital technologies to drive the digital transformation process is not enough and that it also uses digital capabilities, strategies, culture and talent development" [3].

The effects of DT take place in three key areas: business model, operational processes and customer experience [4, 5]. Some authors advocate for the inclusion of employees in the digital transformation journey [6]. Other researchers explore impacts on organizational structure [7] or relationships [8]. As a result, the transformed areas considered for the general description of DT should include both customer and organization [2]. Consequently, the three areas proposed by [5] are kept in the comprehensive definition.

In this paper, we adopt the definition from Morakanyane and Grace: "[DT is] an evolutionary process that leverages digital capabilities and technologies to enable business models, operational processes and customer experiences to create value" [2]. Table 1 describes a simple definition for each of these concepts.

Table 1. Keywords from global definition of DT [2].

Keyword	Simple definition
Evolutionary process	A gradual and ongoing series of activities that brings radical change over a period of time
Digital capabilities	Technology skills possessed or required by employees, customers and other stakeholders in different areas that can enable the organization to thrive in a digital environment
Digital technologies	New and emerging technologies
Business models, operational processes and customer experiences	Different areas of the organization which are bound to transform due to the digital transformation process
Value creation	Organization wide effects and benefits realized as a result of the digital transformation effort, realized by both the organization and the customer

3.2 Digital Business Strategy and IS/IT Strategic Planning

Digitalization, driven by rapid technological development, fundamentally changes how organizations operate, compete, and strategize [9]. The strategies for Information Systems (IS) and Information Technologies (IT), attainable through IS/IT strategic planning, are evolving into Digital Business Strategy (DBS). It has moved from exploiting existing technologies to exploring new innovative opportunities enabled by digital technologies. This proactive shift positions IS as a driver of business innovation and transformation. IS/IT strategy now integrates with broader business objectives, reflecting the central role of digital technologies in business operations. Digital strategy shapes and drives business strategy in the digital age, beyond just supporting it.

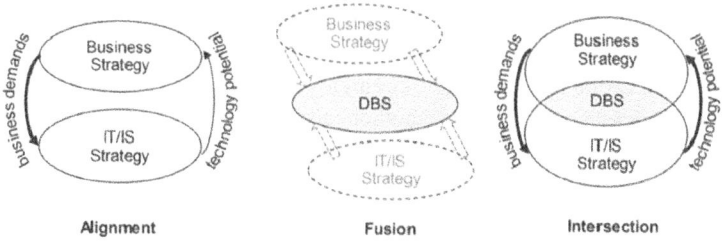

Fig. 1. DBS between the poles of business and IS/IT strategy [9].

In Fig. 1, the traditional alignment view perceives IS/IT strategy as subordinate to business strategy, which is true for the "departmental plan" and "strategy support" conceptions but not for the "shared view" and "master plan" conceptions. While there are concerns about subordinating IS/IT strategy, fusing both strategies (fusion view) risks making them indistinguishable, leading to confusion.

DBS is neither an upgrade of IS/IT strategy nor simply a modern form of business strategy. Both strategies maintain distinct logics that intersect where IT plays a crucial role in value creation. Unlike the fusion view, which merges business and IS/IT strategies, DBS should be seen as their intersection, particularly where digital technologies are integral to production or products themselves.

The study identifies a shift from traditional to evolving conceptions of IS/IT strategy in the digital age. Traditionally, IS/IT strategy was seen in three main ways. First, as a support to business strategy, where IS/IT strategy provided necessary IS/IT facilities to implement business strategies and gain competitive advantages. Second, as a master plan, which involved detailed planning of IS/IT resources and capabilities to support future business success. Third, as a shared view within the organization, focusing on achieving a consensus on the role and importance of IS/IT.

In the digital age, these traditional conceptions are being challenged and redefined. The emerging concept of DBS integrates IS/IT and business strategies, addressing the strategic role of digital technologies in enabling new business models and competitive advantages. DBS is viewed as a business strategy specifically designed for the digital era, reflecting the intertwined nature of IS/IT and business objectives. This evolving conception recognizes that digital technologies are integral to business strategy, not just supportive tools, and emphasizes the need for strategies that are agile, innovative, and capable of navigating the complexities of digital ecosystems.

4 Research Design

Digital Transformation (DT) may involve a profound shift in organizational operations, processes, and culture driven by the integration of digital technologies. Our ongoing research is focusing on key success factors, challenges, and outcomes. Research in this area usually has a practical nature involving models, and the creation of something new (such as new tools, new approaches, new processes, new methods, etc.) that could be useful to organizations in general, or to a specific institution [10]. For this reason, this DT needs to be planned, developed and validated using an appropriate research method.

To ensure that DT efforts are aligned with its overall business goals and in order to handle the impact of the required changes within the organization an IS/IT Strategic Plan is required. Strategic planning in IS/IT involves aligning technology initiatives with organizational goals to enhance performance, competitiveness, and innovation.

Based on the challenges highlighted by aMSP in the previous section, we identified the following research question:

- **RQ1**. How to design, plan and execute a successful DT effort for improving the key processes of a healthcare risk prevention organization?

The proposed main methodology to address the research is Action Research (AR) in several iterations of diagnosing, action planning, action taking, evaluating and specific learning according to Baskerville's description [11]. AR was chosen since it addresses real-world problems and issues while simultaneously aiming to expand scientific knowledge [12]. Unlike other research methodologies, which involve the researcher studying but not altering organizational phenomena, AR aims to create organizational change while studying the change process. In other words, AR emphasizes both change and reflection, requiring active participation from researchers and practitioners in organizational change initiatives. This approach can generate valuable insights and make significant contributions to both theory and practice.

To be more precise, we decided to conduct three iterations with well-defined goals: cover key processes, include the rest of processes, and refine. We also had an initial exploratory phase with a literature review. Each of the iterations inside the AR cycles are inspired in Design Science Research (DSR), for which we follow the principles defined in [13].

In order to ensure the rigor and the quality of the research method, we follow the framework proposed by McKay & Marshall [14] who encourage reflective and reasoned action around four categories: Conduct of the Research, Conceptual Significance of the Research, Practical Significance of the Research and Presentation of the Research.

5 aMSP Digital Strategic Review and Challenges

In response to RQ1, this section provides a strategic review of aMSP and highlights key challenges.

5.1 aMSP Organization and Key Processes in Occupational Risk Prevention

The Occupational Safety and Health Administration (OSH) has established an EU Framework directive [15] defining the tasks to be performed by prevention services when assessing and supporting associated entities. According to this directive, all tasks derive from hazard identification and risk assessment. Based on the identified risks, four technical specialties—hygiene, security, ergonomics, and psychosociology—and one healthcare specialty are to be involved. The technical specialists create technical reports assessing specific risk situations and establishing preventive measures. On the other hand, the healthcare specialist develops protocols based on workplace risk exposures, and monitors employees' health.

The head of these five specialties, under the coordination of the paper's first author, worked together in a series of dedicated meetings to identify the key processes in occupational risk prevention, and reached the following agreement:

- Health surveillance and monitoring. Regularly monitoring the health of employees to detect early signs of work-related illnesses or injuries.
- Hazard identification, risk assessment, and risk control measures. Systematically identifying all potential sources of harm in the workplace and evaluating their likelihood and severity of harm.
- Planning, implementing, and following up the identified risk control measures.
- Psychosocial risk assessment. Identifying and evaluating workplace factors that may impact employees' mental health, well-being, and social dynamics.
- Incident/accident reporting and investigation.
- Emergency and self-protection plans. Designed to manage emergency situations in the workplace and ensure the safety of employees.

- Specific studies and reports on any of the mentioned specialties (healthcare, hygiene, security, ergonomics or psychosociology).
- Training on job-specific risks and on various workplace hazards.

5.2 aMSP Digital Strategy Current State Assessment (as of Beginning of 2023)

To establish an initial strategic analysis, we have adapted and used the PENSI methodology [16] for DBS planning, developed and used at UPC for teaching/learning DBS and IS/IT strategic planning. This approach is oriented around the traditional SWOT analysis, enriched with several IS/IT analysis techniques. The information derived and obtained from the strategic analysis phase is used directly without any additional transformation in the strategic formulation phase, integrating both business and IS/IT.

PENSI is an iterative methodology that allows us to establish a quick initial cycle with less detailed information, which we will complete in subsequent cycles. The main advantage of this approach is that it facilitates the use and inclusion of highly structured techniques.

The first stage begins with business analysis. This stage has been adapted considering the particularities of the nonprofit healthcare and social healthcare risk prevention environment. It involves analyzing the general environment, the competitive sector, an internal analysis of aMSP, and the organization's value systems.

The second stage consists of IS/IT analysis, where existing information systems are analyzed, along with the potential impact of new information systems on business areas, current information technologies, and the potential impact of new information technologies.

From here, we have modified its third stage to adapt it to the DBS [9], as described in Sect. 3.2. Essentially, DBS is about the intersection between business strategies and IS/IT strategies. Stage 3 then involves determining the strategic positioning of business and IS/IT, determining and selecting strategic business and IS/IT actions, and defining specific IS/IT projects related to the previously mentioned actions.

SWOT Analysis. The SWOT analysis has been elaborated through several participative sessions with a representation of each of the technical and healthcare specialties referred in Sect. 5.1, as well as from IS area and aMSP management. The sessions were structured using an adapted Metaplan methodology [17]. Metaplan is a structured method for group discussions and idea generation. It is particularly useful in workshops, meetings, and strategy sessions. This methodology focuses on visualizing thoughts and ideas to enhance group dynamics and ensure a structured process. Each session is structured in several questions. The participants write anonymous answer cards that are sticked in a panel. Once all participants have finished answering the question, there is some discussion on the answers.

The questions were structured using a SWOT matrix to identify strengths, weaknesses, opportunities, and threats across the business, application, and technology dimensions. Priorities and proposed actions were established in a second session, taking in consideration what were the involved processes. Table 2 and Table 3 include a subset of the SWOT matrix, comprising only those items that were found relevant for the DBS.

Table 2. Summarized SWOT matrix (Strengths and Weaknesses)

	Strengths	Weaknesses
Business	**BS1.** aMSP scientific approach	**BW1.** Current systems do not allow easily data analysis and decision making
	BS2. Long-term relationships with the associated entities	**BW2.** Low number of scientific publications found
	BS3. Aim for data-driven decisions	**BW3.** Service delivery not standard across the organization
Application	**AS1.** New core application GeISS ready for implementation	**AW1.** Core application "Prevenet" only partially implemented (1)
		AW2. TecnoPreven, provider of Prevenet, failed in 2020 (2)
		AW3. Entities have new information needs
Technology	**TS1.** New core application "GeISS" is SaS	**TW1.** Current core application Prevenet too rigid and lacks flexibility

(1) Current core application "Prevenet" was only partially implemented due to reluctances from some of the associated entities. Some of them using different systems (Excel, Access, Prevenet...)
(2) In 2019, TecnoPreven, owner of Prevenet, officially stopped supporting the software and finally failed in 2020. aMSP was left without any possible support, not even administration access to the database or updated documentation

Table 3. Summarized SWOT matrix (Opportunities and Threats)

	Opportunities	Threats
Business	**BO1.** Increase of the relevance of our services to associated entities due to legislation shift (1)	**BT1.** Risk of associated entities leaving aMSP (2)
		BT2. Limited growth capacity (3)
		BT3. No hierarchy within the organization (4)
Application	**AO1.** Increase in the demand from associated entities of a health surveillance software solution	**AT1.** ErgosUp, provider of the new core application GeISS, acquired by eCoordina
		AT2. Dependency on integration with HR database within each associated entity
		AT3. Core application new bidding in 2026
Technology	**TO1.** Cloud technologies available	**TT1.** Ransomware is increasing in healthcare sector

(1) The application of legislation is shifting towards more strict requirements. This increases the relevance of our services for associated entities.
(2) Risk of associated entities leaving aMSP in case they feel aMSP is not providing them enough added value
(3) Restricted to public entities in the healthcare sector within the Catalan region
(4) aMSP is an association of more than 35 different entities, without a hierarchical link. Changes in any IT related tools must be embraced bottom up by the Risk Prevention area users from each of the associated entities

Current IS/IT Usage Across Key Processes. We have categorized the key processes previously identified by responsibility, assigning them either to aMSP or the associated entities. Table 4 highlights the IS/IT currently used across these processes. Manual processes are not receiving IS/IT support, while automated or semi-automated processes benefit to varying extents, depending on the adoption and usage of the IS/IT by the associated entities.

5.3 Main Challenges

After the SWOT analysis meetings, a final participative session with the same team was held to develop a list of potential challenges related to the DT challenge to be proposed to aMSP management. Using the SWOT analysis as a foundation, participants proposed and discussed actions related to each SWOT element. These actions were grouped by topic, and related topics were combined and defined as challenges that the organization would need to address. Each of them was associated with a list of SWOT elements, with some elements appearing in multiple groups due to their impact in more than one challenge. The list was finally endorsed by aMSP management. We have highlighted a total of three challenges in Table 5, Table 6 and Table 7.

Table 4. IS/IT usage across key processes

	Process	Degree of automation	Support IS/IT	Associated entities (1)	Covered employees
Associated entities	P1. Health surveillance and monitoring	Semi-automated	Prevenet	15	5100
	P2. Incident/accident reporting and investigation	Semi-automated	Office-Access	22	13,177
	P3. Planning, implementing and following up risk control measures	Manual	Office	0	0
aMSP	P4. Hazard identification, risk assessment, and risk control measures	Automated	Prevenet	35	23,900
	P5. Psychosocial risk assessment	Manual	Office	0	0
	P6. Emergency and self-protection plans	Manual	Office	0	0
	P7. Specific studies and reports	Manual	Office	0	0
	P8. Training	Manual	Office	0	0

(1) The number of associated entities, out of 35, and employees, from a total of 23,900, benefiting from IS/IT support in each process. Manual processes are not receiving this IS/IT support.

Table 5. Challenge 1

Challenge	Aligning business and IS/IT strategy by using the new core application GeISS and improving the key business processes
SWOT element	**AS1.** New core application GeISS ready for implementation
	BS3. Aim for data-driven decisions
	BS1. aMSP Scientific approach
	TS1. New core application GeISS is SaaS
	BW3. Service delivery not standard across the organization
	BW1. Current systems do not allow easily data analysis and decision making
	AW1. Core application Prevenet only partially implemented
	BW2. Reduced number of scientific publications
	TW1. Current core application Prevenet too rigid and lacks flexibility

Challenge 1 is key for the future of aMSP and can be approached by using the following academic methods:

- Digital Transformation. This should take into account the implementation of the new core application and getting the clinics and occupational risk prevention professionals to accept and adopt the new applications and processes.
- Digital Business Strategy as a fusion of business and IS/IT strategy [9]

Table 6. Challenge 2

Challenge	Strengthen the links with the associated entities
SWOT element	**BS2.** Long-term relationships with the associated entities
	AS1. New core application GeISS ready for implementation
	AW3. Entities have new information needs
	TW1. Current core application Prevenet too rigid and lacks flexibility
	AW1. Core application "Prevenet" only partially implemented
	BW2. Reduced number of scientific publications
	BO1. Stricter requirements for associated entities due to legislation shift
	BT1. Risk of associated entities leaving aMSP
	BT2. Limited growth capacity
	BT3. No hierarchy within the organization

Challenge 2 can be approached with the following tools/actions:

- Sharing a common platform GeISS for health surveillance, planning risk control measures and accident reporting and investigation, and being able to use the data to improve the quality of the Risk Prevention service.
- Involve the board of directors in the digital transformation process and create a DT steering committee.
- Strengthen the perception of aMSP internal professionals as leaders in acquiring knowledge in the field of occupational risk prevention and its application, using scientific methodologies. Prioritize and incentivize publications.

Table 7. Challenge 3

Challenge	Reduce dependency on the software provider
SWOT element	**AW2.** TecnoPreven, provider of Prevenet, failed in 2020 **AT1.** ErgosUp, provider of the new core app., acquired by eCoordina
	AT3. Core application new bidding in 2026

Challenge 3 can be approached through the following actions:

- Document processes and operations. Document as well software requirements for the core application so they can be used for the new bidding in 2026.
- Explore alternatives in the market. Explore other existing potential software packages or even the possibility of inhouse building.
- Ensure that data entered into the application can be easily exported without requiring assistance from the software provider.

6 Enterprise Modeling and Architecture for aMSP

aMSP business challenges cannot be addressed by simply adding or changing a few systems [18]. Instead, a complete restructuring of the organization's operational and organizational framework is necessary. In this section we reflect on the use of Enterprise Architecture (EA) as the vehicle to drive this transformational journey.

Enterprise Architecture Definition. An EA can be formally defined as the "representation of the structure and behavior of an enterprise's IS/IT landscape in relation to its business environment (reflecting) the current and future use of IS/IT in the enterprise, and providing a roadmap to reach a future state" [18]. EA defines the organization's structure and operation through models—abstract representations using words, graphics, and other formal depicts [19, 20]. These models outline the functionalities and operational behavior of the enterprise, identifying operational activities and relevant information to reduce complexity and help achieve current and future objectives [21]. EA integrates business, data, information, and technology into a coherent whole [22].

Aligning Business and IT. EA's goal is to guide the enterprise from a disorganized, complex state towards a more rational and efficient state [18]. This transformation requires significant changes to eliminate duplication, reduce costs, improve reliability, and increase agility. EA provides a strategic foundation for business enablement.

6.1 Using Enterprise Architecture for Digital Transformation

As mentioned in Sect. 3.2, the initial point of DT is developing a DBS, integrating IT-based processes that expand capabilities and increase complexity, requiring new methods and tools for effective implementation [23]. Creating a DT strategy that includes key decisions on technology, structure, finances, and value creation is recommended [7]. Business models [24] clarify strategies by detailing value creation but lack in process and service implementation planning.

EA provides a comprehensive description of an enterprise, detailing essential business artifacts and their relationships [23]. It includes principles, methods, and models to help design and realize organizational structures, business processes, information systems, and infrastructure.

Criticism on EAs as an Instrument for DT. EA appears to be a promising support for DT, but it is not widely used in this context [23]. Key reasons include:

- Gap between EA and business transformation: EA is IT-centric and does not adequately consider strategy, while business transformation focuses on processes.
- Complexity: Frameworks like TOGAF are complex and require extensive training, making them difficult to implement.
- Inflexibility: EA follows a traditional, detailed planning approach, conflicting with the agile, iterative methods needed for digital transformation.

DT requires rapid time-to-market, customer inclusion, and deep integration of digital strategies and business models, that EA frameworks do not currently support. While effective in developing and documenting information systems, EA is seen as too complex and IT-focused for today's business needs. There is a need for new, lightweight, business-focused planning tools that support agile methods and are understandable by all stakeholders.

Proposed Approach for DT. Goerzig and Bauernhansl [23] proposed a new EA approach for DT for solving the above-mentioned weaknesses emphasizing agility and customer proximity. The approach is divided into a macro and micro cycles, as shown in Fig. 2. The macro cycle defines the architecture of the entire organization, while in the micro cycle single functions are implemented and tested. Both cycles are incrementally developed. The digital business strategy is the initial point of the approach. It is essential to derive a transformation strategy out of the digital business strategy [7]. Here, technological and organizational principles for the implementation are defined.

The first step of the macro cycle derives the business model from the digital business strategy. As described earlier, the business model contains information like value proposition, customer segments or revenue streams. The second step is to elaborate an ideal architecture, detailing the business model in a simplified manner. The ideal architecture outlines main processes, main IS/IT services and necessary information without restrictions, encouraging innovative ideas without legacy system constraints.

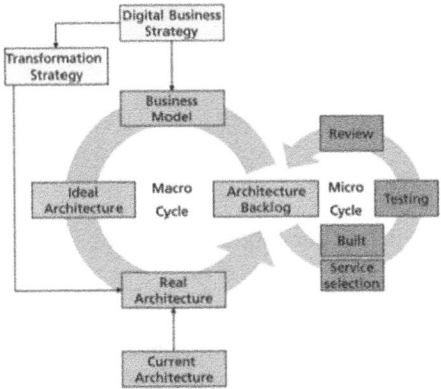

Fig. 2. Agile enterprise architecture for digital transformation [23]

Subsequently, the real architecture is derived from the ideal architecture. In this step, both transformation strategy and current architecture are considered. The architecture backlog follows similar ideas as the product backlog in the scrum approach. Based on the differences between current and real architecture, user stories are defined in the architecture backlog.

6.2 Proposed Methodology

Based on the previous approach we propose a methodology for driving aMSP digital transformation comprising an initial exploratory phase followed by three iterations. The methodology is depicted in Fig. 3. The initial exploratory phase, includes design of the research plan, research approach and the initial digital business strategic review (DBS). Each iteration uses the DBS from the previous iteration, and the current architecture, initially described in the exploratory phase and updated after each iteration. The output is the new real architecture, that becomes the current architecture for the next iteration.

The first iteration focuses on key processes and their application implementation. The second addresses support processes, and the third one involves refining the systems and processes implemented in previous iterations.

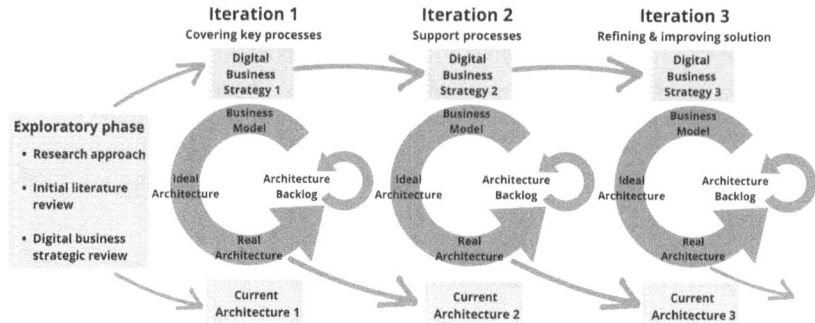

Fig. 3. Proposed methodology based on three AR iterations

6.3 Objectives

The EA implementation will have the following objectives related to the three identified challenges:

- O1: Define and implement new business processes to improve the quality of the service (Challenge 1). This should address standardization Service delivery across the organization, and facilitate improving and optimizing services.
- O2: Implement the new core application according to the new defined processes (Challenges 1 and 2). The new core application is key for aligning business and IS/IT objectives as well as being able to take decisions based on data.
- O3: Expand the usage of the new core application to the associated entities, as a common platform, including the detected new information needs (Challenge 2). This is key to ensure strengthen the links with the associated entities by providing an important tool for them.
- O4: Increase the number of scientific publications (Challenge 2). In order to become a referent for the associated entities.
- O5: Document the defined processes, operations (Challenge 3). Include software requirements for the core application as well so they can be used for the new bidding in 2026.
- O6: Explore alternatives in the market (Challenge 3). This includes other existing potential software packages or even the possibility of inhouse building.

These objectives will include the corresponding metric definitions and will be refined in subsequent iterations.

7 Conclusions

Ensuring the safety and well-being of healthcare workers is crucial for improving the quality of care. Technologies offer such organizations a unique opportunity to improve their services, by helping to become more data-intensive and process-oriented. DT can significantly improve those services, but may involve a profound shift in its operations, processes and culture. This restructuring of the enterprise's operational and organizational framework is the main challenge of our project, and we believe that it can be done successfully with the help of an EA.

After intensive research, we could not find any documentation describing references of an EA in risk prevention for healthcare professionals, not even in occupational risk prevention in general. As far as we know, this project will develop the first documented EA for risk prevention for healthcare professionals.

Thus, this research is based on improving a concrete case, and we do not expect our results to be directly generalizable to other organizations. However, we believe that it may offer valuable insights and inspiration for similar cases, such as for-profit prevention services, but we leave it to each of those organizations to assess how our findings may be applicable to their own particular context.

Acknowledgments. The research work behind this paper has been partially funded by the Catalan program for Industrial Doctorates under the project DI2022115. We also thank Antoni Carrillo, aMSP Chief Technical Officer, for his collaboration and support in this project.

References

1. World Health Organization: World Health Organization fact-sheets: Occupational health: health workers. https://www.who.int/news-room/fact-sheets/detail/occupational-health-health-workers. Accessed 29 July 2024
2. Morakanyane, R., Grace, A., O'Reilly, P.: Conceptualizing Digital Transformation in Business Organizations: A Systematic Review of Literature. In: Digital Transformation – From Connecting Things to Transforming Our Lives, pp. 427–443. University of Maribor Press (2017). https://doi.org/10.18690/978-961-286-043-1.30
3. Kane, G.C., Palmer, D., Phillips, A.N., Kiron, D.: Is your business ready for a digital future? MIT Sloan Manag. Rev. **4** (2015)
4. Santarsiero, F., Schiuma, G., Carlucci, D., Helander, N.: Digital transformation in healthcare organisations: the role of innovation labs. Technovation **122**, 102640 (2023) https://doi.org/10.1016/j.technovation.2022.102640
5. Westerman, G., Bonnet, D., Mcafee, A.: The nine elements of digital transformation. Opin. Anal. MIT Sloan Manag. Rev. **3** (2004)
6. Bouee, C.: Digital transformation doesn't have to leave employees behind. Harv Bus Rev. (2015)
7. Matt, C., Hess, T., Benlian, A.: Digital transformation strategies. Bus. Inf. Syst. Eng. **57**, 339–343 (2015). https://doi.org/10.1007/s12599-015-0401-5
8. Loebbecke, C., Picot, A.: Reflections on societal and business model transformation arising from digitization and big data analytics: a research agenda. J. Strateg. Inf. Syst. **24**, 149–157 (2015). https://doi.org/10.1016/j.jsis.2015.08.002
9. Teubner, R.A., Stockhinger, J.: Literature review: understanding information systems strategy in the digital age. J. Strateg. Inf. Syst. **29**, 101642 (2020). https://doi.org/10.1016/j.jsis.2020.101642
10. Cruz, E.F., da Cruz, A.M.R.: Design science research for IS/IT projects: focus on digital transformation. In: 2020 15th Iberian Conference on Information Systems and Technologies (CISTI), pp. 1–6. IEEE (2020). https://doi.org/10.23919/CISTI49556.2020.9140972
11. Baskerville, R.L.: Investigating information systems with action research. Commun. Assoc. Inf. Syst. **2** (1999). https://doi.org/10.17705/1CAIS.00219
12. Varajão, J., Magalhães, L., Freitas, L., Rocha, P.: Success management – from theory to practice. Int. J. Project Manag. **40**, 481–498 (2022). https://doi.org/10.1016/j.ijproman.2022.04.002

13. Hevner, M.: Park, ram: design science in information systems research. MIS Q. **28**, 75 (2004). https://doi.org/10.2307/25148625
14. McKay, J., Marshall, P.: Quality and rigour of action research in information systems. In: European Conference on Information Systems (ECIS) (2000). http://aisel.aisnet.org/ecis2000/38
15. European Agency for Safety and Health at Work: Legislation: EU directives: The OSH Framework Directive, 1989. https://osha.europa.eu/en/legislation/directives/the-osh-framework-directive/the-osh-framework-directive-introduction. Accessed 29 July 2024
16. Pastor, J.A., Sánchez, F.: Método integral de planificación estratégica de SI-TI. Nota técnica 2 (2007)
17. Metaplan SARL: Moderating group discussions using the Metaplan approach
18. Bente, S., Bombosch, U., Langade, S.: Enriching EA with Lean, Agile, and Enterprise 2.0 practices. In: Collaborative Enterprise Architecture, pp. i–ii. Elsevier (2012). https://doi.org/10.1016/B978-0-12-415934-1.00016-9
19. United States Government Accountability Office: Enterprise Architecture. Leadership Remains Key to Establishing and Leveraging Architectures for Organizational Transformation
20. Vernadat, F.: Enterprise modeling in the context of enterprise engineering: state of the art and outlook. Int. J. Prod. Manag. Eng. **2**, 57 (2014). https://doi.org/10.4995/ijpme.2014.2326
21. Kosanke, K., Vernadat, F., Zelm, M.: CIMOSA: enterprise engineering and integration. Comput. Ind. **40**, 83–97 (1999). https://doi.org/10.1016/S0166-3615(99)00016-0
22. Boar, B.H.: Constructing Blueprints for Enterprise IT Architectures. Wiley, New York (1998)
23. Goerzig, D., Bauernhansl, T.: Enterprise architectures for the digital transformation in small and medium-sized enterprises. Procedia CIRP **67**, 540–545 (2018). https://doi.org/10.1016/j.procir.2017.12.257
24. Osterwalder, A., Pigneur, Y.: Business Model Generation: A Handbook for Visionaries, Game Changers, and Challengers. Wiley, Hoboken (2010)

Fostering Digital Progression of Society: Exploratory Case Studies of Third Place for Services

Jolita Ralyté(✉) and Michel Léonard

University of Geneva, ISS, CUI, Route de Drize 7, 1227 Carouge, Switzerland
{jolita.ralyte,michel.leonard}@unige.ch

Abstract. The digital transformation of an organization, and more broadly of society, consists in the evolution of its digital infrastructure with new information services and service systems supporting its progress. The most remarkable innovation comes with transdisciplinary services. Building such services requires the involvement and contribution of all relevant actors as well as an approach to lead a fruitful co-creation. Recently we have introduced an approach, called Third Place for Services (TPS), aiming to serve this purpose. TPS focuses on building a heterogeneous network of contributors and guides the co-creation of transdisciplinary information services in an exploratory way. Since then, we have conducted several experimental TPS as case studies aiming to validate the applicability of the approach and to refine its definition based on feedback from participants and our observations. In this paper, we present the current definition of the TPS method and the case studies that demonstrate its value.

Keywords: Information service · Digital Transformation · Third Place for Services · Contributory approach · Co-creation

1 Introduction

Digital transformation is omnipresent in the life of today's society: paper-based activities are progressively digitalized, partnerships and collaborations are being established via digital channels, products are being dematerialized, and new services take on digital form. The progress largely depends on society's ability to conduct this digital transformation: to innovate through new digital technologies, and to create new value propositions through digital information assets taking form of information services and service systems. This transformation is at the core of Society 5.0, which envisions a human-centered society integrating digital and physical spaces to achieve balanced economic and social progress [1, 2]. In the context of digital transformation, being human-centered means ensuring the inclusion of all concerned people not only during service usage but also in service creation. This highlights the need for contributory approaches in which each stakeholder – be it public institution, private company, non-profit organization, or individual citizen – actively participates in the co-creation of information services.

Collaborative building of services ensures that digital transformation initiatives are inclusive and address the needs and aspirations of all societal members. This participatory process not only fosters innovation but also builds a sense of ownership and responsibility among participants. People feel included, understood, and accountable for the development of their company, association, and even society. By contributing to these efforts, they can take pride in their achievements and the collective progress made.

In this context, we recently introduced an approach called Third Place for Services[1] (TPS), whose goal is "to build information services in a contributory way involving actors from various disciplines and domains aiming to innovate and co-create value as common information assets, and so, to contribute to the digital progress of Society" [3]. The notion of Society is used here in a broad sense, it can be a public institution, a non-profit organization, a small or large company or an eco-system of various organizations and individuals. Therefore, TPS can be conducted in various situations and serve various purposes. For example, a consortium of health organizations could benefit from this approach to establish a regulation on patients' data sharing via a common service system. In a much narrower context, a private company can use TPS to involve employees from various departments in the creation of new companywide services, like company portal.

The TPS method introduced in [3] is our first attempt to formalize the approach. Since 2018, we have been conducting several exploratory TPS with the aim to test the applicability of the approach in various contexts and the ability to support different purposes, and to make evolve the approach based on the insights gained from these explorations. These explorations allowed us to collect feedback from participants and refine the approach.

The work presented in this paper shows how we are progressing towards a formal definition of TPS as a method, i.e., in terms of metamodel and process model, the ultimate goal being to build a modular method following the principles of Situational Method Engineering [4].

The rest of the paper is organized as follows; in Sect. 2 we briefly present the foundations of the TPS approach. Section 3 provides an overview of the TPS method, while in Sect. 4 we report on three exploratory TPS conducted in the context of a continuing education program. In Sect. 5 we discuss the relevance of the TPS method on the context of Society 5.0 and draw conclusions in Sect. 6.

2 Background

TPS approach is grounded in Service Science and is based on the concept of transdisciplinary information service. It also takes inspiration from social science and in particular the notion of Third Place.

2.1 Service Science

Service science [5, 6] is an interdisciplinary field of study of services and service systems aiming to drive business and social innovation through value co-creation. It combines

---

[1] In [1] it is called Tiers-Lieu for Services, where Tiers-Lieu comes from French and means Third Place.

concepts, knowledge and theories from multiple disciplines such as economy and management, social sciences, design and engineering. The key constructs of service science are service-dominant logic and services system.

Service-dominant logic [7–10] is a theoretical foundation for understanding the notion of service and value co-creation from a service perspective. A service is defined as "the application of resources for the benefit of another" [7]. In order to create value, actors engage in interdependent and reciprocally beneficial resource integration and service exchange.

Service system is defined as "a value-coproduction configuration of people, technology, other internal and external service systems, and shared information (such as language, processes, metrics, prices, policies, and laws)" [11, 12]. In other words, a service system aims to connect people, technology and information through value propositions with the aim of cocreating value for the service systems participating in the exchange of resources within and across systems [8]. In the context of digital transformation of organizations and digital progression of Society, service science provides a background for innovation by co-creating information services and service systems.

2.2 Transdisciplinary Information Service

Information service is a concept built on the principles and properties of two disciplines: service science and information systems engineering. An information service is a service embodied in an autonomous, consistent and interoperable digital information infrastructure that provides capabilities to perform business activities and has resources (data, rules, roles) to realize these capabilities [13, 14]. Information services and service systems allow to build organization's digital information infrastructure in agile and iterative way, taking into consideration new business situations and value propositions. Originally, [13–15] the concept of information service was proposed to deal with business development and evolution of information systems. Then, in [17] it is seen as a common goods and as an engine for innovation. Indeed, the aim of information services and service systems is to enable interactions of various actors aiming to co-create value via information (co)creation and exchange. In this way, existing business and public activities are transformed and new ones created. In the context of digital transformation, information service is a key notion to deal with innovation and digital progress of the Society [3, 16].

When an information service encounters a transdisciplinary context, it must also become transdisciplinary. Transdisciplinarity according to Nicolescu [18] "concerns that which is at once between the disciplines, across the different disciplines, and beyond each individual discipline". Based on the knowledge, theories, concepts, methods, and tools of involved disciplines it allows to create new ones. Therefore, when an information service transcends disciplinary, organizational, or even country boundaries we call it respectively transdisciplinary, trans-organizational, trans-national. For simplicity, in the rest of the paper we use the notion of transdisciplinary service as a generic notion covering different service levels and scopes.

A transdisciplinary information service supports collaborative activities of several actors from different professional fields, representing different business or societal disciplines and having different needs, aims and responsibilities. It unites them around a common intention and enables them to share information assets and to co-create new ones. Each of these actors is a potential information (resource) provider and consumer. The service does not belong exclusively to any of the contributing actors or organizations but nevertheless contributes to the progress of each of the involved disciplines and organizations.

Therefore, a collaborative approach involving a heterogeneous group of contributors is necessary to create and implement transdisciplinary information services. The approach has to offer a shared conceptual framework drawing together disciplinary-specific theories, concepts, and approaches and allowing to explore the potential solutions to reach a common intention.

2.3 Third Place for Services

The notion of third place comes from social science, also called "a great good place" [19] and designates an intermediate environment between home (first place) and workplace (second place) offering facilities for social interactions and community life. It can be physical or virtual, and dedicated to relaxing and/or coworking activities.

During the recent years, the notion of Third Place has evolved towards a contribution space motivating collaborations, creativity and co-creation of common assets. Burret [20] defines a Third Place as: "a social configuration where the encounter between individual entities intentionally engages in the conception of common representations". Léonard [21] states that it can be easily adapted "to the characteristics of informational propulsions and information common goods, in order to make it the place of their construction under the name of Third Place for Service (TPS)". In [17] the authors propose to use Tiers-Lieu (third place) as a social environment for service-centered innovations. They see it as an open environment "that motivates collaboration, intellectual creativity and surpasses the limits of traditional disciplines-defined collaborative spaces, by allowing defining new services". Finally, in [21] TPS is defined as "a social configuration between different entities whose encounter intentionally engages them in the conception of common informational representations, expressed by means of informational models, in order to construct information services assembling in an information common good". Therefore, we see the notion of TPS as a background framework for the co-creation of transdisciplinary information services and systems, and we aim to build a method based on it. From the related literature we identify the main TPS principles, that we consider as method requirements for building the TPS method:

- TPS must be initiated and driven by a shared intention to overcome a remarkable situation by co-creating information services as common goods in the context of digital progression.
- TPS needs a heterogeneous network of contributors exercising different professions, with varied responsibilities and skills, and potentially coming from different organizations. The more variety there is, the more likely the co-creation will be rich and innovative. Eight roles are proposed in [3, 21] to specify the responsibility of contributors: initiator, builder, facilitator, observer, historian, developer, regulator, and concierge, the most important and mandatory being initiator and builder.
- TPS needs a regulatory framework which defines the rules on the contribution and sharing of the co-creation outcomes.

- TPS is a protected place, because outside their organizations, contributors can freely express their opinions and focus on reaching informational consensus.
- TPS aims for a democratic, accountable and inclusive co-creation, because all points of view are important, and access is open to all willingness to contribute.
- TPS is an exploratory approach based on conceptual modeling aimed at finding an informational consensus.

3 Overview of the TPS Method

The TPS method is being developed for conducting a contributive development of information services in the context of digital evolution of Society. The aim of the method is to provide a contribution framework, including concepts, roles and regulations, and to guide the explorations leading to the design and implementation of common information goods as information services [3, 16]. TPS is intended to support transdisciplinary, accountable and inclusive development of information services. Everyone concerned by digital progression of Society can be initiator of and/or contributor to a TPS. Thus, contributors can be from diverse horizons: evolving in different professions, representing public or private institutions, exercising various responsibilities, or simply intervening as responsible individuals.

The development of the TPS method follows the Design Science Research (DSR) [22] and Situational Method Engineering (SME) [4] methodologies. While DSR provides general guidance for building a design artifact, SME offers guidance for building a modular and flexible method adaptable to different service implementation contexts. As a design artefact, the method includes a product part represented by a metamodel, and a process part formalized as a process model.

3.1 Metamodel of TPS

Figure 1 depicts the revised version of the TPS metamodel, which defines the main concepts organized in four spaces: context (yellow), regulation (pink), organization (orange), and contribution (green).

Context. A TPS can only be initiated in a specific *context* which is defined by a couple <*situation, intention*>. The situation explains the reason of opening a TPS. It can be specified in terms of *issues* to deal with (e.g. economic, political, environmental problems), *opportunities* to seize (e.g., new emerging technologies) and/or *obligations* to comply (e.g., new laws or regulations). The intention expresses the will to overcome the situation and move Society forward trough digital transformation. Multiple expertise from various discipline is usually needed in the TPS context to face the situation and to contribute to the achievement of the intention. The context of the TPS determines its organization and the expected contribution. For example, in the TPS on reducing carbon footprint presented in the next section, the situation is described by the problem of global warming and all related issues, and the intention is to offer a system of services to eco-responsible organizations/citizens to measure, reduce and/or offset their carbon footprint in a sustainable manner. The context of TPS also defines the *required expertise* from different *disciplines* to deal with the situation and contribute to reaching the intention. For example, experts in the environmental science should clearly be involved in the TPS on reducing carbon footprint.

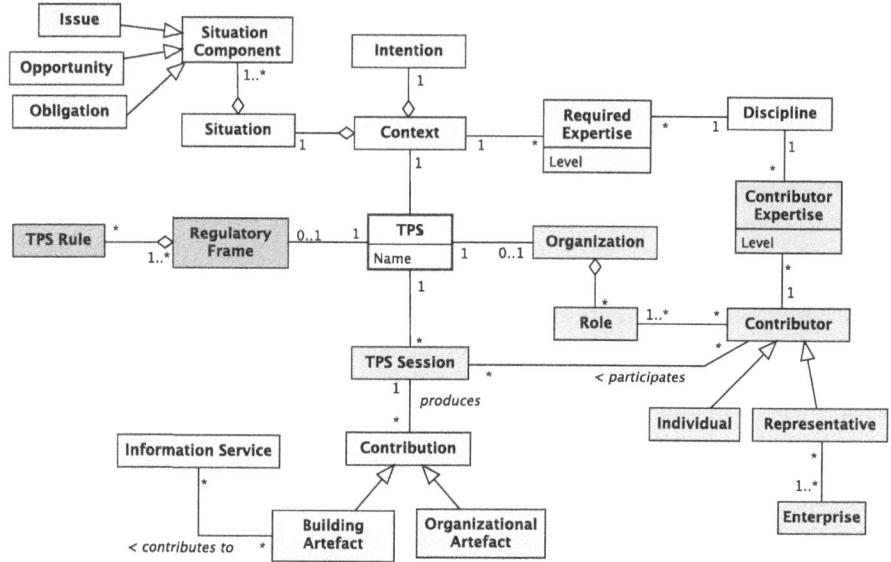

Fig. 1. Metamodel of TPS

Regulation. Since the goal of a TPS is to build common information goods in a collaborative way, a clear *regulatory frame* must be established in the form of a set of *TPS rules*. On one hand, rules must be established regarding the participation of contributors, exploration and co-creation activities, sharing and use of artifacts produced in the TPS, intellectual property, management of the TPS and responsibilities of different roles, etc. On the other hand, this framework should also guarantee the rights of contributors and allow to create an inclusive and free space for collaboration.

Organization. TPS can only exist thanks to *contributors* who, depending on the context, can be *representatives* of *enterprises*[2] or ordinary *individuals* concerned with the purpose of the TPS and willing to contribute to it. Each contributor can play one or more *roles* in a TPS. The typical roles are initiator, builder, facilitator, observer, historian, developer, regulator, and concierge. The more detailed description of roles is available in [3, 21]. TPS requires several builders who will do the main exploratory work and co-design the information services. Facilitators and regulators may be necessary depending on the builders' expertise in using various analysis and design approaches and knowledge in regulations related to the TPS context.

A TPS usually requires several *sessions*. Contributors may be free to participate in all or only some of the sessions. The physical location to organize a TPS is not so

---

[2] The term enterprise is used here in a broad sense, it covers any type of public or private organization.

important as far as it works for all participants. However, we recommend avoiding formal places belonging to one of the contributors. The face-to-face form is preferred, but our recent experience shows that the virtual is also possible thanks to today's communication technologies.

Contribution. This space defines the artefacts created during different TPS sessions. They are classified into *organizational* and *building* artefacts. Organizational artefacts, such as various reports, social media posts, agenda, are created by organizational, management and communication activities. Building artefacts contribute to the exploration, design and implementation of *information services*. They may include various conceptual models, specifications, documentation, code, etc. The models shown in the following section (Fig. 3, 4, 5 and 6) are examples of building artefacts.

3.2 TPS Process Model

It should be noted that the TPS method is not intended to become yet another software development method. The goal of the TPS method is to enable and guide collaborative explorations aimed at achieving actionable results in the form of transdisciplinary information services. Technical design and development may follow dedicated methods provided that they are consistent with the TPS framework (Fig. 1).

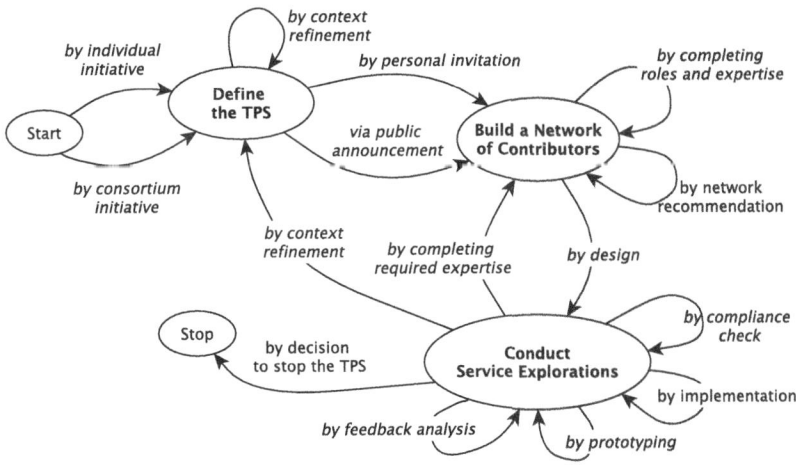

Fig. 2. Process model of TPS

The process model depicted in Fig. 2 proposes a high-level guidance for conducting a TPS. It is expressed by using Map [23] process modeling formalism, where nodes of the graph represent process intentions and arcs represent strategies to achieve the intentions. Conducting a TPS consists in achieving three main intentions, namely *Define the TPS Context*, *Build a Network of Contributors* and *Conduct Service Explorations*. The model indicates that there are various ways (represented in the model by different strategies) to achieve the intentions and that the process may require several iterations. Since the intentions are defined at a high abstraction level, reaching each of them includes several activities. Each activity is then formalized as a method chunk following the [24] SME approach. This level of details is out of scope of this paper.

Define the TPS. In principle, anyone can launch a TPS by defining its context, i.e., its situation and intention, and identifying related disciplines and expertise required. We identify two types of initiatives: *individual* and *consortium*, each of them representing a different strategy. An individual initiative can be started by a responsible organization or individual (or a small group of individuals) with the aim of finding followers, other organizations and citizens, aware of the TPS context and willing to contribute. The initiative launched by a consortium of organizations is already based on an agreement on the cause. The regulatory frame of the TPS, complying with the general TPS rules, must also be agreed at this stage. The context can be refined at any time as the situation changes, for example when new issues or opportunities arise, and/or the intention evolves. This is formalized by the strategy *by context refinement*.

Build a Network of Contributors. The success of attracting contributors depends on many factors, including attractiveness, trend, criticality, and urgency of the context. The first set of contributors is usually collected by the TPS initiators through *personal invitations* or via *public announcements* paying attention to the required expertise and roles. At this moment, the most important is to find interested builders, regulators and a concierge. The network can then be progressively extended based on the *network recommendations* of already agreed contributors and by *completing the missing roles and expertise* progressively. Heterogeneity of contributors is one of the important characteristics to be reached when building the network. Depending on the duration of the TPS, the network can evolve more or less significantly. The rules governing entry and exit from the network must be defined within the TPS regulatory frame.

Conduct Service Explorations. Here, the builders start to work with the help of other supporting roles, notably facilitators and regulators. This step is critical to the success of the TPS, as it requires all these heterogeneous contributors to find a way to collaborate, communicate, co-create actionable outcomes in the form of information services, and agree on the related value propositions. The TPS method promotes exploration *by design* – the usage of various conceptual modeling techniques and methods. To conduct the exploration, contributors need a common language to avoid cognitive confusion due to differences in their professional background. According to [21], this should be an "information language" and an informational approach. Therefore, the *by design* strategy recommends combining various conceptual modeling methods and techniques supporting, among others, value proposition [25, 26], business modeling [27], creativity [28], goal modeling [29], process modeling [23], data modeling, and service description [30]. The design of services undergoes several iterations through refinement of conceptual artifacts until informational consensus is reached. Regulators are responsible for *compliance check* of proposed services with related regulations. Through *prototyping* and/or *development* strategies, services gradually reach their digital form and become actionable artefacts. It may be necessary to extend the network of contributors to complement the required implementation skills. The method also recommends collecting and *analyzing feedback* form service users and using it as input to further iterations and evolutions of the services. How long will last the TPS depends on its scope and the degree of volatility of the TPS context.

4 Exploratory Case Studies of TPS

Since 2018, in the context of our continuing education program at the University of Geneva, we have conducted several exploratory TPS where the participants of the program played the role of contributors, mainly builders, and the teachers played the supporting roles, mainly facilitators. All TPS, except the last one, were initiated by an entity external to the program. The primary goal of these explorations was to experiment the TPS approach in real or close to real societal contexts and to measure the capability to co-create transdisciplinary information services in these contexts. The second goal was to observe the participants, to collect their feedback, and then to refine the TPS method. The method revision presented in the previous section is based on this feedback. Table 1 provides the list of the TPS conducted, including their name, initiator, the number of participants, duration and participation mode (f2f – face-to-face or online via zoom), and the design techniques used during the TPS sessions.

Table 1. Summary of the conducted TPS.

ID	Name	Initiator	Part	Duration	Techniques
TPS1	Dolometer & Wristband	Unige	16	2 days f2f	BMC, Creativity triggers, DCM
TPS2	Neighborhood Local Plans (NLP)	Geneva NLP initiative	17	2 days f2f	BMC, Actor model, DCM
TPS3	ServiceBox	SIG	12	2 days online	VPC, VMC, SMC, DCM, UCM, Map
TPS4	Eternitee Token	TECH-ID	15	2 days online	VPC, VMC, SMC, DCM, UCM, Map
TPS5	Carbon Footprint	Unige	10	4 days f2f	VPC, VMC, SMC, DCM, UCM, Map, Goal modeling

BMC – Business Model Canvas [27], VPC – Value Proposition Canvas [25], UCM – Use Case Model, Creativity triggers [28], SMC – Service Model Canvas [30], Map [23], Goal model [29], DCM – Domain conceptual model (class/relational diagram)

The continuing education program that served as a field of exploration focuses on business development using information services. It lasts 5 months with lessons one day a week and is worth 15 ECTS credits. The course admits practitioners from various organizations and having different roles and responsibilities related to the digital transformation and progression of their organizations. The heterogeneity of the participants allows us to consider that they constitute a network of contributors close to that of a real TPS. The program includes courses and training on service science and business development with services and on various conceptual modeling and design approaches to be used for this purpose, including an introduction to the TPS approach. Two sessions of two days each are dedicated to set up a TPS environment and to explore transdisciplinary information service co-creation. Therefore, we consider that participants of the course have enough knowledge and skills to actively contribute to a TPS.

Since the definition of the context of each TPS was done beforehand and the respective networks of contributors were already established (participants of the program), the five TPS mainly focused on the exploration of services by design.

The first two TPS listed in Table 1, are already documented in our previous publications [3, 16]. TPS1 explored how a novel digital artefact, a new technology, can be used as a source for innovation in terms of digital services. We call such situation a technology push. TPS2 explored the societal push to information service development – services were identified and designed to support a collective design of Neighborhood Local Plans (NLP) in the Canton of Geneva. In these explorations we experimented various conceptual modeling techniques and we found that participants who mastered different modeling techniques performed better. Below we summarize the last three TPS.

4.1 TPS3 – ServiceBox

TPS3 was proposed by a representative of Geneva Industrial Services (SIG) which has set up a secure locker cabinet in one of its buildings to manage the company's car keys. The removal and deposit of the keys of borrowed cars must be done via this cabinet, while the reservation of cars is made via a booking system. This innovation was well accepted by all related actors: drivers, receptionists, car managers. With the outbreak of Covid-19 and all the related restrictions and distancing rules, ideas of other potential usages to this cabinet started to emerge. The intention of the TPS was formulated as follows "To design a ServiceBox as a set of services that would extend the use of lockers to other services allowing to reduce human contact in the daily activities of the organization".

After the initiator introduced the topic and a general brainstorming, the builders (i.e. program participants) organized themselves into small groups and used breakout rooms to develop different ideas. Facilitators (teachers) moved from room to room, observing and helping to use the design techniques.

After identifying a few new services for SIG, participants decided to give the TPS a broader context. Since all Society was concerned by the restrictions of Covid-19, the intention was enlarged to explore the use of similar lockers in larger social and commercial contexts, such as services for shopkeepers who might use lockers for the delivery of goods, and services for citizens who can use lockers to exchange and/or sell various goods. As design techniques, the participants used domain conceptual modeling (class/relational diagrams) to reach a common understanding of the domain. To identify new services and agree on their value propositions, they applied VPC [25] and BMC [27]. Process modeling with Map [23] and use cases were developed to explore the usability of the identified services. Then, services were described with SMC [30] and information service models integrating four service spaces: static, dynamic, rule and role [14, 15]. The exploration also identified regulatory issues, the clarification of which would require contributors with expertise in this area. One example of models produced during the exploration is shown in Fig. 3.

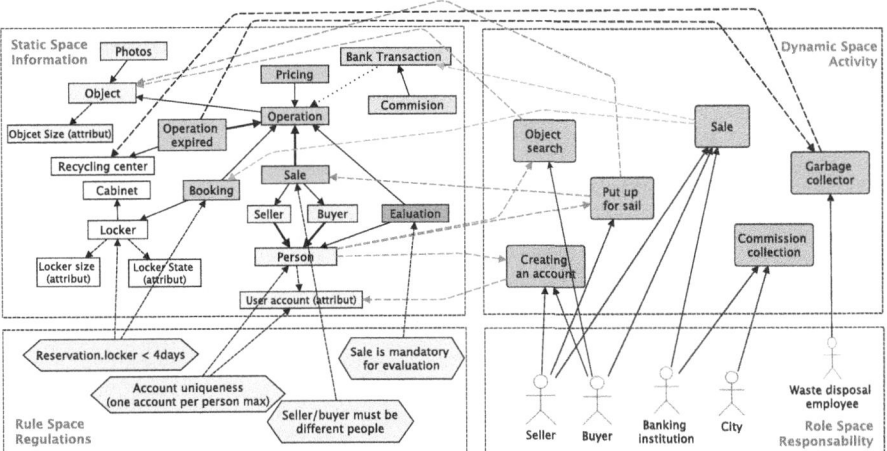

Fig. 3. Example of a conceptual model of a complex information service enabling the sale and distribution of goods via a locker. The model includes four spaces: the static space (domain concepts and their relationships), the dynamic space (activities supported by the service), the rule space (regulations and integrity constraints) and the role space (business roles and their responsibilities represented as actors).

4.2 TPS4 – Eternitee Token

TPS4 was initiated by an association called TECH-ID based on their project Eternitee aiming to promote societal participation and voluntary contribution of individuals. The intention of the TPS was to explore what kind of information services could allow to value the voluntary actions and recognize the voluntary work. Indeed, the voluntary contribution of individuals has no measured recognition or certification, which explains the difficulty to attract people. As a starting point, the concept of digital token was proposed as means to quantify and/or qualify the voluntary work. The initiators of the TPS stressed that the area is strategic, and the situation was never worked on from a digital service perspective. Nevertheless, the identified services and value propositions produced by the contributors during the TPS sessions, in the form of conceptual models of the proposed services, demonstrate the creative power of the approach. TPS4 was held online (due to Covid-19 restrictions) for two days and was organized in different types of sessions: brainstorming, group work in breakout rooms by using different design techniques, plenary presentations of intermediate results, and final restitution. A service platform supporting volunteers' registration, certification, attribution of tokens, exchange of tokens for goods or services with participating partners, was explored and conceptualized. Again, various design artefacts were produced with the aim to identify services and their value propositions. To illustrate a different artifact, Fig. 4 shows a service model canvas representing a complex service called Volunteer Platform.

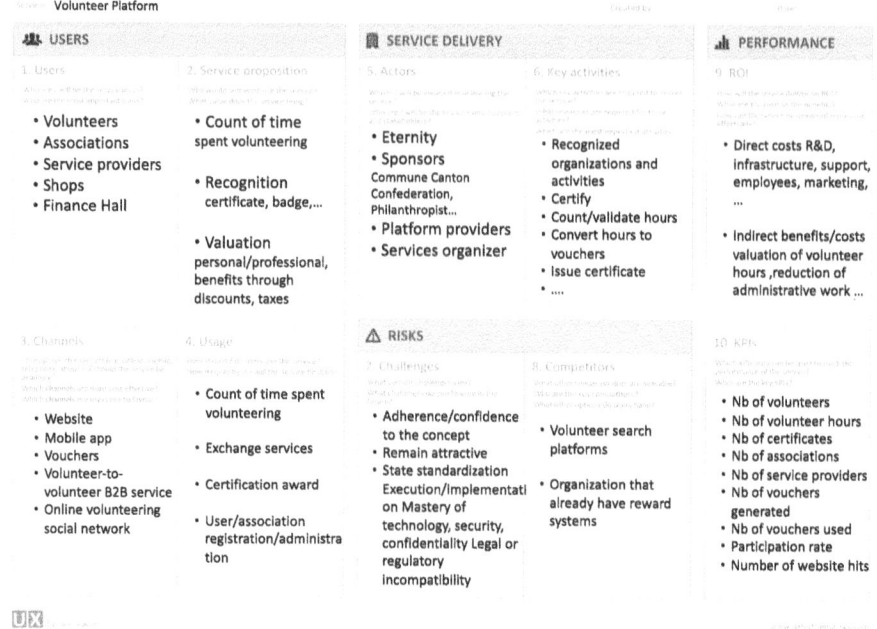

Fig. 4. Example of a service model canvas produced during the TPS4 Eternitee Token.

4.3 TPS5 – Carbon Footprint

In 2022, we chose a hot topic of carbon footprint reduction as the situation for the TPS5. The intention was defined as "offering a system of services to eco-responsible organizations/citizens to measure, reduce and/or offset their carbon footprint in a sustainable manner". The participants spent 4 days exploring the topic and trying to answer the questions: How to make people and organizations eco-responsible? How to value their actions? How to make them sustainable? How to move from individual actions to collective and coordinated ones? After the presentation of the context and a general brainstorming, participants created two groups: one taking as subject responsible citizens and the other – green enterprises. The four days of co-creation ware organized in work in groups sessions and plenary presentations and discussions. To explore the context and identify potential value propositions and services to enable them, participants produced goal models [29], VPC [25], BMC [27] and domain conceptual models. Then, selected services were designed with the help of SMC [30], use cases and information service models. The group working on the proposal for citizens has developed a design for a service system, which they have called Smart Challenge Co2050. This system aims at providing several services for community building, organizing events and actions to reduce carbon footprint, participating in these events, sharing one's own experience and tips for daily Co2 reduction. The value proposition canvas of this service system is illustrated in Fig. 5.

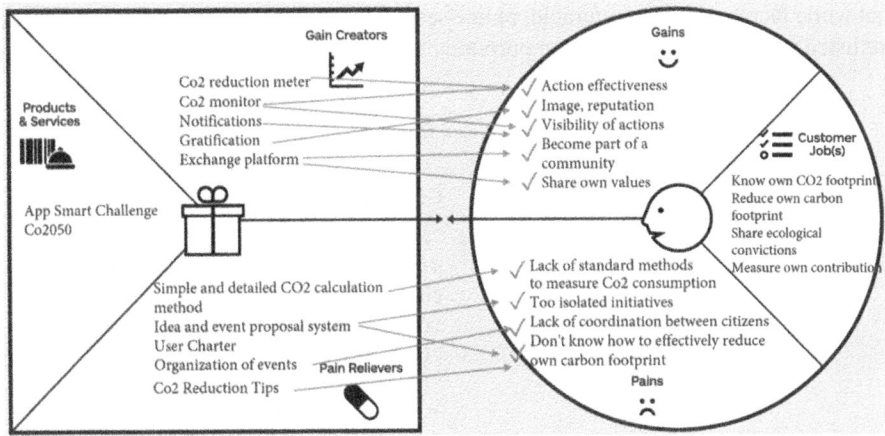

Fig. 5. Example of a value proposition canvas created in the TPS Carbon Footprint.

The group working on the proposal for green enterprises has developed a proposal to create an entity specialized in eco-responsible management of businesses. The entity will be offering services of advice how to reduce enterprise carbon footprint and its environmental impact via a digital platform including a dashboard and a Co2 meter, and a comparison system between companies (Compar ECO). Figure 6 illustrates a goal model that led to the identification of these services.

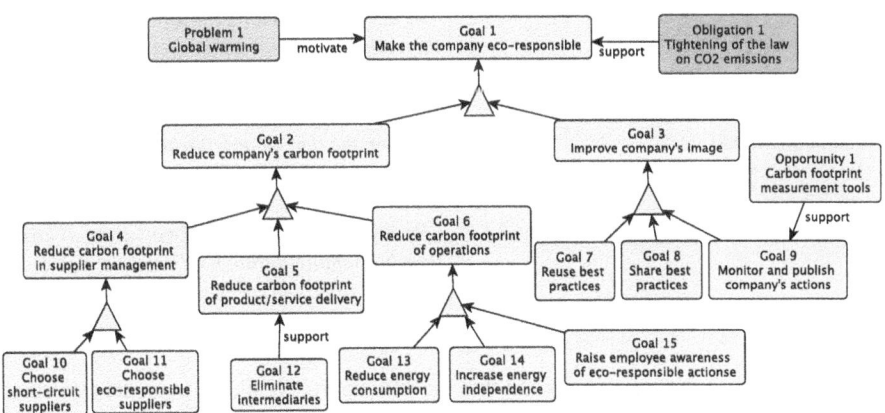

Fig. 6. Example of a goal model created in the TPS5 Carbon Footprint.

4.4 Feedback from Participants and Lessons Learned

At the end of each TPS, we asked the participants including the initiators to give their feedback. Overall, all participants were positively surprised by the ability to co-create within the TPS framework, recognized the value of conceptual modeling, and agreed that while face-to-face is preferable, online sessions also worked well. Same comments are listed in Table 2 for illustration purposes.

Table 2. Feedback from participants

Subject	Comments
Participation and heterogeneity of participants	*"Extraordinary group dynamic, each person was able to bring something to the work of the group"*, *"Group dynamics, extraordinary result."* *"Collective intelligence worked well."* *"I liked the concept of Third Place. The exchanges were rich because of the difference in our professions and our experiences."*
Usage of conceptual modeling	*"The difficulty of getting out of your comfort zone and aligning yourself with others was finally overcome thanks to modeling"*, *"The models help to understand a new domain, to imagine services beyond the basic subject, to anticipate future services"*, *"All the techniques and models used were complementary, they made it possible to explore services from different angles, different perspectives, complement and align them"* *"At first, I didn't think we were going to get there, the result exceeded expectations., we begin to understand service through these various models"*
Participation mode	*"Online the time of appropriation of the subject is longer. Everything takes longer and suddenly fewer breaks."* *"We explore and suddenly we progress. It takes iterations, more iterations. Doing the design remotely (by zoom) is new but it worked well."*

From our observation, we can add that the TPS approach allows to create synergies between people from different professions, to put into practice knowledge and expertise from different disciplines and to set up a transdisciplinary co-creation of information services. Conceptual modeling proves to be a formidable tool for creating these synergies and fostering collective intelligence. It is worth noting that the expertise of the participants in the design approaches used during the TPS was very diverse. Some were just discovering them. However, it was sufficient for just one participant to master a particular design approach to guide the exploration using it. Of course, the role of the facilitators was not negligible either.

5 TPS in the Context of Society 5.0

In the context of Society 5.0 [1, 2], the TPS approach aims to support the co-creation and collaboration across various sectors of society. By involving diverse actors in the exploratory creation and evolution of information services, TPS embodies the principles of Society 5.0, which promote inclusion, innovation, and the integration of advanced technologies to improve quality of life.

Digitalization, as seen through the lens of Society 5.0, is not just about technological advancement but also about ensuring that these advancements contribute positively to societal well-being. By fostering transdisciplinary, trans-organizational and even trans-national environments where various actors co-create information services, TPS contributes to the goal of Society 5.0 to create a super-smart and people-centric society. The method ensures that digital transformation efforts are inclusive, addressing the needs and aspirations of all members of society, and leading to the services that are sustainable, scalable, and beneficial for the broader community. Moreover, by focusing on the co-creation of information services, TPS helps build a sense of ownership and responsibility among contributors, aligning with Society 5.0's objective of creating a society where individuals feel empowered and engaged in the continuous improvement of their surroundings. We are convinced that this approach can significantly enhance the effectiveness and acceptance of digital transformation initiatives, ensuring they meet the diverse needs of society, and contribute to the overall goal of creating a more advanced and human-centered society. Despite our enthusiasm, applying the method in practice remains challenging.

6 Conclusion

In the context of the digital progression of business and society, the paper presents a new method, called Third Place for Services (TPS), for driving the contributory development of transdisciplinary information services. The TPS method is founded on the principles of Service Science and the concept of information service, drawing inspiration from Social Science. Five exploratory case studies were conducted to validate the applicability of the approach and refine its definition. Each case study had a distinct context – a societal situation requiring the contribution of various actors where transdisciplinary information services would bring value to each of them and beyond. A real TPS would certainly require several sessions and could last weeks, months, or even years, depending on its scope, type of contributors, and the nature of the related business or societal activity. However, even though these TPS sessions were relatively short, we found the results promising. Even brief explorations supported by adequate conceptual tools resulted in the creation of artefacts allowing progress in the quest for the digital transformation of society. Therefore, we argue that the TPS method supports the co-creation of transdisciplinary and trans-organizational information services contributing to the societal progression. The TPS method, is formalized in the form of a metamodel and a process model. The modularity of the process model, embodied in intentions and strategies, allow it to be easily formalized in terms of method chunks as recommended by [4, 24]. This formalization is our current preoccupation. Further experimentation of the method in real cases and the collection of more formally structured feedback from participants will help us continue its refinement and gain its acceptance in practice.

References

1. Deguchi, A., et al.: What is Society 5.0? In Society 5.0: A People-Centric Super-Smart Society, pp. 1–24. Springer, Cham (2020)
2. Salgues, B.: Society 5.0: Industry of the Future, Technologies, Methods and Tools. Wiley (2018)
3. Ralyté, J., Léonard, M.: Tiers-Lieu for services: an exploratory approach to societal progression. In: Nóvoa, H., Drăgoicea, M., Kühl, N. (eds.) IESS 2020. LNBIP, vol. 377, pp. 289–303. Springer, Cham (2020). https://doi.org/10.1007/978-3-030-38724-2_21
4. Henderson-Sellers, B., Ralyté, J., Ågerfalk, P., Rossi, M.: Situational Method Engineering. Springer, Cham (2014)
5. Maglio, P.P., Spohrer, J.: Fundamentals of service science. J. Acad. Mark. Sci. **36**(1), 18–20 (2008)
6. Maglio, P.P., Kieliszewski, C.A., Spohrer, J.C. (eds.): Handbook of Service Science. Springer, Boston (2010)
7. Vargo, S.L., Lusch, R.F.: Service-dominant logic: what it is, what it is not, what it might be. In: Lusch, R.F., Vargo, S.L. (eds.) The Service-Dominant Logic of Marketing: Dialog, Debate, and Directions, pp 43–56. M.E. Sharpe, Armonk (2006)
8. Vargo, S.L., Akaka, M.A.: Service-dominant logic as a foundation for service science: clarifications. Serv. Sci. **1**(1), 32–41 (2009)
9. Vargo, S.L., Akaka, M.A.: Service-dominant logic: continuing the evolution. J. Acad. Mark. Sci. **36**(1), 1–10 (2008)
10. Lusch, R.F., Vargo, S.L.: Service-Dominant Logic: Premises, Perspectives, Possibilities. Cambridge University Press, New York (2014)
11. Spohrer, J., Maglio, P.P., Bailey, J., Gruhl, D.: Steps toward a science of service systems. Computer **40**(1), 71–77 (2007). https://doi.org/10.1109/MC.2007.33
12. Maglio, P.P., Vargo, S.L., Caswell, N., Spohrer, J.: The service system is the basic abstraction of service science. IseB **7**(4), 395–406 (2009)
13. Arni-Bloch, N., Ralyté, J.: MISS: a metamodel of information system service. In: Papadopoulos, G.A., Wojtkowski, W., Wojtkowski, G., Wrycza, S., Zupancic, J. (eds.) Information Systems Development, pp. 177–186. Springer, Heidelberg (2008). https://doi.org/10.1007/b137171_19
14. Arni-Bloch, N., Ralyté, J., Léonard, M.: Service-driven information systems evolution: handling integrity constraints consistency. In: Persson, A., Stirna, J. (eds.) PoEM 2009. LNBIP, vol. 39, pp. 191–206. Springer, Cham (2009). https://doi.org/10.1007/978-3-642-05352-8_15
15. Ralyté, J., Khadraoui, A., Léonard, M.: Designing the shift from information systems to information services systems. Bus. Inf. Syst. Eng. **57**(1), 37–49 (2015)
16. Ralyté, J., Léonard, M.: Exploring the concept of "Tiers-Lieu" for information services: the value of conceptual modeling. In: Joint Proceedings of the ER Forum and Poster & Demos Session, ER 2019. CEUR Workshop Proceedings, vol. 2469, pp. 98–107 (2019). http://ceur-ws.org/Vol-2469/
17. Yurchyshyna, A.: Towards contributory development by the means of services as common goods. In: Nóvoa, H., Drăgoicea, M. (eds.) IESS 2015. LNBIP, vol. 201, pp. 12–24. Springer, Cham (2015). https://doi.org/10.1007/978-3-319-14980-6_2
18. Nicolescu, B.: Manifesto of Transdisciplinarity. State University of New York (SUNY) Press, New York. (2002)

19. Oldenburg, R.: The Great Good Place: Cafes, Coffee Shops, Bookstores, Bars, Hair Salons, and Other Hangouts at the Heart of a Community, Da Capo Press (1998)
20. Burret, A.: Étude de la configuration en Tiers-Lieu – la repolitisation par le service (Third Place Configuration Study - Repolitization Through Services). Ph.D. thesis, Université des Lumières, Lyon, France (2017)
21. Léonard, M.: Informational Lights from Service Science for the Progression of Society, EDP Sciences (2020). https://doi.org/10.1051/978-2-7598-2467-0
22. Peffers, K., Tuunanen, T., Rothenberger, M.A., Chatterjee, S.: A design science research methodology for information systems research. J. Manag. Inf. Syst. **24**(3), 45–77 (2007). https://doi.org/10.2753/MIS0742-1222240302
23. Rolland, C., Prakash, N., Benjamen, A.: A multi-model view of process modelling. Requirements Eng. J. **4**(4), 169–187 (1999)
24. Mirbel, I., Ralyté, J.: Situational method engineering: combining assembly-based and roadmap-driven approaches. Requirements Eng. **11**(1), 58–78 (2006)
25. Osterwalder, A., Pigneur, Y., Bernarda, G.: Value Proposition Design: How to Create Products and Services Customers Want. Wiley (2014)
26. Gordijn, J., Wieringa, R.: E3value User Guide. Designing Your Ecosystem in a Digital World. The Value Engineers B.V., Soest, NL (2021). ISBN 978-90-828524-3-1
27. Osterwalder, A., Pigneur, Y.: Business Model Generation: A Handbook for Visionaries, Game Changers and Challengers. Wiley (2010)
28. Burnay, C., Horkoff, J., Maiden, N.: Stimulating stakeholders' imagination: new creativity triggers for eliciting novel requirements. In: 2016 IEEE 24th International Requirements Engineering Conference (RE). IEEE (2016). https://doi.org/10.1109/RE.2016.36
29. Sandkuhl, K., Stirna, J., Persson, A., Wißotzki, M.: Enterprise Modeling: Tackling Business Challenges with the 4EM Method. Springer, Heidelberg (2014)
30. Turner, N.: Introducing the service model canvas. https://www.uxforthemasses.com/updated-service-model-canvas/

Using Enterprise Modeling for Dealing with Complexity of Elderly Care in Sweden

Erik Perjons[1], Ilia Bider[1,2(✉)], and Martin Henkel[1]

[1] Stockholm University, Borgarfjordsgatan 12, 164 55 Kista, Stockholm, Sweden
{perjons,ilia,martinh}@dsv.su.se
[2] University of Tartu, Ülikooli 18, 50090 Tartu, Estonia

Abstract. Elderly care in Sweden is quite complex due to the many different actors involved. Actors are governed by different regulatory authorities and use many IT systems that often are not connected to each other. This paper describes the usage of Enterprise Modeling to pinpoint the problematic areas in the coordination between the actors and to suggest solutions. The first stage of the project, which is described in this paper, is to build as-is models and identify the problematic areas. This is done based on the previous project that analyzed the state of elderly care in the county of Stockholm with the goal of suggesting how to connect various IT systems used by the involved actors. The previous project did not use enterprise modeling but produced enough information for building and analyzing such models. The as-is models presented in this paper are built using the Fractal Enterprise Modeling technique. The models and discovered problems will be used to suggest solutions in the form of to-be models.

Keywords: elderly care · enterprise modeling · fractal enterprise model · FEM

1 Introduction

There are many agents that provide elderly care in Sweden. They include:

- home services, which provide assistance to elderly individuals with daily living activities in their own homes and apartments
- nursing homes, which are residential facilities for elderly that provide both assistance with daily living activities and medical care
- primary care, which provides general medical care
- special care, which provides special medical care (e.g. eye surgery)
- hospitals, which provide emergency or advanced care

Different agents are under the control of different authorities and are regulated by different legislations. Home services and nursing homes are under municipality authority, while the rest are under county authority. Also, the actors can be private or public. Lack of coordination between the actors that take care of the elderly results in the ineffectiveness of total care and non-optimal usage of resources. A simple example of the latter is as follows. If an elderly person is accepted to a hospital, home services might not know this and send a worker to his/her home to provide service.

The problems related to providing elderly care were investigated in the DISVO project [1, 2]. This project has a special focus on integrating various IT systems used by the different agents that provided the elderly care. The project listed the problems in cooperation between the agents and suggested some solutions, especially those related to integrating various systems used by the agents. The DISVO project used scenarios of what might happen to an elderly person, how the agents behaved, what means they used, including IT systems, and what problems existed in coordinating various agents.

Now, we are embarking on the next project that will result in more concrete solutions for the discovered problems. We plan to use enterprise modeling for this end. The first step is to use the information gathered during the DISVO project to build and analyze as-is models, as this has not been done in the DISVO project. The models should also incorporate the changes that have happened since the DISVO project was finished. The second step is to build to-be models that incorporate solutions to the problem discovered in the first step. The current paper is devoted to the first step of the new project. The idea behind using enterprise modeling is to give a structured overview of the discovered problems and show how they are related to healthcare agents and the tasks for which they are responsible. Moreover, examining if and how the problems and solutions can be represented in a model paves the way for creating a methodology of structured model-driven analysis that can be used in similar projects.

For building the models, we use a technique called Fractal Enterprise Model (FEM) [3, 4]. FEM has been chosen (1) because we believe it has enough capability to highlight the existing problems and support identification of solutions and (2) because it is our invention; thus, we have enough knowledge about its structure, and we have experience in using it for creating enterprise models.

FEM has a form of a directed graph with two main types of nodes, *processes,* and *assets,* where the arrows (edges) from assets to processes show which assets are used in which processes, and arrows from processes to assets show which processes help to have specific assets in "healthy" and working order. The arrows are labeled with meta-tags that show how a given asset is used, e.g., *workforce, infrastructure,* etc., or how a given process helps to have the given assets "in order", i.e., *acquire, maintain,* or *retire.*

This paper belongs to the topic "Empirics of enterprise modeling" listed in PoEM call for papers [5]. It can be classified as a "modeling practice" or "case study" of using modeling to better understand organizational problems and find solutions for them. The rest of the paper is structured according to the following plan. In Sect. 2, we present a background of the project and introduce FEM using an example related to the current project. In Sect. 3, we present models built so far, which include a depiction of the problems discovered. In Sect. 4, we analyze and reflect on our experience and draw some conclusions. In Sect. 5, we summarize our experience and suggest future directions.

2 Research Background

2.1 Research Approach

The project to which this paper belongs has two goals, one practical and one research. The practical goal is to define the problems in the current elderly care and suggest solutions to them. The research goal is to investigate how well FEM works for detecting problems in cooperation between multiple organizational agents in pursuing a common goal and for supporting the identification of solutions for the detected problems.

The achievement of the practical goal can be judged by the results. Firstly, whether the suggestions are accepted, and secondly, whether the accepted solutions have improved the cooperation between different agents. The appropriateness of FEM for the task can be measured by how well the problems are presented and whether the presentations give a clue for possible solutions. As we are at the beginning of our journey, the evaluation of the practical results cannot be done at this point. Regarding the appropriateness of FEM for the task, we can use our own reflections, as suggested in [6], as we function as practitioners in the project. Our reflection will be presented in Sect. 4, "Discussion".

FEM has been tested and found useful in several practical projects, such as [7, 8]. However, most of its usage was in modeling activities of one organization. An exception is the paper [9], where a model represents cooperation between different organizational agents. However, the goal of the paper [9] is different from the current one. In the former, FEM was used to analyze already completed changes; in the current project, FEM is used as a tool to formally identify the weaknesses in cooperation and suggest improvements.

For building and analyzing the models, we use information gathered in the previous project [1, 2], as well as the experience of the current authors, two of which has been active participants in the previous project.

2.2 Introduction to Fractal Enterprise Model

As FEM is not a widely spread enterprise modeling technique, we will present the basic concepts and the relations used in this technique based on an example. The example concerns cooperation between three different players in total elderly care, namely, home services, primary care, and hospitals. The model is presented in Fig. 1. In it, elements that belong to the different actors have a special color for their borders. Home services elements have blue borders, primary care elements have green borders and hospital elements have yellow borders. In addition, the shape that represents the elderly clients has a red border to show that this is the focus of the model.

The model gives only a general view of cooperation between the three actors in elderly care; in it, many details are omitted. The model uses two main FEM concepts for describing the structure of the business: a process – a repetitive behavior – represented as an oval, and an asset – a set of things or actors that are needed for the behavior to become repetitive – represented as a rectangle. A relation between a process and an asset is represented by an arrow. FEM differentiates two main types of relations between processes and assets. The first – *used-in* relation – is a relation of a process "using" an asset; in this case, the arrow points from the asset to the process and has a solid line. The second – *managed-by* relation – is a relation of a process managing the asset, e.g., adding elements; in this case, the arrow points from the process to the asset and has a dashed line.

Processes and assets have properties, several of which are presented visually. For example, a double-lined border of a process shows that this is a primary process – the process that produces some value for the beneficiary of the process. The beneficiary is identified by the corresponding label on a used-in relation between a process and an asset.

In FEM, a label inside an oval names the given process, and a label inside a rectangle names the given asset. Arrows are also labeled to show the meaning of relations between the processes and assets. A label on an arrow pointing from an asset to a process identifies the role the given asset plays in the process, for example, *Workforce* or *Infrastructure*. A label on an arrow pointing from a process to an asset identifies how the process manages (i.e., changes) the asset. In FEM, an asset is considered as a set of entities capable of playing a given role in a given process. Labels leading into assets from processes reflect how the set is affected; for example, the label *Acquire* identifies that the process can/should increase the set size. Note that having more than one label on an arrow is possible; it shows that the asset fulfills several roles in a process or that the process manages an asset in several ways.

Labels inside ovals (representing processes) and rectangles (representing assets) are not standardized. They can be set according to the terminology accepted in the given domain or be specific to a given organization. Labels on arrows (which represent the relations between processes and assets) are standardized. This is done using a relatively limited set of abstract relations, such as *Workforce* or *Acquire*, which are clarified by the domain- and context-specific labels inside ovals and rectangles.

Note that standard labels on relations are quite abstract, which forces the modeler to uncover the essence of the relations between the elements. This does not affect the readability of the models for the stakeholders, as they understand the models based on the labels inside the shapes. Standardization of the labels on the relations facilitates the formal analysis of the models and the usage of patterns based on the labels on relations, which is essential for this work.

While several types of relations show how an asset is used in a process (see example in Fig. 1), only three types of relations describe how a process manages an asset – *Acquire*, *Maintain*, and *Retire*. *Acquire* means, as mentioned above, that new elements are added to the asset, *Retire* means that elements are removed from the asset, and *Maintain* means that elements are changed so that they can continue to be part of the asset engaged in the respective process.

The *Stock* label on used-in relation has a special meaning. It indicates that one or more of the asset elements are consumed in each run of the process. This means that the asset should be filled in constantly. The *Stock* label can be alone, which means that the asset has some consumable parts, or it can be accompanied by some other label that clarifies the essence of the elements of the asset. For example, the *Stock* label can be accompanied by the label *Tech & info infrastructure*, which may mean that the elements of the asset provide information for the process; see an example of such a case in Fig. 1. Note that if *Stock* is added as a label to the relation, its visualization changes, namely, two additional short lines are added to the tail of the arrow that expresses the relation.

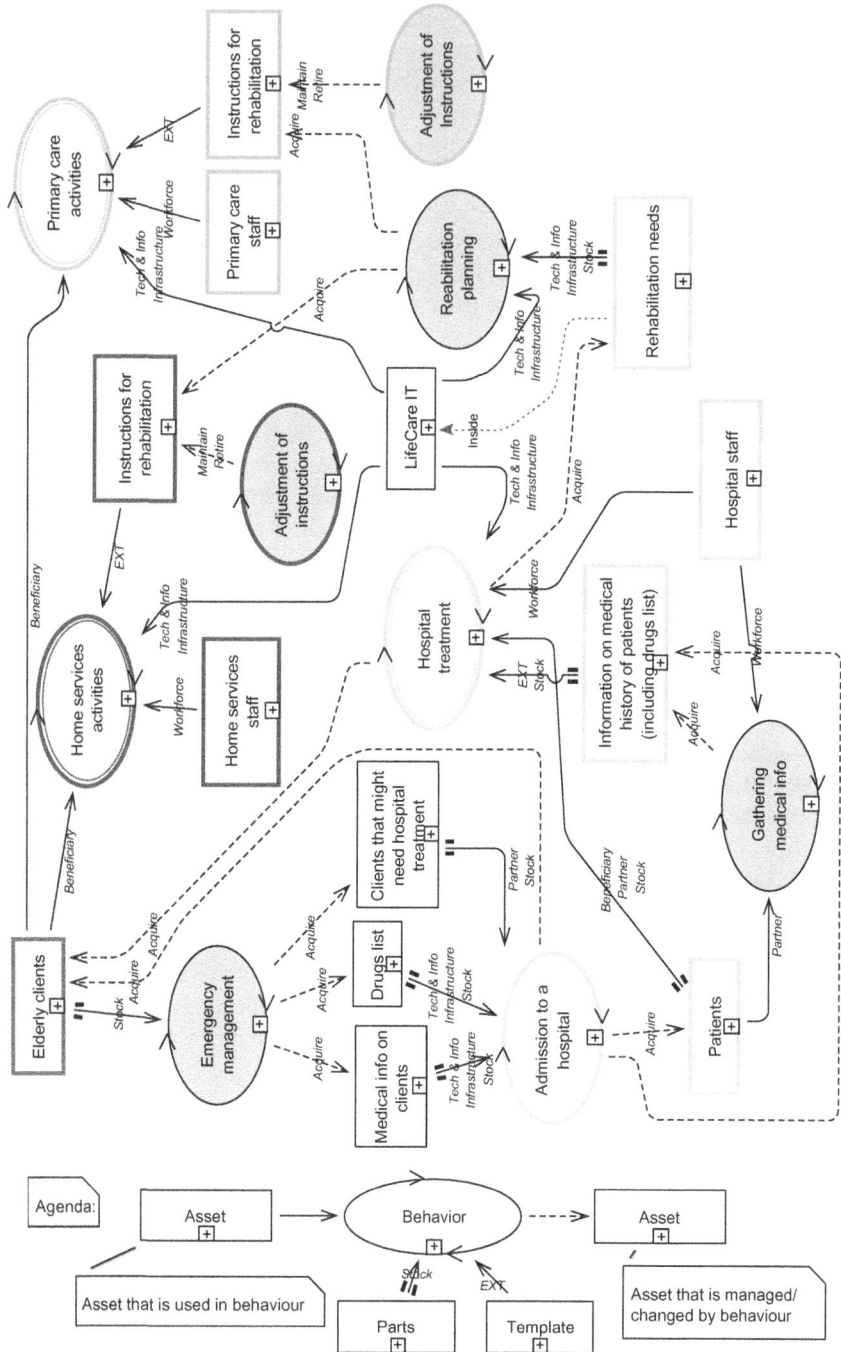

Fig. 1. A partial FEM for elderly care

The *EXT* (Executable Template) label has a special meaning; it shows that the asset is used as a controlling element of a process. Such an asset can include manuals, policy documents, and instructions. It can also include workflow systems that control the flow of activities. *EXT* can be used alone or in combination with other labels; see Fig. 1.

The model in Fig. 1 shows that elderly clients are considered as beneficiaries of home services and primary care. In case of emergency, they become patients of a hospital and remain there until they are discharged. When they are admitted to the hospital, there is a need for cooperation with primary care to establish their medical history (not shown in the model in Fig. 1). After discharge, the elderly may need rehabilitation, which is provided by both home services and primary care, and these agents need to coordinate their efforts. Also, the home services need to know that the patient is in the hospital, and when he/she is discharged. Otherwise, they would send their people to the patient's home to compete some services.

The above introduction to FEM includes concepts that are needed for understanding most of Sect. 3. Additional concepts, such as background colors, are introduced as the needs arise. Readers who are interested to know more about FEM and why it has the term *fractal* in the name are referred to papers [3, 4].

2.3 Suitability of FEM for the Task

As was already discussed, we use enterprise modeling for detecting problems in cooperation between the agents, as well as suggesting solutions for these problems. Therefore, it is important to differentiate in the model activities where only one agent participates from activities where there is cooperation between the agents. When using FEM, this is done by using border colors. In Fig. 1, we use border color to represent areas of responsibilities of different agents. Elements that have no special border color represent multi-actor actions and assets. Thus, the attention is given mostly to the processes that have neutral (black) border color.

Furthermore, we need to understand which agents and tools are engaged in activities that require cooperation. In FEM, this is done by using the concept of asset and its connection to the action. As mentioned earlier, FEM has two types of such connection *used-in* and *managed-by*; both are used in the model in Fig. 1. *Managed-by* is used to explicate the essence of action (what effect it produces), and *used-in* is used to explain in what capacity an asset is used. Several of such capacities are useful in our case. W*orkforce* and *partner* shows who is engaged in the activity, and their border color shows the agents to which they belong. *Tech & Info infrastructure* shows what tools are used in the activities, and *EXT* shows the steering mechanisms of the actions. Again, the border color shows to which agents they belong.

Whenever needed, an association relation could be used to depict a relation between the model elements that cannot be expressed with *used-in* and *managed-by* relations. In Fig. 1, we have one such association between *LifeCare IT* and *Rehabilitation needs*. The free text label on this association explains the connection, namely that *Rehabilitation needs* are stored in *LifeCare IT*. This is an example of an asymmetric association expressed by a dashed blue arrow that has an arrowhead only at one end. Besides the asymmetrical, symmetrical association can be used, which has arrowheads on both ends (there are no examples in this paper). The association is a very general relation; it should be explained by a label attached to it.

The deliberation above shows that a priory FEM is a good candidate for the task of creating a model that includes multi-organizational cooperation in order to discover problems and suggest solutions. This does not mean that another modeling language could be as good or even better for this task. It only means that FEM is worth trying, and this paper is devoted to such a trial and analysis of its results.

2.4 A Short Literature Review

The topic of modeling interactions between various agents has a long history. For example, the paper [10] published in year 2000 discusses the modeling of the processes that cross the organizational boundary using the workflow perspective. However, the example taken in [10] is not of the same kind as in our case; [10] discusses the interaction between companies that have different goals, such as providers, buyers, suppliers, etc. In our case, we consider cooperation between the organizations that have a common goal – providing care for the third party – elderly persons. Besides, the workflow perspective is too detailed for our case. For now, we are not interested in the details of the processes but in what tools and agents are engaged and in what way cooperation does not work. From the time the paper [10] was written, the topic of inter-organizational business processes was extensively discussed in the research literature devoted to Business Process Management (BPM). However, as they belong to BPM, they are not especially relevant to our research on the reasons mentioned above.

There is also a body of literature that discusses modeling of cooperation between various actors using not workflow but more general enterprise modeling languages. For example, [11] uses i* modeling language to model situations where organizations collaborate on some issues and compete on other issues. The paper introduces a set of requirements for modeling languages to model such situations, such as presenting two (2) or more actors, added value, etc. Only some of these requirements are related to our project, as we describe collaboration without competition. Moreover, most of the literature is devoted to situations where the partners can decide with whom to cooperate and need to create a contract that regulates the cooperation. This is not true for our case. Cooperation between the partners is defined by the laws and regulatory documents produced by the central and local governments. Therefore, our focus is on finding the problems in the tools and procedures in use rather than in the contracts and the level of trust between the partners.

There is also a large body of literature related to cooperation in healthcare. For example, the paper [12] presents an approach to healthcare system analysis and design by integrating socio-technical systems (STS) theory with enterprise modeling (EM). The study utilizes various enterprise modeling techniques, such as goal modeling, process modeling, resource modeling, and agent modeling, to capture and visualize the complex interactions and dependencies within the healthcare system. By applying these models to a healthcare scenario, the paper demonstrates how combining STS and EM can enhance coordination among stakeholders, improve resource allocation, and optimize healthcare delivery. However, this paper [12] takes a very broad view of healthcare; in our project, we concentrate on finding problems in the existing collaboration between the agents in the Swedish context. Thus, our task is much narrower and more to the earth.

Concluding this short overview of the existing literature, we can conclude that there is a vast body of literature that is devoted to multi-organizational cooperation in general, and in healthcare in particular. However, most of the literature takes a more general view of this cooperation than is needed for our project. Besides, we use a modeling technique that was not tested in similar projects. Therefore, our endeavor has a possibility to produce results not published previously.

3 Analysis of the Current Situation

In this section, we extend the model presented in Fig. 1 with details that concern cooperation between various agents and the problems that exist in the way how the cooperation is organized. The light green background color attached to some processes in Fig. 1 represents elements that are covered in more detail in this section. More exactly, we will discuss the following scenarios:

1. *Emergency management* – when the elderly person has a problem that might require hospital treatment
2. *Gathering medical info* on the elderly patient admitted to the hospital
3. *Rehabilitation* of the elderly person after he/she is discharged from the hospital. This scenario extends the model in Fig. 1 that concerns elements: *Rehabilitation planning* and *Adjustment of instruction* (two elements in Fig. 1).

3.1 Emergency Management

There are four different scenarios in which the decision to take an elderly person to the hospital is taken. The first scenario is when a home service worker visiting an elderly person discovers that something has happened to him; for example, an elderly person has fallen and might have broken a bone. In this case, the home service worker contacts primary care and waits until a worker from this service arrives. The primary care worker determines the need to send the elderly person to a hospital. The FEM for this scenario is presented in Fig. 2.

In this model, the elements taken from the model in Fig. 1 have a special visual form; they have a thick arrow in the upper right corner. This arrow shows that the element already exists somewhere else, e.g. in another model. An element with a thick arrow in the upper right corner is called a ghost. In the FEM toolkit that we use for producing the models [4], a user can move from the ghost to the original element by clicking on the arrow. There is also a possibility to find all ghosts of the given element, (if there are any). New elements in Fig. 2 that do not exist in the model of Fig. 1 have the usual visualization; there is only one such element in Fig. 2 – *Primary care IT*. In this scenario, the primary care worker uses their IT system to provide full information on medical history and the current drug list.

In the next scenario, Scenario 2, a home service worker finds an elderly person in a condition that demands immediate action, i.e., call an ambulance that would take the elderly to the hospital. This situation is presented in the model in Fig. 3. The difference from scenario 1 is that the home service has no access to the medical history, but it can provide a drug list that normally exists in a printed form in the elderly person's home.

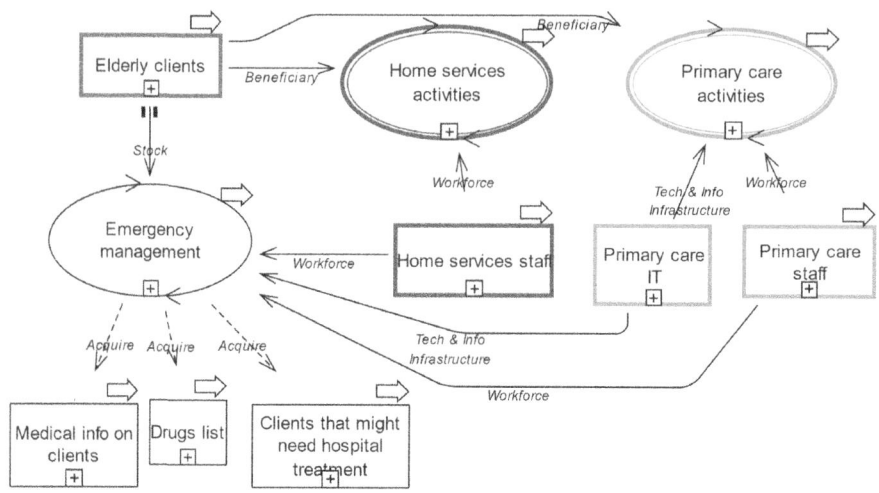

Fig. 2. Emergency management – Scenario 1.

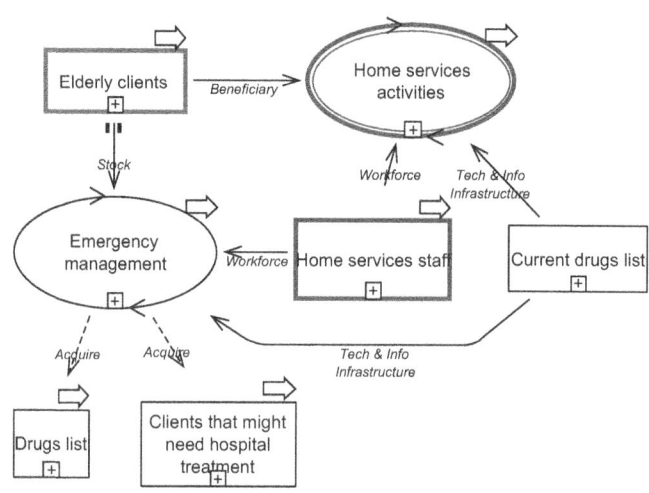

Fig. 3. Emergency management – Scenario 2.

In the next two scenarios, neither home services nor primary care workers are present. In Scenario 3, an elderly person him-/herself calls emergency service and is taken to the hospital. The model that represents this case is presented in Fig. 4. It is possible, though, but there is no guarantee that the elderly person will take the printed drug list to the hospital. This scenario differs from the previous two in that neither home services nor primary service knows that the elderly person has disappeared from the asset *Elderly clients*. The information on the event will come to them only after the elderly person has been admitted to the hospital. This can take quite a long time, up to half a day. Without this knowledge, activities of home services and primary care planned for this person are not canceled, which can result in a loss of resources. This fact is represented in the model in Fig. 4 by using the rose background color on the affected elements. In addition, a note is added to the model that is connected with these elements; The note[1] explains the problem via the text inside it.

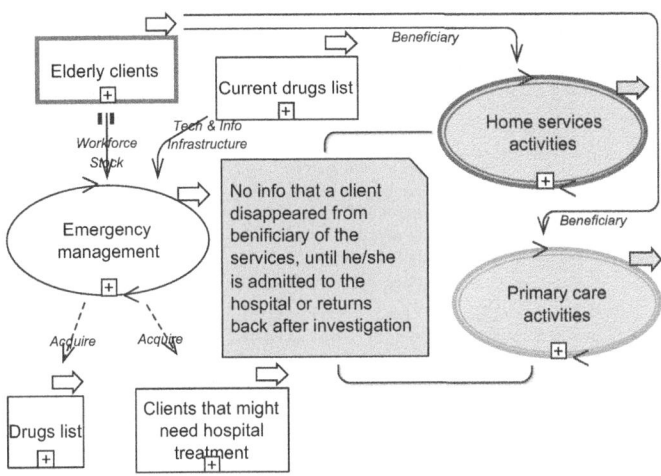

Fig. 4. Emergency management – Scenario 3.

The last scenario related to emergency management is when a relative of the elderly person discovers that something is wrong with the latter and arranges his/her transfer to the hospital, either via ambulance or using his/her own car. In this case, most probably, no information on medical history or drug list follows the elderly to the hospital. This scenario is presented in the model in Fig. 5. The difference from Fig. 4 is that a new asset – *Relatives* – is added to the model as a partner for *Emergency management*, and the asset *Drug list* disappears from the model.

3.2 Gathering Medical Info

As follows from the previous section, the medical information about the elderly person admitted to the hospital might be missing or incomplete. However, having such information is crucial for prescribing the right treatment. As the patient is an elderly person, it is not, in some cases, possible to rely on him/her to know all the details of his medical history. Therefore, the hospital needs to contact the person's primary care to get the missing information. A more detailed model of this process is presented in Fig. 6.

---

[1] A note is a special element introduced in the FEM toolkit. It includes free text, and can be connected to any element of the model.

62 E. Perjons et al.

The major problem for gathering medical info on the elderly is as follows. Information that the hospital needs is stored in the Primary care IT and, as a rule, is accessible only to *Primary care staff*. This fact is shown in the model using an asymmetric association – a blue dashed arrow – that connects Primary care IT with Primary care staff. The meaning of this association is explained by the label attached to the association – *Accessible only to*.

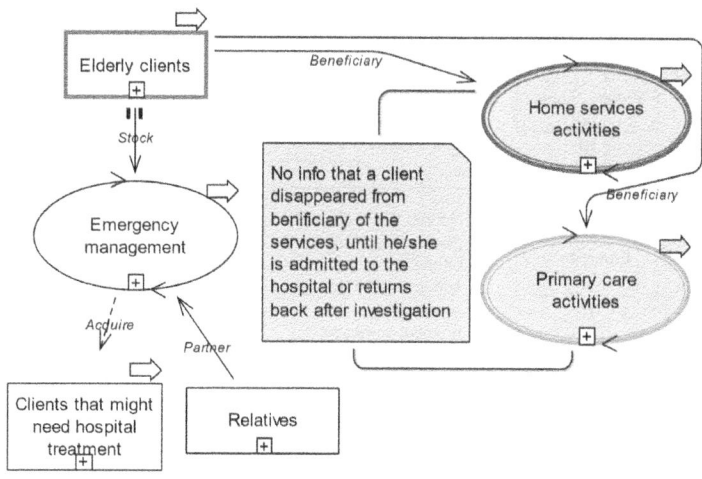

Fig. 5. Emergency management – Scenario 4.

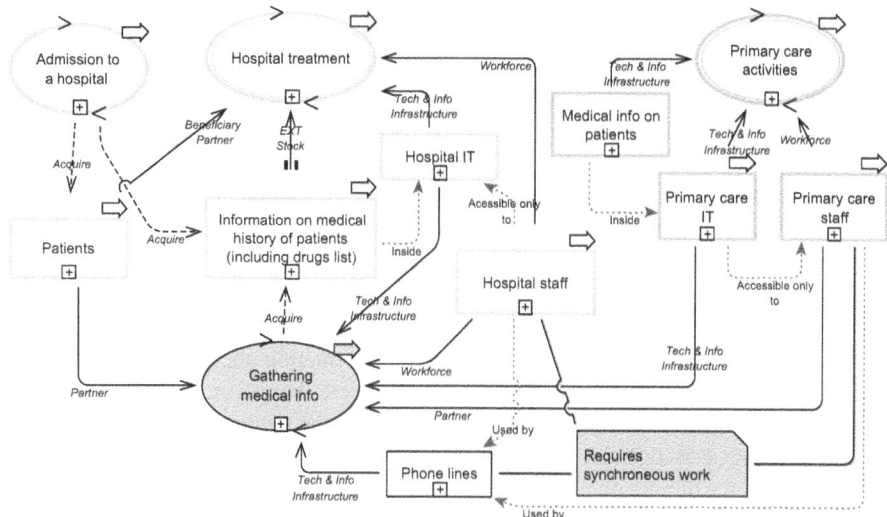

Fig. 6. Gathering medical info

Currently, the transfer of medical information that exists in *Primary care IT* into *Hospital IT* requires synchronous communication between a member of the *Hospital staff* and a member of the *Primary care staff* over the *Telephone lines*. This is difficult to arrange; that is why the process *Gathering medical information* has a rose background color, which means that there is a problem. The problem is explained in a note, which also has a rose background color. There is an exception to this rule in case both the hospital and the primary care are using the same kind of IT. In this case, the hospital staff may have access to the medical information. We did not present a model of this case in the paper, as it does not have a problem that needs to be solved.

3.3 Rehabilitation

From the model in Fig. 1, we can see that one of the results of *Hospital treatment* is a document *Rehabilitation needs* that is produced before the patient is discharged from the hospital. This document resides in *LifeCare IT*, which is an IT system specifically designed for cooperation between different agents engaged in caring for elderly people. This document is used to produce rehabilitation instructions for *Home service* and *Primary care*. A more detailed model depicting the rehabilitation is presented in Fig. 7.

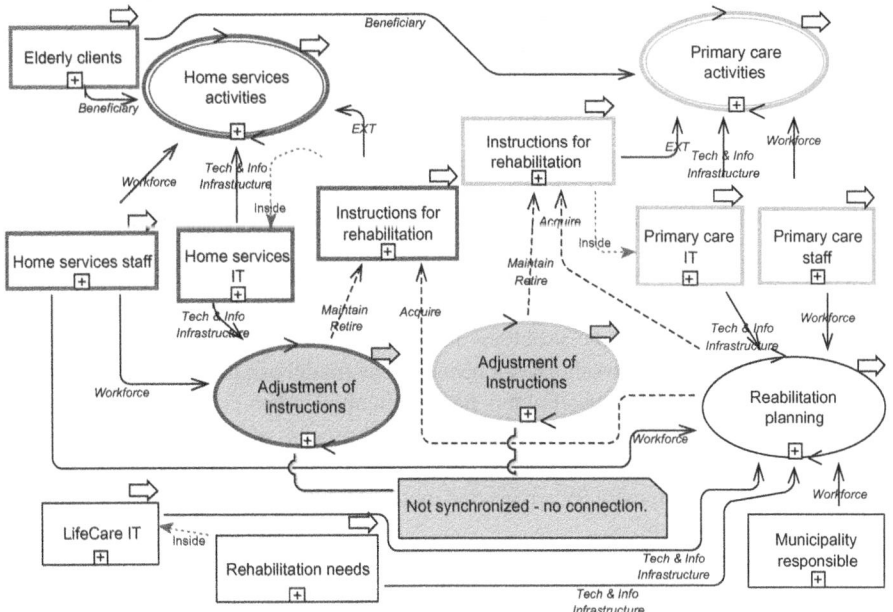

Fig. 7. Rehabilitation

As can be seen from the model in Fig. 7, several agents participate in *Rehabilitation planning*, namely: *Municipality responsible*, *Home service staff*, and *Primary care staff*. This activity results in two sets of instructions – one for *Home services* and one for *Primary care*. These instructions serve as *EXT* for the respective activities. The instructions are placed in the IT systems of each agent, which are accessible only to the staff that belong to the particular agent. With the passing of time, there might be a need to adjust the instructions, which is done independently by each partner, as shown in the model in Fig. 7. This can break the alignment between the instructions, which is the major problem in the current way of treatment of elderly persons. To highlight the problem, the adjustment processes have a rose background (the problem color), and a note is added to the model (also with the rose background) to explain the problem.

4 Discussion

In the previous section, we presented a set of models that highlighted the problems in cooperation between the agents taking care of elderly persons in Sweden. This set presents only some scenarios of problems in cooperation. In reality, there are more agents than the three discussed in this paper and more scenarios that need cooperation between the agents.

Based on the work done so far, we can draw a number of conclusions. Building FEM models in a case of multi-organizational cooperation, on its own, does not indicate problems or suggest solutions. That said, the models themselves provide help to do both.

Firstly, it is possible to differentiate activities that fall into the responsibility of one partner from activities where several partners cooperate. This is done by assigning a border color to each partner. Secondly, essential elements of the cooperative activities are presented in the models as assets, depicting the landscape of each cooperative activity. This facilitates detecting the problems connected to a specific asset. For example, using phone lines in *Gathering medical info* (Fig. 6) points to the requirement of synchronous communication, which can pose challenges, such as knowing whom to contact, lack of synchronous agent availability, interpretation issues, and the risk of missing the sharing of important information during phone communication.

Detecting problems requires additional information to the one needed to build the models. This information can be obtained either from the stakeholders or from the existing texts that describe the problems in an informal way. In the first case, either interviews or facilitating workshops can be used. The model can be used to design some questions, like whether the stakeholders have difficulties when cooperating with other organizations in the frame of a certain activity. In the process of detecting the problems, questionable processes and assets can be colored in some way to show that there is a problem, and also its intensity. When needed, notes can be added to the model to explain the nature of the problem.

The models also help to generate hypotheses for possible solutions. Consider, for example, a problem identified in models of Fig. 4 and 5 – the agents do not know that the elderly client has disappeared from their asset until he/she is admitted to the hospital or returns back home. The solution is to inform on disappearance earlier. As the partners already have *LifeCare IT* for cooperation, one solution can be to automatically inform the agents early in the process of *Admission to the hospital* (see Fig. 1). In this case, information on the client's disappearance will appear much earlier – at the moment he/she is registered as a client of the hospital emergency service. Currently, *LifeCare IT* is only used when an agent at the hospital has time to open it and report the admission, which usually happens only when the elderly individual is admitted to a ward, potentially taking several hours.

Regarding the understandability of the models for the business stakeholders, this issue has not been investigated in the current project. We aim to do it in the near future. From our past experience, we know that in some cases, the FEM models were understandable by business stakeholders, and they could comment on them [7]. In other cases [8, 13], the stakeholders were not interested in looking at the models. In the latter cases, the models were still useful for business analysts to understand the situation, and suggest solutions. However, the solutions in these cases were formulated by using other means than models, e.g., as text [8] or tables [13]. Our experience regarding showing models to the stakeholders corresponds to the experience of other business consultants. For example, Patrick Hoverstadt, who uses the Viable System Model (VSM) [14], stated that in his business practice models are only shown if the stakeholders want to see them. Otherwise, the conclusions made based on the models are communicated.

Summarizing the project so far, we have achieved some progress in both our practical and research goals. We have built several models that depict cooperation between three partners and pinpointed the problems in cooperation. We also tested FEM for this task and found it quite useful, so we will continue to use it in the project.

5 Conclusion and Plans for the Future

The objective of this paper is to report on the progress of the project of detecting problems and finding solutions in elderly care in Sweden. The complexity of the project is due to several partners being engaged in providing care, and the project is aimed at investigating cooperation between the partners. This project, in difference from the previous one, uses enterprise modeling as a tool to present problems and solutions in a relatively formal way. The problems are depicted in as-is models by using background colors for questionable elements and notes to explain them. The solutions will be presented as to-be models.

The FEM technique has been used for the project. Partly this choice is justified by the technique being suitable for the task (see Sect. 2.3) and partly because it is the author's own invention, which means that the modelers know the advantages and limitations of this technique. In addition, choosing FEM resulted in adding a research goal to the project, namely evaluation of FEM for a particular task. As was discussed in the previous section, so far, we have found it useful for the task of identifying and visualizing problems and for hypothesizing about possible solutions.

If no contradictory discoveries are made during the rest of the project, the results could give rise to the next project. Namely, developing a methodology of using FEM for detecting problems in complex multi-organizational settings related to cooperation between the partners and developing solutions for them. In its nature, it will be a design science project [15].

Acknowledgments. The DISVO project was partially funded by Region Stockholm. The work of the second author was partly supported by the Estonian Research Council (grant PRG1226). The authors are also grateful to the anonymous reviewers whose comments helped improve the text.

References

1. Lappalainen, F., Fors, U., Henkel, M., Sjöberg, C., Perjons, E.: Digitalisering inom vård och omsorg: Ett projekt om samverkan inom och mellan Region Stockholm och Stockholms stad. Technical report no. 21-003, Stockholm University, Stockholm
2. Henkel, M., Perjons, E., Lappalainen, K., Fors, U., Johannesson, P., Sjöberg, C.: Digitalization of health and social care collaboration: identification of problems and solutions. In: RCIS Workshops. CEUR, vol. 3674 (2024)
3. Bider, I., Perjons, E., Elias, M., Johannesson, P.: A fractal enterprise model and its application for business development. SoSyM **16**(3), 663–689 (2017)
4. Bider, I., Perjons, E., Klyukina, V.: Tool support for fractal enterprise modeling. In: Karagiannis, D., Lee, M., Hinkelmann, K., Utz, W. (eds.) Domain-Specific Conceptual Modeling, pp. 205–229. Springer, Cham (2022). https://doi.org/10.1007/978-3-030-93547-4_10
5. PoEM 2024: Call for Papers. In: PoEM 2024. https://poem2024.dsv.su.se/call-for-papers/
6. Mott, V.: Knowledge comes from practice: reflective theory building in practice. In: Rowden, R.W. (ed.) Workplace Learning: Debating Five Critical Questions of Theory and Practice, pp. 57–63. Jossey-Bass, San Francisco (1996)
7. Leego, S., Bider, I.: Using fractal enterprise model in technology-driven organisational change projects: a case of a water utility company. In: 23rd IEEE Conference on Business Informatics, CBI 2021, vol. 2, pp. 107–116 (2021)
8. Klyukina, V., Bider, I., Perjons, E.: Does fractal enterprise model fit operational decision making? In: Proceedings of the 23rd International Conference on Enterprise Information System, ICEIS 2021, vol. 2, pp. 613–624 (2021)
9. Henkel, M., Koutsopoulos, G., Bider, I.P.: Using the fractal enterprise model for interorganizational business processes. In: ER Forum/Posters/Demos 2019, vol. CEUR, vol. 2469, pp. 56–69 (2019)
10. Aalast Van der, W.: Loosely coupled interorganizational workflows: modeling and analyzing workflows crossing organizational boundaries. Inf. Manag. **37**(2) (2000)
11. Pant, V., Yu, E.: Modeling simultaneous cooperation and competition among. Bus. Inf. Syst. Eng. **60**(1), 39–54 (2018)
12. Fayoumi, A., Williams, R.: An integrated socio-technical enterprise modelling: a scenario of healthcare system analysis and design. J. Ind. Inf. Integr. **23** (2021)
13. Leego, S., Bider, I.: Improving IT governance, security and privacy using fractal enterprise modeling: a case of a highly regulated company. In: Hinkelmann, K., López-Pellicer, F.J., Polini, A. (eds.) BIR 2023. LNBIP, vol. 493, pp. 199–213. Springer, Cham (2023). https://doi.org/10.1007/978-3-031-43126-5_15
14. Hoverstadt, P.: The viable system model. In: Systems Approaches to Managing Change: A Practical Guide, pp. 87–133. Springer, London (2010)
15. Johannesson, P., Perjons, E.: An Introduction to Design Science. Springer, Cham (2014)

Evaluation of Categorization Patterns for Conceptual Modeling of IoT Applications

Mathis Wyffels[1]([✉]), Zahra Ahmadi[1]([✉]), Estefanía Serral[1], Irene Vanderfeesten[1], and Monique Snoeck[2]

[1] Research Centre for Information Systems Engineering (LIRIS), KU Leuven, Warmoesberg 26, 1000 Brussels, Belgium
mathis.wyffels@gmail.com, zahra.ahmadi@kuleuven.be

[2] Research Centre for Information Systems Engineering (LIRIS), KU Leuven, Naamsestraat 69, 3000 Leuven, Belgium

Abstract. The Internet of Things (IoT) plays a crucial role in applications for the emerging Industry 5.0 and Society 5.0. However, due to the complex nature of IoT systems, it is essential to have well-defined conceptual models for effective understanding. A good way to enhance this understanding is by incorporating categorization into the conceptual models, which can be achieved through the use of categorization patterns. This paper evaluates how different categorization patterns have an impact on the quality of IoT systems. Specifically, two categorization patterns (Inheritance and Type pattern) and a base model are used to create conceptual models in an IoT setting and are evaluated by the Quality Model for Object-Oriented Design (QMOOD) metric. We examine the impact of these patterns on different design properties and quality attributes, such as reusability, flexibility, understandability, functionality, extendibility, and effectiveness. Additionally, we use the MERODE framework, which allows us to automatically transform the models into code, enabling a more comprehensive evaluation of the patterns' impact through the generated code. To evaluate the patterns we use two IoT use cases: 1) employees' well-being in a smart factory (Industry 5.0), and 2) the daily behavior of solo residents in a smart home (Society 5.0). The results indicate that the Inheritance model exhibits the highest reusability and functionality in comparison to the other models, making it well-suited for complex projects with significant reuse requirements. This evaluation provides valuable and extensive insights for developers, helping them in understanding the impact of different categorization patterns in the final system.

Keywords: Internet of Things · Conceptual modeling · IoT use case · Categorization patterns · QMOOD · MERODE

1 Introduction

In Industry 5.0 and Society 5.0, the Internet of Things (IoT) is emerging as a central technology. In Industry 5.0, IoT supports the path toward more human-centric, sustainable and resilient processes [3]. Meanwhile, in Society 5.0, IoT enhances sustainability, safety and comfort for individuals in their living environments [19]. However, the multitude of smart objects that communicate with each other in IoT systems makes them inherently complex [10]. Conceptual modeling, within the object-oriented design (OOD) domain, allows us to formally describe these complex IoT systems in an understandable way [17].

To enhance the understanding of the information system being developed, the necessary concepts of the physical and digital world are abstracted into "categories" through categorization or classification techniques [6]. This abstraction allows objects or entities to be grouped under higher-level, more abstract objects or entities. For example, sensor types fall under the category "Sensor", while actuator types fall under "Actuator". In the Unified Modeling Language (UML) class diagrams, the most widely used conceptual modeling language for information systems, there are existing concepts and patterns that enable this categorization. However, clear guidelines for applying these concepts and patterns are lacking. While several options exist, each with its specific application, there is no straightforward method to evaluate their impact and determine the most suitable one. Given the inherent complexity of IoT systems, it is essential to provide clear guidelines on the most effective conceptual representation of categories according to specific IoT requirements.

In this paper, we aim to provide more clarity on the representation of categories in a conceptual model by comparing two categorization patterns as well as establishing guidelines for their use. The representation of categories in a conceptual model involves two key decisions. On the one hand, the decision of whether to include categorization at all. To explore this, we compare a base model without categorization to one using the generalization/specialization concept from standard UML class diagrams, which can represent categorization. On the other hand, when representing categories, the question arises of whether the categories remain static or need to change over time. For this, we compare the generalization/specialization concept with the type object pattern-a fundamental version of the dynamic object model that uses the composition concept of UML and, according to the authors, allows for the creation of new categorizations dynamically (at runtime). Based on these potential choices in representing categorizations, we compare three models: a basic model, a model with the generalization/specialization concept and type object pattern. In this work, these models are referred to as the Base model, the Inheritance model and the Type Pattern model, respectively [13,18]. We evaluate the base model and two categorization patterns (Inheritance and Type Pattern) using two IoT use cases, an Industry 5.0 application and a Society 5.0 application, and focusing on the representation of one of the most important IoT components: sensors. The Industry 5.0 application uses sensors in a smart factory setting to measure workers' well-being, while the Society 5.0 application uses sensors in a smart home setting to track the residents' activities.

The two categorization patterns are evaluated and compared with each other and the Base model using the Quality Model for Object-Oriented Design

(QMOOD) [4]. The QMOOD model is a very comprehensive and well-supported suite to evaluate object-oriented design quality [9,16]. The conceptual model itself will be developed using the MERODE modeling method [22]. This method is chosen due to its ability for rapid prototyping and validation of the model. Using the MERODE modeling method, findings from the QMOOD evaluation can be assessed through testing. This comprehensive evaluation and testing allow us to establish clear guidelines for the use of categorization approaches within the context of conceptual models for IoT applications. These guidelines make it possible to apply the most appropriate conceptual model for concrete IoT systems.

The paper is structured as follows. Section 2 provides related work on conceptual modeling in an IoT context. Section 3 presents the methodology that is followed for the evaluation of the two categorization patterns and Base model. Section 4 provides the results of this evaluation, utilizing the QMOOD model and MERODE rapid prototyping. In Sect. 5 the results are further discussed. Finally, Sect. 6 presents the conclusion.

2 Related Work

This section offers an overview of relevant works within the field of conceptual modeling for IoT applications.

As early as 2011 and 2013, the work of [21] and [11] appeared with a comprehensive conceptual or reference model for IoT. During these early years of IoT, there was a lot of hype around the technology, but it was often not fully understood resulting in different views. Through the creation of a reference or domain model, the authors sought to determine the relevant IoT concepts and their relationships. The model of [11] is more comprehensive and builds on the one of [21]. In addition, the work of [11] discusses some example models for possible use cases. Some classes in their UML conceptual model appear in the models of our two use cases such as device, sensor and user.

In a similar way, [12] also tries to create clarity and a common understanding of the IoT field by designing a metamodel. Within their designed architecture of models, this metamodel serves as an aid for developers to build their concrete model for an IoT solution. The metamodel they describe in their work was based on previous reference models by [21] and [11].

While the earlier works focus on establishing a reference model to achieve a common understanding and help in the creation of models for concrete IoT use cases, the work of [5] proposes a UML class model based on IoT use cases. Based on eleven IoT use cases that the system must be able to accomplish, a comprehensive and detailed class model is created. However, this work focuses on the development of user interfaces of IoT systems and therefore mostly models the IoT application's users and the organization structure and its customers.

Finally, the work of [7] is also notable. The authors establish a domain model for Digital Twins (DTs) using the *Semantic Sensor Network* (SSN) and *Sensor, Observation, Sample and Actuator* (SOSA) IoT ontologies. Although DTs is a different technology, it often implements a form of IoT. The striking thing about this work is that they also use the MERODE approach in their work and apply their domain model in a real-life IoT use case.

Although the models proposed in this work include some similar classes as in previous works, our focus is on understanding the impact of different design choices on the final system quality. This is realized by modeling two different cases and comparing three modeling variants in each use case using the QMOOD quality assessment and MERODE rapid prototyping. Based on the evaluation of these models, we can not only select the best categorization pattern for each case but also establish important guidelines about the different design options to represent sensors in UML class models. Unlike previous conceptual models, this approach allows developers to easily apply a clear categorization pattern from the start, tailored to the needs of their IoT system.

3 Methodology

For each of the two use cases representing different IoT applications, we develop three models using UML class diagrams, two categorization patterns and a Base model. The fundamental workings of these two patterns are explained following the use cases. We evaluate these three models using the QMOOD assessment methodology. Subsequently, we apply the MERODE approach to generate information systems for both use cases based on the models. These generated information systems are then tested using four test cases derived from the requirements outlined in the use cases.

3.1 Use Cases

In the following sections, we describe the two use cases used to apply and evaluate the categorization patterns: a smart factory and a smart home. The description of the two use cases below is used to construct the class diagrams in Sect. 4.

Smart Factory in Industry 5.0. In a smart factory, IoT sensors are used to observe worker well-being. This information is utilized to improve social sustainability. By having information about the well-being of workers, health aspects can be taken into account that can impact productivity, product quality and overall sustainability of workers [24]. To measure these aspects as accurately as possible, several IoT sensors will be worn by each worker via smart wearables such as smartwatches, smart headbands, smart rings, smart shirts or smart glasses. The following sensors are used: ECG (heart rate), EEG (electric brain waves), PPG (oxygen in blood), ST (skin thermometry) and GSR (skin conductance). These sensors are based on the description of [15] and are widely used in currently available wearables.

To optimise this application, there is a requirement besides the description. The smart factory is designed with a future-oriented approach, emphasizing openness to new wearables and sensor types. Consequently, the system requires the flexibility to integrate new types of sensors as they become available.

Smart Home in Society 5.0. One of the uses of smart homes is to find the relationship between human behavior and health conditions. Changes in daily habits can be early signs of diseases such as dementia. For this purpose, behavior monitoring by sensors in a smart home can help detect these diseases. This use case focuses on a house with a single resident where ambient sensors, a wristband and a smartphone are used to capture data about the resident. The smart home includes multiple PIR (passive infrared) sensors indicating the presence of the resident in various areas of the house; a power usage sensor showing TV usage; contact sensors highlighting the opening and closing of the bathroom, WC, and closet doors; temperature sensors monitor the house's temperature and a gas detection sensor for detecting cooking. Additionally, the smartphone and the wristband are used to provide information on activities and their duration such as walking (steps), and sleeping (night sleep time, duration, and quality) [8].

The smart home also has a requirement with the IoT application. Unlike the smart factory, the type of sensors here will most likely not change. During the evaluation with the MERODE test environment, we use these requirements to determine the test cases.

3.2 Categorization Patterns

As mentioned earlier, three models are established for both use cases: a Base model, an Inheritance model and a Type Pattern model. Using these last two models, categorization for the type of sensors can be represented. This section gives a brief description of these two categorization patterns that are evaluated.

The Inheritance model, using the generalization/specialization concept, has existed within UML class diagrams for a long time. In this approach, a generalized superclass manages specialized subclasses. For example, 'Sensor' is the generalized superclass, while each type of sensor is a specialized subclass. Here, an instance or object in a specialized subclass (type of sensor) is also an instance or object in the generalized superclass (sensor). Furthermore, specialized subclasses inherit attributes and methods from the superclass but can also contain additional attributes unique to them. This inheritance allows subclasses to extend the functionality of the superclass while maintaining their distinct characteristics [20].

The Type Pattern model is based on the composition concept from UML class diagrams. In this type of association between classes, instances of the category class (such as sensor types) are the owners of instances in the component class (the sensors themselves). As a result, the components cannot exist without their associated owner. For example, the sensor "ECG1" in the Sensor class is associated with the sensor type "ECG" and cannot exist without this type. In other words, if the sensor type "ECG" is deleted, then the sensor "ECG1" is also deleted [13, 18, 20]. While the composition concept in the Type Pattern model, as described in UML, represents the relationship and dependency between objects, it also serves an additional purpose in the Type Pattern model by facilitating categorization. Unlike the Inheritance approach, the Type Pattern does not create a separate class for each sensor type; instead, it uses instances to represent different sensor types.

3.3 The QMOOD Assessment Methodology

Over the years, a series of object-oriented design quality assessment models have been proposed that aim to assist the programmer in developing qualitative information systems. Developing these assessment models is inherently difficult because of the different viewpoints and opinions on what quality means [14]. However, our viewpoints on quality are in line with the QMOOD model that we apply in this paper. Not only does it link to the ISO 9126 quality attributes, but it is also considered the most comprehensive OOD quality assessment model [9,16].

Table 1. Quality attributes definitions based on QMOOD [4]

Quality attribute	Definition
Reusability	Reflects the presence of object-oriented design characteristics that allow a design to be reapplied to a new problem without significant effort
Flexibility	Characteristics that allow the incorporation of changes in a design. The ability of a design to be adapted to provide functionally related capabilities
Understandability	The properties of the design that enable it to be easily learned and comprehended. This directly relates to the complexity of the design structure
Functionality	The responsibilities assigned to the classes of a design, which are made available by the classes through their public interfaces
Extendibility	Refers to the presence and usage of properties in an existing design that allows for the incorporation of new requirements in the design
Effectiveness	This refers to a design's ability to achieve the desired functionality and behavior using object-oriented design concepts and techniques

The model is divided into four levels with links between these levels. The first level represents the abstract design quality attributes based on the ISO 9126 attributes. These attributes and their definitions according to the QMOOD model are visible in Table 1. Due to their abstract nature, these are not directly observable. Therefore, the second level introduces design properties that can be directly assessed via the structures, relationships and functionalities of the design (Table 3). Through this clear and measurable description of design properties, design metrics can be established in the third level. These design metrics enable precise measurement of the design property. The fourth and final level contains the design components that define and identify the architecture of an OOD. Thus, these are the objects, classes and relationships between them. Finally, to connect the four levels described above and transition from level four to level one for evaluating each quality attribute, there are three links [4].

To evaluate and compare the three models, we use the first two levels of the QMOOD model. This has the following two reasons. First, our focus is on describing the semantic differences to provide a reasoned evaluation of the proposed models. Second, the models are high level mainly focusing on the distinction between Iinheritance and Type Pattern without discussing variations in attributes and methods.

We start our evaluation from level two, using the definitions of the design properties from the QMOOD model that can also be found in Table 3. Since a numerical evaluation of the models is not possible using the definitions in level two, we use the following qualitative scores to distinguish the results of the models: 'Lowest', 'Moderate', and 'Highest'. 'Moderate' may be omitted if two or all three models achieve similar results.

Table 2. Quality attributes (columns) with design properties (rows) relationships based on QMOOD [4]

	Reusability	Flexibility	Understandability	Functionality	Extendibility	Effective
Design size	↑		↓	↑		
Hierarchies				↑		
Abstraction			↓		↑	↑
Encapsulation		↑	↑			↑
Coupling	↓	↓	↓		↓	
Cohesion	↑		↑	↑		
Composition		↑				↑
Inheritance					↑	↑
Polymorphism		↑	↓	↑	↑	↑
Messaging	↑			↑		
Complexity			↓			

To convert the design properties into quality attributes from level one (level two to level one), we use Table 2 which shows the relationship between the design properties and quality attributes. This table, also from the QMOOD model, allows transforming qualitative results from level two to level one without numerical calculations. An up arrow indicates a positive relationship between the design property and quality attribute while a down arrow indicates a negative relationship between the design property and quality attribute [4]. Table 2 also shows that not every design property affects every quality attribute, as established in the QMOOD model.

3.4 The MERODE Approach

Nowadays, a multitude of approaches exists for conceptual modeling information systems. In this paper, the MERODE approach was chosen due to its ability for rapid prototyping and validation of the model. The approach is based on UML: MERODE uses a part of UML constructs and extends it with proprietary notions. Using MERODE, it is possible to generate fully functioning code using three views: an Existence Dependency Graph (EDG) based on UML class diagrams, an Object Event Table (OET) and a Finite State Machine (FSM) for every class in the EDG, based on UML state machines. Our focus in this paper is on the EDG, the OET and FSMs are set up in a default manner. The EDG represents the domain classes and the associations between them. These associations express existence dependency, which is based on the most interesting features of the principle of composition along with simple and clear semantics. With this, each instance in a class with a parent class is related to a specific instance from that parent class. This form of association provides a classification with more simplicity, less ambiguity and the possibility for more quality control [23]. The EDG, together with the OET and FSM models, can be created using a web-based tool called Merlin [1,2,22]. The Merlin tool includes features to check the consistency and readiness of the models as well as automatic code generation. The code generation itself is done through a standalone Java application. This code generator, called Merlin Prototyper, creates a default Graphical User Interface (GUI) which displays each class in a separate tab. Instances can be created, viewed or ended in each tab. Additionally, the GUI provides feedback when an action cannot be carried out [2,22].

The Merlin Prototyper allows further verification of the evaluation from the QMOOD assessment method. This allows for the verification of quality attributes such as reusability, flexibility, functionality, and effectiveness. To achieve this, we build six EDG models (three for each use case) using the web-based Merlin tool and generate a test environment with the Merlin Prototyper. The focus in both use cases is to find an appropriate categorization pattern for the types of sensors. Additionally, the requirements in both use cases differ regarding the future needs for types of sensors. Based on this, we establish the following four test cases for the two use cases: 1) add a new type of sensor, 2) add a new sensor instance, 3) delete the sensor instance, and 4) delete the type of sensor. In this context, a type of sensor refers to a general category of sensors, such as ECG in the smart factory use case. A sensor instance refers to an individual sensor, such as ECG1.

4 Results

This section presents a comprehensive evaluation of our three EDG model variants (Base, Inheritance, and Type Pattern) using the QMOOD framework and the test cases performed with the Merlin Prototyper. We aim to assess each model's design properties and quality attributes to evaluate their suitability for our use cases.

4.1 Models Use Cases

In the next section, we discuss the construction of conceptual models for the two use cases presented in Sect. 3.1. These diagrams were built in the web-based Merlin tool using the MERODE approach to create the test environments afterwards. The EDG diagrams (UML class diagrams in MERODE approach) in this section are presented with UML class diagram notation for intelligibility.

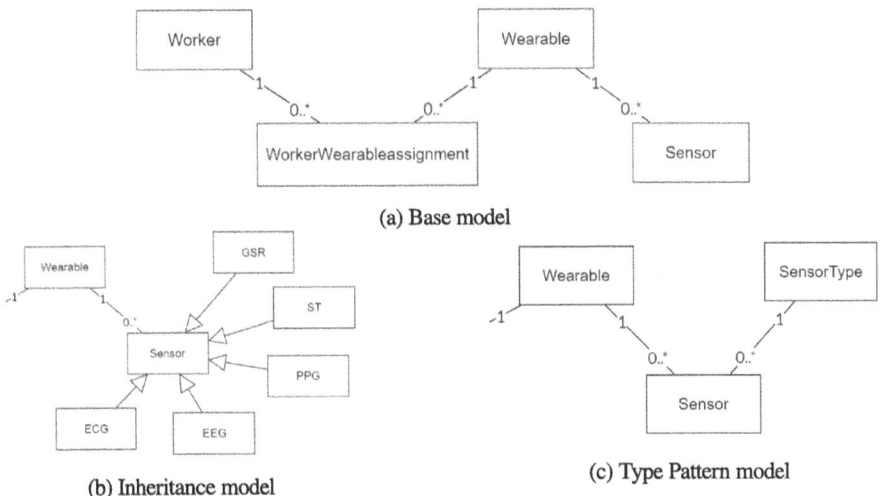

Fig. 1. UML class diagrams for the smart factory use case

Smart Factory in Industry 5.0. To display the smart factory correctly in a system, the company must be able to capture the following elements: the various sensors used for data collection, the wearables where these sensors are embedded, the specific worker each wearable is connected to, and the specific data each sensor observes. This creates the following classes in our UML class diagram: Worker, Wearable and Sensor. Additionally, the class 'WorkerWearableAssignment' is created to assign the worker with the wearable s/he uses. Due to the existence of dependency in the MERODE approach, every association between the classes has a 1 or direct link along one side of the association. Along the other side of the association, the link is 0 or many. This ultimately resulted in the Base model for the presented use case in Fig. 1a. The use case shows the need for the categorization of sensor types. This categorization of the type of sensors is represented in two ways. Figure 1b presents the Inheritance model, while Fig. 1c shows the Type Pattern structure. To simplify these models, the diagrams show only the most important elements and omit the common parts. These three models are compared and evaluated in the following sections.

Smart Home in Society 5.0. To correctly represent the second use case on the smart home in a system, the following is needed in the diagram: the smart homes containing sensors, the resident staying in the house, the rooms with sensors, the smartwatch and smartphone being used and finally the sensors hanging in the rooms. For this, the following classes are created: Sensor, Room, SmartHome, Resident, Smartwatch and SmartPhone. The associations between classes contain more constraints in this use case than in the previous one including the use of 1 to many or 0 to 1. The Base model for this use case is shown in Fig. 2a. Figure 2b presents the Inheritance model and Fig. 2c the Type Pattern model.

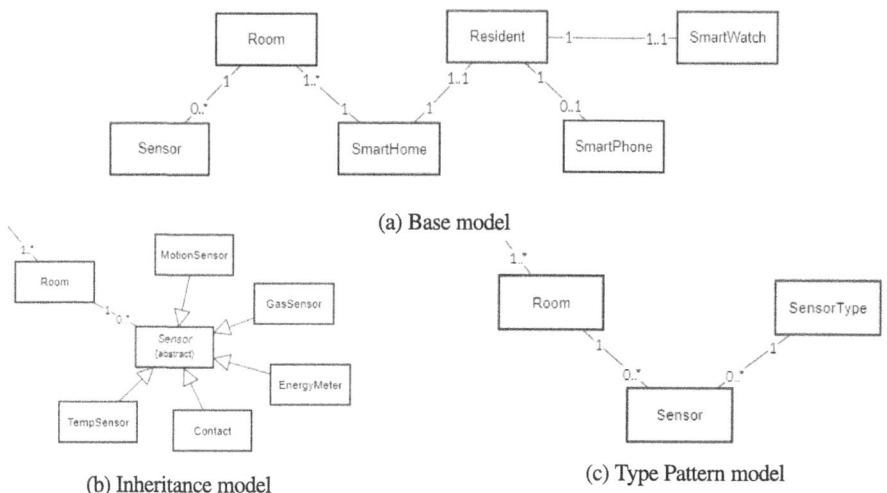

Fig. 2. UML class diagrams for the smart home use case

4.2 QMOOD

We applied the QMOOD model to assess the three different model variants of our two use cases. Since the differences between the three variants are the same in both use cases, there is only one evaluation comparing the three different variants for both use cases. The most appropriate categorization pattern for both use cases depends on their requirements. Table 3 shows the evaluation of the design properties for the three models described. This evaluation is based on the measurement description for each property. The evaluation results of the three models for level two can be found in their corresponding columns. There are two design properties that have the same result for all three models: Encapsulation and Messaging. Encapsulation is evaluated by the number of private attributes the classes contain. Since we use default attributes in all models, the number of private attributes is the same for each class. Similarly, the Messaging property measures the number of public methods per class, which is also consistent across the three standard models.

Table 3. Evaluation of the three models using design properties with definitions based on QMOOD

Design property	Measurement description	Base	Inheritance	Type Pattern
Design size	Amount of classes in the design	Lowest	Highest	Moderate
Hierarchies	The number of classes that have children in a design	Lowest	Highest	Moderate
Abstraction	The amount of classes that inherit information from other classes	Lowest	Highest	Lowest
Encapsulation	The degree to which the implementation details of a class are hidden from other classes	Highest	Highest	Highest
Coupling	Amount of direct dependencies between classes	Lowest	Highest	Moderate
Cohesion	Amount of relatedness between methods and attributes in a class with generalization being highest followed by composition, aggregation and association	Lowest	Highest	Moderate
Composition	Amount of aggregation relationships	Lowest	Lowest	Highest
Inheritance	Amount of generalization/specialization relationships	Lowest	Highest	Lowest
Polymorphism	Amount of methods that exhibit polymorphic behavior	Lowest	Highest	Lowest
Messaging	Amount of public methods in a class	Lowest	Lowest	Lowest
Complexity	Amount of complexity within the design, including factors such as the number of classes, methods, and relationships, as well as the overall structure and organization	Lowest	Highest	Moderate

As mentioned earlier, we convert the design properties (level two) in Table 3 to quality attributes (level one) via the specified relationships in Table 2. These quality attributes are shown in Table 4. The design properties that affect the given quality attribute are listed in this table. Based on the calculation, we display the score for each design property using the following circles: empty (○) indicating no value, half-full (◐) indicating moderate value, and full (●) indicating high value. For design properties with a negative influence, a high design property score is represented by an empty circle and for properties with a positive influence, a high design property score is represented by a full circle and vice versa. To clarify with an example: if a given model receives a bad score on a design property, it will translate to a good score in the quality attribute if there is a negative relationship between the design property and the quality attribute. Conversely, it will retain a bad score if there is a positive relationship. By summing the amount of filled or half-filled circles using the amount of black space, we can identify which categorization pattern is the best for a given quality attribute. The results of the design properties are shown in Table 4.

Table 4. Evaluation of the three models on quality attributes using design properties results

Quality attributes	Base model	Inheritance model	Type Pattern model
Reusability	*Design size:* ○ *Coupling:* ● *Cohesion:* ○ *Messaging:* ○ Result: **worst**	*Design size:* ● *Coupling:* ○ *Cohesion:* ● *Messaging:* ○ Result: **best**	*Design size:* ◐ *Coupling:* ◐ *Cohesion:* ◐ *Messaging:* ○ Result: **moderate**
Flexibility	*Encapsulation:* ● *Coupling:* ● *Composition:* ○ Result: **moderate**	*Encapsulation:* ● *Coupling:* ○ *Composition:* ○ Result: **worst**	*Encapsulation:* ● *Coupling:* ◐ *Composition:* ● Result: **best**
Understandability	*Design size:* ● *Abstraction:* ● *Encapsulation:* ● *Coupling:* ● *Cohesion:* ○ *Complexity:* ● Result: **best**	*Design size:* ○ *Abstraction:* ○ *Encapsulation:* ● *Coupling:* ○ *Cohesion:* ● *Complexity:* ○ Result: **worst**	*Design size:* ◐ *Abstraction:* ● *Encapsulation:* ● *Coupling:* ◐ *Cohesion:* ◐ *Complexity:* ◐ Result: **moderate**
Functionality	*Design size:* ○ *Hierarchies:* ○ *Cohesion:* ○ *Messaging:* ○ Result: **worst**	*Design size:* ● *Hierarchies:* ● *Cohesion:* ● *Messaging:* ○ Result: **best**	*Design size:* ◐ *Hierarchies:* ◐ *Cohesion:* ◐ *Messaging:* ○ Result: **moderate**
Extendibility	*Abstraction:* ○ *Coupling:* ● *Inheritance:* ○ *Polymorphism:* ○ Result: **moderate**	*Abstraction:* ● *Coupling:* ○ *Inheritance:* ● *Polymorphism:* ● Result: **best**	*Abstraction:* ○ *Coupling:* ◐ *Inheritance:* ○ *Polymorphism:* ○ Result: **worst**
Effectiveness	*Abstraction:* ○ *Encapsulation:* ● *Composition:* ○ *Inheritance:* ○ *Polymorphism:* ○ Result: **worst**	*Abstraction:* ● *Encapsulation:* ● *Composition:* ○ *Inheritance:* ● *Polymorphism:* ● Result: **best**	*Abstraction:* ○ *Encapsulation:* ● *Composition:* ● *Inheritance:* ○ *Polymorphism:* ○ Result: **moderate**

Table 5. Overview of results based on quality attributes evaluation

Quality attribute	Base model	Inheritance model	Type Pattern model
Reusability	○	●	◐
Flexibility	◐	○	●
Understandability	●	○	◐
Functionality	○	●	◐
Extendibility	◐	●	○
Effectiveness	○	●	◐
Overall	○	●	◐

By displaying the results for each quality attribute for all three model variants using circles, we can present an overview in Table 5. This table summarizes the quality attribute results for each model, allowing us to identify which categorization modeling approach performed best overall across all quality attributes.

Through the evaluation shown in Table 3, we observe that the Inheritance model has the highest values for design properties such as design size, hierarchies, and abstraction, indicating a more complex structure compared to the Base and Type Pattern models. In contrast, the Base model is the least complex, with the Type Pattern model falling in between.

Also, based on the results shown in Table 4, the models show the following features:

- **Reusability:** The Inheritance model shows the highest reusability due to its complex structure and high cohesion. It can be quickly applied in a new situation due to the already created classes for sensor types.
- **Flexibility:** The Type Pattern has the most flexibility due to the use of composition and low coupling. This allows designs to be easily changed.
- **Understandability:** The Base model is the easiest to learn and comprehend due to its simplicity, despite having the lowest cohesion.
- **Functionality:** The Inheritance model demonstrates the highest functionality through more classes, hierarchy and cohesion, making it the most feature-complete option.
- **Extendibility:** The Inheritance model exhibits high extendibility. This is due to the high scores in abstraction, inheritance, and polymorphism achieved by using the generalization/specialization concept. Thus, new requirements can be easily integrated into the design.
- **Effectiveness:** For similar reasons to extendibility, the Inheritance model is also the best in terms of effectiveness, indicating they meet performance requirements efficiently.

Overall, the Inheritance model stands out as the most comprehensive choice, balancing reusability, functionality, and effectiveness. The Type Pattern model is good for its flexibility, while the Base model is perfect in understandability.

4.3 MERODE Test Environment

After the evaluation of the three models using QMOOD, we compare them in the test environments provided by the MERODE approach and Merlin Prototyper. The test cases are described in Sect. 3.4. These test cases were established based on expected changes to the online systems of the two use case models. In addition, they are aligned with the requirements of both use cases and address the quality attributes reusability, functionality, and effectiveness. Since both categorization patterns were applied in the same way in both use cases, the results of the test cases are identical for both scenarios. More detailed information about the tests and test environments for all model variants and both use cases can be found via the following reference GitHub Repository. The results of these tests are visible in Table 6.

Table 6. Test cases with results for the three model variants

Test cases	Base model	Inheritance model	Type Pattern model
Add new sensor type	Not possible	Not possible, new class must be added offline	A new sensor type can directly be added in the class 'SensorType'
Add new sensor instance	New instances can be added in the class 'Sensor', but are not linked to a sensor type	Instances can be directly added to the correct specialization sensor type class (e.g. 'ST') without the need of linking the sensor with the sensor type	Instances can be added to the class 'Sensor', but these need to be linked to the correct sensor type instance in class 'SensorType' (e.g. 'ST') which needs to exist
Delete sensor instance	Instances can be removed from the class 'Sensor'	Instances can directly be removed from the correct specialization sensor type class	Instances can be removed from the class 'Sensor'
Delete sensor type	Not possible	Not possible, class needs to be deleted offline	Instance can be removed from the class 'SensorType'

The MERODE test cases reveal several important insights for each model:

- The Base model lacks the functionality to link sensors to sensor types, putting it at a disadvantage. While the Inheritance and Type Pattern model can link the added sensor with the correct sensor type, the Base model cannot.
- The Inheritance model allows for easy addition and removal of sensors but requires offline adaptation to add new sensor types. To add a new type of sensor, an entirely new class must be created. In contrast, the Type Pattern model enables easier addition of new sensor types by simply creating a new instance in the 'SensorTypes' class.
- The Type Pattern model and the Inheritance model can easily add new sensors to the 'sensor' class. However, adding and linking these sensors to the

correct sensor type is easier in the Inheritance and less error-prone. In the Inheritance model, they can be directly added in the correct sensor type class while they need to be linked manually to the correct sensor type in the type pattern model.

This evaluation provides a precise understanding of the model suitable for various application scenarios, which we discuss in the next section.

5 Discussion

Before moving on to general guidelines and potential limitations of this study, we discuss some conflicting results between the QMOOD evaluation and Merlin prototyper testing. The QMOOD evaluation shows that the Inheritance model scored best in reusability, functionality, and effectiveness, among others. However, the Merlin prototyper tests indicate that the Type Pattern model can more easily add and remove new categories compared to the Inheritance model. This discrepancy raises doubts about whether the Inheritance model genuinely excels in reusability, functionality, and effectiveness, and whether the QMOOD evaluation alone is sufficient to accurately assess these quality attributes. However, it is important to note that the definitions of these quality attributes can be quite subjective, and the most appropriate model depends on the specific requirements. Additionally, the QMOOD evaluation correctly identifies the Type Pattern model as the most flexible, consistent with the results from test cases.

To address potential shortcomings of the QMOOD evaluation, it is advantageous to combine this evaluation with tests conducted in a test environment like Merlin prototyper testing. This combined approach is crucial for providing a comprehensive and accurate evaluation of a model's quality. Based on this approach, we can formulate the following guidelines for the use of categorization patterns in IoT applications.

Choosing the best categorization pattern significantly impacts IoT software development; selecting a model that aligns with system requirements can streamline the development process. The Inheritance model demonstrates the highest reusability, functionality, extendibility and effectiveness. This suggests that this model is well-suited for components requiring extensive reuse and capable of managing complex operations. Its high effectiveness indicates strong performance in scenarios that leverage its comprehensive structure and relationships. Testing also showed its ease of use. Additionally, the Inheritance model, unlike the Type Pattern and Base models, creates a separate subclass for each specialization (type of sensor). This approach enables the inclusion of specific attributes and methods tailored to each specialization, allowing for more precise and specialized functionality within the model. However, because new subclasses and their corresponding attributes and methods can only be added offline during the model-building process, this inheritance model has low flexibility when it comes to adding new categories. In contrast, the Type Pattern model offers greater flexibility because it allows for the easy addition of new categories and is suitable for environments where frequent changes and developments occur. While new categories can be added quickly, this model is more complex and requires additional training and experience to use correctly and avoid errors. The Base model, with its simplicity, is easier to understand despite having the lowest cohesion. This makes it an excellent choice for IoT systems where understandability and maintenance are critical priorities.

Using these guidelines, we can make a decision on the most appropriate categorization pattern for both use cases. For the smart factory use case, where there is a need for new sensor types in the future, the Type Pattern model is the best option. In contrast, for the smart home use case, where there is no anticipated need for new sensor types, the Inheritance model is more suitable and is easier to use.

While this study provides valuable insights regarding IoT and conceptual modeling, it has several limitations and challenges and further work is necessary. Firstly, the evaluation focused on design properties using the QMOOD in two levels, and excluding other relevant metrics to evaluate the models. Considering other metrics can help us to evaluate and choose the best model more accurately for the system. Secondly, while the evaluated categorization patterns can potentially be applied to other modeling use cases, the findings of this study are based on specific IoT use cases, which may limit the model's applicability to other software systems and development environments. Finally, the subjective nature of interpreting design properties and quality attributes introduces a level of subjectivity as a significant challenge. Although an independent team of experts conducted a separate evaluation based on their perspective and expertise, it is not possible to ignore biases and their impact on the evaluation.

In our future work, we want to address these limitations and explore additional aspects of our proposed methodology; we want to consider a wider range of metrics to provide a more comprehensive evaluation of the models. In addition, we want to conduct empirical studies with more use cases to validate our findings and enhance the generalizability of our approach and minimize potential biases in evaluation. Lastly, the extended version of the Type Pattern, known as the dynamic object model, can also be evaluated and compared with the categorization patterns presented in this work using the QMOOD methodology and the MERODE test environment.

6 Conclusion

In this paper, different conceptual models of IoT systems were designed using a base model and two different categorization patterns: Inheritance and Type pattern. The QMOOD metrics were used to compare and evaluate the design properties and quality attributes in IoT systems. The models were implemented using a code generator and the MERODE tools. The results for each model by using two different smart factory and smart home use cases show that the Inheritance model has the highest reusability, functionality, extendibility and effectiveness, the Type Pattern model excels in flexibility, and the Base model has the highest understandability. The choice of the categorization pattern significantly has impacts on development efficiency, maintenance, and scalability.

With this work, we hope to have provided new insights for system developers and modelers applying categorization patterns within conceptual models in an IoT context or other domains. Limitations such as the scope of metrics and generalization, suggest areas for future research to provide a more comprehensive evaluation. In conclusion, understanding the trade-offs between different design properties and quality attributes for IoT systems enables developers to make decisions and select the most appropriate model for their specific needs.

References

1. Merlin. https://merlin-academic.com/login
2. Research on enterprise modelling at KU Leuven. https://merode.econ.kuleuven.be/index.html
3. Akundi, A., Euresti, D., Luna, S., Ankobiah, W., Lopes, A., Edinbarough, I.: State of industry 5.0-analysis and identification of current research trends. Appl. Syst. Innov. **5**, 27 (2022). https://doi.org/10.3390/ASI5010027
4. Bansiya, J., Davis, C.G.: A hierarchical model for object-oriented design quality assessment (2002)
5. Brambilla, M., Umuhoza, E., Acerbis, R.: Model-driven development of user interfaces for IoT systems via domain-specific components and patterns. J. Internet Serv. Appl. **8**, 1–21 (2017). https://doi.org/10.1186/S13174-017-0064-1/TABLES/8
6. Carvalho, V.A., Almeida, J.P.A.: Toward a well-founded theory for multi-level conceptual modeling. Softw. Syst. Model. **17**, 205–231 (2018). https://doi.org/10.1007/S10270-016-0538-9/FIGURES/15
7. Compagnucci, I., Snoeck, M., Asensio, E.S.: Supporting digital twins systems integrating the MERODE approach (2023)
8. Cook, D.J., Schmitter-Edgecombe, M.: Fusing ambient and mobile sensor features into a behaviorome for predicting clinical health scores. IEEE Access **9**, 65033–65043 (2021)
9. El-Wakil, M., El-Bastawisi, A., Boshra, M., Fahmy, A.: Object-oriented design quality models a survey and comparison (2004)
10. Guillemin, P., Gusmeroli, S., Milano, P.D., Sundmaeker, H.: Internet of Things strategic research roadmap (2009)
11. Haller, S., Serbanati, A., Bauer, M., Carrez, F.: A domain model for the Internet of Things. CPSCom **2013**, 411–417 (2013). https://doi.org/10.1109/GREENCOM-ITHINGS-CPSCOM.2013.87
12. Hassine, T.B., Khayati, O., Ghezala, H.B.: An IoT domain meta-model and an approach to software development of IoT solutions. In: IINTEC 2017, pp. 32–37 (2017). https://doi.org/10.1109/IINTEC.2017.8325909
13. Johnson, R., Woolf, B.: The type object pattern (1996)
14. Kitchenham, B., Pfleeger, S.L.: Software quality: the elusive target. IEEE Softw. **13**, 12–21 (1996). https://doi.org/10.1109/52.476281
15. Loizaga, E., Eyam, A.T., Bastida, L., Lastra, J.L.: A comprehensive study of human factors, sensory principles, and commercial solutions for future human-centered working operations in industry 5.0 (2023). https://doi.org/10.1109/ACCESS.2023.3280071
16. Neelamegam, C., Punithavalli, M.: A survey - object oriented quality metrics. Glob. J. Comput. Sci. Technol. (2009)

17. Olivé, A.: Conceptual Modeling of Information Systems (2007)
18. Riehle, D., Tilman, M., Johnson, R.: Dynamic object model (2000)
19. Rojas, C.N., et al.: Society 5.0: a Japanese concept for a superintelligent society. Sustainability **13**, 6567 (2021). https://doi.org/10.3390/SU13126567
20. Selic, B., et al.: OMG Unified Modeling Language (Version 2.5) (2015). http://www.omg.org/spec/UML/2.5
21. Serbanati, A., Maria, C., Biader, U.: Building blocks of the internet of things: state of the art and beyond. Deploying RFID - Challenges, Solutions, and Open Issues (2011). https://doi.org/10.5772/19997
22. Snoeck, M.: Enterprise Information Systems Engineering: The MERODE Approach (2014)
23. Snoeck, M., Dedene, G.: Existence dependency: the key to semantic integrity between structural and behavioral aspects of object types. IEEE Trans. Softw. Eng. **24**, 233–251 (1998). https://doi.org/10.1109/32.677182
24. Vanderfeesten, I.: Advanced Dynamic Actor Assignment. Edward Elgar Publishing (2024). https://www.e-elgar.com/shop/gbp/handbook-on-business-process-management-and-digital-transformation-9781802206081.html

Advances in Enterprise Modelling Techniques

SmartCML: A Visual Modeling Language to Enhance the Comprehensibility of Smart Contract Implementations

Simon Curty[✉][iD] and Hans-Georg Fill[iD]

Digitalization and Information Systems Group, University of Fribourg, Bd de Pérolles 90, 1700 Fribourg, Switzerland
{simon.curty,hans-georg.fill}@unifr.ch
https://www.unifr.ch/inf/digits/en/

Abstract. One of the most notable capabilities of blockchain technology, exemplified by the Ethereum platform, is the decentralized execution of deterministic code, commonly referred to as smart contracts. This can be employed to develop business services that capitalize on the unique properties of blockchain technology, including the ability to maintain immutable, transparent, and persistent records on a distributed ledger. Nevertheless, even experts may find the process of writing smart contracts challenging. In addition to cost, optimization, and security concerns, it is essential to ensure that the smart contracts align with the business case and the associated rules. To address this issue, we propose *SmartCML*, a domain-specific visual modeling language to draft smart contracts, with the primary objective of facilitating the communication of the codified information among relevant stakeholders. The modeling language has been implemented using the ADOxx metamodeling platform. Smart contract models can then be transformed into fully functional code for the Ethereum virtual machine. The application of the modeling language is demonstrated with the help of two use cases.

Keywords: Blockchain · Smart contracts · Visual programming · Ethereum · Model-driven engineering · Domain-specific modeling language

1 Introduction

Blockchain technology is commonly related to cryptocurrencies and finance. This is largely due to the Bitcoin electronic cash system, conceived in 2008 [26], that popularized this technology. The combination of a decentralized ledger and cryptographic schemes enables the persistent and tamper-proof storage of transaction records without the necessity of a central controlling party [2,13]. These intrinsic properties of blockchains offer promising potential for the digital transformation of businesses, facilitating the emergence of novel business cases [20,32].

The advent of program code that is executed in a decentralized, transparent, and traceable manner has significantly enhanced the versatility and viability of this technology for a multitude of business models. These so-called *smart contracts* were popularized by the Ethereum blockchain platform [3] and have since been adopted by many other blockchain implementations. Smart contracts allow for the realization of business services and novel decentralized business models that benefit from the aforementioned blockchain properties. Despite the potential for blockchain technology to disrupt existing business models and facilitate the development of innovative business cases, the adoption of this technology within organizational contexts is still hindered by a multitude of challenges.

Organizational barriers such as unavailability of financial and human resources, regulatory involvement, and lacking knowledge of the technology in the organization can prevent practical adoption [4]. The successful implementation of a blockchain-based business model requires the alignment of institutional, market, and technological factors, which can be achieved through a comprehensive approach that addresses the inherent complexity of these interrelated elements [21]. In addition, the complexity and relative immaturity of the technology's ecosystem [15], as well as specific technical challenges [23], further impede its adoption. While ongoing technological advancements have mitigated some concerns, such as high energy consumption [11] and scalability issues [27], the implementation of blockchain-based applications and business services remains a demanding and complex endeavor. The intrinsic properties of blockchains present a double-edged sword for smart contract development. On the one hand, the persistent and transparent nature of the ledger, and by extension the code deployed, fosters security, data privacy, and functional issues. On the other hand, these very properties enable smart contracts in the first place. Previous research on methods to support technical smart contract development predominantly focus on the engineering challenges related to these issues. However, interrelation of business and technological factors in blockchain-based business cases remains sparsely researched [10]. This includes in particular the alignment of business services and their associated rules with smart contract implementations. To support this, we propose a modeling method to increase the comprehensibility of smart contracts and thereby facilitate communication among stakeholders and the alignment of the business case with the code. In particular, we present a domain-specific visual modeling language, named *SmartCML*, designed for use with Ethereum-compatible smart contracts. *SmartCML* is intended to serve two distinct functions. First, it can be used to facilitate communication regarding smart contracts for business cases. Second, it can be employed to generate code written in the Solidity language.

The remainder of the paper is structured as follows: In Sect. 2 we introduce the necessary foundations of blockchain technology and smart contracts, followed by an overview of previous modeling approaches that relate to this work. In Sect. 3, we present the extended the domain-specific modeling language, including the requirements, metamodel and graphical notation. Section 3.4 presents a prototypical implementation of the language and code generator. In Sect. 4, we demonstrate the proposed language with two use cases. Finally, in Sects. 5 and 6 we summarize our contribution and provide an outline for future research.

2 Foundations and Related Work

The following section presents a concise overview of blockchain technologies, with a particular focus on smart contracts. Further, it provides an analysis of previous research on visual modeling languages for the development of smart contracts.

2.1 Blockchain Technology

A blockchain consists of an electronic ledger that is organized in cryptographically linked blocks of digitally signed transactions between authorized parties. This ledger is stored decentralized on a peer-to-peer network. A consensus mechanism defines the rules on how transactions are validated, recorded, and propagated among the network nodes, thereby ensuring a consistent and valid state of the distributed ledger [2,13]. Depending on the specific blockchain implementation, transactions may include the transfer of funds, digital assets or, more generally, the storage of data. In some blockchain systems, transactions may also include executable code in the form of smart contracts to be stored on the ledger [1]. Subsequent invocation of such smart contracts results in the decentralized execution of deterministic code, which can be reenacted trustfully given the original parameters and environment. These smart contracts can be used to build business services, as part of decentralized applications, which leverage core blockchain properties, such as transparency of records and shared data access. These properties can be regarded as powerful disruptors to business models [6,20]. Blockchain-based smart contracts were popularized by the Ethereum blockchain technology [3] and its application on the publicly available network of the same name. Ethereum-compatible smart contracts are compiled into bytecode for the Ethereum Virtual Machine (EVM), which is the decentralized execution environment on the network nodes. Bytecode instructions are assigned a cost value that serves as a measure of the complexity of the code to be executed. In public networks, this cost is to be paid by the invoking party as part of transaction fees. Several other blockchains use the EVM as an execution environment[1], so that smart contracts written for Ethereum are portable. Smart contracts targeting the EVM are often written in Solidity, a high-level, statically typed programming language resembling JavaScript [30].

2.2 Visual Modeling Languages for Smart Contracts

The programming of smart contracts is subject to challenges that are not encountered in such a profound way in traditional development. This is partly due to the nature of blockchain technology and its idiosyncrasies, but also due to the intricacies of specific implementations, programming languages, and development practices [23]. This complexity renders smart contracts vulnerable to problems

---
[1] e.g., Avalanche and Polygon.

that are difficult to remedy once the contract is deployed. These include security vulnerabilities that can result in the loss of funds, or poorly optimized code that leads unnecessary transaction costs [23]. In order to support the development of smart contracts and to address the challenges associated with them, several approaches have been discussed in the academic community, including visual modeling languages [18]. In the following, we highlight selected previous visual modeling languages for developing smart contracts and the subsequent generation of code, that are most relevant to the approach presented here. For a comprehensive overview of model-driven approaches to distributed application development, we refer to a recent literature review [10].

Previous visual modeling approaches for smart contracts are based either on an existing language, propose a domain-specific language or rely on a mixture of the two, for example, in the form of domain-specific extensions or profiles. An approach by Jurgelaitis et al. can be classified within the first group [22]. It utilizes UML class diagrams to model the structure of smart contracts. The behavioral logic is then modeled with UML state charts. The UML diagrams serve as input for the generation of executable Solidity code. The code generation of this approach is based on model transformations using the Eclipse ATL platform, with the main goal of facilitating the implementation process. Another approach relies on Petri nets to model smart contracts [35]. Here, the focus lies on the prevention of security issues at design time. This is achieved by first modeling contracts platform-independent and then simulating the resulting Petri net workflows in order to detect vulnerabilities such as deadlocks. Solidity template code can subsequently be generated from the workflows. The generated code may then serve as secure basis for further developments.

Designing a domain-specific language promises flexibility in terms of the representation of smart contract or blockchain platform-specific features. As such, several domain-specific languages for smart contract development have been proposed over the years. The modeling language iContractML aims to facilitate the development of language-independent smart contracts [17]. It features a visual notation for representing smart contracts in terms of participants, transactions, and assets at a high abstraction level. From the high-level models, the structure of smart contract code and partial behavioral logic can be derived using a template and transformation rule-based code generation paradigm. It allows to target multiple languages and platforms. Tan et al. presented a tool specifically targeting Solidity [29]. The modeling process relies on a combination of form-based definition of the structure of Solidity contracts and their implementation as action graphs. These are defined visually in a notation resembling flow-charts. From the definitions, Solidity code can be generated. A particular focus thereby lies on the estimation and optimization of execution costs. Based on Google's Blockly framework, SmartBuilder is a tool for visually programming smart contracts for the Hyperledger Fabric blockchain platform [24]. Code control structures and statements are represented as building blocks that can be combined together in a drag-and-drop fashion to compose smart contracts. This approach is intended to aid in learning smart contract coding.

Partially relying on Blockly as well, is the language Das Contract [28], in which Blockly is used to specify the behavior of a contract. Das Contract pertains to the last group of modeling approaches. For the conceptual representations of smart contracts it reverts to modified DEMO and BPMN models. Another approach combines UML class diagrams with a domain-specific language [19]. Thereby, language elements of the target smart contract language are mapped to UML class diagram elements. These diagrams are further complemented by models of operations in a domain-specific language. The models are then transformed into a platform-independent target language.

The modeling language presented in this work shares similarities with existing approaches, adopting several design decisions and ideas. However, previous work has mostly focused on facilitating the development activity in terms of model-based code generation or aims to make writing smart contracts more accessible to non-experts. Our approach instead seeks to enhance the comprehensibility of the implementation to facilitate its alignment with the business case. Therein, a focus lies on abstractions on the algorithmic level and explicit modeling of information access.

3 Domain-Specific Language Design

The *SmartCML* language has been designed and developed in accordance with the macro process as outlined by Frank and considering principles of modeling method engineering [16,34]. The methodology comprises seven cyclical phases (micro processes), which serve as guidelines for designing a domain-specific modeling language (DSML). These phases are summarized as follows:

1. *Clarification of scope and purpose*: visual modeling of Ethereum-compatible smart contracts to enhance the comprehensibility of behavioral logic.
2. *Analysis of generic requirements*: These requirements are, in essence, applicable to every DSML. We revert to the catalog of generic requirements as outlined by Frank [16] and adopt them accordingly to our purposes as outlined in Sect. 3.1.
3. *Analysis of specific requirements*, that is, requirements that apply to the modeling artifact in particular. We will present these in Sect. 3.1.
4. *Language specification*: The metamodel will be presented in Sect. 3.2 in semi-formal notation. Formal specifications may be added later, e.g. using FDMM [14].
5. *Design and documentation of graphical notation*: The graphical notation of the visual smart contract modeling language will be shown in Sect. 3.3.
6. *Development of modeling tool*: The prototypical implementation of the language using the ADOxx metamodeling platform and the supplementary code generation are discussed in Sect. 3.4.
7. *Evaluation and refinement*: In accordance with the macro process, the modeling language and its constituent parts were subject to continuous evaluation and refinement cycles in alignment with the collected requirements. In Sect. 4 we show the applicability of the language for visually modeling smart contracts by means of two exemplary use cases.

3.1 Requirements

The macro process distinguishes between *generic* and *specific* requirements. Thereby, generic requirements may relate to appropriate conceptual representation of the target domain, levels of abstraction, or pragmatics such as comprehensibility and ease of use. We have specified 6 generic requirements ($\mathbf{GR}_{1-6}$) that are adopted from the catalog proposed by Frank [16]:

The visual smart contract language contains concepts that are familiar and recognizable to smart contract experts ($\mathbf{GR}_1$). The visual notation serves to differentiate between discrete concepts and is readily comprehensible to both experts and non-experts alike ($\mathbf{GR}_2$). The concepts of the language allow the modeling of smart contracts in such a way that common features of the Solidity language can be represented adequately ($\mathbf{GR}_3$). The modeling language includes all the essential concepts so that models can convey all the necessary information to be transformed into Solidity as the target representation ($\mathbf{GR}_4$). Additional concepts can be added via an extension mechanism to accommodate future smart contract features ($\mathbf{GR}_5$). In order to prevent the model from becoming overloaded and to ensure the correct interpretation, the language provides different levels of abstraction where appropriate ($\mathbf{GR}_6$).

We further derived six specific requirements ($\mathbf{SR}_{1-6}$), which detail the modeling artifacts' capabilities and features. The requirements have been formulated based on features of previous approaches and use case scenarios. The latter category encompasses tasks for which the method is considered to be applicable, as well as concrete smart contracts that one should be able to replicate in terms of functionality through the use of the language. The fundamental use scenario of the language is for the visual modeling of an Ethereum-compatible smart contract by an expert, with the objective of conveying implementation details to other stakeholders for the purpose of aligning the implementation and the business case. The particular specifications were as follows:

$\mathbf{SR}_1$ Visual smart contracts can be transformed to executable Solidity code as target representation. The produced code is fully consistent with the behavioural logic and contract structure as defined in the corresponding visual contract model. Ethereum has been selected as the target platform due to its status as the dominant blockchain technology with smart contract capabilities in both academic and industrial contexts [10]. Moreover, selecting Solidity, which compiles to EVM bytecode, permits compatibility with blockchains that rely on the EVM as an execution environment in general.

$\mathbf{SR}_2$ Common programming language structures and features, namely if-else conditions, while loops, parameterized functions, function calls, arithmetic and Boolean operations, and variable assignments can be modeled or represented equivalently. The rationale for this requirement is that the language must be sufficiently expressive to enable the representation of general algorithms. Furthermore, these concepts are intuitively known to programmers.

$\mathbf{SR}_3$ Concepts related to Solidity-specific language features are included, such that these features can be modeled or derived from the model. In particular, this includes the emission of events and errors, conditional transaction guards, data location of reference types and multiple return values. The mapping and array data structures, as well as user-defined structs shall be supported. This selection is informed by an analysis of over 400.000 Solidity smart contracts on their use of language features and structures. The languages have been obtained from the thousand most popular public GitHub repositories that contain Solidity code. Subsequently, these have been parsed and analyzed on a language grammar level.

SR_4 Native solidity types, builtin functions, and custom complex composite types, such as structs and arrays of structs, can be defined by the user. These definitions are used in visual smart contracts and can be shared among them. This requirement relates to **GR_4** and **GR_6** in particular. Solidity is a statically typed language, and ideally, the required information for deriving correct types is present within smart contract models.

SR_5 Interactions that result in a change of the contract state are explicitly denoted. Any write operation that commits data to the contract state storage is permanently recorded in the context of a transaction on the blockchain. As a result, such interactions are subject to transaction fees and the committed information becomes immutable.

SR_6 The notation of the modeling language is suitable for drafting visual smart contracts with pen and paper. The rationale here is that a strict requirement for a tool would compromise one of the core goals of the modeling language, which is to facilitate communication, since the method could not be used as easily in workshops, on whiteboards, and so on.

3.2 Metamodel

Based on the formulated requirements the metamodel of *SmartCML* was specified in seven steps (MM_{1-7}), as shown in Fig. 1. The language is inherently flow-based and follows a similar paradigm as process languages and transition systems. The fundamental concept is based on the representation of smart contracts as a set of interfaces, with each interface accompanied by a graph of operations that can be regarded as a transition system. In the following, a detailed examination of the individual components of the metamodel will be presented. For the sake of clarity, terms in *italics* relate to their respective metamodel class.

MM_1 The language elements are assigned to two distinct *Model Types*, namely the *Definitions Map* and the *Visual Smart Contract*. The former is comprised of shared definitions of types and builtins. The latter models a single contract in terms of structure, state, behavioral logic, and communication interfaces. A *Visual Smart Contract* model may reference elements of one or several definition maps and definition maps can be shared among models. This segregation relates in particular to **GR_6**.

MM_2 A *Definitions Map* model defines *Builtin Functions* that are part of the execution environment, and data types. A type is either a *Struct*, *Mapping*,

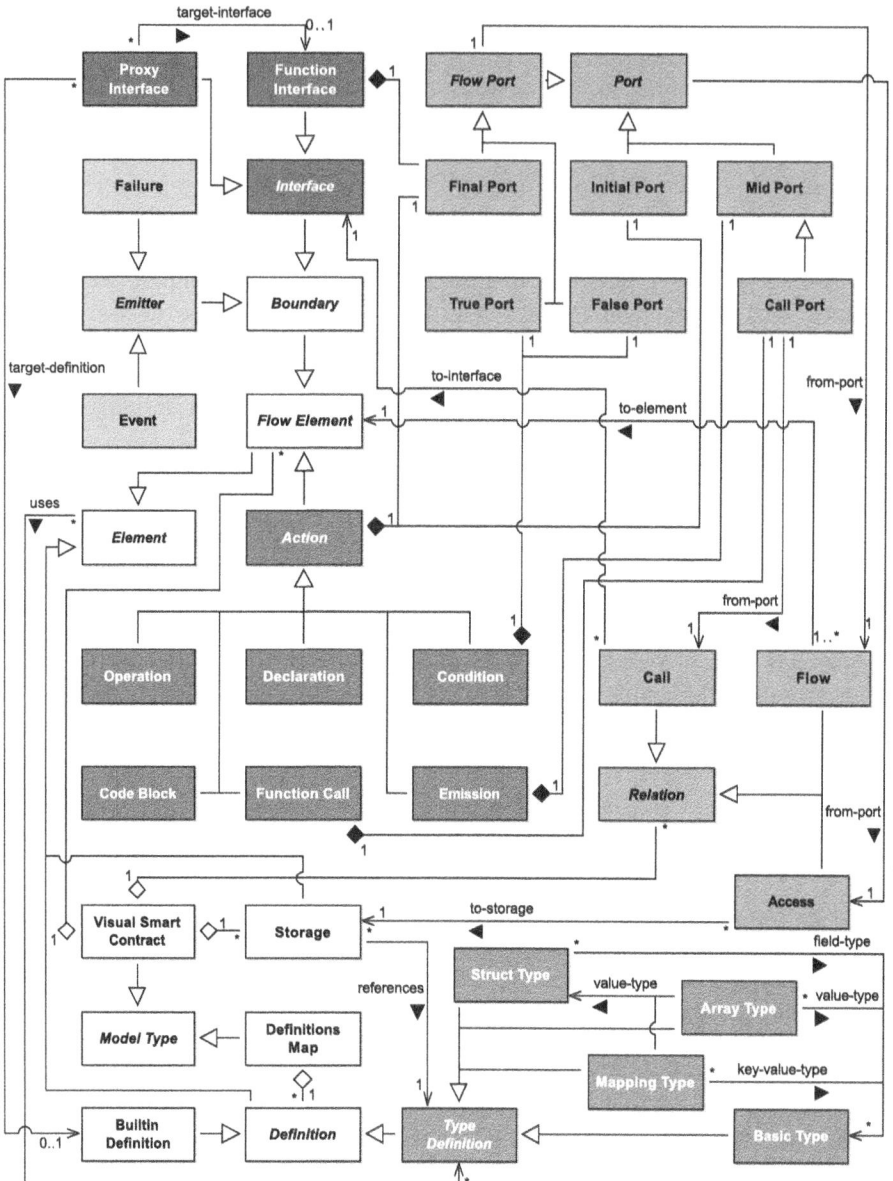

Fig. 1. Metamodel of the proposed domain-specific modeling language *SmartCML*. Attributes are omitted. The coloring is intended as reading aid.

Array or *Basic Type* (**GR**$_4$, **SR**$_4$). The former three reference further types. E.g., a mapping has a key and a value type. Elements are defined by the user. This allows to accommodate for future additions and changes of the execution environment (**GR**$_5$).

MM$_3$ *Boundaries* define the bounds of a contract in terms of communication. An *Interface* defines a scope of execution with defined input and output. The *Function Interface* models a contract function, while the *Proxy Interface* is used to relate other interfaces or *Builtin Functions*. Further, *Emitters* allow for the signaling of *Events* and *Failures* during executions (**GR$_3$**, **SR$_2$**, **SR$_3$**).

MM$_4$ An *Action* represents a discrete unit of work within a flow. This may take the form of an arithmetic or Boolean *Operation*, a branching *Condition*, the *Declaration* of an instance, a *Function Call* or the *Emission* of a signal (**SR$_2$**, **SR$_3$**). The *Code Block* element accommodates the inclusion of logic that cannot be modeled otherwise or whose explicit representation would be inappropriate for the targeted abstraction level (**GR$_3$**, **GR$_5$**, **GR$_6$**). One potential usage example is the incorporation of EVM assembly code.

MM$_5$ *Actions* and *Boundaries* are *Flow Elements*, i.e., are within a flow. Each such element has a number of *Ports* that define the available outgoing relations. The *Flow* relation allows to specify a subsequent *Flow Element* from an outgoing *Flow Port*. Elements may differ in what ports they have. All *Actions* have an *Initial* and a *Final Port*, while a *Condition* additionally has a *True* and *False Port*. Each *Port* has a priority that defines in which order operations are to be executed. The sequence in which ports are activated and the action is performed is as follows: initial, action execution, mid or call, true, false, and final. This allows to model branching logic with well-defined sequences of actions while accommodating for some flexibility in modeling (**GR$_1$**, **GR$_4$**, **SR$_2$**).

MM$_6$ The *Storage* class represents a state variable of a contract. To be available within an action, state variables must explicitly be accessed with the *Access* relation. Furthermore, the relation indicates the nature of the access, whether it is a read or write operation. As a result, contract functions that access state variables or modify them can be readily identified (**GR$_4$**, **SR$_3$**, **SR$_5$**).

MM$_7$ The *Call* relation delineates the invocation of a function from the outgoing port. This may be in the form of an internal function call; in which case the target element is a *Function Interface* in the same model. Alternatively, the call may target a *Proxy Interface*, referencing either a *Builtin Function* or some external function (**GR$_1$**, **GR$_3$**, **SR$_2$**).

3.3 Graphical Notation

The concrete subclasses of the *Element* and *Relation* metamodel classes are available as modeling elements in one of the model types. As such, these have a designated graphical representation. In Table 1, a summary of the elements of the *Visual Smart Contract* model type is shown. The design of the graphical notation concerns mainly the requirements **GR$_2$** and **SR$_6$**. The visual language is based on simple geometric shapes where related elements share design elements. Each *Action* type is denoted with a distinctly decorated circle and has an annotation that designates what the action represents. For example, a *Condition* could have the annotation ≪ *if* ≫ or ≪ *while* ≫, depending on whether the

Table 1. Graphical notation of the modeling elements that comprise a *SmartCML Visual Smart Contract* model.

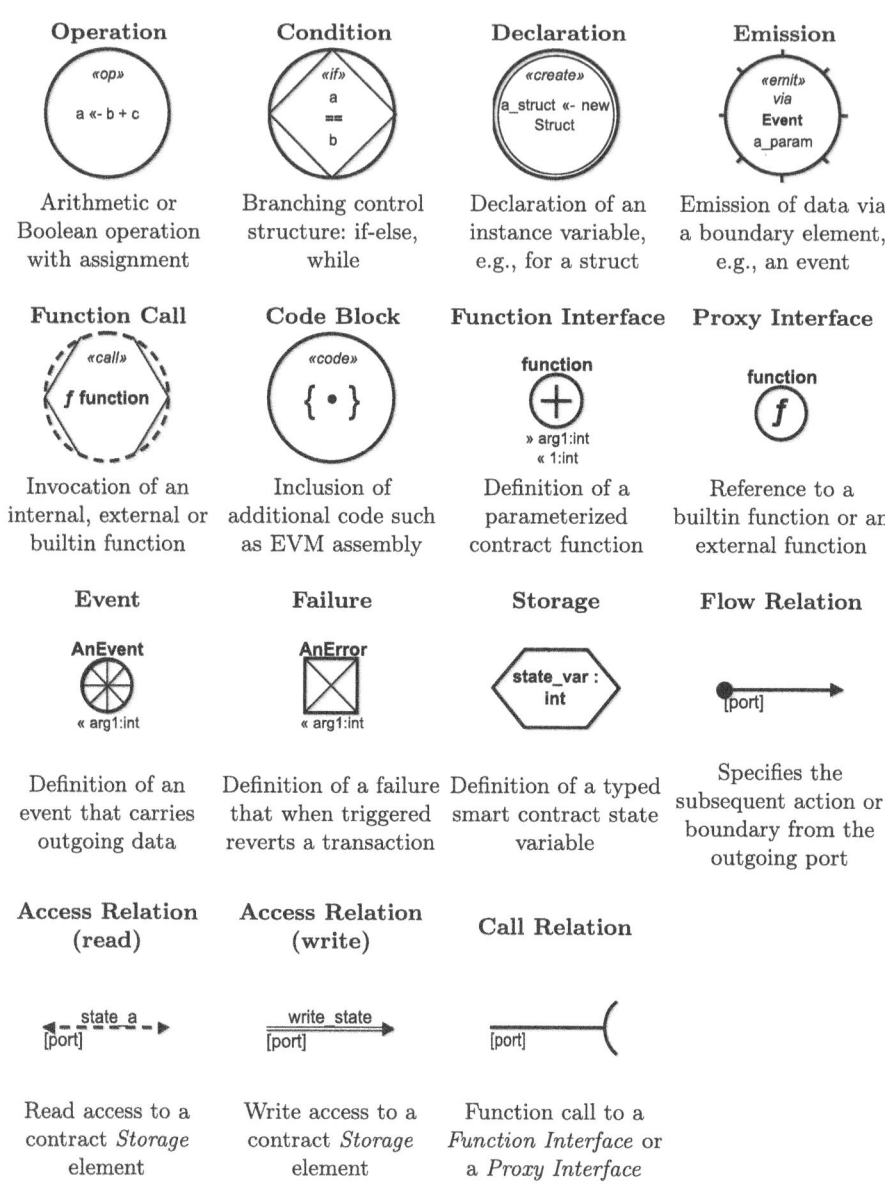

element translates to an if-else statement or a while loop. *Boundary* elements, that is, *Interfaces* and *Emitters*, are uniquely named as they represent a distinct definition in the smart contract, e.g., of an error. Further, *Boundaries* display what data is transmitted in the form of parameters and return values. Each relation shows the port from which it is triggered. The visualization of the *Access* relation is based on the access mode, and additionally denotes the variables read from, or written to state, represented by the *Storage* element. The straightforward shapes and the subtle visual design elements enable models to be drafted by hand (SR_6). The descriptive elements, such as the annotations, and the distinct visual representation facilitates comprehensibility and the differentiation of the concepts (GR_2).

3.4 Implementation

The proposed domain-specific modeling language has been developed and implemented as a prototype using the ADOxx metamodeling platform [12]. ADOxx was selected for its maturity, acceptance in both academic and industrial contexts, and suitability for the prototyping of modeling methods. It has previously been successfully employed for the implementation of modeling languages with varying purposes [6,25]. In order to implement a metmodel for a custom modeling language, it is necessary to extend the ADOxx metamodel in the development toolkit and export it as a library. In order to facilitate this process, the ADOxx metamodel provides a set of pre-defined classes, relations, and attribute types that can be leveraged to simplify implementation. ADOxx further offers the capability to specify model types for which specific elements and relations are available (MM_1). The *Flow*, *Access*, and *Call* relations (MM_{5-7}) are realized as relation classes. However, ADOxx does not natively support the concept of ports. To circumvent this limitation, outgoing ports are imitated by an attribute of the relation classes. The references to *Definitions* (MM_2) are realized with attributes of the *Interref* type, which allows to link instances of elements across models. The linked *Type Definitions* are then leveraged by a type-checking system to verify that the typed variables are being utilized in a consistent manner. The typing system is implemented with the internal scripting language and constitutes an integral part of the modeling library. The code generator, on the other hand, is implemented as a separate Node.js application that takes ADOxx models exported as XML as input. The XML models are transformed into a syntax tree that conforms to the Solidity grammar, and the code is then generated from this syntax tree. The *SmartCML* modeling library for ADOxx and the Solidity code generator are openly available [7].

4 Exemplary Use Cases

In accordance with the macro process, the modeling language was subject to continuous evaluation and refinement cycles. Among other measures, the continuous analysis of use cases contributed to the refinement of the method. The application of the modeling language for the visual design of smart contracts is demonstrated through the analysis of two use cases.

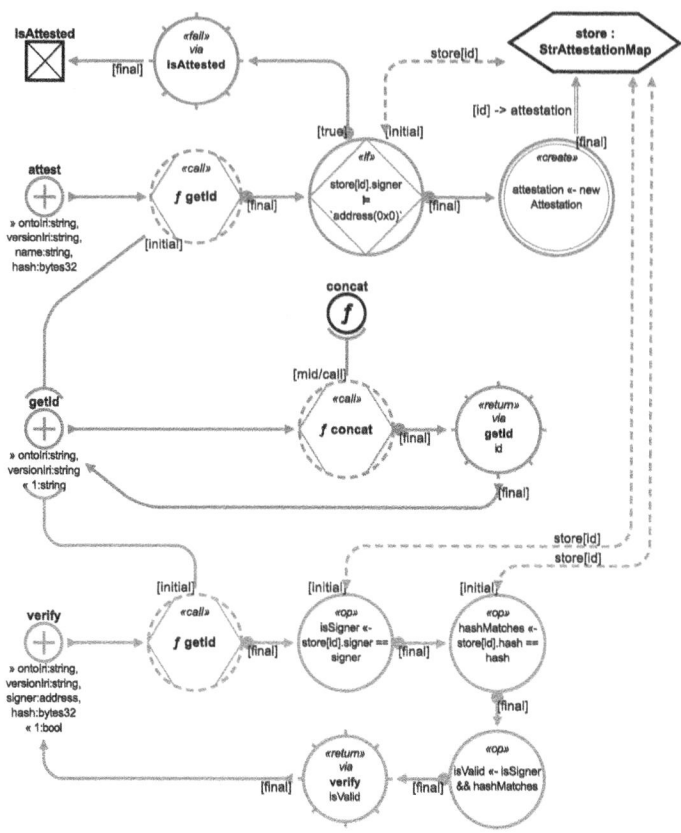

Fig. 2. *Visual Smart Contract* model for recording and verifying attestations of OWL ontologies.

4.1 Ontology Attestation

The decentralized attestation of information is a common topic of discussion with regard to the potential applications of blockchain technology. The persistence of records ensures the immutability of previous attestations, without the need to employ additional technological measures. This particular use case revolves around the proposal to utilize blockchain technology and smart contracts for the purpose of attesting to the provenance of OWL ontologies. As illustrated in Fig. 2, the visual smart contract aligns with an architectural framework for this specific purpose that has been previously proposed [8].

This visual smart contract contains three *Function Interfaces* that correspond to the contract functions *attest, verify*, and the helper function *getId*. A specific version of an OWL ontology is identified by the ontology IRI and a version IRI. Accordingly, attestations are mapped to ontologies using these identifiers. The *getId* function constructs a key from the identifiers by calling a builtin function *concat*, that concatenates strings. To record a new attestation, the *attest* function takes as input the identifiers, a name, and a hash of the ontology. A unique key is obtained through an internal invocation of *getId*. Subsequently, it is checked whether an attestation with the same key already exists by reading from the state storage mapping. The mapping maps the string keys to structs that contain the attestation information such as the address of the signer. If the signer is already set for this key, the ontology is already attested and an error *IsAttested* is emitted, and the transaction reverted as a result. Otherwise, a new attestation struct is created and stored in the mapping. Listing 1 show the code that is generated from this part of the model. Similarly, given an ontology version's identifiers, its hash, and the address of the supposed signer, it can be verified whether this version has been attested by the given signer.

```
function attest(string calldata ontoIri, string calldata versionIri, string
    calldata name, bytes32 hash) public {
  string memory id = getId(ontoIri, versionIri);
  if (store[id].signer != address(0x0)) {
     revert IsAttested();
  }
  Attestation memory attestation = Attestation(msg.sender, name, block.
     timestamp, hash);
  store[id] = attestation;
}
```

Listing 1. Generated solidity code that corresponds to the *attest* function interface flow.

4.2 Decentralized Auctions

In order to demonstrate the viability of proposed languages for the visual modeling of more complex smart contracts, we revert to the use case of decentralized auctions [5]. The smart contract that corresponds to the model illustrated in Fig. 3, allows the posting of auctions for items with a fixed duration. In this context, the blockchain fulfills the function of executing the auction process and recording of the involved bids. This enables the reenactment of the auction process in the event of disputes without the necessity of a trusted third party [5]. It should be noted that, in this illustration, the smart contract does not serve as a payment channel; however, it could be adapted to include this capability.

Auctions are stored as structs in an array, represented as the *auctions Storage* element. Publishing a new auction simply involves appending a new auction struct to the array, represented by the first *Declaration* action and subsequent write *Access* relation to the *Storage* element. The index of the new array element is then returned and serves as future identifier for the auction. The visualization allows to easily identify each access to the state storage. The distinction between read and write access further allows to identify at a glance which functions may alter the contract state, and thus require to be invoked in a transaction context. That is, posting, bidding and closing an auction may change the state and is thus recorded on the blockchain.

Furthermore, the boundary elements serve as clearly identifiable points of data exchange that may be further processed by applications. The emitters

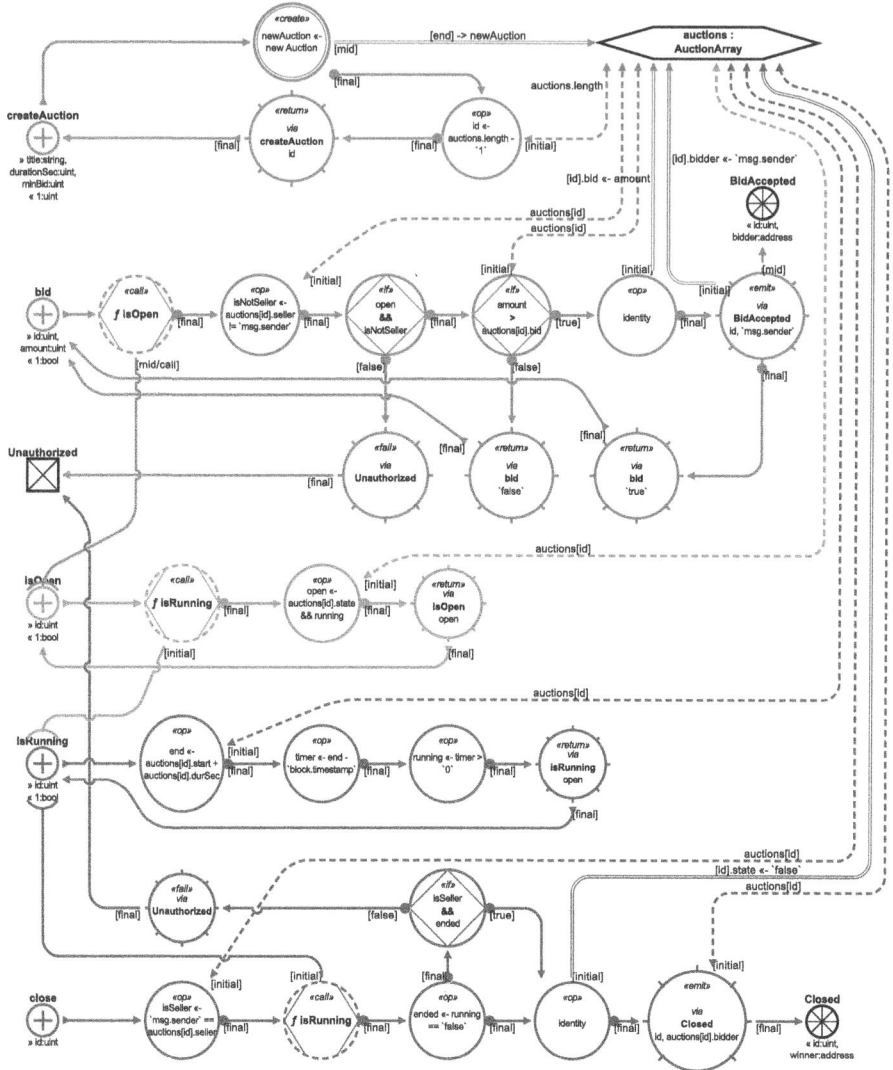

Fig. 3. *Visual Smart Contract* model for decentralized, timed auctions.

Unauthorized, BidAccepted, Closed are shared across flows. That is, these elements, same as the *Storage* are defined on the contract scope. This is indicated by the black coloring of these elements.

5 Discussion

Domain-specific languages are particularly well-suited for addressing the complexities inherent to the adoption of blockchain technology. This is due to the fact that intrinsic properties can be captured in great detail within the context of such languages. Thus, several modeling methods have been proposed that aim to address the many inherent challenges. Common objectives of modeling methods are related to security concerns [31] or model-driven development [9,33], while methods to support the alignment of blockchain technology and business aspects remains sparsely researched [10]. This work aims to leverage the advantages of model-driven engineering methods for the development of smart contracts, while providing a visualization of the implementation that facilitates communication of the behavioral logic. As such, the presented *SmartCML* may serve as a tool to discuss smart contract implementations among stakeholders. To achieve this, the modeling language has been rigorously designed following the *macro process* [16]. The demonstration underlines the languages applicability for visually modeling smart contract that can be transformed into executable Solidity code, without the need of any further manual programming ($\mathbf{GR}_{1,3,4}$, $\mathbf{SR}_{1-4}$). An emphasis in the language's design has been placed on the explicit modeling of smart contract states and which interaction cause a state change ($\mathbf{SR}_5$). The immediate practical benefit is the straightforward identification of interaction in a transaction context and all consequences thereof. Moreover, this offers the opportunity to further link business models with smart contract implementations regarding information spaces, e.g., for ensuring fulfillment of regulatory requirements. The graphical notation is based on simple shapes, which allows for drafting models by hand ($\mathbf{SR}_6$), thus facilitating use on whiteboards.

6 Conclusion and Future Work

In this paper we presented *SmartCML*, a domain-specific modeling language for the visual programming of Ethereum-compatible smart contracts. A focus has been put on a simple graphical notation that aims to facilitate the comprehensibility of the implementation and explicit representation of state changing interactions. The visual smart contract model can be transformed to readily deployable and executable smart contract code. Opportunities for future work include the integration with business modeling approaches, e.g., e^3value, model-based formal verification methods, and the specification of modeling procedures. Further evaluations, for example in the form of expert interviews or ontological analysis, are required to validate the language beyond the initial feasibility demonstration.

Acknowledgments. This work was supported by the Swiss National Science Foundation project Domain-Specific Conceptual Modeling for Distributed Ledger Technologies [196889].

Disclosure of Interests. The authors have no competing interests to declare that are relevant to the content of this article.

References

1. Antonopoulos, A.M., Wood, G.: Mastering Ethereum: Building Smart Contracts and Dapps. O'reilly Media (2018)
2. Banafa, A.: Introduction to Blockchain Technology. River Publishers, New York (2023). https://doi.org/10.1201/9781003426264
3. Buterin, V.: A Next-Generation Smart Contract and Decentralized Application Platform (2013). https://ethereum.org/en/whitepaper/
4. Clohessy, T., Acton, T., Rogers, N.: Blockchain adoption: technological, organisational and environmental considerations. In: Treiblmaier, H., Beck, R. (eds.) Business Transformation through Blockchain, pp. 47–76. Springer, Cham (2019). https://doi.org/10.1007/978-3-319-98911-2_2
5. Curty, S., Fill, H.G.: Exploring the systematic design of blockchain-based applications using integrated modeling standards. In: Bork, D., et al. (eds.) Proceedings of the PoEM 2022 Workshops and Models at Work Co-Located with Practice of Enterprise Modelling 2022, London, United Kingdom, 23–25 November 2022. CEUR Workshop Proceedings, vol. 3298. CEUR-WS.org (2022)
6. Curty, S., Fill, H.G.: A domain-specific e3value extension for analyzing blockchain-based value networks. In: Almeida, J.P.A., Kaczmarek-Heß, M., Koschmider, A., Proper, H.A. (eds.) The Practice of Enterprise Modeling, vol. 497, pp. 74–90. Springer, Cham (2024). https://doi.org/10.1007/978-3-031-48583-1_5
7. Curty, S., Fill, H.G.: SmartCML ADOxx Application Library and Code Generator (PoEM 2024) (2024). https://doi.org/10.5281/zenodo.13899102
8. Curty, S., Fill, H.G., Gonçalves, R.S., Musen, M.A.: An architecture for attesting to the provenance of ontologies using blockchain technologies. In: Shishkov, B. (ed.) Business Modeling and Software Design. LNBIP, pp. 182–199. Springer, Cham (2022). https://doi.org/10.1007/978-3-031-11510-3_11
9. Curty, S., Härer, F., Fill, H.G.: Blockchain application development using model-driven engineering and low-code platforms: a survey. In: Augusto, A., Gill, A., Bork, D., Nurcan, S., Reinhartz-Berger, I., Schmidt, R. (eds.) BPMDS EMMSAD 2022. LNBIP, vol. 450, pp. 205–220. Springer, Cham (2022). https://doi.org/10.1007/978-3-031-07475-2_14
10. Curty, S., Härer, F., Fill, H.G.: Design of blockchain-based applications using model-driven engineering and low-code/no-code platforms: a structured literature review. Softw. Syst. Model. (2023). https://doi.org/10.1007/s10270-023-01109-1
11. Fernando, Y., Saravannan, R.: Blockchain technology: energy efficiency and ethical compliance. J. Governance Integrity **4**(2), 88–95 (2021). https://doi.org/10.15282/jgi.4.2.2021.5872
12. Fill, H.G., Karagiannis, D.: On the conceptualisation of modelling methods using the ADOxx meta modelling platform. Enterprise Model. Inf. Syst. Archit. (EMISAJ) **8**(1), 4–25 (2013). https://doi.org/10.18417/emisa.8.1.1
13. Fill, H.G., Meier, A. (eds.): Blockchain: Grundlagen, Anwendungsszenarien und Nutzungspotenziale. Edition HMD, Springer Fachmedien, Wiesbaden (2020). https://doi.org/10.1007/978-3-658-28006-2
14. Fill, H.-G., Redmond, T., Karagiannis, D.: Formalizing meta models with FDMM: the ADOxx case. In: Cordeiro, J., Maciaszek, L.A., Filipe, J. (eds.) ICEIS 2012. LNBIP, vol. 141, pp. 429–451. Springer, Heidelberg (2013). https://doi.org/10.1007/978-3-642-40654-6_26

15. Flovik, S., Moudnib, R.A., Vassilakopoulou, P.: Determinants of blockchain technology introduction in organizations: an empirical study among experienced practitioners. Procedia Comput. Sci. **181**, 664–670 (2021). https://doi.org/10.1016/j.procs.2021.01.216
16. Frank, U.: Domain-specific modeling languages: requirements analysis and design guidelines. In: Reinhartz-Berger, I., Sturm, A., Clark, T., Cohen, S., Bettin, J. (eds.) Domain Engineering, pp. 133–157. Springer, Heidelberg (2013). https://doi.org/10.1007/978-3-642-36654-3_6
17. Hamdaqa, M., Met, L.A.P., Qasse, I.A.: iContractML 2.0: a domain-specific language for modeling and deploying smart contracts onto multiple blockchain platforms. Inf. Softw. Technol. **144**, 106762 (2022). https://doi.org/10.1016/j.infsof.2021.106762
18. Härer, F., Fill, H.G.: A Comparison of Approaches for Visualizing Blockchains and Smart Contracts. Jusletter IT Weblaw (2019). https://doi.org/10.5281/zenodo.2585575. ISSN 1664-848X
19. Heckel, R., Erum, Z., Rahmi, N., Pul, A.: Visual smart contracts for DAML. In: Behr, N., Strüber, D. (eds.) ICGT 2022. LNCS, vol. 13349, pp. 137–154. Springer, Cham (2022). https://doi.org/10.1007/978-3-031-09843-7_8
20. Iansiti, M., Lakhani, K.R.: The truth about blockchain. Harv. Bus. Rev. **95**(1), 118–127 (2017)
21. Janssen, M., Weerakkody, V., Ismagilova, E., Sivarajah, U., Irani, Z.: A framework for analysing blockchain technology adoption: Integrating institutional, market and technical factors. Int. J. Inf. Manag. **50**, 302–309 (2020). https://doi.org/10.1016/j.ijinfomgt.2019.08.012
22. Jurgelaitis, M., Ceponiene, L., Butkiene, R.: Solidity code generation from UML state machines in model-driven smart contract development. IEEE Access **10**, 33465–33481 (2022). https://doi.org/10.1016/j.ijinfomgt.2019.08.012
23. Kannengiesser, N., Lins, S., Sander, C., Winter, K., Frey, H., Sunyaev, A.: Challenges and common solutions in smart contract development. IEEE Trans. Softw. Eng. (2021). https://doi.org/10.1109/TSE.2021.3116808
24. Merlec, M.M., Lee, Y.K., In, H.P.: SmartBuilder: a block-based visual programming framework for smart contract development. In: 2021 IEEE International Conference on Blockchain, Blockchain 2021, Melbourne, Australia, 6–8 December 2021, pp. 90–94. IEEE (2021). https://doi.org/10.1109/Blockchain53845.2021.00023
25. Muff, F., Fill, H.G.: A domain-specific visual modeling language for augmented reality applications using WebXR. In: Almeida, J.P.A., Borbinha, J., Guizzardi, G., Link, S., Zdravkovic, J. (eds.) Conceptual Modeling, pp. 334–353. Springer, Cham (2023). https://doi.org/10.1007/978-3-031-47262-6_18
26. Nakamoto, S.: Bitcoin: a peer-to-peer electronic cash system (2009). https://web.archive.org/web/20140320135003/https://bitcoin.org/bitcoin.pdf. Accessed 24 July 2024
27. Nguyen, C.T., Hoang, D.T., Nguyen, D.N., Niyato, D., Nguyen, H.T., Dutkiewicz, E.: Proof-of-stake consensus mechanisms for future blockchain networks: fundamentals, applications and opportunities. IEEE Access **7**, 85727–85745 (2019)
28. Skotnica, M., Pergl, R.: Das contract - a visual domain specific language for modeling blockchain smart contracts. In: Aveiro, D., Guizzardi, G., Borbinha, J. (eds.) EEWC 2019. LNBIP, vol. 374, pp. 149–166. Springer, Cham (2020). https://doi.org/10.1007/978-3-030-37933-9_10

29. Tan, S., Bhowmick, S.S., Chua, H.E., Xiao, X.: LATTE: visual construction of smart contracts. In: Proceedings of the 2020 International Conference on Management of Data, SIGMOD Conference 2020, Online Conference, Portland, OR, USA, 14–19 June 2020, pp. 2713–2716. ACM (2020). https://doi.org/10.1145/3318464.3384687
30. The Solidity Team: Solidity—Solidity 0.8.26 documentation. https://docs.soliditylang.org/en/v0.8.26/. Accessed 24 July 2024
31. Tolmach, P., Li, Y., Lin, S., Liu, Y., Li, Z.: A survey of smart contract formal specification and verification. ACM Comput. Surv. **54**(7), 148:1–148:38 (2022). https://doi.org/10.1145/3464421
32. Treiblmaier, H., Clohessy, T. (eds.): Blockchain and Distributed Ledger Technology Use Cases: Applications and Lessons Learned. Progress in IS. Springer, Cham (2020). https://doi.org/10.1007/978-3-030-44337-5
33. Varela-Vaca, Á.J., Quintero, A.M.R.: Smart contract languages: a multivocal mapping study. ACM Comput. Surv. **54**(1), 3:1–3:38 (2021). https://doi.org/10.1145/3423166
34. Visic, N., Fill, H., Buchmann, R.A., Karagiannis, D.: A domain-specific language for modeling method definition: from requirements to grammar. In: IEEE RCIS 2015, pp. 286–297. IEEE (2015). https://doi.org/10.1109/RCIS.2015.7128889
35. Zupan, N., Kasinathan, P., Cuellar, J., Sauer, M.: Secure smart contract generation based on Petri nets. In: Rosa Righi, R., Alberti, A.M., Singh, M. (eds.) Blockchain Technology for Industry 4.0. BT, pp. 73–98. Springer, Singapore (2020). https://doi.org/10.1007/978-981-15-1137-0_4

Assessing Model Quality Using Large Language Models

Anne Gutschmidt and Benjamin Nast(✉)

University of Rostock, Rostock, Germany
{anne.gutschmidt,benjamin.nast}@uni-rostock.de

Abstract. Recently, researchers have explored whether large language models (LLMs) can be used as a substitute for domain experts to elicit information that should be represented in an enterprise model. This paper examines a slightly different application purpose, assessing an existing model's quality using an LLM. We will analyze which aspects of model quality can be evaluated using an LLM in principle, referring to the established model quality framework SEQUAL. We will present a first test of assessing perceived semantic quality using ChatGPT. To examine the effect of different prompting strategies, we compared our results to the assessments of human domain experts. Our results suggest that LLMs are suitable for assessing the perceived semantic quality of models and provide a basis for considering further quality dimensions in future work.

Keywords: Model Quality · Conceptual Models · Perceived Semantic Quality · Large Language Models

1 Introduction

Recently, researchers have explored whether large language models (LLMs) can be used for generating enterprise models [31]. In particular, LLMs were used as a substitute for domain experts, testing to what extent the LLM can deliver domain knowledge that is eventually to be represented in a model. This paper focuses on the assessment of a model's quality using an LLM, assuming that an initial model has already been created by domain experts. We address the following research questions (RQs):

- **RQ1:** Which aspects of model quality can be assessed by an LLM?
- **RQ2:** How can these quality aspects be measured by human raters?
- **RQ3:** Can the same metrics be used in a quality assessment with an LLM?
- **RQ4:** What should a prompt for such quality assessment look like, what information does it have to include?

For the first question, we chose SEQUAL [18] as a model quality framework, giving us a structure of quality dimensions we could systematically analyze. Concerning the second research question, finding validated metrics for the assessment of the different quality dimensions is still challenging. Our basic idea is to test whether these metrics can be transferred to quality assessments by LLMs, as stated in the third question. To explore the feasibility of this approach, we decided to concentrate on perceived semantic quality as a first example, because we consider this quality dimension as particularly important. Stakeholders will only accept and utilize a model, such as for implementing the measures it represents, if they perceive it as both accurate and complete. We chose metrics from the literature and adapted and supplemented them according to our needs. These metrics alone will, however, not suffice for measuring model quality with an LLM. We had to test how to embed these metrics in suitable prompts, leading to the fourth question.

The paper is structured as follows: Sect. 2 provides an overview of model quality and prompt engineering, as well as insight into current applications of LLMs in enterprise modeling. Section 3 addresses the question of which aspects of model quality can be assessed by an LLM. The study in which we explore the feasibility and possible strategies to assess perceived semantic quality with an LLM is described in Sect. 4. Limitations and implications for future work are discussed in Sect. 5.

2 State of the Art

2.1 Model Quality

Conceptual models may serve different purposes. They may be used to capture the requirements of information systems (IS) or as a documentation of the IS that developers can use later when they need to maintain or change the system [29]. Conceptual models may be used to help people understand the current situation and to support people's communication about a current or a future state [20]. Further purposes comprise computer-assisted analysis or quality assurance [20]. This list of purposes makes the importance of the models' quality very obvious. If the model is not "good", it will not properly serve the intended purpose. For example, if the requirements contained in the model are wrong, this will lead to the development of a system that will not provide the desired functions. If a model is not readable or comprehensible, its users will not be able to use it for sense-making or communication. According to [30], measuring quality is important to check whether supposed quality improvements in a model are actually perceived by a user. Another motivation that drove us was to have the possibility of evaluating different approaches to modeling, e.g. in studies that compare participatory and conventional modeling [7,8]. We see the need for a measuring instrument with which we can assess the quality of models that have been created under different preconditions.

The question is what makes a "good" model and what is a "bad" model. To consider model quality as only a general term would be too simple. The extensive list of quality features that have been considered and empirically investigated [5,21] demonstrates the many facets of model quality. Consequently, authors have come up with frameworks that are to cover as many of these facets as possible. These frameworks should either give orientation for creating models of good quality or serve for evaluating an existing model's quality or both, such as the SEQUAL framework [18]. While SEQUAL is focussing on the quality of the product, i.e., the model itself, frameworks such as the Conceptual Modeling Quality Framework (CMQF) try to take into consideration both product, where it even builds on SEQUAL, and modeling process [28,29]. This makes CMQF, however, very complex.

As our analysis should concentrate on evaluating the model as a product, we chose SEQUAL as a basis. SEQUAL dates back to the 1990s with its early version [21] that was soon extended [17]. Krogstie demonstrated SEQUAL's applicability to business process models [19], requirements specification models [18], and data models [13]. SEQUAL was examined empirically with regard to process models in a company [10]. The early version of the framework was tested with regard to entity relationship models, also evaluating how well raters get along with the proposed quality dimensions [27]. All in all, it is an established framework that seems to capture the most important aspects of model quality and has matured over the last decades.

SEQUAL is based on the basic concepts domain, knowledge, model externalization, language, and actor interpretation. The major quality dimensions refer to relations between these concepts. Moreover, each quality dimension has its own goals, and the framework suggests means to achieve these goals [17,18]. It is important to note that these quality dimensions should not be seen as independent but as influencing each other [18,27,28].

Physical Quality means that the externalized model is persistent, current, and available [18]. The model should, for example, be protected against loss and damage. If the domain is rapidly changing, the model should present the latest information. Moreover, the model should be easy to access by the designated audience, be it technical or human.

Empirical Quality mainly refers to readability. The model should be provided in such a way that when reading or creating a model, the audience understands it and makes as few mistakes as possible [18,19]. Usually, best practices for modeling concerning wording, colors, and further aesthetics should provide for this type of quality [28].

Syntactical Quality aims at syntactical correctness, i.e., the model externalization follows the rules of the modeling language [18].

Semantic Quality refers to the goals' completeness and validity. A model should present reality in a correct way, which is also referred to as model validity, and it should present all parts that are relevant to the audience. This also means that the model should not contain elements that are not needed, i.e., it should not be redundant but minimal. It should also be consistent and unambiguous [21].

Perceived Semantic Quality refers to the correspondence between the actors' interpretation of the model and their knowledge, while semantic quality represents the correspondence between the domain (reality) and the model externalization [19]. So, in this quality dimension, actors judge how well they think the model depicts what they know about the world.

Pragmatic Quality represents the correspondence between model externalization and model interpretations. The goal is that the model should be understood. The authors underline that this type of quality is not about comprehensibility but about comprehension [5,21]. Other authors, however, have mixed these terms, assigning understandability generally to pragmatic quality [11]. Thus, although quality frameworks such as SEQUAL exist, this does not necessarily mean that all connected terms are defined and distinguished in the same way. Furthermore, SEQUAL distinguishes two kinds of pragmatic quality. While social pragmatic quality refers to human understanding, technical pragmatic quality means that the model can be correctly interpreted by a tool [18,29].

Social Quality is about the agreement, either absolute or relative. Relative agreement with regard to the model, its interpretation, or knowledge of different stakeholders would mean that all contained statements are consistent, while absolute agreement would mean the statements are the same [19].

Deontic Quality means that all the statements contained in the model serve the goal that should be attained with the modeling. It also means that all the modeling goals are addressed in the model [19].

In Sect. 3, we will discuss how these quality facets can be measured and whether and how an LLM could be of assistance for such an assessment.

2.2 The Art of Prompting

LLMs belong to the broader category of deep learning models, address the area of natural language processing, and are designed to interpret and generate text similar to that produced by humans. The capabilities of LLMs include a range of tasks, such as translation, summarization, and question-answering. These can be achieved without task-specific training data [12]. One of the key features of those models is their ability to generate coherent, diverse, and contextually relevant text over long passages. OpenAI's GPT (Generative Pre-trained Transformer) models, which are equipped with a chatbot frontend (ChatGPT[1]), can also be utilized for translation, grammar correction, or email composition [4].

In order to achieve meaningful and optimal results in the context of working with LLMs, it is of great importance to design and formulate appropriate input requirements (prompts). A prompt can be defined as a set of instructions provided to an LLM that programs the LLM by customizing it and/or enhancing or refining its capabilities [24]. Improved prompts lead to better results across a wide range of tasks [24,33,35]. White et al. [36] describe a catalog with general prompt patterns that enhance the interaction with LLMs. Prompt patterns are structured instructions for LLMs which improve the quality of outputs and tailor them to the needs of users. The catalog contains a multitude of patterns, which have been classified into six distinct categories:

---

[1] https://chat.openai.com.

- **Input Semantics** addresses the manner in which an LLM processes input and translates it into a format that can be utilized to generate output. *Meta Language Creation*
- **Output Customization** is concerned with the modification of the types, formats, structures, and other properties of the outputs generated by the LLM. *Output Automater, Persona, Visualization Generator, Recipe, Template*
- **Error Identification** is focused on the identification and resolution of errors in the output generated by LLMs. *Fact Check List, Reflection*
- **Prompt Improvement** is concerned with enhancing the quality of both the input and the output. *Question Refinement, Alternative Approaches, Cognitive Verifier, Refusal Breaker*
- **Interaction** focuses on the interaction between the user and the LLM. *Flipped Interaction, Game Play, Infinite Generation*
- **Context Control** regulates contextual data within the operational parameters of the LLM. *Context Manager*

Another concept of prompt engineering is contextual learning, which involves the user instructing the LLM to perform a specific action based on the context. A distinction is made between three different approaches [2, 9]: In what is known as zero-shot learning, the LLM is tasked with performing a given operation without prior examples. In this case, the model is presented with a natural language description of the task, devoid of specific examples. In one-shot learning, a single example of a solution is provided for the LLM to emulate during execution. This allows the model to discern the desired format and solution approach. In few-shot learning, multiple examples are presented to illustrate the anticipated solution to the task. In this approach, the model is conditioned with multiple examples of the task. Typically, an example comprises a context and a desired completion.

The term prompt chain is used to describe the process of utilizing two or more prompt templates in sequence. The output of the prompt generated by the initial prompt template is employed to parameterize the subsequent pattern, continuing until all patterns have been utilized [37]. A prompting technique can be defined as "a blueprint that describes how to structure a prompt, prompts, or dynamic sequencing of multiple prompts. A prompting technique may incorporate conditional or branching logic, parallelism, or other architectural considerations spanning multiple prompts" [33].

2.3 Using LLMs for Enterprise Modeling

To identify existing work and results from other scholars that could inform the investigation of the potential for assessing model quality with LLMs, we conducted a literature search. We employed Kitchenham's approach for systematic literature reviews (SLR) [14]. The literature databases employed were Scopus, IEEE Xplore, and AISeL. The search string utilized in Scopus was *("Enterprise Modeling" OR "Process Modeling") AND ("Large Language Model" OR "LLM" OR "Neural Text" OR "ChatGPT")*. This string was modified accordingly for the other databases. The search was conducted in July 2024 and yielded 106 results (20 in Scopus, no in IEEE Xplore, 86 in AISeL). As inclusion criteria, we have defined that a paper is relevant for us if the utilization of LLMs in the context of enterprise modeling is discussed. Papers that merely mention the potential usefulness of these for specific questions are not relevant to us.

The process of excluding papers was conducted in two stages. In the initial prescreening phase, six papers were excluded due to their status as conference proceedings containing papers on either enterprise modeling or LLMs, but lacking any papers that covered both topics. Following this initial phase, a second iteration was undertaken, in which papers were excluded on the basis of both abstract and content. Specifically, if the abstract did not provide any indication of the application of LLMs in enterprise modeling, the paper was excluded. In the event that a paper required further examination due to the absence of an initial exclusion criterion, it was excluded on the grounds of its content being irrelevant to the scope of our study. Based on the second iteration, 92 papers were excluded. Eight papers were relevant to our work [1, 6, 15, 16, 22, 26, 31, 34].

Table 1 presents a summary of the diverse applications of LLMs in EM as identified in the relevant papers.

Table 1. Applications of large language models in enterprise modeling

Application	Papers
business process model creation without domain knowledge	[6, 31]
execution of business process models	[23]
create formal representations from textual process descriptions	[15, 34]
generate modeling suggestions to improve quality of business process models	[1]
generation and refinement of models based on textual descriptions	[16]
improve the quality of generated text explanations for process models	[26]

The work of Görgen et al. [6] and Sandkuhl et al. [31] describe the creation of business process models using an LLM without domain knowledge. The objective was to get an idea of the extent to which a domain expert can be substituted by an LLM. Lins et al. [23] present the execution of existing business process models with LLMs, while the papers of Klievtsova et al. [15] and Simon et al. [34] describe the creation of formal representations from textual process descriptions. Kourani et al. [16] do the same, but they also try to refine the models in this process. Ayad and AlSayoud [1] use an LLM to generate modeling suggestions in order to improve the quality of business process models. Minor and Kaucher [26] improve the quality of generated text explanations for process models using an LLM. The results show that assisted working with LLMs is already possible in the context of enterprise modeling [1, 6, 15, 16, 22, 26, 31, 34]. All authors state that further experimentation is necessary to ensure the generalizability of the results. Furthermore, [6, 23, 31, 34] advise the application of diverse LLMs to substantiate findings or contrast disparate performances for analogous tasks between them.

Another crucial subject for future work is the systematic engineering of prompts [6,31,34]. This can be enhanced, e.g., by experimenting with diverse patterns to ascertain their impact on outcomes or by developing a model-driven prompt design tailored to domain-specific use in the enterprise context. In conclusion, no papers were identified that address quality assessment with LLMs. Therefore, the literature reviewed does not provide any information that can be used to answer our RQs.

3 How LLMs Could Help Assessing Model Quality

In this section, we will address RQ1. We will make a first exploration of how LLMs could be used for assessing the different facets of model quality. We will use the quality dimensions of SEQUAL as we consider it to be an established quality framework that has been shown to be applicable to different kinds of models. The feasibility of these suggestions will, however, have to be thoroughly investigated in future research. Consequently, this section also presents a first basis for a systematic research agenda for the future.

Physical Quality: To assess the availability, currency, and persistence of a model, one has to check the corresponding conditions given in the individual company. An LLM would probably not be of much assistance here, as it cannot judge a company's situation, unless it is explicitly given.

Syntactical Quality: There exist already plenty of modeling tools that help in preventing, detecting, and correcting syntactical errors [18]. Future research has to show whether LLMs have particular benefits, either when being integrated into such tools or on their own, and how this can be implemented. What is needed is a description of the syntax rules and the model to execute the task. A special advantage an LLM could bring would be context-sensitive feedback. So, instead of a standard error message, the LLM could provide users with more meaningful and individual feedback.

Empirical Quality: In SEQUAL, Krogstie suggests following guidelines for modeling and visual aesthetics to attain empirical quality, which will eventually support actual understanding, i.e., pragmatic quality [18]. For example, the LLM could check whether a model follows guidelines such as 7PMG for process modeling [25] or SMART rules for goal modeling [32]. It could not only give hints on possible shortcomings but also give explanations and recommendations for improvement. By now, ChatGPT can handle visual input, such that a graphical representation could also be judged by the system. The complexity of a model is also an important factor influencing the readability and understandability of a model [28]. Nevertheless, tools for counting elements, etc., already exist. Future research might deal with how we can make the LLM give recommendations on how we could reduce model complexity and still keep its validity and completeness.

According to Krogstie [5], stakeholders need to understand only those parts of the model that are relevant to them. One might test whether an LLM could give feedback on whether the model is designed and visualized in such a way that a specific type of stakeholder can understand it.

Semantic Quality: Recently, it was shown that, to some extent, an LLM can substitute a domain expert and provide the information needed to create a model [31]. The model was checked by domain experts which is rather an assessment of perceived semantic quality than semantic quality. If a model can be created from textual descriptions [16], it might also be possible to assess semantic quality by checking the model against existing documentation, textual or visual, examining if the model is correct and consistent. To check for completeness and redundancy, it might be necessary to inform the LLM about the modeling scope, e.g., by giving information about the modeling purpose and target audience. Moody suggested using user requirements as a basis for comparison [27].

Perceived Semantic Quality: While the quality dimensions mentioned before can be objectively measured, perceived semantic quality is a subjective criterion. It requires actual users to rate how far they think the model is correct and complete. So, we would have to make the LLM mimic a human reaction to the model. A human's interpretation of a model is something we cannot see and, thus, cannot equip the LLM with. We can, however, give the LLM context in the form of a description of the recipient and his or her background, e.g., is the user a developer or a system architect? To substitute a human rater with an LLM rater would, nevertheless, mean that we require a suitable measuring instrument to capture correctness and completeness. Here, an LLM could assist in an additional way by helping in developing a measuring instrument, i.e., developing a set of statements about the model to be rated. Furthermore, the LLM could be used to make recommendations on how to improve a model. Future research could investigate how useful domain experts find these recommendations and whether such recommendations are useful to different degrees in the different phases of a modeling project.

Pragmatic Quality: While empirical quality addresses understandability, pragmatic quality is about understanding, in particular, human understanding, when considering social pragmatic quality. Again, we would have to make the LLM mimic a human reaction. Houy et al. list several ways of testing human understanding [11], some of them might be used for an LLM. Like with human actors, one could test if the LLM can correctly answer questions about the model or whether it can solve problems or apply an example to the model. Systematic research must be done to explore what according prompts would have to look like.

Concerning technical pragmatic quality, usually, formal models, in terms of syntax and semantics, are required [18]. Thus, one major influencing factor for this is syntactic quality. Consequently, an LLM could check the model against syntax rules, as stated above, and against verbalized tool requirements. Formal models can also be obtained by transformation [18]. Sometimes, a formal model is less understandable to social actors. To find a compromise, one could let the LLM transform a less formal model into a model that can be correctly interpreted by a tool based on transformation rules.

Social Quality: Comparing real actors' actual knowledge and their interpretation of a model is not feasible for an LLM. Nevertheless, the LLM could compare different models to check their extent of agreement. Thus, given different models, the LLM could point out contradictions between them. Future research must, moreover, examine how well an LLM can find joint content.

Deontic Quality: A model should help increase the stakeholders' knowledge and help change the domain, e.g., improve a process such that it is faster or less costly [18]. It is questionable whether an LLM would be better than or as feasible as user feedback and objective performance measures to assess the attainment of such goals. As long as the goals can be verbalized and compared to the model, using an LLM could be considered.

To sum up, we have given only a broad overview of ideas on how LLMs could be used for the assessment of model quality. In each case, it is to be tested what kind of input the LLM needs besides the model itself, e.g. a set of rules or requirements. Additionally, often, a set of questions representing the respective quality dimension or exact definitions of the quality dimension might be needed. Systematic prompt engineering is needed to find the best strategies for the evaluation of the different quality facets.

4 Study

In this small pilot study, we wanted to explore the feasibility and possible strategies to assess perceived semantic quality with an LLM. Only if stakeholders consider a model as correct and complete, will they accept the model and use it, e.g., for implementing the measures represented in the model. First, we needed, however, to address RQ2 and find a suitable measuring instrument that could also be used with human raters. Subsequently, we could address RQ3 and RQ4 using the same measuring instrument and exploring different prompting strategies.

4.1 Method

Models and Sample: The models we used for this study originate from an experiment we conducted in 2022[2] [8]. Small groups of students and university teachers had to create goal models in a limited amount of time. The main topic of discussion was how to improve learning and teaching at universities through technology. The participants were asked to draw from their experience during the pandemic and gather mainly goals serving the given major goal, and problems that might hinder these goals. This experiment is not the subject of this paper, but we used three of the models generated in that experiment for the analysis presented in this paper. We let six other students and five teachers rate the quality of these models. Thus, model creators and evaluators belonged to the same domain. Two students and one teacher rated two models; the others rated one model. On the whole, we obtained 14 ratings, five ratings each for two

---

[2] https://doi.org/10.5281/zenodo.13882534.

models and four ratings for one model. The average age was 27.4 years (between 20 and 39). The raters' experience in general modeling was 3.8 ($\sigma = 0.6$) and 3.2 ($\sigma = 1.1$) for 4EM, the modeling language used in the model, given a scale from 1 for no experience to 5 for expert level.

We assessed perceived semantic quality with an online questionnaire. In the next section, we will describe the measures we used in detail.

Measures: To measure perceived semantic quality, we used a set of items suggested in [30]. The authors empirically tested the scale. It covers important features of semantic quality as proposed by [17] and [21]: correctness, validity, minimality, and consistency. However, the scale was applied to entity relationship diagrams and UML class diagrams. An application to 4EM goal models required several adaptations and extensions. First of all, the goal of reaching completeness in such a creative task is questionable. In the first publications on SEQUAL, the authors underlined that *feasible* completeness is to be aspired [17,21], accepting that total completeness is impossible to reach. In our context, completeness is even less to be expected. Moreover, in a creative task, it might not be appropriate to judge ideas as *correct* or *wrong*. Thus, we removed items that did not seem appropriate to us and adapted items to fit our context, but we kept items from an early version of the scale to have a sufficient list of initial items. Table 2 lists the final items in English. The participants could decide whether they wanted to fill out the questionnaire in English or German, yet only one participant used the English version.

Table 2. English items used to assess perceived semantic quality and addressed quality features

No	Item	Quality feature
1	All the elements are relevant for the representation of possible goals, problems, and connected ideas in the given domain	correctness
2	All goals, problems, and connected ideas make sense in the given domain	
3	There are no elements or relations contained in the model that seem absurd to me	
4	All relations make sense to me and are logically comprehensible	
5	All ideas in the model seem sensible and logical to me	
6	In my opinion, all relations have the right direction	
7	Elements must be added to faithfully represent important ideas on the subject	completeness
8	The model covers the given topic "Improving learning and teaching at the university through technology" very well in terms of content	
9	The model takes into account essential aspects in order to represent the given topic well	
10	From my point of view, there are obvious relationships between the elements, but these have not been drawn	
11	The model contains redundant elements	redundancy
12	The model contains contradicting elements	consistency

Procedure: In the initial phase of the investigation with ChatGPT to address RQ3 and RQ4, the three models under investigation were transformed into .csv files. The list of concepts was sorted according to type, which will eventually serve as input. Subsequently, a prompt engineering process was initiated with the objective of identifying the best possible prompt that would yield the most accurate results across the three models. This entailed identifying the prompt with the least deviation from the average values of the human ratings. Finally, the extent to which the LLM can be utilized to assess the perceived semantic quality of models was evaluated, employing the developed measuring approach. In order to ensure the reproducibility of the procedure, the relevant material (human ratings, prompts, and LLM output) has been uploaded to Zenodo[3].

As the models under consideration are the result of a creative task, it is questionable whether they can be better evaluated by providing exemplars for how to solve the task to the LLM. Furthermore, it can be assumed that when evaluating models, there are often no suitable models that could be used as exemplars. Consequently, we have decided to apply zero-shot learning.

The initial prompt was designed to be as close as possible to the original instructions for human raters. A variety of prompt patterns and combinations have then been tested. It was our intention to ensure that no modifications were made to our predefined statements (see Table 2), as our objective was to evaluate their suitability for utilization in ChatGPT. The utilization of the patterns *Persona*, *Cognitive Verifier*, and *Question Refinement*, for instance, yielded results that were no more favorable than those obtained with our final prompt. Additionally, the description of the topic and objective of the model demonstrated no notable impact. When prompted, ChatGPT was able to respond to these inquiries in all three models, indicating that the elements of the models were sufficient to make those clear. It was also found that the description of the structure in which we provided the models was not significant. The part of the prompt describing the model only contained a line of information regarding the components (*ID; Type; OriginalID; Text*) and relations (*From; To; Text*), which seemed to be exhaustive enough.

The final prompting technique (see Fig. 1) developed for assessing the model quality for all three models contained two prompt patterns: *Context Manager* and *Template* [36]. The *Context Manager* pattern is to provide users the ability either to specify or remove context to a conversation, giving them greater control over the statements the LLM considers or ignores when generating output. *Template* pattern guarantees that the output of an LLM adheres to a defined structure. This enables the user to direct the LLM to generate its output in a format that differs from its typical approach for the specific type of content being produced. The *Context Manager* part starts with an exhaustive description of the [Modeltype] (in our case, the goal model), containing the general structure and a short explanation of its elements and relations. Afterward, the actual [Model] under consideration is given as text copied from the .csv file. To get the required output, we defined the [Task] and finally provided the [Statements] of

---

[3] https://doi.org/10.5281/zenodo.13882605.

our questionnaire (see Table 2). The structure of our prompting technique should allow for adaptation to different model types and models. It remains to be tested whether this structure is also suitable for the assessment of other quality aspects.

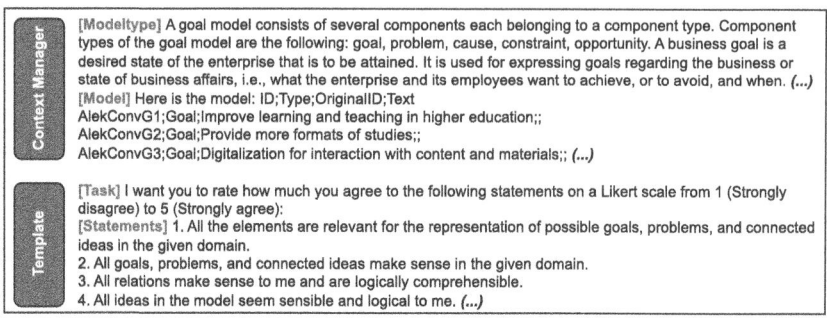

Fig. 1. Prompting technique

Data Evaluation: To address RQ2, we had to first check our measuring instrument for perceived semantic quality. Our study cannot provide a sufficient validity check, but we tried to stick to the definitions and descriptions of semantic quality. Moreover, we used exploratory factor analysis (with principal axis factorization and Varimax rotation) to check how many factors can be found statistically [3]. We checked the reliability of the measuring instruments using Cronbach's Alpha [3]. Items that have a strong influence on reliability will be removed. To analyze the congruence between human ratings and the ratings of ChatGPT, we examined both the congruence based on the single items and based on scores. We calculated scores for those quality features that were measured using several items, namely correctness and completeness, using the average value of item ratings per person.

4.2 Results

Analysis of Measuring Instruments: For the analysis, we had to transform items 7 and 10, as they expressed completeness in an inverse form, striving for homogeneity among the items for completeness. The factor analysis showed a solution with four factors, both using eigenvalue and screeplot. The rotated factor matrix reveals, however, weaknesses in the measuring instrument. Items 1, 2, 4, and 5 show factor loadings greater than 0.8. They represent correctness and seem to measure this feature quite clearly. The remaining items are, however, difficult to clearly assign to one factor, taking into consideration what each corresponding statement is supposed to express. Table 3 shows the factor loadings of all items in the rotated factor matrix. A reliability analysis for correctness was conducted both with all items and without items 3 and 6 leading to Cronbach's Alpha of

0.804 and 0.914, which are both good [3]. To calculate a correctness score, we decided to remove items 3 and 6 due to the improvement in reliability this brings. A reliability analysis for completeness was conducted with all corresponding items, leading to a Cronbach's Alpha of 0.436, which is very poor [3]. Removing any item did not bring any improvement. Consulting the rotated factor matrix, we decided to use only items 7 and 8 to calculate a score for completeness since items 9 and 10 both seem to mix with redundancy and consistency.

Table 3. Rotated factor matrix resulting from the exploratory factor analysis

Item	Quality feature	Factor 1	Factor 2	Factor 3	Factor 4
1	correct	0.887	0.043	0.056	−0.146
2	correct	0.834	−0.015	0.141	−0.081
3	correct	0.206	0.901	−0.119	0.201
4	correct	0.824	0.088	0.075	−0.146
5	correct	0.879	0.401	0.009	0.108
6	correct	0.066	0.057	0.014	−0.688
7	complete	−0.350	0.142	−0.020	0.840
8	complete	0.314	0.432	0.183	0.493
9	complete	0.063	0.167	0.682	0.041
10	complete	0.018	−0.336	0.456	0.253
11	redundant	−0.036	−0.707	−0.519	0.152
12	consistent	−0.142	0.020	−0.895	0.103

Comparing Quality Assessments Table 4 shows the results of the assessments for the different models divided into the human ratings (_hum) and the ratings of ChatGPT (_GPT). In terms of the score for correctness, it can be stated that the output of ChatGPT produced the same ranking as the human raters. All models were rated the same for completeness, which resulted in the greatest deviation for the $M3$ model.

Table 5 shows the differences between the ratings only for the remaining relevant items (_diff = deviation of the assessments). The average deviations (AVG) in the items concerning correctness and completeness are pretty similar, with the exception of the $M3$ model. A comparison of the results reveals that ChatGPT exhibits a notably low degree of variation in the score for correctness, with no deviation observed for the $M3$ model. The results of the completeness score reveal higher deviations. The deviations in the assessment of consistency are pretty low for all three models. Otherwise, no other particular deviations that are particularly similar in all models can be identified. The average deviation of the results across all items is quite similar, with the lowest for the $M1$ model and the highest for the $M2$ model.

Table 4. Mean values of the human ratings and ChatGPT ratings per item and for the scores of correctness and completeness

Item	Feature	M1_hum	M2_hum	M3_hum	M1_GPT	M2_GPT	M3_GPT
1	correct	4.2	4.3	4.4	4	5	4
2	correct	3.8	4.8	4.2	4	4	4
4	correct	3.6	3.8	3.2	3	4	4
5	correct	3.4	3.8	4.0	4	4	4
7	complete	3.6	3.3	3.8	3	3	3
8	complete	4.0	3.5	4.6	4	4	4
11	redundant	2.4	3.5	2.6	2	2	3
12	consistent	1.8	2.0	2.2	2	2	2
score	CORRECT	3.8	4.2	4.0	3.8	4.3	4
score	COMPLETE	3.8	3.4	4.2	3.5	3.5	3.5

4.3 Discussion

Factor and reliability analysis have shown how challenging it is to come up with a suitable measuring instrument for certain quality aspects, particularly completeness. This may be connected to the kind of model. Usually, a company uses a goal model to document its specific objectives. With models that are already very subjective by nature, such as the goal model, it is questionable whether third parties who are not involved can judge completeness. In practice agreement on correctness and completeness by other stakeholders would, however, be required. Thus, measuring completeness seems to be more challenging, but our particular setting may have made the measuring more difficult. More effort has to be invested in developing valid and reliable scales for perceived semantic quality. It is a facet of quality that relates to the stakeholders' acceptance of a model. During the prompt engineering process, we realized that many patterns were not suitable for our specific case. One reason for this may be that the evaluation is very subjective, and there is no "best" solution for such models that can be used as guidance. In addition, it proved difficult to use patterns that give the LLM a better understanding of the task. This is mainly because we wanted to check how well the same statements that humans were given were suitable for the LLM. Nevertheless, we were able to achieve fairly good results for the considered models. We have structured the prompting technique so that we can initially validate it with several similar models and also apply the structure to other models, model types, and quality aspects. This can also be seen as a basis for further development, e.g., developing a more effective sequence of prompts or considering several ways to input the respective model to the LLM.

Table 5. Difference between the human ratings and ChatGPT ratings per item, for the scores of correctness and completeness, and for all items on average

Item	Feature	M1_diff	M2_diff	M3_diff
1	correct	0.2	0.7	0.4
2	correct	0.2	0.8	0.2
4	correct	0.6	0.2	0.8
5	correct	0.6	0.2	0
7	complete	0.6	0.3	0.8
8	complete	0	0.5	0.6
11	redundant	0.4	1.5	0.4
12	consistent	0.2	0	0.2
score	CORRECT	0.1	0.1	0
score	COMPLETE	0.3	0.1	0.7
AVG	correct	0.4	0.5	0.4
AVG	complete	0.3	0.4	0.7
AVG	**ALL ITEMS**	**0.35**	**0.53**	**0.43**

5 Limitations and Implications

We have compiled an initial collection of ideas for the potential use of LLMs for model quality assessment (RQ1). This provides a basis for further investigations in this field. It was difficult to design the measurement instrument (RQ2), and some items were excluded from the results analysis. Further efforts are needed to make it valid and reliable. The process of prompt engineering described in this work should only be seen as an initial investigation. The results of our pilot study indicate that the statements are also suitable for use with an LLM (RQ3). Before improving the prompting, however, the validity and reliability of the scales should be improved in order to obtain more reliable reference values. These should then also be collected with a larger sample that would enable us to conduct statistical tests and analyses such as t-tests for comparing the ratings (dependent variable) between human and machine raters (independent variable), or inter-rater reliability.

Initially, the prompting technique should be applied to several models in order to subsequently examine the transferability to other model types or quality aspects. Nevertheless, this paper presents an initial approach to the development of a prompt for quality assessment (RQ4). The models considered in this work further received a favorable human rating. It will be interesting to see whether LLMs can deliver similarly good results for models of particularly poor quality, where it may be more challenging to grasp the meaning. The use of the *Persona* pattern did not result in the desired improvements in responses in our study. However, it may be worthwhile to explore whether the results would be more favorable if ChatGPT were to conduct multiple iterations of the survey with the roles we employed in real life (student and lecturer) to ascertain whether the averages would align more closely with those of humans. Since we compared the averages of the human raters with ChatGPT's integer values in our study, exact correspondence was only possible for very few items.

In our analysis, we assumed that the LLM would have a similar domain knowledge as the human raters. We must further examine this aspect, e.g., by comparing pragmatic quality assessments of LLMs and humans. The study showed that at least a general understanding of the LLM was given.

Our discussion of possible uses of LLMs for the assessment of model quality offers only a first glimpse into the topic. Each quality dimension will have to be explored and investigated both in theory and empirically.

The SLR can be expanded in terms of the classification of results and the utilization of supplementary synonyms within the search string. In addition to LLMs, related technologies could also be considered, and a systematic overview of quality aspects could be compiled.

On the whole, our paper introduces LLMs as tools for validating enterprise models. In the future, it will be important to investigate how people interact with such validation tools, particularly in terms of the usefulness of the explanations and descriptions they provide for quality assessment. When chatbots offer improvement suggestions, it will be crucial to assess how helpful these suggestions are perceived to be.

References

1. Ayad, S., AlSayoud, F.: Exploring ChatGPT prompt engineering for business process models semantic quality improvement. In: Rocha, Á., Adeli, H., Dzemyda, G., Moreira, F., Poniszewska-Marańda, A. (eds.) WorldCIST 2024. LNCS, vol. 987, pp. 412–422. Springer, Cham (2024). https://doi.org/10.1007/978-3-031-60221-4_39
2. Brown, T., et al.: Language models are few-shot learners. In: Advances in Neural Information Processing Systems 33, pp. 1877–1901 (2020)
3. Field, A.: Discovering Statistics Using IBM SPSS Statistics, 6th edn. Sage, London and Thousand Oaks and New Delhi and Singapore (2024)
4. Floridi, L., Chiriatti, M.: GPT-3: its nature, scope, limits, and consequences. Minds Mach. **30**(4), 681–694 (2020). https://doi.org/10.1007/s11023-020-09548-1
5. Genero, M., Poels, G., Piattini, M.: Defining and validating measures for conceptual data model quality. In: Pidduck, A.B., Ozsu, M.T., Mylopoulos, J., Woo, C.C. (eds.) CAiSE 2002. LNCS, vol. 2348, pp. 724–727. Springer, Heidelberg (2002). https://doi.org/10.1007/3-540-47961-9_54
6. Görgen, L., Müller, E., Triller, M., Nast, B., Sandkuhl, K.: Large language models in enterprise modeling: case study and experiences. In: Proceedings of the 12th International Conference on Model-Based Software and Systems Engineering, pp. 74–85. SCITEPRESS - Science and Technology Publications (2024). https://doi.org/10.5220/0012387000003645
7. Gutschmidt, A., Lantow, B., Hellmanzik, B., Ramforth, B., Wiese, M., Martins, E.: Participatory modeling from a stakeholder perspective: on the influence of collaboration and revisions on psychological ownership and perceived model quality. Softw. Syst. Model. **22**(1), 13–29 (2023). https://doi.org/10.1007/s10270-022-01036-7

8. Gutschmidt, A., Verbruggen, C., Snoeck, M.: A study on the impact of the level of participation in enterprise modeling. In: Almeida, J.P.A., Kaczmarek-Heß, M., Koschmider, A., Proper, H.A. (eds.) PoEM 2023. LNBIP, vol. 497, pp. 193–208. Springer, Cham (2024). https://doi.org/10.1007/978-3-031-48583-1_12
9. Hadi, M.U., et al.: Large language models: a comprehensive survey of its applications, challenges, limitations, and future prospects (2023). https://doi.org/10.36227/techrxiv.23589741.v4
10. Heggset, M., Krogstie, J., Wesenberg, H.: Understanding model quality concerns when using process models in an industrial company. In: Gaaloul, K., Schmidt, R., Nurcan, S., Guerreiro, S., Ma, Q. (eds.) CAISE 2015. LNBIP, vol. 214, pp. 395–409. Springer, Cham (2015). https://doi.org/10.1007/978-3-319-19237-6_25
11. Houy, C., Fettke, P., Loos, P.: Understanding understandability of conceptual models – what are we actually talking about? In: Atzeni, P., Cheung, D., Ram, S. (eds.) ER 2012. LNCS, vol. 7532, pp. 64–77. Springer, Heidelberg (2012). https://doi.org/10.1007/978-3-642-34002-4_5
12. Huang, W., Abbeel, P., Pathak, D., Mordatch, I.: Language models as zero-shot planners: extracting actionable knowledge for embodied agents. https://doi.org/10.48550/arXiv.2201.07207
13. Krogstie, J.: Quality of conceptual data models (2013). https://api.semanticscholar.org/CorpusID:57996387
14. Kitchenham, B.: Procedures for performing systematic reviews **33**(2004), 1–26. Keele University, Keele (2004)
15. Klievtsova, N., Benzin, J.V., Kampik, T., Mangler, J., Rinderle-Ma, S.: Conversational process modelling: state of the art, applications, and implications in practice. In: Di Francescomarino, C., Burattin, A., Janiesch, C., Sadiq, S. (eds.) BPM 2023. LNBIP, vol. 490, pp. 319–336. Springer, Cham (2023). https://doi.org/10.1007/978-3-031-41623-1_19
16. Kourani, H., Berti, A., Schuster, D., van der Aalst, W.M.P.: Process modeling with large language models. In: van der Aa, H., Bork, D., Schmidt, R., Sturm, A. (eds.) BPMDS EMMSAD 2024. LNBIP, vol. 511, pp. 229–244. Springer, Cham (2024). https://doi.org/10.1007/978-3-031-61007-3_18
17. Krogstie, J., Lindland, O.I., Sindre, G.: Defining quality aspects for conceptual models. In: Falkenberg, E.D., Hesse, W., Olivé, A. (eds.) Information System Concepts. IAICT, pp. 216–231. Springer, Boston, MA (1995). https://doi.org/10.1007/978-0-387-34870-4_22
18. Krogstie, J.: Model-Based Development and Evolution of Information Systems: A Quality Approach. Springer, London (2012). https://doi.org/10.1007/978-1-4471-2936-3
19. Krogstie, J.: Quality of business process models. In: Sandkuhl, K., Seigerroth, U., Stirna, J. (eds.) PoEM 2012. LNBIP, vol. 134, pp. 76–90. Springer, Heidelberg (2012). https://doi.org/10.1007/978-3-642-34549-4_6
20. Krogstie, J.: A semiotic approach to data quality. In: Nurcan, S., et al. (eds.) BPMDS/EMMSAD -2013. LNBIP, vol. 147, pp. 395–410. Springer, Heidelberg (2013). https://doi.org/10.1007/978-3-642-38484-4_28
21. Lindland, O.I., Sindre, G., Solvberg, A.: Understanding quality in conceptual modeling. IEEE Softw. **11**(2), 42–49 (1994). https://doi.org/10.1109/52.268955
22. Ling, T.W. (ed.): Conceptual Modeling - ER '98: 17th International Conference on Conceptual Modeling, Singapore, November 16–19, 1998; Proceedings. LNCS, vol. 1507. Springer, Heidelberg (1998). https://doi.org/10.1007/b68220

23. Lins, L.F., Nascimento, N., Alencar, P., Oliveira, T., Cowan, D.: Comparing generative chatbots based on process requirements: a case study. In: 2023 IEEE International Conference on Big Data (BigData), pp. 4664–4673. IEEE (2023). https://doi.org/10.1109/BigData59044.2023.10386251
24. Liu, P., Yuan, W., Fu, J., Jiang, Z., Hayashi, H., Neubig, G.: Pre-train, prompt, and predict: a systematic survey of prompting methods in natural language processing. ACM Comput. Surv. **55**(9), 1–35 (2023). https://doi.org/10.1145/3560815
25. Mendling, J., Reijers, H.A., van der Aalst, W.: Seven process modeling guidelines (7PMG). Inf. Softw. Technol. **52**(2), 127–136 (2010). https://doi.org/10.1016/j.infsof.2009.08.004
26. Minor, M., Kaucher, E.: Retrieval augmented generation with LLMs for explaining business process models. In: Recio-Garcia, J.A., Orozco-del Castillo, M.G., Bridge, D. (eds.) ICCBR 2024. LNCS, vol. 14775, pp. 175–190. Springer, Cham (2024). https://doi.org/10.1007/978-3-031-63646-2_12
27. Moody, D.L., Sindre, G., Brasethvik, T., Solvberg, A.: Evaluating the quality of information models: empirical testing of a conceptual model quality framework. In: Clarke, L. (ed.) Proceedings of the 25th International Conference on Software Engineering, pp. 295–305. ACM Conferences. IEEE Computer Society, Washington, DC (2003). https://doi.org/10.1109/ICSE.2003.1201209
28. Moreno-Montes de Oca, I., Snoeck, M., Reijers, H.A., Rodríguez-Morffi, A.: A systematic literature review of studies on business process modeling quality. Inf. Softw. Technol. **58**, 187–205 (2015). https://doi.org/10.1016/j.infsof.2014.07.011
29. Nelson, H.J., Poels, G., Genero, M., Piattini, M.: A conceptual modeling quality framework. Softw. Qual. J. **20**(1), 201–228 (2012). https://doi.org/10.1007/s11219-011-9136-9
30. Poels, G., Maes, A., Gailly, F., Paemeleire, R.: Measuring the perceived semantic quality of information models. In: Akoka, J., et al. (eds.) ER 2005. LNCS, vol. 3770, pp. 376–385. Springer, Heidelberg (2005). https://doi.org/10.1007/11568346_41
31. Sandkuhl, K., Barn, B., Barat, S.: Neural text generators in enterprise modeling: can ChatGPT be used as proxy domain expert? In: Proceedings of the 31st International Conference on Information Systems Development. International Conference on Information Systems Development, Instituto Superior TécnicoLisbon, Portugal (2023). https://doi.org/10.62036/ISD.2023.44
32. Sandkuhl, K., Stirna, J., Persson, A., Wißotzki, M.: Enterprise Modeling: Tackling Business Challenges with the 4EM Method. Springer, Heidelberg (2014). https://doi.org/10.1007/978-3-662-43725-4
33. Schulhoff, S., et al.: The prompt report: a systematic survey of prompting techniques.https://doi.org/10.48550/arXiv.2406.06608
34. Simon, C., Haag, S., Zakfeld, L.: Experiments on GPT-3 assisted process model development. In: 37th ECMS 2023 (2023)
35. Wei, J., et al.: Chain-of-thought prompting elicits reasoning in large language models. https://doi.org/10.48550/arXiv.2201.11903
36. White, J., et al.: A prompt pattern catalog to enhance prompt engineering with ChatGPT. https://doi.org/10.48550/arXiv.2302.11382
37. Wu, T., Terry, M., Cai, C.J.: AI Chains: transparent and controllable Human-AI interaction by chaining large language model prompts. In: Barbosa, S., et al. (eds.) CHI Conference on Human Factors in Computing Systems, pp. 1–22. ACM, New York (2022). https://doi.org/10.1145/3491102.3517582

Grass-Root Enterprise Modelling: How Large Language Models Can Help

Peter-Alexander Kolev[1], Hauke Hansen Pruss[1], Jim Robert Wilken[1], and Kurt Sandkuhl[1,2]

[1] The University of Rostock, Rostock, Germany
{peter-alexander.kolev,hauke.pruss,jim.wilken,
kurt.sandkuhl}@uni-rostock.de
[2] Jönköping University, Jönköping, Sweden
kurt.sandkuhl@ju.se

Abstract. Conceptual modelling has turned out to be a promising application field for large language models (LLM). The paper reports the results of a study in the field of enterprise modelling (EM) aiming at generating multi-perspective models. The results indicate that LLM can be seen as assistive technology for certain tasks in EM. Thus, the paper also discusses if LLM can be considered as a tool for grass-roots EM, i.e., modelling by stakeholders without solid EM training. The main contributions of the paper are (1) an analysis of the state of research in LLM use in EM, (2) a study on LLM use for producing multi-perspective enterprise models, and (3) to position LLM in the roadmap for increasing the reach of EM.

Keywords: Enterprise Modeling · Large Language Model · Grass-Root Modelling · ChatGPT · Modelling Assistance

1 Introduction

Since the introduction of OpenAI's service ChatGPT and its enormous echo in the industry and society, numerous new application fields for large language models (LLM) have been explored, among them the LLM use for tasks in conceptual modelling [8]. The LLM potential in business process [7] and enterprise modelling (EM) [1] was investigated for different tasks, such as generating models from textual specifications or preparing modelling teams by providing relevant domain knowledge (cf. Sect. 3). In our previous work, we gained promising results when using LLM to reduce the workload of domain experts in EM [19]. Encouraged by the results, we conducted a study with the aim to produce multi-perspective models. This study is the first research activity presented in this paper (see Sect. 4). The research question for this part is (RQ1): In the context of EM, can LLM be used to produce multi-perspective enterprise models?

The results of RQ1 confirm the findings of other scholars (cf. Sect. 3.1) that LLM can be considered as an assistive technology for certain tasks in EM. When investigating the impact of this finding, the question arises if LLM could be a vehicle to increase the reach of EM in organisations, for example, as a tool for grassroots enterprise modelling (RQ2). This question is the second research activity addressed in the paper. Grass-root enterprise modelling has been used as a term to describe EM by stakeholders without solid EM training. The aim is to move from expert discipline to common practice in an organisation. A roadmap has been proposed by [20], which identifies various research needs, like, for example, embedding modelling in everyday work or softening the requirements to model completeness. By tackling RQ2, we aim to position the results of our work on RQ1 in the roadmap and to identify necessary future LLM-related work.

The main contributions of our work are (1) an analysis of the state of research in LLM use in EM (see Sect. 3.1), (2) a study on LLM use for producing multi-perspective enterprise models (see Sect. 4), and (3) to position LLM in the roadmap for increasing the reach of EM (see Sect. 5). The paper is structured as follows: Sect. 2 introduces the background for our work from EM and LLM. Section 3.2 summarizes related work and the potential of LLM use in EM. Section 4 investigate the generation of models by LLM using 4EM as modelling language. Section 5 positions the results of Sect. 4 in the roadmap towards grassroots EM. Section 6 discusses implications for EM and future work.

2 Background and Related Work

2.1 Enterprise Modeling

EM is addressing the "systematic analysis and modeling of processes, organisation structures, product structures, IT-systems or any other perspective relevant for the modeling purpose" [25]. The variety of methods, languages and tools supporting EM is visible in work on research roadmaps and future directions from the information systems community (see, e.g., [20]) and from industrial organisation (e.g., [24]).

Enterprise Modeling (EM) is meant to support organisations in coping with a broad range of challenges, including managing organisational change in dynamic market environments, aligning organisational goals and information systems to support these goals, as well as explicating and consolidating knowledge from various stakeholder groups. The role of EM usually is to provide methods, tools, and practices for capturing and visualising the current ("as-is") situation and to develop the future ("to-be") situation. In particular, a model of the current situation forms one of the fundamentals for supporting the future development. Given the complexity of enterprises, there seems to be an agreement in the literature related to EM that a key feature of enterprise models is that various perspectives are included. Depending on the modelling language, the perspectives are represented by different sub-models or in the same model.

For the investigation into LLM use to generate high-quality EM in the first part of our paper (i.e., Sect. 4), we selected 4EM [22], a multi-perspective EM language used in many universities for teaching EM. 4EM distinguishes several modelling perspectives that are summarised with their focus, issues to model and main components in Fig. 1.

	Goals Model (GM)	Business Rules Model (BRM)	Concepts Model (CM)	Business Process Model (BPM)	Actors and Recourses Model (ARM)	Product/Service (P/S)	Technical Components Model (TCRM)
Focus	Vision and strategy	Policies and rules	Business ontology	Business operations	Organizational structure	Products and Services	Information system needs
Issues to model	What does the organization want to achieve or to avoid and why?	What are the business rules, how do they support organization's goals?	What are the things and "phenomena" addressed in other sub-models?	What are the business processes? How do they handle information? and material?	Who are responsible for goals and process? How are the actors interrelated?	What product and services components exist? What are core features?	What are the business requirements to the IS? How are they related to other models?
Components	Goal, problem, external constraint, opportunity	Business rule	Concept, attribute	Process, external proc., information set, material set	Actor, role, organizational unit, individual	Product, service, component, feature	IS goal, IS problem, IS requirement, IS component

Fig. 1. 4EM perspectives and method components

2.2 Large Language Models

The release of ChatGPT by OpenAI marked a significant moment in integrating AI into mainstream applications and problem-solving tasks. The model behind ChatGPT operates with 175 billion parameters and utilises datasets that include nearly a trillion words sourced from various corpora [2]. Its training involves predicting the next sequence of tokens based on given contexts, which enables it to generate realistic and novel word sequences. LLMs like GPT-4 are pre-trained in a task-agnostic manner [11], which allows for flexible customization through in-context learning during runtime via natural language prompts. This advancement facilitates experimentation and prototyping in AI without the need for initial model training. LLM can perform tasks like summarization, translation, grammar correction, and more, providing accessible AI tools across various fields.

Prompt engineering has emerged as a crucial discipline in LLM utilization, conceptualized by [16]. It involves formulating prompts that effectively "program" the AI to perform desired tasks. Research shows that prompt design lacks standardized methods, relying heavily on trial and error [17]. This has led to the developing of domain-specific languages like Impromptu to support consistent, platform-independent prompt creation [27], highlighting the need for more structured approaches in prompt engineering. Significant discussions in the literature focus on the need for meta-models and software tools to support effective prompt design, allowing prompts to be reused in various contexts (see, e.g. prompt chainer [29]) and helping manage their complexity akin to traditional programming. However, there is still a notable gap in comprehensive methods for prompt design, calling for method-driven tools that integrate expert knowledge to enhance the validity and effectiveness of LLM interactions [6].

3 Potential of LLM Use in Enterprise Modelling

An investigation into the potential of LLM use in EM should include at least two aspects: (1) what LLM uses in EM have been reported in the literature, and (2) what usage areas would theoretically be possible? We conducted a literature analysis to tackle the first aspect (Sect. 3.1). For the second aspect, we propose to structure the EM field according to modelling phases and tasks (Sect. 3.2).

3.1 Literature Analysis on LLM Use in Enterprise Modelling

The state of research into LLM use in EM was investigated in a systematic literature review (SLR) using the procedure suggested by Kitchenham [12] that consists of six steps. The first step is to develop research questions (RQ) to be answered by the SLR. For our work, the RQ is: *What previous scientific work is visible in publications about using LLM in EM?* The process of paper identification starts with defining the overall search space (step 2), which requires determining the literature sources. We selected Scopus, IEEE Xplore and AISeL to reach a broad coverage in information systems and computer science. Paper identification continues with the population phase (step 3), which includes search string development and the search in the literature sources. Our search string is shown in Table 1 and consists of the terms "LLM" and "enterprise modelling", synonyms for both terms, and closely related terms, such as "conceptual modelling" and "process modelling". The search was performed on June 15, 2024. The number of hits is also shown in the table. In step 4, the "paper selection" follows by defining inclusion and exclusion criteria and a manual selection of relevant papers. We only included papers that address the actual use of LLM in conceptual modelling and excluded those who happen to have only both keywords in the paper or describe LLM use as future work. The data collection phase (step 5) has its focus on extracting the information relevant for the RQ from the set of relevant papers. The last step is the analysis of data and interpretation, i.e., to answer the RQ.

Table 1. Results of the literature analysis

Query	No. of Hits			
	Scopus	AISeL	IEEE Xplore	Relevant
(("neural text" OR "ChatGPT" OR "LLM" OR "large language model") AND ("enterprise modelling" OR "conceptual modelling" OR "process modelling"))	29	1	0	9
Total				9

In Scopus, among the 29 hits for the modified query were six conference proceedings and fourteen papers applying LLM in mathematics, chemistry, education and economics. These papers were not relevant. The remaining nine relevant papers include our own previous work (three papers; see below) and six recently published papers:

Klievtsova et al. [13] focus explicitly on process modelling and take the perspective of conversational modelling, defined as 'creating and improving process models and process descriptions based on the iterative exchange of questions/answers between domain experts and chatbots'. The paper contributes practical recommendations for LLM application in process modelling that might be relevant for the business processes perspective usually included in enterprise models. The paper by Fill et al. [8] is closely related to our work: the authors present the results of a series of experiments that investigate the engineering of prompts for generating and interpreting conceptual models. ChatGPT is used to generate ER, BPMN, UML, and Heraklit models and large parts of the models are correctly generated. One of the results of the paper is that the potential of LLM for supporting modelling tasks is substantial if a textual problem description of the domain to be modelled exists. The paper also investigates the interpretation of models. [14] propose a framework that leverages LLMs for the automated generation and iterative refinement of process models. The framework takes textual descriptions as a starting point and includes a prompting strategy, the generation of Partially Ordered Workflow Language (POWL) models, model refinement and the correction of potential errors in the model. This paper is also related to our work, but focuses on process models only and uses an intermediary language for representing the modelling results. [26] investigate typical tasks of the business process management (BPM) lifecycle, such as process identification, discovery, analysis or implementation, and discuss LLM application opportunities and future research directions. The paper intends to explore opportunities for LLM use and propose application scenarios, i.e., it does not contain any experiments or in-depth studies. [4] collect and structure what is expected from LLM as support for semantics-driven systems engineering. Many expectations formulated in the paper are consistent with our view about the potential of LLM in EM, like the support of multiple perspectives in EM or the importance of semantics. However, the paper does not present solutions and takes the wider scope of systems engineering. [5] focus in the use of LLM in the context of the Legal Goal-oriented Requirements Language.

In our previous work, we investigated if domain experts in EM projects could partly be substituted by LLMs [19] when preparing EM projects, modelling the as-is situation or developing alternatives for change in an organisation. We conducted experiments comparing the output of ChatGPT with the results of a human expert. The results showed that ChatGPT produced good results that cannot substitute but support domain experts. In an additional study [10], we extended this experiment into larger modelling tasks that confirmed the results of the experiments. Furthermore, we proposed a meta-model for integrating enterprise models, reusable prompts and domain terminology and investigated the effects of LLM use on EM methods [1].

In AISeL, the only relevant paper is one of our own publications mentioned above: [19].

3.2 Structuring the LLM Potential in Enterprise Modelling

The aim of this section is to structure the potential usage areas of LLM in EM. For this purpose, we propose to consider three aspects that can be used to position the results of the literature analysis: the different phases of EM projects, the potential stakeholders to be supported by LLM, and the perspectives included in enterprise models.

According to [15], the most relevant modelling phases to be distinguished are scoping of the modelling project, preparation of the modelling project, modelling of the current situation ("as is"), analysis of the "as is" and modelling of alternatives for addressing identified change needs, modelling of the future situation for the selected alternative ("to be"), and applying the "to be" model for the designed purpose. Most papers found in the SLR address all lifecycle phases (i.e., [13,14,19,26] and [4]). [8] focus on model generation and interpretation; [5] focus on preparation for modelling ans model generation.

What tasks to perform in these modelling phases depends on the role. [23] describes various roles that belong to two main groups: modelling experts and domain experts. Modelling experts include, e.g., facilitators of modelling sessions, modellers and tool operators. Domain experts usually are non-EM experts who participate in modelling projects. However, we also have to consider non-EM experts who perform modelling-like activities outside EM projects. Only [4] and our own work differentiate between different roles in modelling projects. [4] distinguish primarily between end-users and engineering-facing roles, whereas we use the above-mentioned categories by [23].

[9] points out that enterprise modelling has to include different perspectives that reflect the concerns of different stakeholder groups and roles. These different perspectives of EM, such as processes, organisation structures, products and services, or the IT infrastructure, are visible in all modelling phases. [13,26] and [14] focus on business processes only; [5] does not consider EM but domain-specific modelling (of legal compliance). [8] consider different conceptual modelling languages for information, processes and service-oriented infrastructure modelling. [4] include multiple perspectives for modelling systems.

In our own work, we have been investigating the potential of LLM use in the perspectives included in 4EM (see Sect. 2.1). This showed that all the above-mentioned phases involve domain experts and can be LLM-supported for all perspectives More concretely, structuring and refining domain knowledge as preparation for modelling, generating/producing models from this domain knowledge that is often available in documents and improving or checking existing models are typical tasks. The same tasks can be expected to be also relevant for the knowledge workers. Additionally, already existing model-like content hidden in documents, presentations, and drawings has to be converted into models, as investigated by Reiz et al. [18].

So far, the majority of existing research has focused on the use of LLM to support modelling experts in performing routine tasks. Only a few papers distinguish between modelling experts and non-EM experts. Most papers focus on process modelling. There is no work on generating multi-perspective models.

4 LLM for Generating Multi-perspective Models

Our previous work (see Sect. 3.1) investigated where it makes sense to use LLM in EM, how to adapt LLM for specific modelling languages, and how to make the prompts reusable. Essentially, we showed that for a given modelling task described in natural language, LLM can generate XML specifications of the content of all 4EM sub-models. What was not part of previous work was (1) whether multi-perspective EM could be generated and (2) how to produce model representations for actual modelling tools. The latter do not only require XML model content but also information required for displaying the model (position of components, symbols, colors, performed operations etc.). The challenge in multi-perspective models is that many model elements are present in several perspectives. The naming and usage of these model elements must be consistent across all perspectives. Example from 4EM: if certain information is required as input to a business process, required for a business rule, part of a goal specification, and specified in the concepts model, the LLM has to make sure that this information has identical identifiers and naming in all sub-models generated. Thus, the research questions for this section are:

- RQ1-1: Can LLM produce models in a native EM tool format?
- RQ1-2: Can LLM generate multi-perspective models consisting of sub-models?

The above RQ are sub-questions of the RQ1 presented in the introduction. Investigating these RQ requires generating models from textual descriptions, an activity also required for grass-roots EM. To tackle the RQ, we begin with the required toolchain for generating EM models (Sect. 4.1), followed by a study on the generating of multi-perspective models with this toolchain (Sect. 4.2).

4.1 LLM Toolchain for Generating Multi-perspective Models

The core functionality of the toolchain has to be to generate an enterprise model from a natural language description for a given modelling language and modelling tool. The natural language description could be the output of a preceding LLM task or authored by a human. Previous experiments showed that LLM can generate structured descriptions (e.g., XML or JSON) of enterprise model content following a defined meta-model if prompts define the response structure. Furthermore, we investigated the XML formats tailored for the import in modelling tools, such as the 4EM tool (i.e., ADO.xx-based modelling tools). Here, we discovered that the XML format basically consists of a specific prefix, the model content following the tool-specific DTD and a suffix. Using this discovery, we designed the tool chain as follows: The toolchain has a Client Server Architecture. The client generates a specific prompt for every model of the 4EM modelling portfolio. Already conducted research on the topic in [21] proposed the use of preprompting. A textual scenario which is to be modelled is used as input for the LLM to generate a comprehensive list of the key features for a scenario to be modelled. The prompt for each model of 4EM is manually fit to match the different model parameters. An example of such a prompt is shown in Fig. 2. The resulting list of key features is used as the content for a call to the LLM, resulting in a list of all components and relations as defined in the prompt. After this first prompt, the LLM is familiar with the classes and relations for a given 4EM sub-model.

| I am trying to capture vision and strategy of an organization using a goal model (GM) as follows: it has concepts of "Goal", "Opportunity", "Problem" (i.e., "Threat" and "Weakness"), "Cause", and "Constraint". Goals are refined by sub-goals and they are connected with its parent goal using "AND" and "OR" relationships. All concepts may have binary relationships with other concepts of the type "supports" and "hinders". Please be less verbose and detailed outcome. Create a List of all Components and Relationships for the following scenario: | ```
INSTANCE <Goal - [Individual Name]> : <Goal> \\
ATTRIBUTE <Position>
VALUE "NODE x:5cm y:3cm w:4cm h:1.5cm index:2"
ATTRIBUTE <External tool coupling>
VALUE ""
ATTRIBUTE <Description>
VALUE "The goal is.."
ATTRIBUTE <Criticality>
VALUE "Low"
ATTRIBUTE <Priority>
VALUE "Low"
ATTRIBUTE <Intermodel-Relations>
VALUE
ATTRIBUTE <Decomposition>
VALUE ""
ATTRIBUTE <Defined by>
VALUE ""
ATTRIBUTE <Attributes>
VALUE
// END
``` |
|---|---|

Fig. 2. Prompt excerpts [left: prompt describing the features of 4EM goal model] [right: minimal example how to represent the goal model in ADL]

In the next step, a prompt is built that concatenates the known component syntax for a model as well as the scenario which is to be generated. The model syntax for each model was manually extracted from the 4EM Platform in the ADL format. Figure 2 shows a minimal example of such a component for the goal model. With the overall syntax of the 4EM Model component relations already known to the LLM, the most crucial part is to train it on the specific semantics of the ADL format for each model. For this purpose, the pretrained model is provided with another prompt containing the above semantics of the ADL format for a given model as well as the scenario which is to be modelled. The full workflow of the toolchain is illustrated in the pseudocode below:

The Functions "getAllIntroductionsForModelByName", "getAllComponentsByModelName" and "getScenarioFromUserInput" load the discussed introductions, ADL semantics, and Scenarios from the database. The loaded Introduction is used first to pre-train the LLM on a given 4EM Model. Next, the resulting "chatState" is used to send another prompt to the LLM providing it with the ADL semantic as well as the to be modeled Scenario. The LLM returns the generated Model, which then can be imported into the ADO.xx-based 4EM tool. This approach was influenced by the best practice approaches in [28].
```

Algorithm 1. Prompt generation Service

$Introduction \leftarrow getAllIntroductionsForModelByName(ModelName)$
$ModelComponents \leftarrow getAllComponentsByModelName(ModelName)$
$Szenario \leftarrow getScenarioFromUserInput(UserInput)$

$ChatState \leftarrow generateModelService(Introduction)$

$Prompt \leftarrow ModelComponents + Szenario$

$GeneratedModel \leftarrow generateModelService(ChatState, Prompt)$

4.2 Experiment in Generating Multi-perspective Models

This section details a study to analyse the feasibility of using LLM for generating multi-perspective enterprise models. We used 4EM as modelling language, ChatGPT 4o as LLM and the toolchain discussed in the previous section. In the following, the study design is introduced followed by the data collection and a comprehensive interpretation of the results.

The **study design** corresponds to a quasi-experiment with a defined modelling task as study object, the modelling by an expert modeller and an LLM as treatments of the study object, and the evaluation by comparing the results of the modelling using defined criteria. The defined modelling task is based on a textbook [22] that illustrates the use of 4EM method with scenarios. For the six sub-models, we used a scenario from the book (complex scenario) and produced a simplified version. For each scenario, the expert modeller developed the 4EM sub-models. Another modeller performed a quality check of the developed models. The resulting models for the textual description were used as "gold standard" in the evaluation. Each textual scenario was processed through the toolchain, and its output, which represents the modelled scenario, was integrated into an .adl file, the input format for the 4EM modelling tool. After the import into the 4EM tool, the evaluation phase began. The evaluation focuses on the following criteria:

Importability (Basic Requirement): This assesses whether the LLM-generated output can be seamlessly re-imported into ADL tools. It checks if the output adheres to the required formats and standards, ensuring error-free integration. Importability is fundamental; if a model cannot be imported due to errors, it is deemed unusable.

Component Completeness: This measures how completely the components in the output match the intended architectural components. It includes: Identification: Ensures all necessary components are correctly identified and named. Attribute Completeness: Verifies the correctness of component attributes. Mapping Completeness: Assesses the completeness of mapping abstract concepts to concrete components.

Relationship Precision: This evaluates the accuracy and clarity of relationships between components. It includes: Identification of Relationships: Ensures all relevant relationships are identified. Correctness of Connections: Verifies the accuracy of relationships, such as hierarchies and dependencies. Clarity: Assesses how clearly relationships are defined.

Although relationship precision includes the aspect of completeness similar to component completeness, we prefer the term precision, as in addition to the existence and correct type of the relationship, the degree (binary, tertiary) is also relevant.

Data Collection: To analyse and subsequently rate the used method, we applied our toolchain and collected data. If a generated output passed the importability criteria (see above) it became viable for further evaluation. Regarding component completeness and relationship precision, a comparison with the gold standard was conducted by two expert modellers. A component was accurately represented by the LLM output if the given component existed in both output and gold standard. This resulted in a similarity degree which equals the percentage of classes in the gold standard that are also represented in the LLM output following the evaluation criteria. The same logic is applied to the relationship accuracy.

As mentioned above, the toolchain was utilised to generate six outputs consisting of simple and complex scenarios. This was repeated for a second scenario resulting in a dataset of 24 outputs. Although we managed to produce 24 outputs that could be evaluated, the importability rate was not 100 %. Five outputs for complex scenarios were not importable after the initial run. The analysis of the outputs showed that parts of the XML file required for the import into ADO.xx were missing in these outputs, i.e., the LLM generation was incomplete or interrupted. In these cases, we had to restart the whole generation process and repeat the run to generate importable output. The search for an explanation for the faulty output resulted in the conjecture that the token length exceeded the maximum permitted in the ChatGPT-4o license used. This technical limitation requires further investigation. In conclusion, the answer to RQ1-1 is that LLM can produce models in a native EM tool format (in our case ADO.xx), but the robustness of the generation process needs further work.

The results of the study for the first scenario (simple and complex) are visualised using a bar graph approach in Fig. 3. The abbreviations for the 4EM sub-models can be found in Fig. 1. The results for the second scenario were very similar and, thus, require no additional discussion.

Interpretation of Results: The bar chart in Fig. 3 (left side) illustrates the results achieved in the simple scenario. Overall, a component completeness of between 44.44 % and 100 % was achieved. Particularly noteworthy is the TCRM component, which achieved a perfect component completeness of 100 % and a high relationship precision of 89.74 %. This shows that in clearly structured and less complex scenarios, the LLM was able to precisely identify all necessary components and map their relationships, including the ones between sub-models, largely correctly. However, it should be noted that the component completeness scores also reflect some challenges; the lowest score of 44.44 % indicates potential problems in these scenarios. One reason for this discrepancy could be the

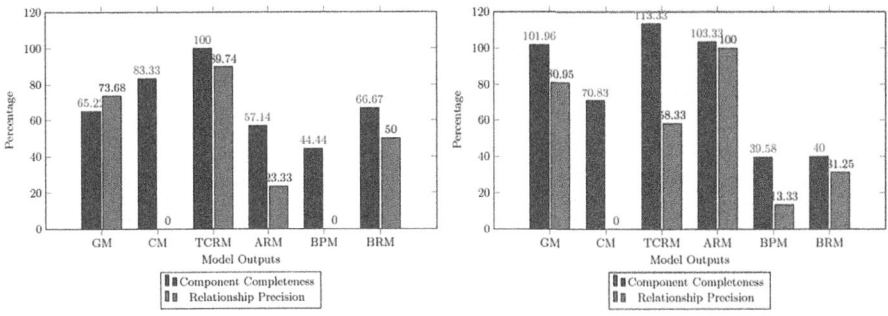

Fig. 3. Evaluation of Model Outputs [left: simple] [right: complex]

complexity of the scenarios, which may have resulted in ambiguous or more complex relationships and requirements. The CM model also achieved a component completeness of 83.33 %, despite relationship completeness of 0 %, which indicates a selective but precise identification. For the complex scenarios in Fig. 3 (right side) a component completeness of over 100 % was achieved for the GM, TCRM, and ARM models. More than 100 % were possible as we also counted the components in the generated model not included in the gold standard but deductible from the scenario and, therefore, accurate. For example, as the gold standard focuses on the essential goals for the modelling purpose, the scenario potentially includes additional goals that could be discovered during the generation of the GM. Thus, a percentage value above 100 shows that the outputs from these models included more components than initially specified, indicating potential overestimation in component identification. It should be particularly emphasized that there were hardly any components with different names across the sub-models that had to be counted as incorrect. Furthermore, the relationship precision in the ARM model is 100 %, which indicates the exact and precise mapping of the relationships between the components.

In summary, the results show how strongly the performance of the models depends on the complexity of the scenarios. While in simple scenarios, a high precision in identifying and mapping the relationships was achieved, in more complex scenarios, difficulties were encountered, leading to over- or underrepresentation of the components. This highlights the need to further refine and adapt the prompts to ensure consistent performance across different scenario types. Thus, the answer to RQ1-2 is that, in principle, it is possible to generate multi-perspective models with LLM as shown for our simple scenario. However, for more complex scenarios, shortcomings in creating thoroughly interlinked sub-models became clearly visible. Additional work is required to determine the exact technical causes for the shortcomings and how to extend the current limits of model generation.

This study faced several problems, which the authors want to share. The evaluation process was conducted twice. In the first iteration, two more evaluation criteria were considered: notation consistency and description accuracy. Due to the following problems in evaluating these criteria, they were not included in the final evaluation. Notation consistency was meant to measure if a goal in the gold standard remains a goal in the output. However, this was a duplicate of the component completeness because both measured the same metric. Description accuracy is intended to evaluate the textual description attribute that many model components in 4EM have, for example, the textual description of goals or problems. This was very subjective in its evaluation due to the evaluator having to choose which description matches the gold standard and which did not.

5 LLM Support for Grass-Roots Enterprise Modelling

How to support enterprise modelling of non-experts as a way to increase the reach of enterprise modelling has been an ongoing discussion in the EM community for several years. The results of the state of research analysis in Sect. 3.2 and our LLM study in Sect. 4 indicate that there is a lot of potential for using LLM for non-expert modelling, such as using LLM to produce a model from a given textual process description, but also a number of limitations, such as the incompleteness of LLM-generated models experienced in our study. To some extent, these findings were unsurprising as the strengths of LLM, according to their developers and current research [3], are in natural language understanding and generation, maintaining context over long passages of text, or assisting in creative processes. In this section, we shift the focus of our paper to the question of whether LLM could be a vehicle to increase the reach of EM in organisations, for example, as a tool for grass-roots enterprise modelling. The section is divided into two parts: Sect. 5.1 uses two scenarios of LLM support for non-expert modellers to illustrate the new possibilities that LLM create. In Sect. 5.2, we widen the perspective from functional to organisational and methodical considerations by considering the roadmap for increasing the reach of EM.

5.1 Scenarios of LLM Use in Grass-Roots Modelling

Using two simple scenarios, this section aims to illustrate what new possibilities LLMs offer for supporting non-EM experts in modelling. The non-EM experts to be supported can roughly be divided into knowledge workers producing results in their daily work that preferably should be documented or represented as enterprise models instead of texts, drawings or PowerPoint files, and participants in EM projects as domain experts or company representatives. The knowledge worker group is much larger, very heterogeneous and can include any kind of administrative role in an enterprise. For each group, we defined a simple scenarios that can be used to show what possibilities LLM unlock as compared to modelling without LLM support:

– Scenario A: A knowledge worker (KW) from a certain local practice with no modelling background explains in natural language the essential facts (of a process, product design, system structure, business model, etc.) worth representing in a model, and the LLM produces the model based on this description.

– Scenario B: A domain expert (DE) who is part of the modelling team and aware of the objective of the modelling project, but no expert in modelling wants to contribute domain knowledge to the project that is represented in the modelling language used in the project.

We structure the scenario analysis by considering the different phases of model development. Along these phases, we identify what new opportunities LLMs offer for the individual phase and what has already been investigated in the research.

Table 2. Potential of LLM Use in Grass-Roots-Modelling

Model Dev. Phase	Relevant for Scenario	Potential of LLM use	Existing Research
prepare modelling	B	DE lets LLM summarize the relevant context documents for modelling team	[19]
select modelling language and tool	B	no modelling tool needed; phase is reduced to selecting prompt for modelling language	[1]
provide essential knowledge	A, B	essential task of KW or DE; LLM use should be avoided	
improve knowledge description	A, B	LLM improve description and add context information	[13]
develop model based on description	A, B	LLM generates model based on textual input	[8, 10, 19]
check quality of model	B	[8]	
put the model into usage	B		[8]

The first column in Table 2 reflects a model development process consisting of preparatory work for modelling (scoping, retrieving and providing existing documents from the enterprise), selection of modelling language and tool, providing the essential knowledge to be captured in the model for the defined scope (for example as verbal description), the actual model development, checking the quality of the model (adherence to modelling language, completeness), and putting the model into usage (for example by providing final form descriptions or converting it into executable formats). The column dedicated to the potential makes clear that all phases relevant to scenario A could be performed by LLM with the exception of the provision of the knowledge to be captured in a model. The phase of selecting the modelling language and tool is reduced to selecting prompts for the language. For scenario B, LLMs also offer assistive functions, like summarizing background information for the modelling team or the additional step of checking the description of the knowledge to be modelled. Furthermore, the existing research column shows that all model development phases have already been addressed in research.

Shortcomings of current solutions could be explained by the need for more advanced prompts or prompt chains, or by the need for CustomGPTs or combinations of LLM and VectorDBc that are specially supporting modellers. Both paths have to be explored.

5.2 Positioning LLMs in Roadmap for Increasing the Reach of EM

The roadmap outlining research required in this field was published in 2018 and is summarized below. The roadmap is based on the vision that in the future, *the majority of organizational stakeholders uses enterprise modelling (often without noticing it) to capture, store, distribute, integrate and retrieve essential knowledge relevant for their local practices in a way that supports long-term, cross-concern organizational objectives* [20]. The roadmap defines research topics along seven dimensions to investigate (e.g., what stakeholders are creating and using models, what factors are affecting the value and quality, what scope or concern/purpose models have) and different aspects required to implement the vision. The identified aspects are:

- Modelling is embedded in everyday work. Non-EM experts perform modelling without special training, sometimes even without knowing it;
- more flexibility in using different kinds of models in combination, for example by extracting or integrating different content and formats "on demand"
- Local practices of different stakeholder groups in capturing knowledge and using modelling remain unchanged and integrated with other local practices
- Grass-roots modeling and professional modelling can be combined. Models are not primarily developed for one specific purpose, but can be more flexibly used for several purposes;
- Completeness, coherence and rigor requirements to models are softened towards incomplete, partly formalized and contradictory model components

Our position is that LLM can contribute to many of these aspects, but should not be used for all of them: As visible in the scenarios discussed in the previous Sect. 5.1, LLM has much potential for *embedding modelling in everyday work*. This possibly is the most promising contribution of LLM to the roadmap. When it comes to *model combination and integration on demand*, our view is that the existing modelling environments and tools should be used for this purpose, i.e. we should try to produce syntactically and semantically correct models with LLM and switch to applying dedicated modelling tools for tasks, such as integration and combination, as modelling tools offer a richer set of functionalities.

Local practices are expressed with concerns, terminology and even processes specific and sometimes different from other stakeholder groups. Besides the task of generating models from textual descriptions, translating or adjusting between different terminologies could be a task suitable for LLM. LLM can be asked to take specific roles ("personas"), which in many cases also lead to the use of terminology associated with this role (if the terminology is included in the LLM). If explaining a certain situation from one role to another role can help solve terminology issues, it should be explained. The development of future solutions often happens in *collaboration with different stakeholders* who contribute their background knowledge, experiences and ideas. This participatory way of working makes the different stakeholders co-designers of future solutions and increases acceptance. Replacing domain experts' or stakeholders' input with LLM generated might, in some cases, contribute to the stakeholders' knowledge but does not substitute the consensus-developing process. Furthermore, we still need the domain experts to judge the correctness and completeness of LLM output, which probably is less work than generating the input but still puts workload on the domain experts. For this kind of work, local practices have to be established.

6 Concluding Remarks

The research presented in this paper had the aim to investigate the use of LLM for generating multi-perspective enterprise models (RQ1) and to discuss the potential of LLM for grass-roots EM (RQ2). The literature analysis confirmed that the research community's interest in LLM use in EM is increasing quickly. Meanwhile, all phases of EM projects and all stakeholder groups involved in EM have been identified as potential usage areas, or initial studies were performed.

Our study confirmed the potential of LLM for model generation but also revealed limitations, mainly for model generation from textual descriptions of complex scenarios and interrelations between different sub-models of multi-perspective EM. In the context of grass-roots EM, the large potential of LLM as assistive technology was confirmed, i.e., LLM can help non-EM experts in enterprise modelling. However, the intensive use of LLM with the associated optimisation efforts carries the danger that we achieve the goal of being able to do EM without training in EM at the price of the need for training in LLM prompting and toolchains instead. So far, the simplicity of LLM has been one of their important success factors, and this factor should be seen as essential and maintained when using LLM for grass-roots modelling. There is a lot of potential for future work on LLM use in EM and in grass-roots modelling, some of which is discussed in Sect. 5.2. Future work is also required for the question of what tasks should be supported by LLM during grass-roots modelling. Our work started from typical activities of EM projects, but there might be additional demands from non-EM experts beyond these activities. An empirical study into the actual demands of non-EM experts is recommended to validate the view reflected in the roadmap.

Limitations of our work result from the fact that we used only one LLM (ChatGPT), only one target modelling language and only one scenario with two complexity levels. A larger study would be worthwhile that compared several LLMs and/or the performance of LLMs for different modelling languages in different scenarios. In this context, our interpretation of what is complex and what is simple needs discussion.

References

1. Barn, B.S., Barat, S., Sandkuhl, K.: Adaptation of enterprise modeling methods for large language models. In: Almeida, J.P.A., Kaczmarek-Heß, M., Koschmider, A., Proper, H.A. (eds.) PoEM 2023. LNBIP, vol. 497, pp. 3–18. Springer, Cham (2023). https://doi.org/10.1007/978-3-031-48583-1_1

2. Brown, T.B., et al.: Language models are few-shot learners. In: Larochelle, H., Ranzato, M., Hadsell, R., Balcan, M.F., Lin, H. (eds.) Advances in Neural Information Processing Systems 33, pp. 1877–1901. Curran Associates, Inc. (2020)
3. Bubeck, S., et al.: Sparks of artificial general intelligence: early experiments with GPT-4. arXiv preprint arXiv:2303.12712 (2023)
4. Buchmann, R., et al.: Large language models: expectations for semantics-driven systems engineering. Data Knowl. Eng. **152**, 102324 (2024)
5. de Kinderen, S., Winter, K.: Towards taming large language models with prompt templates for legal GRL modeling. In: van der Aa, H., Bork, D., Schmidt, R., Sturm, A. (eds.) BPMDS EMMSAD 2024. LNBIP, vol. 511, pp. 213–228. Springer, Cham (2024). https://doi.org/10.1007/978-3-031-61007-3_17
6. Du, R., et al.: Rapsai: accelerating machine learning prototyping of multimedia applications through visual programming. In: Proceedings of the 2023 CHI Conference on Human Factors in Computing Systems, pp. 1–23 (2023)
7. Dumas, M., et al.: AI-augmented business process management systems: a research manifesto. ACM Trans. Manag. Inf. Syst. **14**(1), 1–19 (2023)
8. Fill, H.-G., Fettke, P., Köpke, J.: Conceptual modeling and large language models: impressions from first experiments with ChatGPT. Enterp. Model. Inf. Syst. Architect. (EMISAJ) **18**, 1–15 (2023)
9. Frank, U.: Multi-perspective enterprise modeling: foundational concepts, prospects and future research challenges. Softw. Syst. Model. **13**, 941–962 (2014)
10. Görgen, L., Müller, E., Triller, M., Nast, B., Sandkuhl, K.: Large language models in enterprise modeling: case study and experiences, vol. 1, pp. 74–85 (2024). Cited by: 0. All Open Access, Hybrid Gold Open Access
11. Huang, W., Abbeel, P., Pathak, D., Mordatch, I.: Language models as zero-shot planners: extracting actionable knowledge for embodied agents. In: International Conference on Machine Learning, pp. 9118–9147. PMLR (2022)
12. Kitchenham, B., Brereton, O.P., Budgen, D., Turner, M., Bailey, J., Linkman, S.: Systematic literature reviews in software engineering-a systematic literature review. Inf. Softw. Technol. **51**(1), 7–15 (2009)
13. Klievtsova, N., Benzin, J.-V., Kampik, T., Mangler, J., Rinderle-Ma, S.: Conversational process modelling: state of the art, applications, and implications in practice. In: Di Francescomarino, C., Burattin, A., Janiesch, C., Sadiq, S. (eds.) BPM 2023. LNBIP, vol. 490, pp. 319–336. Springer, Cham (2023). https://doi.org/10.1007/978-3-031-41623-1_19
14. Kourani, H., Berti, A., Schuster, D., van der Aalst, W.M.P.: Process modeling with large language models. In: van der Aa, H., Bork, D., Schmidt, R., Sturm, A. (eds.) BPMDS EMMSAD 2024. LNBIP, vol. 511, pp. 229–244. Springer, Cham (2024). https://doi.org/10.1007/978-3-031-61007-3_18
15. Krogstie, J.: Quality of business process models. In: Krogstie, J. (ed.) Quality in Business Process Modeling, pp. 53–102. Springer, Cham (2016). https://doi.org/10.1007/978-3-319-42512-2_2
16. Liu, P., Yuan, W., Jinlan, F., Jiang, Z., Hayashi, H., Neubig, G.: Pre-train, prompt, and predict: a systematic survey of prompting methods in natural language processing. ACM Comput. Surv. **55**(9), 1–35 (2023)
17. Oppenlaender, J.: Prompt engineering for text-based generative art. arXiv preprint arXiv:2204.13988 (2022)
18. Reiz, A., Sandkuhl, K., Smirnov, A., Shilov, N.: Grass-root enterprise modeling: issues and potentials of retrieving models from powerpoint. In: Buchmann, R.A., Karagiannis, D., Kirikova, M. (eds.) PoEM 2018. LNBIP, vol. 335, pp. 55–70. Springer, Cham (2018). https://doi.org/10.1007/978-3-030-02302-7_4

19. Sandkuhl, K., Barn, B., Barat, S.: Neural text generators in enterprise modeling: can ChatGPT be used as proxy domain expert? In: Proceedings ISD 2023 Conference (2023)
20. Sandkuhl, K., et al.: From expert discipline to common practice: a vision and research agenda for extending the reach of enterprise modeling. Bus. Inf. Syst. Eng. **60**, 69–80 (2018)
21. Sandkuhl, K., Stirna, J., Holz, F.: Modeling products and services with enterprise models. In: Grabis, J., Bork, D. (eds.) PoEM 2020. LNBIP, vol. 400, pp. 41–57. Springer, Cham (2020). https://doi.org/10.1007/978-3-030-63479-7_4
22. Sandkuhl, K., Stirna, J., Persson, A., Wißotzki, M.: Enterprise Modeling. Springer, Heidelberg (2014). https://doi.org/10.1007/978-3-662-43725-4
23. Stirna, J., Persson, A.: Enterprise Modeling. Springer, Cham (2018). https://doi.org/10.1007/978-3-319-94857-7
24. Vernadat, F.: Enterprise modelling: research review and outlook. Comput. Ind. **122**, 103265 (2020)
25. Vernadat, F.B.: Enterprise modelling and integration. In: Kosanke, K., Jochem, R., Nell, J.G., Bas, A.O. (eds.) Enterprise Inter- and Intra-Organizational Integration. ITIFIP, vol. 108, pp. 25–33. Springer, Boston (2003). https://doi.org/10.1007/978-0-387-35621-1_4
26. Vidgof, M., Bachhofner, S., Mendling, J.: Large language models for business process management: opportunities and challenges. In: Di Francescomarino, C., Burattin, A., Janiesch, C., Sadiq, S. (eds.) BPM 2023. LNBIP, vol. 490, pp. 107–123. Springer, Cham (2023). https://doi.org/10.1007/978-3-031-41623-1_7
27. White, J., et al.: A prompt pattern catalog to enhance prompt engineering with ChatGPT. arXiv preprint arXiv:2302.11382 (2023)
28. White, J., et al.: A prompt pattern catalog to enhance prompt engineering with ChatGPT (2023). arXiv:2302.11382
29. Wu, T., et al.: PromptChainer: chaining large language model prompts through visual programming. In: CHI Conference on Human Factors in Computing Systems Extended Abstracts, pp. 1–10 (2022)

Investigating the Effectiveness of Feedback-Driven Exercises on Deadlock Detection Skills in Conceptual Modelling

Vlada Mekhryukova[1]((✉)) ⓘ, Felix Cammaerts[2]((✉)) ⓘ, and Monique Snoeck[2]((✉)) ⓘ

[1] Naamsestraat 69, 3000 Leuven, Belgium
mekhryukovavlada@gmail.com
[2] LIRIS, Naamsestraat 69, 3000 Leuven, Belgium
{felix.cammaerts,monique.snoeck}@kuleuven.be

Abstract. Conceptual modelling (CM) has gained prominence in software development, especially with the rise of low-code/no-code development techniques rooted in model-driven development (MDD), which simplify coding complexity and bridge the gap between business and IT. However, these approaches are not without issues, as errors in models can lead to unreliable, error-prone software. One particular challenge for modellers is that of potential deadlock situations which can obstruct the system's components and make it unable to finish the assigned tasks. This paper reports a study that aimed to explore how an Automated Feedback System (AFS) can assist novice modellers in identifying and rectifying possible deadlock situations in conceptual models. The study consisted of a two-group posttest-only experimental design, allowing to assess the impact of an AFS-enhanced approach on novice modellers' ability to identify and correct deadlock-related errors in the context of a CM course. Unfortunately, the experiment did not conclusively demonstrate that the AFS-enhanced approach significantly improves novice modellers' performance. Nonetheless, after performing additional post-hoc statistical tests on the behavioural data collected from the participants during the CM course prior to the experiment, we were able to conclude that this negative result was in part due to an imbalanced experimental group division. Subsequently, we redivided the participants based on the self-reported usage of a model-simulation tool during the experiment, which did allow us to find evidence for one of our hypotheses. We conclude the paper by proposing several improvements to the used experimental design as well as the implications for teaching conceptual modelling based on the already found results.

Keywords: Conceptual modelling · Deadlock detection · Automated feedback

1 Introduction

Nowadays, it is hard to imagine a business operating without IT integration. Conceptual modelling (CM) is widely used in this area in various applications such as requirements analysis, system design, data management, process optimisation, decision support, and enterprise architecture. CM is also more relevant than ever in software development due to the recent emergence of low-code/no-code development techniques that stem from model-driven development (MDD) [1]. These development approaches are used for further abstraction from the complexity of computer coding. Due to the code-agnostic nature of models, using low-code/no-code and MDD principles further helps practitioners bridge the gap between business and IT, as deep technical expertise is not critical for understanding models. These novel development techniques aim to save time and resources while reducing debugging and software maintenance efforts. Gartner [2] predicts that by 2025, 70% of software developed will use low-code/no-code technologies, up from just under 25% in 2020. ReportLinker [3] estimates the Low-Code Development Platform market at $7.61 billion in 2021 and expects it to reach $36.43 billion by 2027.

However, low-code/no-code and MDD are not a panacea for development problems, as it can still suffer from bugs and errors of various nature, just like any code-based development approach. In the case of low-code/no-code and MDD, the errors may originate in the model created by human practitioners due to semantic or syntactic inconsistencies. Such errors inevitably propagate to the code through model-to-code transformations that automatically turn the model into working software with a transformation engine. As a result, error-prone and unreliable software applications are created; deadlocks, a situation in which a software system is unable to proceed, are an example of such errors. According to the CISQ report, only in the USA alone, the losses due to poor software quality reached $2.41 trillion in 2022 [4]. It is therefore essential that CM practitioners deliver high-quality models at the earliest stages of the software development process [5]. However, this field, as crucial for computer science, software engineering, and related disciplines as it is, is a complicated learning task where learners face difficulties in the modelling process [6, 7].

A particularly challenging and common error when modelling a system's behavioural aspects, is that of deadlock situations. Fanti and Zhou [8] define deadlock as a circumstance where a system or a component of it remains indefinitely obstructed and unable to complete its assigned tasks. The problem of deadlocks is well-known in software engineering, however, it may also arise in CM, where deadlocks may occur in the design of interdependent processes, for example.

We believe this issue of deadlock situations in CM should be tackled at the root, namely in education. In fact, Bolloju and Leung [5] suggest that knowing about common errors in CM could help novice practitioners apply error-prevention techniques and deliver higher-quality models. Providing relevant feedback from the very beginning of the training could help to accomplish this task [9]. Moreover, a recent study found that about 40% of students' models which were submitted as homeworks, were not deadlock-free [10].

Consequently, in this research, we investigated the impact of using a set of exercises aimed at teaching students about deadlocks in conceptual modelling. A two-group posttest-only experimental design was used to investigate the effect of the exercises on novice modellers' ability to recognise and correct deadlock-related errors.

As university students have been reported to often be dissatisfied with the traditional feedback they receive from educators, its timeliness and applicability [11], we have opted to integrate our set of exercises in an automated feedback system (AFS) so that the learning process can benefit from personalised and immediate feedback [12].

To find evidence for the effectiveness of the exercises, we conducted an experiment which allowed us to formulate an answer to the following research question: *How effective are feedback-oriented exercises integrated into an AFS for conceptual modelling in teaching novice modelers to detect and eliminate deadlock/livelock-related errors in statechart-based conceptual models?*

The remainder of this paper is structured as follows: in Sect. 2, we provide a technical definition of deadlocks in behavioural CM and discuss existing methods for aiding practitioners in deadlock detection in various tools for different CM languages. Then we motivate our choice for the modelling approach used in our study and discuss its main characteristics. In Sect. 3, we describe our experimental setup and our hypotheses. In Sect. 4 we summarise the obtained data. Section 5 then discusses the results and the limitations of the study, while in Sect. 6 we propose our view of the directions for possible future research.

2 Literature Review

Different CM languages for designing the behavioural aspects of a system can suffer from deadlocks. According to Kersten and Nebel [13], it is very easy to design a deadlock-prone model, yet it is challenging to find the cause of deadlock by manual inspection. That is why there is a high demand for automatic model-checking techniques to aid practitioners in deadlock detection during the model design and testing phases. In the following subsection, we will explore existing methods for automatic deadlock detection for a couple of different CM languages.

Automatic Methods for Deadlock Detection. The Unified Modelling Language (UML) has been steadily gaining popularity ever since it was adopted by the Object Management Group (OMG) as the standard language for "specifying, constructing, visualising, and documenting the artifacts of a software-intensive system" in 1997 [14]. UML can be used for automatic code generation [15, 16]. Initially, the code generators were only able to generate the basic software structure based on class diagrams [17]. However, since the class diagram only represents the structural aspects of a model, generating code from it often does not capture enough of the complexity of the real world [18, 19]. Therefore, software generators based on behavioural models were introduced. The state chart diagram has become the most widely adopted diagram type for generation because it contains states, transitions, events, and actions that can be used to model the behaviour of an object during its lifetime [17, 19].

Yet, erroneous design of behavioural diagrams like statecharts or flowcharts, in turn, can result in deadlocks. Although UML is one of the best-known and well-suited tools for designing general software systems, it lacks formalism and "support for reasoning" [10, 20]. Due to this lack of formal semantics, many existing methods for automatic checking first translate behavioural diagrams into some formal notation and perform an automated assessment afterwards [20]. For example, Schäfer et al. [21] developed a tool called HUGO that helps to verify that a set of interacting state machines can realise the interactions expressed by a UML collaboration diagram. In order to do that, UML state machines are translated into a PROMELA model, while collaboration diagrams are turned into sets of Büchi automata. The HUGO tool was able to identify deadlock situations for the dining philosophers problem in less than one second, while larger UML models can take "well over a minute" to be solved. Extended checking times occur because model states are generated with a linear factor during verification, which is manageable for smaller models but can impact performance for larger ones. Similarly, Lima et al. [20] propose a deadlock and non-determinism verification method that uses the Communicating Sequential Processes (CSP) algebra, capable of checking complex models for deadlocks in around 30 s. However, the verification time generally depends on the number of nodes and edges in the model and the presence of concurrent flows Although their framework is based on formal methods, it does not require practitioners to be familiar with this formal notation. It can be used as a plug-in for the Astah modelling environment.

Another deadlock-prone modelling language is the Business Process Modelling Notation (BPMN), which is often used to capture business processes in an organisation. In BPMN, one can define a deadlock as a situation where "the workflow is stopped in the current position of the path and cannot be accomplished", as well as a special case of deadlock – livelock, which is a situation that "keeps the operating workflow system in an infinite loop" [22]. Signavio, one of the most popular tools for BPMN modelling designed by SAP, uses coloured Petri Nets for process verification and deadlock detection. Mohammed et al. [23] propose a method for detecting structural errors in BPMN (deadlocks, livelocks, multiple terminations in the BPMN process) that maps the BPMN model to a Kripke structure to express the model's behaviour. Awad [24] introduced BPMN-Q, a visual language for querying repositories of business process models. The corresponding querying method can detect deadlocks, among its other useful properties.

In general, it can be said that researchers face two significant difficulties when designing tools to automatically check models on deadlock situations. The first problem is a lack of formalisation that requires models to be transformed into more formal notations [20–24]. The second problem is the state explosion problem, that arises from the need to exhaustively check for all possible state-transition combinations [10, 20, 25, 26].

Henceforth, in the absence of a universal tool for deadlock detection, we believe it could be particularly beneficial to provide students with deadlock-related automated-feedback exercises as to educate novice modellers on the possible sources of deadlocks as well as ways to eliminate them.

Modelling Approach Selection. For a long time, UML has been the language of choice for MDE practitioners [27]. However, over the years, some controversy has appeared regarding using UML. A study by Grossman et al. [28] revealed that the practitioners' opinion on the effectiveness and maturity of the UML language varies greatly. According to Kobryn [29], users often mention the following downsides of UML: "excessive size, gratuitous complexity, imprecise semantics, non-standard implementations, limited customizability, inadequate support for component-based development, and inability to interchange model diagrams". In order to generate code from UML, a very detailed and intricate design is necessary, which means that practitioners must possess vast knowledge of UML [30]. It is also evident that although UML serves as an ideal base for many domain-specific languages, it cannot be deployed as a universal modelling language in all problem domains [31, 32].

MERODE, which stands for model-driven entity relationship object-oriented development, is a domain-specific UML-based modelling approach that was created to develop conceptual models (or domain models) specifically for enterprise information systems [33]. MERODE tackles the problem of excessive complexity and vastness of UML by providing an approach for creating conceptual models precise enough for code generation while keeping the formal grounding of the modelling approach concealed from the practitioners [30, 33]. Unlike UML, the MERODE approach utilises concepts of CSP, the theory of Finite State Automata and Petri Net theory, which allows easy quality checking for internal consistency, completeness and mutual consistency of models.

MERODE is the modelling approach used in the Architecture and Modelling of Management Information Systems (AMMIS) course provided by KU Leuven[1], in which students who match our target group are enrolled. These are the main reasons MERODE approach was chosen in this study.

Overview of the Relevant Features of MERODE. MERODE supports three basic artefacts: a class diagram called an existence-dependency graph (EDG) for structural modelling, a CRUD-matrix object-event table (OET), which represents a collection of business event types for interaction modelling, and finite-state machines (FSM) for behavioural modelling, where a life cycle description of each business object type can be found [30, 33].

MERODE's uniqueness stems from the existence-dependency (ED) concept, a critical feature that facilitates inter-diagram consistency checking among the three schemes – EDG, OET, and FSM [33]. To better understand the ED concept, we must first define a few concepts used in MERODE. Business object types are "classes that represent a set of similar objects in the universe of discourse of an enterprise". Business object types coexist in the universe of discourse (UoD) and are linked through a relationship type called "association". These definitions of class and association align with those found in UML and the concept of entity and relationship in ER models. However, unlike the class diagram in UML, MERODE's EDG requires all the associations to express existence-dependency, hence the name "existence-dependency graph" [34].

Snoeck [33] provides the following informal definition of ED: "If each object of a class P always is associated with minimum one, maximum one and always the same occurrence of class Q, then P is existence dependent on Q". One can compare associations between UML and MERODE to better understand ED. For associations that already express ED – associations that end with a read-only 1..1 multiplicity – one should substitute the UML type of association with a relationship that aligns with the MERODE notation. Associations that do not express ED have to be reified through the introduction of an object type that only exists while the relationship does [33]. Existence dependency has the same semantics as the notion of weak entities in ER-modelling, be it that the identity of the weak entity is not necessarily derived from the one of the strong entity.

Object lifecycles can be used to further illustrate the ED principle. Snoeck and Dedene [35] define the life of an object as "the span between the point in time of its

---

[1] More info on this course can be found at https://onderwijsaanbod.kuleuven.be/syllabi/e/D0I71AE.html.

creation and the point in time it is ended". Due to the principle of ED the life of an existence-dependent object cannot start before its master has been created, and the life of the master object cannot end before the lives of all its existence-dependent objects have been ended. That is called referential integrity [33]. The EDG, therefore, also establishes a certain order of creation and ending of object-type instances. It can be concluded that the EDG is not a pure structural model, as it also serves as a default behavioural model that constrains objects' lifecycles by inducing the rules for the order in which objects must be created and ended.

To further enhance the behavioural aspects of the model, FSMs and OET are used. Through it, one can define states for each object, as well as business events that facilitate the transition between these states [34]. However, business events cannot happen in an arbitrary order [33]. The OET specifies which events create, modify and end objects of certain object types, while FSMs help restrict the occurrence of events through sequence constraints. Business event types also serve as a basis for object interaction. This means that objects in the UoD can influence each other through business events in which they are allowed to participate. The rule that determines the ability of objects to participate in certain events is called the propagation rule and [33] defines it as follows:

"If P is existence dependent on Q, then Q participates in each event in which P participates. In other words, each event marked for the dependent P must also be marked for the master Q."

The principle of interaction between objects also suggests that multiple objects can be affected by an event [33]. Therefore, the model's global behaviour depends on the individual behaviour of interacting objects. The principle of joint participation in events is based on the process algebra of CSP and states that each object defined to participate in any given event must react to it by either accepting or declining it.

Deadlocks in MERODE. When a practitioner fails to recognise inconsistency between the FSMs, OET, and EDG, the model quality can suffer from the introduction of unwanted errors, such as deadlocks, for example. In the MERODE framework, the simultaneous execution of several interconnected FSMs, where at least one FSM is non-default, can lead to deadlocks. Deadlocks occur when these FSMs reach a state where:

1) None of them can advance any further – typical deadlock situation.
2) They are forced to continuously execute a sequence of events in a loop that lacks events that can lead to the ending of the existing objects' lifetime – livelock situation.

We illustrate a deadlock and a livelock with a fabricated example.

Figure 1 shows a model that contains a deadlock and a livelock situation. The sequence of events *crIdolPosition, crCandidateTrainee, crTraining, crEvaluation, promote* will place the CANDIDATETRAINEE object into the *promoted* state, the TRAINING object into the *completed* state, and the IDOLPOSITION object into the *filled* state. Yet none of these objects will be able to move further since there are missing end methods for the ED objects. As an example, in the FSM of IDOLPOSITION, ending the training can only be done in the state *open*, thus preventing the ending of the TRAINING and the IDOLPOSITION object, since the principle of referential integrity doesn't allow to end master objects without ending their ED objects first. This is a typical deadlock situation.

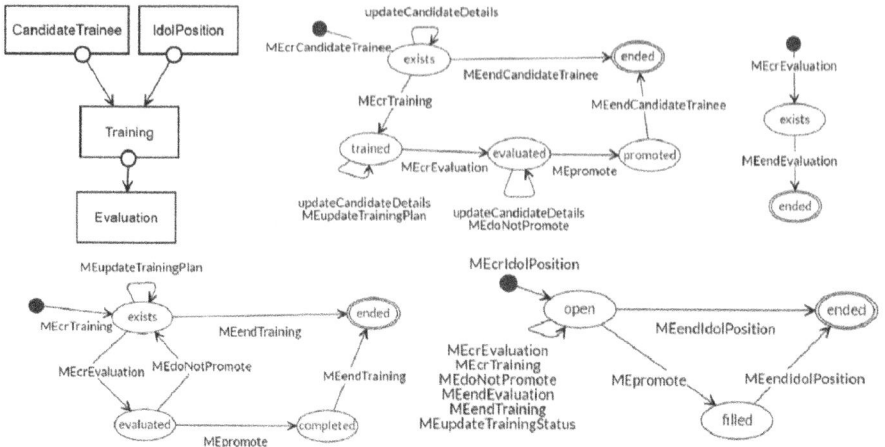

Fig. 1. Model with possible deadlock and livelock situations.

Alternatively, after the sequence of events *crIdolPosition, crCandidateTrainee, crTraining, crEvaluation,* and *doNotPromote,* the CANDIDATETRAINEE object will end up in the *evaluated* state and the TRAINING object will end up in the *exists* state. After this, the CANDIDATETRAINEE object can participate in the event *updateCandidateDetails*, yet no further actions will be possible. This is a typical livelock example.

A manual inspection of MERODE models submitted by students from previous year reveals that there are three main reasons deadlocks may occur in the model:

1) Missing ending methods for ED object types in the masters' FSMs;
2) Missing and/or misplaced modifying methods for ED object types in the masters' FSMs;
3) Backward inaccessible states. These are states from which it is not possible to reach an end state.

Before one can start checking the correctness of a model, one should define the intended behaviour of a model and the properties this model must satisfy [25]. Creating an FSM design methodology that would always yield deadlock-free models is difficult. However, MERODE practitioners can follow some general guidelines to ensure that a model is deadlock-free:

1) Ending methods for ED object types should be placed in a self-loop in the state that precedes the ended state in the FSMs of their master object types.
2) Modifying methods that facilitate the transition of the ED object types through their lifecycle should be present in the FSMs of the master object types.
3) Business rules that cannot be expressed through EDG, OET, and FSM diagrams must be expressed as method constraints using Object Constraint Language (OCL).
4) Models should be thoroughly tested before implementation.

Automatic Deadlock Detection in MERODE. Intelligent tool support was developed to aid modellers, who use MERODE approach: namely a modelling environment MERLIN and a Code Generator [36]. The MERLIN modelling environment helps to create a model in MERODE modelling language. The Code Generator can generate runnable Java code from a MERODE model created using MERLIN, producing a prototyper application for simulation and testing. MERLIN and the Code Generator currently provide no formal automatic deadlock detection functionality. However, MERLIN can check models for internal consistency and provide on-demand feedback that can detect backwards and forward inaccessible states and unused events. This feedback aids practitioners in detecting important sources of some, but not all, potential deadlocks. Additionally, the Code Generator can inform modellers about encountered errors with on-the-fly feedback messages during simulation when an action that is not allowed by the model's constraints is attempted. These messages can be of use when debugging models for potential deadlocks. Both tools are readily available for all students, who take AMMIS course.

Relevance of the Study. To validate the study, we analysed 127 homework assignments submitted by students taking AMMIS course in previous years. We excluded models with default FSMs as these models are proven to be deadlock-free [37], as well as models with severe semantic errors, resulting in 109 usable models. The analysis showed that nearly 70% of those models contained deadlocks, livelocks, or both. The most common cause, found in 92% of erroneous models, was missing end methods for ED object types. The second most common issue, affecting 23% of erroneous models, is inconsistency between FSMs caused by missing/misplaced modifying methods.

3 Method

3.1 General Context

The experiment was conducted during the 2023–2024 academic year during one lab session of the AMMIS course. The course uses the Blackboard (LMS) learning environment for general communication and the edX Edge educational platform, where course material is available. Students can also use the MERLIN modelling tool and the Code Generator. The respondents are master students of various backgrounds enrolled in the AMMIS course; the majority follow either the Master of Business and Information Systems Engineering degree or the Master of Information Management degree. They thus have a non-technical background.

3.2 Experimental Setup

The study employed a two-group posttest-only experimental design to investigate the impact of feedback-oriented exercises (independent variable) on the ability to identify and rectify deadlocks and livelocks in conceptual modelling using the MERODE approach (dependent variable).

The experiment was set up during a lab session. Lab attendance is voluntary, and the moment was chosen so that students were sufficiently familiar with behavioural modelling. Once randomly assigned to either test group A or control group B, participants received detailed guidelines on the experiment and a brief introduction to deadlocks in conceptual modelling. Following this introduction, group A was offered a set of exercises focusing on recognising and rectifying deadlock situations. These exercises are reminiscent of the exercises available in the course material and introduce no new concepts apart from deadlocks. Subsequently, group A proceeded to a testing phase where they were offered a pre-designed Scooter Rental[2] model in which we fault-seeded deadlocks and livelocks. Students were first asked to analyse the case by answering ten true or false questions and filling out one open-question. This part of the test measures students' ability to detect potential deadlock-related problems in the model. The second part of the test offers students a chance to rectify previously identified problems.

In contrast, after the initial introduction, control group B was immediately offered the Scooter Rental model without prior exposure to the preparatory exercises. To mitigate potential learning disadvantage to participants in group B, they are presented with a set of preparatory exercises after completing the Scoter Rental case. Additionally, to explore the impact of automated feedback on their learning progress, students in the control group can review the models they submitted in the last part of the Scooter Rental exercise. This review aimed to identify and address any potential deadlocks they might have missed during the initial phase of the experiment. Additionally, during the testing phase of the experiment, students in both groups were encouraged to use the MERLIN tool and the Code Generator. Their performance in identifying and rectifying deadlock-related issues (dependent variable) is to be analysed to test the proposed hypotheses.

After completing the preparatory exercises and the Scoter Rental case, all students were asked to fill in a post-experimental survey that ascertains their previous experience with conceptual modelling, deadlocks, the tools used during the experiment, and the perceived usefulness of the exercises with respect to the AMMIS course using a Likert scale. Due to institutional guidelines and ethical considerations, demographic data was not collected to safeguard participants' anonymity and rights. Figure 2 gives a schematic overview of the experimental setup. With this experimental design, we aim to test the following hypotheses:

Hypothesis 1: Providing feedback-oriented exercises that focus on deadlock detection and elimination improve students' ability to detect possible deadlock situations in conceptual models.

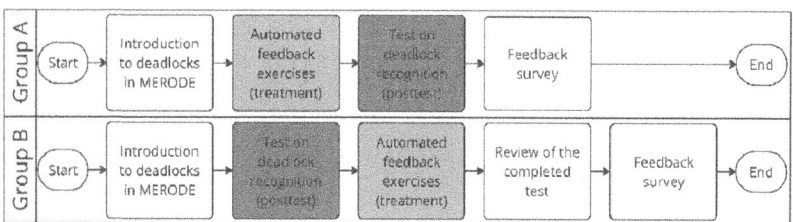

Fig. 2. Experimental setup outline.

---

[2] The full model can be found on https://merode.econ.kuleuven.be/cases/index.asp.

Hypothesis 2: Providing feedback-oriented exercises that focus on deadlock detection and elimination improve students' ability to rectify possible deadlock situations in conceptual models.

Validation of the Experimental Setup. Two pilot experiments were conducted to validate the setup. The goal was to gather qualitative feedback and determine an appropriate timeframe for each part of the experiment. Two former students who took the AMMIS course in the previous academic year participated, providing feedback on the setup and content. Feedback from the first pilot revealed mixed opinions, highlighting errors and shortcomings in the setup. After incorporating this feedback with input from all co-authors, a second pilot experiment was conducted with one participant. Their feedback was used to refine the setup further.

4 Results

4.1 Data Analysis

In total, 65 participants took part in the experiment. However, not all the participants completed each part of the experiment. We recorded 40 participants who provided their group numbers correctly in the post-experimental questionnaire. One of the participants in group A did not complete the treatment part of the experiment and was therefore excluded from the final data set. Consequently, for hypothesis testing we decided to move forward with 39 participants, with 19 belonging to group A and 20 belonging to group B. The data recorded for the remaining participants who did not mention their group is still used for qualitative insights. For finding evidence for H1, we looked at the answers for the 11 questions that focused on deadlock detection. For this part, we got 18 responses from group A and 20 responses from group B. For H2, we analysed the received responses concerning the rectification of deadlocks in the Scooter model. For this part, we received 14 responses from group A and 15 responses from group B. As for the review of the completed post-test that participants of group B were offered, we have only received two reviewed models. Statistical analysis of such a small data set is not possible, so we omitted these submissions.

The Scooter Rental case was designed with three deadlocks, two typical deadlocks and one livelock. Participants could get one point for each true or false question, while a fully correct open question and submitted model could each yield three points. One point was granted for each found (or corrected) deadlock. However, some deadlocks could be partially found (or corrected), resulting in half a point.

The true or false questions were graded automatically. At the same time, grading open questions and the submitted models required manual effort. The first few responses were graded by all co-authors. The rest of the responses were divided among the co-authors and then cross-checked. If assigned grades differed, we discussed the response together to determine the correct grade.

Hypothesis 1. Table 1 presents the basic statistics for submitted responses to the questions on deadlock detection for groups A and B.

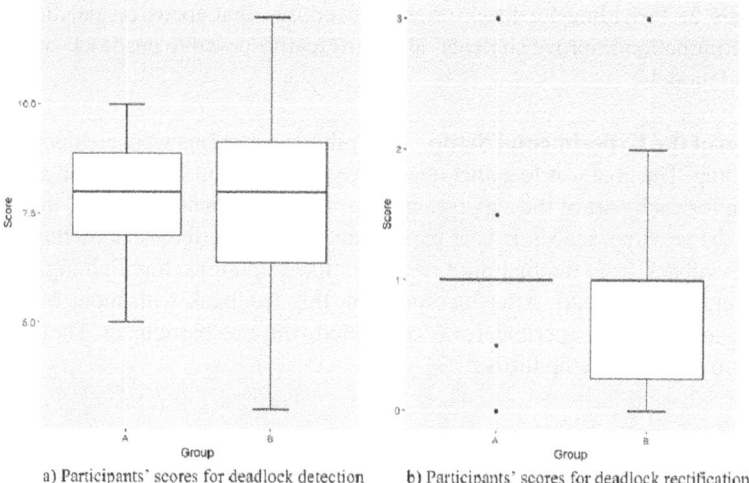

a) Participants' scores for deadlock detection   b) Participants' scores for deadlock rectification

Fig. 3. Participants' scores boxplots.

Table 1. A statistical summary for questions about deadlock detection.

Group	n	Mean	sd	Median	Min	Max
A	18	7.92	1.51	8	5	10
B	20	7.82	2.23	8	3	12

Figure 3a illustrates the distribution of participants' scores for the first 11 questions in the Scooter Rental case, which shows how well group A and group B respondents performed in deadlock detection. Group B has a wider spread and a longer interquartile range compared to group A, suggesting a more dispersed distribution.

To test for normality, we conducted a Shapiro-Wilk test. Both group A ($p = 0.25$) and group B ($p = 0.54$) are normally distributed. Then, we conducted a Welch Two-Sample t-test, which yielded a p-value equal to 0.88. We, therefore, are unable to confidently conclude that the mean grades of groups A and B in the first 11 questions of the Scooter Rental case are different.

Hypothesis 2. Table 2 presents the basic statistics for submitted responses to the questions on deadlock rectification for groups A and B, and Fig. 3b depicts the distribution of scores for both groups.

The box plots show that group B is more dispersed than group A. For group B, 50% of the data points are spread between 0.25 and 1. Group A's box plot has the most data points lying at 1. This boxplot has no whiskers, while the first and the third quartile coincide with the median. It is interesting to note that in each group, there is only one respondent who successfully rectified all three deadlocks.

An initial Shapiro-Wilk test was performed on the data from groups A and B to investigate the normality. In this case, both group A ($p < 0.01$) and group B ($p < 0.01$)

Table 2. A statistical summary for question about deadlock rectification.

Group	n	Mean	sd	Median	Min	Max
A	14	1.04	0.72	1	0	3
B	15	0.867	0.812	1	0	3

are not normally distributed. Therefore, we performed a non-parametric Wilcoxon rank-sum test for the second null hypothesis. The p-value was found to be 0.34. We are unable to reject the null hypothesis and therefore conclude that the mean grades of groups A and B for deadlock rectification exercise do not differ significantly.

Post-hoc Analytics. As to our surprise we did not find any evidence for either of our hypotheses. We also analysed the distribution of the students based on their prior performance in the course. More specifically, we looked at the usage logs of the students when simulating models with the Code Generator during the lab sessions prior to the experiment. Herein, we exhaustively logged all the actions the students have performed on the simulated models. These actions were labelled based on their intended behaviour, such as checking for allowed or disallowed scenarios. A Welch Two Sample t-test shows that the students in group B performed significantly ($p = 0.03$) more actions on the simulated models. Specifically, for positive testing, in which a user checks that a scenario which should be allowed is indeed allowed in the model, a significant difference ($p < 0.01$) was found favouring group B. This shows that the groups were not fairly distributed, meaning that group B consisted of students already performing better in the course prior to the experiment.

The Confounding Factor. Based on this insight, we redistributed the students based on their self-reported usage of the Code Generator for the experiment. Herein, participants using the Code Generator to solve the Scooter Rental case, regardless of group, identified more deadlocks than those who didn't ($p < 0.01$ according to the Wilcoxon rank-sum test) (Table 3).

Table 3. A statistical summary of scores for open-ended test question based on self-reported use of the Code Generator.

Code Generator	n	Mean	sd	Median	Min	Max
Used	20	0.63	0.54	0.5	0	2
Not used	15	0.13	0.40	0	0	1.5

Simultaneously, the analysis of submitted models revealed no significant difference in the number of rectified deadlocks between those students who used the Code Generator and those who did not ($p = 0.93$ according to the Wilcoxon rank-sum test) (Table 4).

Perceived Usefulness. The feedback survey also included several questions that asked participants to evaluate the usefulness of the experiment concerning their studies and the

Table 4. A statistical summary of scores for question about deadlock rectification based on self-reported use of the Code Generator.

Code Generator	n	Mean	sd	Median	Min	Max
Used	20	0.68	0.80	0.75	0	3
Not used	15	0.57	0.59	0.5	0	1.5

AMMIS course. The analysis shows that 75.8% of participants who filled in the survey find the Scooter Rental case at least "somewhat useful", and 82.4% of participants found the multiple-choice questions on edX at least "somewhat useful".

5 Discussion and Limitations

Although we observe a slightly more consistent performance of participants in group A, we do not have sufficient evidence to reject the null hypothesis for H1 nor H2. We believe this to be due to an unequal group division, as evidenced by the significant difference of the participants in behaviour during model simulation prior to the experiment. More specifically, group B had already used the Code Generator more extensively to test their models than participants in group A. In fact, Sedrakyan et al. [38] found that feedback-inclusive rapid prototyping positively affects learners' understanding of interacting statecharts. Therefore, we believe that participants in group B generally had a better understanding of FSM interactions prior to the experiment, which could explain the similar performance between the groups. In future research this issue can be addressed by introducing a pretest in the experiment which would allow us to more accurately measure such group imbalances.

Nonetheless, after redividing the participants based on their self-reported usage of the Code Generator, we found that the participants who used the Code Generator detected more deadlocks than those who relied solely on visual inspection of erroneous model. However, the Code Generator did not improve participants' ability to rectify the detected deadlocks. This can be due to the fact that the Code Generator mostly aids practitioners in the task of locating possible deadlock-related errors via model simulation, yet the usefulness of model simulation remains limited in the more complex task of correcting the deadlocks. This finding can become a basis for a future study on the effects of feedback-inclusive prototyping on deadlock detection among novice modellers.

The collected data allows us to draw some additional conclusions. First, we conducted an analysis of the open-ended questions and submitted models separately to gather qualitative feedback. Our examination revealed that grasping the concept of deadlock was a common difficulty among students. Specifically, some students confused the inability to end instances of object types from all states these object types have with a deadlock situation. This misunderstanding occurred equally often in groups A and B, suggesting that it cannot be solely attributed to the wording of the tasks for treatment or post-test. Moreover, deadlock is often confused with the inability to follow the path participants may perceive as "happy".

Additionally, most participants found the exercises and posttest practice case at least "somewhat useful" in the context of the AMMIS course. This further evidences that it is rather due to an imbalanced group distribution during the experiment, than due to the exercises being ineffective that we did not find any evidence for our initial hypotheses. This makes us hopeful that introducing feedback-augmented exercises will have a long-term positive impact on students' understanding of deadlocks.

Although the experiment was conducted in an educational setting using the MERODE method, we believe the findings have broader applicability. Educators in the field of CM can benefit from incorporating rapid prototyping tools tailored to their chosen CM language. As discussed, it is beneficial to provide novice modelers with comprehensive explanations of deadlock-related errors and to reinforce their understanding through practical exercises. When designing curricula, educators can utilize Bloom's Taxonomy framework, where lower levels (Remembering, Understanding) focus on the theoretical study of deadlocks, and higher levels (Applying, Analysing, Evaluating) emphasize practical experience, all while keeping in mind that the ultimate goal is to achieve the highest level (Creating), where novice modelers can develop deadlock-free models independently.

Threats to Validity. The two-group posttest-only design inherently presents several threats to validity. The lack of a pretest makes it difficult to assess potential selection bias in the random assignment to groups A and B. To address this, participants completed a post-experiment survey measuring their prior familiarity with CM and deadlocks using a Likert scale (1 = no familiarity, 5 = complete familiarity). A Wilcoxon rank-sum test showed no significant differences in familiarity between groups ($p = 0.10$ and $p = 0.37$). However, as described in a previous section, post-hoc analysis indicated that group B participants were already performing better prior to the experiment, making the test results less reliable.

Attrition is another concern, as participation and full completion could not be enforced in an educational setting. To encourage participation, students were offered an opportunity to review correct answers after completing the final survey.

Limitations. First of all, a non-negligible portion of participants had incomplete data, with about one-third of entries unassignable to groups A or B, possibly due to ambiguous instructions. Combined with the limited sample size this can be a possible reason for a lack of significance. Secondly, during the experiment, some students struggled to understand the requirements due to unfamiliarity with concepts like deadlocks and ambiguous instructions, particularly in the feedback-oriented exercises on the edX platform. And lastly, the manual grading of open questions and model submissions introduces a risk of human error, making the evaluation potentially imprecise, highlighting the need for appropriate automated feedback.

To improve the experimental design, we recommend conducting a more extensive pilot test with a diverse group of participants varying in background and CM experience. Additionally, reevaluating the instructions to eliminate ambiguity and developing a more detailed evaluation system that better reflects the complexity of deadlock situations while remaining comprehensible to participants is advised. Adjusting the workload would also enhance the feasibility of replicating the experiment.

6 Conclusion

This paper evaluates the impact of feedback-oriented exercises on learners' ability to identify and resolve deadlock situations in conceptual modelling, employing the MERODE approach. AFS aim to enhance learner engagement and provide timely feedback. To measure the effect of an AFS concerning deadlocks in CM on learners' understanding of deadlocks in CM, we performed a two-group posttest-only experiment, where master students of KU Leuven, taking a course in conceptual modelling for enterprise informational systems, participated. Both groups were given a treatment of multiple-choice exercises with automatic feedback and a posttest that measured their ability to detect and rectify deadlocks.

Unfortunately, the collected experimental data did not yield statistical evidence to confirm that feedback-enhanced exercises positively influence the learners' ability to detect or rectify deadlocks. We believe this to be due to an unfair group division, as we were able to confirm with post-hoc analytics.

Nonetheless, the group where participants received the treatment before the posttest showed less dispersed results than the group that performed the posttest without prior treatment, meaning that the overall level of performance was slightly higher for the first group.

Furthermore, we found that participants who used a feedback-inclusive prototyping tool complementary to MERODE during the experiment performed significantly better in deadlock detection than participants who did not.

Amongst the experiment's limitations, we can highlight the problem of incomplete data, suboptimal experimental design, and human error. While the results of the experiment expose the difficulties of training students' understanding and resolution of deadlocks, the participants believe introducing the exercises and test case was useful to their educational journey in conceptual modelling.

Considering these findings, future research could focus on replicating the experiment while addressing identified limitations. Additionally, exploring the effects of data-driven AFS and on-demand semantic checks integrated into modelling tools could offer valuable insights beyond the scope of this study.

References

1. DiCesare, M.: Model-driven development: the foundation of low-code. Mendix. https://www.mendix.com/blog/low-code-principle-1-model-driven-development/. Accessed 11 Apr 2024
2. Gartner Says Cloud Will Be the Centerpiece of New Digital Experiences, Gartner. https://www.gartner.com/en/newsroom/press-releases/2021-11-10-gartner-says-cloud-will-be-the-centerpiece-of-new-digital-experiences. Accessed 11 Apr 2024
3. Low Code Development Platform Market - Growth, Trends, COVID-19 Impact, and Forecasts (2022–2027), GlobeNewswire News Room. https://www.globenewswire.com/news-release/2022/03/18/2405899/0/en/Low-Code-Development-Platform-Market-Growth-Trends-COVID-19-Impact-and-Forecasts-2022-2027.html. Accessed 11 Apr 2024
4. Krasner, H.: Cost of poor software quality in the U.S.: a 2022 report, CISQ (2022). https://www.it-cisq.org/the-cost-of-poor-quality-software-in-the-us-a-2022-report/. Accessed 11 Apr 2024

5. Bolloju, N., Leung, F.S.K.: Assisting novice analysts in developing quality conceptual models with UML. Commun. ACM **49**(7), 108–112 (2006). https://doi.org/10.1145/1139922.1139926
6. Robinson, S.: Conceptual modelling for simulation part I: definition and requirements. J. Oper. Res. Soc. **59**(3) (2008). Art. no. 3. https://doi.org/10.1057/palgrave.jors.2602368
7. Rosenthal, K., Strecker, S., Snoeck, M.: Modeling difficulties in creating conceptual data models. Softw. Syst. Model. **22**(3), 1005–1030 (2022). https://doi.org/10.1007/s10270-022-01051-8
8. Fanti, M.P., Zhou, M.: Deadlock control methods in automated manufacturing systems. IEEE Trans. Syst. Man Cybern. Part A Syst. Hum.Part A: Syst. Hum. **34**(1), 5–22 (2004). https://doi.org/10.1109/TSMCA.2003.820590
9. Vemuri, P., Poelmans, S., Compagnucci, I., Snoeck, M.: Using formative assessment and feedback to train novice modelers in business process modelling. In: 2023 ACM/IEEE International Conference on Model Driven Engineering Languages and Systems Companion (MODELS-C), pp. 130–137 (2023). https://doi.org/10.1109/MODELS-C59198.2023.00037
10. Cammaerts, F., Snoeck, M.: Assessing the value of incomplete deadlock verification in model-driven engineering. In: CEUR Workshop Proceedings (2023). https://ceur-ws.org/Vol-3618/. https://lirias.kuleuven.be/4142646. Accessed 26 Feb 2024
11. Henderson, M., Ajjawi, R., Boud, D., Molloy, E.: Why focus on feedback impact? In: Henderson, M., Ajjawi, R., Boud, D., Molloy, E. (eds.) The Impact of Feedback in Higher Education: Improving Assessment Outcomes for Learners, pp. 3–14. Springer, Cham (2019). https://doi.org/10.1007/978-3-030-25112-3_1
12. Deeva, G., Bogdanova, D., Serral, E., Snoeck, M., De Weerdt, J.: A review of automated feedback systems for learners: classification framework, challenges and opportunities. Comput. Educ. **162**, 104094 (2021). https://doi.org/10.1016/j.compedu.2020.104094
13. Kersten, M., Nebel, W.: On detecting deadlocks in large UML models: based on an expressive subset. In: Kleinjohann, B., Gao, G.R., Kopetz, H., Kleinjohann, L., Rettberg, A. (eds.) DIPES 2004. IFIPAICT, vol. 150, pp. 11–20. Springer, Boston (2004). https://doi.org/10.1007/1-4020-8149-9_2
14. About the Unified Modeling Language Specification Version 1.1. https://www.omg.org/spec/UML/1.1#document-metadata. Accessed 06 Dec 2023
15. UML Lab, Yatta. https://www.uml-lab.com/. Accessed 06 Dec 2023
16. UML/Code Generation Software, Visual Paradigm. https://www.visual-paradigm.com/features/code-engineering-tools/. Accessed 06 Dec 2023
17. Viswanathan, S.E., Samuel, P.: Automatic code generation using unified modeling language activity and sequence models. IET softw. **10**(6) (2016). Art. no. 6. https://doi.org/10.1049/iet-sen.2015.0138
18. Chu, M.-H., Dao, A.-H.: Automated code generation from use cases and the domain model. Presented at The Seventh International Conference on Research in Intelligent and Computing in Engineering, pp. 75–81 (2022). https://doi.org/10.15439/2022R27
19. Niaz, I.A.: Automatic code generation from UML class and statechart diagrams (2005)
20. Lima, L., Tavares, A., Nogueira, S.C.: A framework for verifying deadlock and nondeterminism in UML activity diagrams based on CSP. Sci. Comput. Program. **197**, 102497 (2020). https://doi.org/10.1016/j.scico.2020.102497
21. Schäfer, T., Knapp, A., Merz, S.: Model checking UML state machines and collaborations. Electron. Notes Theor. Comput. Sci. **55**(3), 357–369 (2001). https://doi.org/10.1016/S1571-0661(04)00262-2
22. Suchenia, A., Wiśniewski, P., Ligęza, A.: Overview of verification tools for business process models, pp. 295–302 (2017). https://doi.org/10.15439/2017F308

23. Mohammed, O., Ahmad, A., Basson, H.: Detecting structural errors in BPMN process models. In: International Multitopic Conference (2012). https://doi.org/10.1109/INMIC.2012.6511490
24. Awad, A.: BPMN-Q: a language to query business processes, pp. 115–128 (2007)
25. Clarke, E.M., Klieber, W., Nováček, M., Zuliani, P.: Model checking and the state explosion problem. In: Meyer, B., Nordio, M. (eds.) LASER 2011. LNCS, vol. 7682, pp. 1–30. Springer, Heidelberg (2012). https://doi.org/10.1007/978-3-642-35746-6_1
26. Esparza, J., Heljanko, K.: Unfoldings. Monographs in Theoretical Computer Science An EATCS Series, Springer, Heidelberg (2008). https://doi.org/10.1007/978-3-540-77426-6
27. Verbruggen, C., Snoeck, M.: Practitioners' experiences with model-driven engineering: a meta-review. Softw. Syst. Model. **22**(1), 111–129 (2023). https://doi.org/10.1007/s10270-022-01020-1
28. Grossman, M., Aronson, J.E., McCarthy, R.V.: Does UML make the grade? Insights from the software development community. Inf. Softw. Technol. **47**(6) (2005). Art. no. 6. https://doi.org/10.1016/j.infsof.2004.09.005
29. Kobryn, C.: Will UML 2.0 be agile or awkward? **45**(1) (2002). Art. no. 1. https://doi-org.kuleuven.e-bronnen.be/10.1145/502269.502306
30. Snoeck, M.: MERLIN: an intelligent tool for creating domain models. In: Dalpiaz, F., Zdravkovic, J., Loucopoulos, P. (eds.) RCIS 2020. LNBIP, vol. 385, pp. 549–555. Springer, Cham (2020). https://doi.org/10.1007/978-3-030-50316-1_37
31. Engels, G., Heckel, R., Sauer, S.: UML—a universal modeling language? In: Nielsen, M., Simpson, D. (eds.) ICATPN 2000. LNCS, vol. 1825, pp. 24–38. Springer, Heidelberg (2000). https://doi.org/10.1007/3-540-44988-4_3
32. Gray, J., Rumpe, B.: UML customization versus domain-specific languages. Softw. Syst. Model. **17**(3), 713–714 (2018). https://doi.org/10.1007/s10270-018-0685-2
33. Snoeck, M.: Enterprise Information Systems Engineering: The MERODE Approach. The Enterprise Engineering Series. Springer, Cham (2014). https://doi.org/10.1007/978-3-319-10145-3
34. Snoeck, M., Wautelet, Y.: Agile MERODE: a model-driven software engineering method for user-centric and value-based development. Softw. Syst. Model. **21**(4), 1469–1494 (2022). https://doi.org/10.1007/s10270-022-01015-y
35. Snoeck, M., Dedene, G.: Existence dependency: the key to semantic integrity between structural and behavioral aspects of object types. IEEE Trans. Softw. Eng. **24**(4), 233–251 (1998). https://doi.org/10.1109/32.677182
36. MERODE Enterprise Modelling Tools. https://merode.econ.kuleuven.be/Tools.html. Accessed 05 Dec 2023
37. Snoeck, M., Dedene, G.: Formal deadlock elimination in an object oriented conceptual schema. Data Knowl. Eng. **15**(1), 1–30 (1995). https://doi.org/10.1016/0169-023X(94)00031-9
38. Sedrakyan, G., Poelmans, S., Snoeck, M.: Assessing the influence of feedback-inclusive rapid prototyping on understanding the semantics of parallel UML statecharts by novice modellers. Inf. Softw. Technol. **82**, 159–172 (2017). https://doi.org/10.1016/j.infsof.2016.11.001

Knowledge Graphs as a Scholarly Data Fabric: A Data Silo Transformation Pipeline with Visualization Semantics

Robert Andrei Buchmann and Ana-Maria Ghiran(✉)

Faculty of Economics and Business Administration, Babeș-Bolyai University, Str. T. Mihali 58-60, 400591 Cluj-Napoca, Romania
{robert.buchmann,anamaria.ghiran}@econ.ubbcluj.ro

Abstract. The paper reports on a Knowledge Graph (KG)-based Data Fabric project in the authors' host institution. The project aimed to lift legacy relational databases that are spread around the institution to an enterprise-grade Ontotext GraphDB server and to provide a visual data navigator to decision-makers. The visualization takes a particular technical approach to be explained in this paper. Complex SPARQL queries are devised not only to retrieve the data to be visualized, but also to gradually transform legacy data towards visual graph structures tailored for diagrammatic navigation through a contextual sliding window. This raises a specific requirement for graph transformations that are valuable as reusable patterns that are more comprehensible compared to the common visual tools we encountered for KG navigation. Therefore the work belongs to the artifact-building genre advocated by Design Science and suggests the importance of a dedicated research direction that should account for the distinction between the semantics of what is stored in the KG and the semantics of visual constructs, of how things are graphically presented – with the help of metadata labelled here as "visualization semantics", a viewpoint that is well established in the field of diagramming but ignored for a long time by the visual interfaces emerging from the KG community.

Keywords: Data fabric · RDF · scholarly data · graph transformations · visualization semantics

1 Introduction

This paper reports on an institutional project that applies semantic lifting to a university's legacy data sources in order to create a scholarly Data Fabric [1]. Knowledge graphs are employed as an integration strategy over a number of isolated data silos containing didactic, research and administrative information. The paper presents a branching out of an earlier report of the same project available in [2]; here with focus on technical aspects pertaining to the enduser-facing graph navigation experience that evolved over multiple Design Science iterations to improve navigability and data findability across the newly connected data silos.

The institution developed over the years several internal decoupled systems running on separated data silos. This legacy lack of connectivity was compensated by a costly synchronization mechanism across numerous databases, that must be executed every 24 h consequently imposing some delays on business processes that need to access the synched information. Data footprints of various entities become difficult to delimit, and occasionally referential errors arise from manual edits across multiple systems dealing with the same entities – e.g. a professor's data, with some overlapping fields and some distinct ones, shows up in all systems for different purposes: course management, administrative management, accounting of the research outputs. Evidently, analytics are drastically hindered and typically requires recollecting the data to be analyzed from stakeholders who already provided that data for prior reporting cases.

By adopting an enterprise grade semantic graph database license (Ontotext GraphBD[1]) our Design Science research team had the opportunity to experiment with building an enterprise-scale data fabric that brough a certain level of data hygiene and structural unification. RDF graph databases were first adopted to lift the legacy data silos to a new integrative schema, then a visualization layer was added. This was intended to be generic enough to enable a contextual sliding window along nodes in the graph, with a searchbox-based entry point exploiting a Lucene index over the graphs and also a path finding functionality between any two searched entities found with the help of the search index.

The project also aims to support graph analytics and graph data retrieval by power users familiar with the RDF technology. For this, it also leverages public identifiers (DOIs, ORCIDs) to support data linking with external graphs already published by open science and scholarly stakeholders.

The university's earlier IT strategy was based on building small scale digitalization projects that responded to stakeholder pressing needs, the pandemic crisis etc. An enterprise architecting top-down approach has been missing and this reflected in cumulative pain points over time, especially pertaining to data integration.

The weak integration capabilities mean that the same data is either synchronized by scheduled mechanisms (imposing delays on business process level) or replicated across different enterprise functions for local reporting purposes. Same individuals would get redundant local identifiers, lacking any documented mapping, relying on improvised matching and requiring improvised solutions of manual data cleaning for some cross-function reports, even improvised namespacing rules (e.g. person X from department Y).

The legacy compromise solution for synchronization across data silos (based on relational databases) was based on Linked Servers [3], using stored procedures scheduled across several DB servers from different vendors and of different performance capabilities. A data service architecture started to develop around this, but only to replicate the data fragmentation to functionality level, and to ensure some modularization in order to facilitate isolation of future incidents or bugs caused by fragmentation.

The knowledge graph approach aimed to mitigate such issues and to facilitate more comprehensive data analytics, partly described in our previous publication [2]. This report focuses on the so-called "visualization semantics", visual graph patterns that

---

[1] https://www.ontotext.com/products/graphdb/.

required SPARQL graph rewriting to map the visualization-agnostic knowledge graph on visualization patterns that were handled by graph visualization libraries, therefore needed similar graph structures but arranged differently than those actually stored. For example, an arrow relating an instance to the number and type of courses being taught is useful as a visualization pattern, but would not make sense to be explicitly stored in a knowledge graph, where instance-to-instance edges would be available regardless of the choice of visual aggregation.

The remainder of the paper is structured as follows: after Sect. 2 will comment on related works, Sect. 3 will present the project context and Sect. 4 will decompose the data engineering pipeline in concrete steps and exemplary situations. Brief conclusions are drawn in Sect. 5.

2 Related Works

The Dagstuhl Seminar indicated recently [4] that Scholarly Knowledge Graphs are an important preoccupation of the Semantic Web community, already instantiated by a number of tools developed experimentally in what can be generally considered design science contexts, as they propose artifacts for a particular usage context. Linked Open-Scholar [5] was introduced for content management systems; the Microsoft Academic Knowledge Graph [6] shared open information about a large corpus of scientific publications; the work of [7] use an automated pipeline to extract paper and patent descriptions from a variety of public sources.

Knowledge Graphs are a well-known approach to Data Fabrics [8]. Universities use heterogeneous and distributed data sources that provide an ideal case to Data Fabrics, to achieve master data management that can integrate scholarly teaching, research and administrative information. Transparency requirements also incentivize universities to share expertise, results or skill profiles in a seamlessly navigable way that does not burden the user with understanding how the underlying data is spread across repositories, even if that data is already available in graph structures. There are inherent differences – stemming from navigability and findability requirements – between how graphs are stored and how they should be displayed, hence our current focus on what we labelled here as "visualization semantics".

Elsevier's Pure platform [9] has been adopted for such a purpose by numerous universities, e.g. Monash University [10], connecting research output to employee networks in a visually navigable way. VIVO [11, 12] is an ontology for academic activity aiming to support the browsing of available scholarly expertise. Springer Nature's SciGraph [13] used to allow visual navigation of research items but has been discontinued. Semantic-Scholar [14], applies AI techniques to establish authorship networks. VOSViewer [15], CiteSpace [16] and Connected Papers [17] aim to facilitate bibliographic navigation. Such systems occasionally provided a visual graph navigation mechanism, however typically a rudimentary one showing direct instance-to-instance connections around the node under focus.

Browser-based interfaces of public knowledge graphs like DBPedia[2] or Wikidata[3] could also benefit, but they traditionally preferred a tabular Webpage with clickable URIs triggering simple dereferencing queries to move along the graph paths. This has been the navigation pattern of choice for multiple works focusing on resource dereferencing, including past contributions to business process navigation based on semantic process steppers [18, 19].

The problem becomes increasingly relevant, as commercial vendors are placing more focus on inducing a visual perception of knowledge graph fragments or navigation experience – this has become evident during recent years in products such as Stardog [20], Ontotext GraphDB [21] or Metaphacts [22]. Our approach aimed to be vendor agnostic as an independent visualization layer that does not have to give its users access to the actual knowledge graph server and can be a Webpage integrated with any data-driven enterprise system.

3 Project Context

The work follows a Design Science approach for the construction of an experimental artifact through non-traditional engineering methods, in response to an organizational problem – in this case, one regarding institutional data management for a semantically integrated vision, with the help of semantic graph database technologies. This project pursued internal data management goals covering a diversity of entities relevant to academic management - including research output (but not for bibliometric analytics which are supported by widely available tools). The Data Fabric developed in this project focuses on relationship navigation and how this can be offered as a visual experience to knowledge graph users.

The developed application addressed use cases shown in Fig. 1. The Data admin role is responsible for enriching the application over time, which is amenable to schema changes without changing the source code, enabled by navigation patterns derived from the relationship types provided by OWL.

The core functionality that we focus on in this paper is the sliding window for navigating interconnected data and entities. The window centers on a node and displays its connections either radially or in a tabular form, according to patterns to be produced by graph transformation rules that prepare the stored graph structure into visualization annotations acting as semantic hints for the front-end rendering components. The current report does not touch on the possibility of interacting with the knowledge graph via natural language integration, as the project was developed just before GraphDB incorporated integration with Large Language Models – therefore such augmentations remain in the scope of subsequent iterations.

The software development process was an exploratory one, testing multiple alternatives in terms of available frameworks, libraries and their integrability. The implementation architecture is depicted in Fig. 2.

---

[2] https://www.dbpedia.org/.
[3] https://www.wikidata.org/.

The front-end component used as ingredients: UI components from the Kendo components package[4]; VisJS for the graph visualization[5]; Angular as the general front-end development framework.

The back-end component used as ingredients: DotNetRDF for communicating with GraphDB and processing graphs in the back end[6]; Kephas adapted to serve a graph-based application as an aspect-oriented framework[7]; .NET as the general back-end development framework.

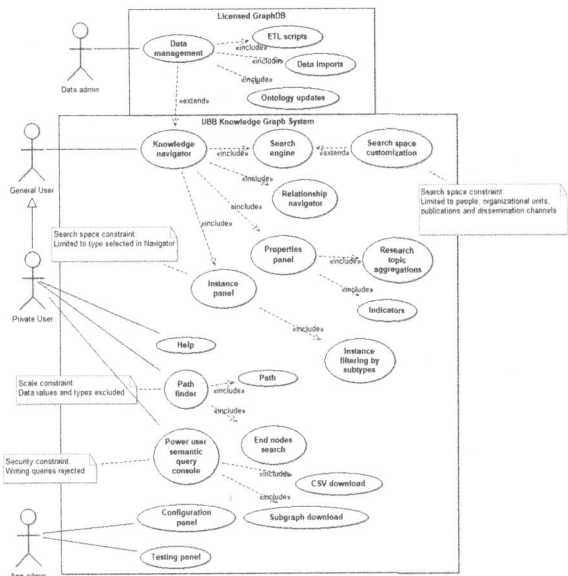

Fig. 1. Project context: the use cases

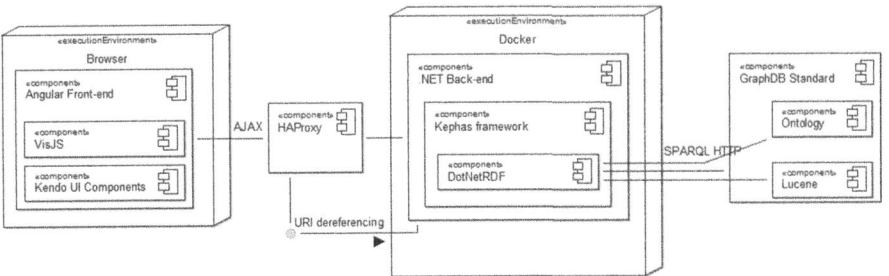

Fig. 2. Project context: the architectural ingredients

---

[4] https://www.telerik.com/kendo-ui.
[5] https://github.com/visjs.
[6] https://dotnetrdf.org/.
[7] https://github.com/kephas-software/kephas.

The data hosting component, where we focus this paper's discussion, was based on a licensed GraphDB server from Ontotext[8] with the Lucene search engine grafted over the graph database[9]; the RDF and OWL standards for graph modelling, SPARQL for graph querying and reasoning; Ontorefine[10] for data cleaning, URI generation, uniformization and general semantic lifting of tabular data sources.

Data procurement and preparation was achieved through a flow of data cleaning, integration, table-graph mapping and graph transformations - both structural and terminological, in order to prepare graph fragments for a visualization based on VisJS. Some of these steps were performed offline to persist in the graph database information as clean as possible, and some of the transformations take place at run-time to facilitate a "knowledge browsing" experience improved over the basic dereferencing pages we found in public systems such as Springer SciGraph or DBPedia.

After some initial attempts with the D2RQ[11] semantic lifting platform we found significantly superior support for data cleaning and transformation streamlining in the Ontotext Refine module, which uses a combination of Google's OpenRefine[12] with its GREL expression language[13], mappings to RDF (for building URIs from legacy identifiers and attribute names) and SPARQL CONSTRUCTS for final graph transformations. Figure 3 presents the flow of transformations applied to the data, showing both offline activities (ingestion into the application and extraction from it by a user-analyst) and runtime activities (the transformations performed by the application regarding presenting graphs for visual navigation).

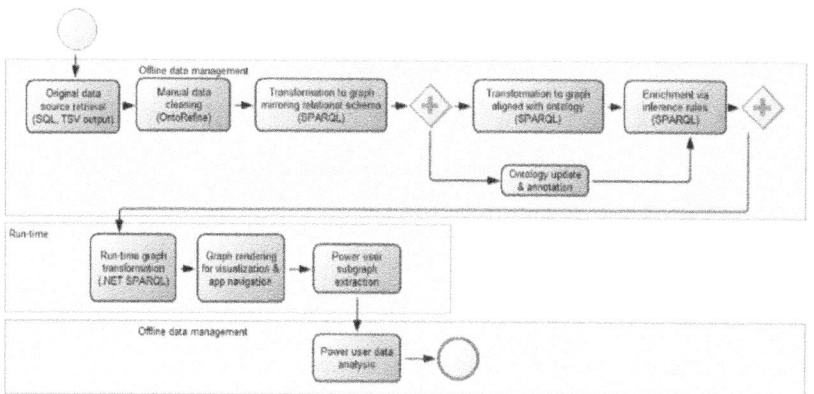

Fig. 3. The flow of data transformations from ingestion of legacy sources to front-end exposure (including a feature for read-only graph queries for power users)

---

[8] https://www.ontotext.com/products/graphdb/.
[9] https://lucene.apache.org/core/2_9_4/queryparsersyntax.html.
[10] https://www.ontotext.com/products/ontotext-refine/.
[11] https://d2rq.org/.
[12] https://github.com/OpenRefine.
[13] https://openrefine.org/docs/manual/grel.

Knowledge Graphs as a Scholarly Data Fabric   163

This flow has been reiterated over multiple relational databases ensuring that the new graph-based structure can preserve most of the information while eliminating inconsistencies, merging redundant data and matching entities based on rules and the semantic similarity index of GraphDB[14].

4 Graph Transformations

4.1 Transformations for Data Cleaning and Data Model Mapping

As an initial data hygiene phase, we had to perform data cleaning, vocabulary conversion (to a hybrid ontology mixing Schema.org and local terminology derived from the legacy data schema) and type enrichment (attaching types from the hybrid ontology). While gathering information about the same entities (e.g. persons) from different data sources (accounting, publications, employments etc.) we identified discrepancies ranging from simple capitalization issues to more complex issues (e.g. remarks on the marital status and name changes in the surname field). Cross-table analysis allowed us to create transformation rules with data cleaning role using the transformation capabilities provided by Ontotext Refine: filtering rows and columns, data type conversions, clustering similar values for syntactic uniformization etc. This could be done partly in the same transformation that generated the graphs, partly in the resulting graph by leveraging SPARQL functions at transformation time. An impression of the visual configuration of such transformations, with mappings from legacy data fields to RDF properties conforming the hybrid ontology, is given in Fig. 4.

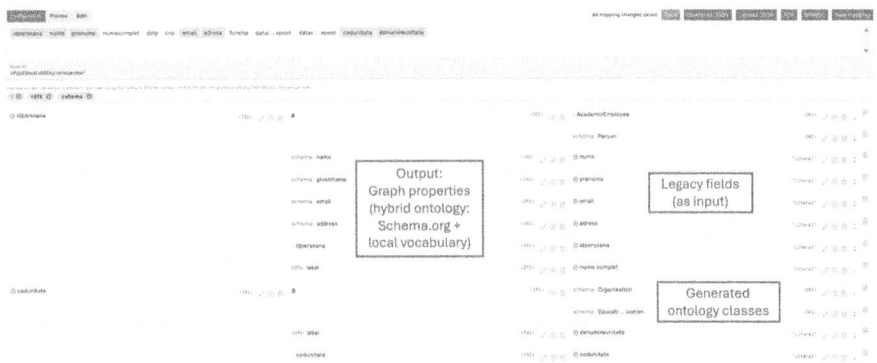

Fig. 4. Ontotext Refine configuration for vocabulary conversion and type enrichment

Such configurations result in CONSTRUCT queries that can be tested and further modified before committing changes, to apply SPARQL-level transformations. The example shown in Fig. 5 reflects the obtained alignments with the hybrid ontology (types generated for ?s1 and ?s2 nodes), granular syntactic refinements on identifiers and data points (BIND clauses applying a chain of SPARQL functions) as well as manually edited

---
[14] https://graphdb.ontotext.com/documentation/10.7/semantic-similarity-searches.html.

changes in the CONSTRUCT transformation for more complex patterns that could not be designed with the visual OntoRefine tool – Fig. 5 shows the ad-hoc generation of a blank node depicting an n-ary relationship derived from an intermediary table. Some fields are redundantly kept for testing reasons – e.g. the old form of the person identifier is visible as a literal besides newly generated URIs.

```
CONSTRUCT {
    ?s1     a                       :AcademicEmployee, schema:Person ;
            schema:name             ?o_name ;
            schema:givenName        ?o_givenName ;
            schema:email            ?o_email ;
            schema:address          ?o_address ;
            :idpersoana             ?o_idpersoana ;
            rdfs:label              ?o_label .
    ?s2     a                       schema:Organization, schema:EducationalOrganization ;
            rdfs:label              ?o_label_2 ;
            :codunitate             ?o_codunitate ;
            :hasMembers             [a                   :Membership;
                                    schema:member       ?s1;
                                    schema:startDate    ?o_startDate;
                                    schema:endDate      ?o_endDate;
                                    :inRole             ?o_functia].
} WHERE {
    SERVICE <rdf-mapper:ontorefine:1780387927014> {
        BIND(IRI(CONCAT(str(?c_nume),"-",replace(STR(?c_prenume)," ","-"),"-", SHA1(STR(?c_cnp)))) as ?s1)
        BIND(IRI(CONCAT(replace(STR(?c_denumireunitate)," ",""),STR(?c_codunitate))) as ?s2)
        #... granular syntactic transformations on identifiers and data points
    }
}
```

Fig. 5. Extending the transformation on SPARQL level

4.2 Transformations for External Identifiers

Similar data preparations have been applied for the purpose of connecting to datasets available in external scholarly repositories – we've experimented with datasets from Springer SciGraph[15] (currently discontinued as a Web navigator, still available as an API) and Dimensions[16], limited to selected university employees to incorporate researcher identifiers or paper identifiers (DOIs). Sample datasets on publications available in such repositories were retrieved in tabular structures and subjected again to the OntoRefine semantic lifting – first to extract additional details on publications, then to apply matching via the clustering and uniformization of syntactically similar names or the semantic similarity index, the goal being to match external identifiers (e.g. ORCIDs) based on name similarities and relationship similarities (e.g. affiliation, coauthors) and to ingest publication details not available in the legacy systems.

Figure 6 shows fragments of SPARQL used for the preparatory steps of ingestion, highlighting some critical features extending the default SPARQL capabilities: the GREL expression language to extract and manipulate the shape of URIs, or the SPIN functions that extend SPARQL in GraphDB[17] (e.g. breaking a comma-separated string of authors names into an RDF collection of author nodes). SPARQL 1.1 functions in their

---

[15] https://communities.springernature.com/users/82895-sn-scigraph.
[16] https://www.dimensions.ai/.
[17] https://graphdb.ontotext.com/documentation/10.7/sparql-ext-functions-reference.html.

default implementations can be insufficient for such real case data uniformization and the GraphDB extensions proved critical for the semantic lifting and ingestion, sometimes complemented by workarounds, e.g. to preserve the open world assumption – the absence of a value in OntoRefine actually built a property with an empty string value, making it necessary to generate an erroneous (1/0) value in order to avoid generating a property entirely (i.e. to avoid the generation of a property for some instances).

Fig. 6. Mixing SPARQL with GREL and SPIN functions for data ingestion

4.3 Transformations for Visual Navigation

The example in Fig. 7 shows an employee with her/his relationships that are revealed graphically by focusing on the relational context of that node, depicted radially. Relations are displayed radially outgoing regardless of their real RDF triple direction – some must be dynamically reversed (e.g. schema:author), others must be homogenized (e.g. coauthor, being a symmetric OWL property would have both incoming and outgoing triples, therefore they are merged in the visualization – OWL was used only for descriptive purposes and not for actually manifesting inferred triples, in order to minimize the knowledge graph size and to generate as much as possible at visualization time).

Other RDF properties are not even visualized as graph patterns, but in side panels showing lists or tables aggregating various properties of the center node: data attributes, external identifiers (to navigate to, for instance, SciGraph), types of the center node, instances of the types visually connected to the center node.

Selecting an element – either from the end of the visual edges or from the instance panels would cause the navigation window to slide to the selected node and update its semantic contextualization with the new relations and attributes found according to visualization metadata. This also ensures the evolution of the application through enrichment with new data, entities or relationships independent of the source code of the application – in other words, the application handles a generic graph data model that extends the RDF metamodel to facilitate the visual rendering and navigation.

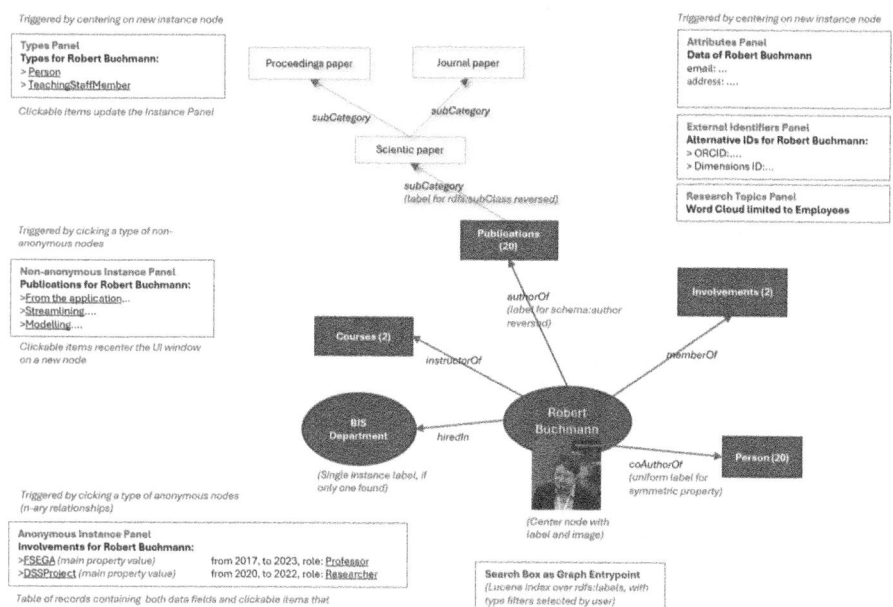

Fig. 7. Mockup of the visual interaction experience (context window centered on the instance Robert Buchmann)

The entry point in the graph can be searched through a Lucene search engine index incorporated in GraphDB[18] and allowing approximate word search[19]. The search space can be limited to selected types (e.g. Persons, Organizational Units, Publications) by parameterizing the Lucene-based SPARQL queries.

Besides properties lifted from legacy data or external sources, some SPARQL-based inference rules would also generate relevant information to be visualized - the most frequent co-author of an employee, aggregate impact factor over journal publications

---
[18] https://graphdb.ontotext.com/documentation/10.7/lucene-graphdb-connector.html.
[19] The query syntax is documented at https://lucene.apache.org/core/2_9_4/queryparsersyntax.html.

of an employee, preferred topics and scientific themes according to the Scopus and Clarivate classifications.

This visualization experience could have been handled by completely decoupling the stored graphs from the visualization logic – e.g. to obtain relevant data as JSON and render it as needed. However we wanted to experiment with a notion of visualization semantics and graph rewriting – we build dynamically at run-time the contextual graph containing all information that must be made available for visualization with no latency. This contextual graph collects all needed information around the center node, however it goes beyond the standard DESCRIBE that collects all direct connections in the typical browsing experience (that we evaluated in e.g. SciGraph or DBPedia). On one hand the contextual graph extends beyond direct connections (e.g. collecting subclasses of the directly assigned type, or properties of connected anonymous nodes); it performs aggregations and calculations (to display an instance count and to avoid visual cluttering of the radial graph by gradually revealing connected instances in separate panels); finally, it also annotates parts of this contextual graph with "visualization semantics" – hints to indicate to the front-end rendering component which properties should be displayed as lists, tables, table keys, in which panel type and which should be shown as radial edges.

Some of these annotations relied on standard terminology (e.g. to differentiate data properties, object properties, symmetric properties in OWL terms), but additional terminology was also needed – e.g. to have a "reverse label" to be displayed when the visualization reverses the triple, without storing inverse relationships that could double the knowledge graph size; to have a "main property" to identify the key property withing an n-ary relationship organized around blank nodes.

Figure 8 shows a transformation rule sample that takes as input the node under focus (current node parameter), collects its edges, the types of the connected individuals, the types of connects and metadata and produces a new RDF graph enriched with visualization semantics that instruct front-end components what visual treatment to apply to each construct – see the *visualMeaning* properties. This ensures the transition from the RDF storage to the visual patterns supporting the UI experience: some RDF predicates become arrows, others become tabular attributes; some arrows are displayed in their natural direction, others in reverse or bidirectional; some arrows connect instances, others connect instances to types annotated with various information (e.g. instance counts for a type).

Thus, the approach employs RDF not only for the semantics at data model level, but also for visualization semantics that determine the user experience and enriches data graphs with visual cues that ultimately act as a visualization ontology.

4.4 Path Finding

A Path Finder functionality was required to perform bidirectional path searches through the network of relationships found in the knowledge graph, parameterized at run-time with specific start and end nodes found by the same search engine that ensures the selection of the focus node in the contextual sliding window. Another run-time parameter is the path length, thus allowing a user to discover chains of connections of desired length between, for instance, two employees – are they connected by some common activities (courses, publications), belonging to units of some relevant granularity (same department, same research center) etc.? The paths lose relevance as length increases therefore users had to be able to adjust length; also paths should avoid extremely common edges that are expected to be found for all or most nodes – either because they are too generic (e.g. rdf:type would take paths through the TBOX, where all paths lead inevitably) or because they are domain-specific but extremely common (e.g. positions/roles available for all employees).

Fig. 8. SPARQL-based graph rewriting: from stored graph to visual graph

Path finding functionality is not supported in a straightforward way by SPARQL 1.1 – first of all because of the absence of a wildcard property chain, with some workarounds being used by practitioners but showing scalability issues or bugs for general path detection[20]. The Ontotext GraphDB SPARQL extension for path search[21] overcomes this, however the visualization of path results requires additional treatments – whether to display path segments in the way they are directed by the path finding algorithm, or the way they are stored; what to display for blank nodes present in the path; how to circumvent certain edges that would explode the number of paths, or certain nodes that would prove irrelevant in connecting certain entities (e.g. the same salary value connecting multiple

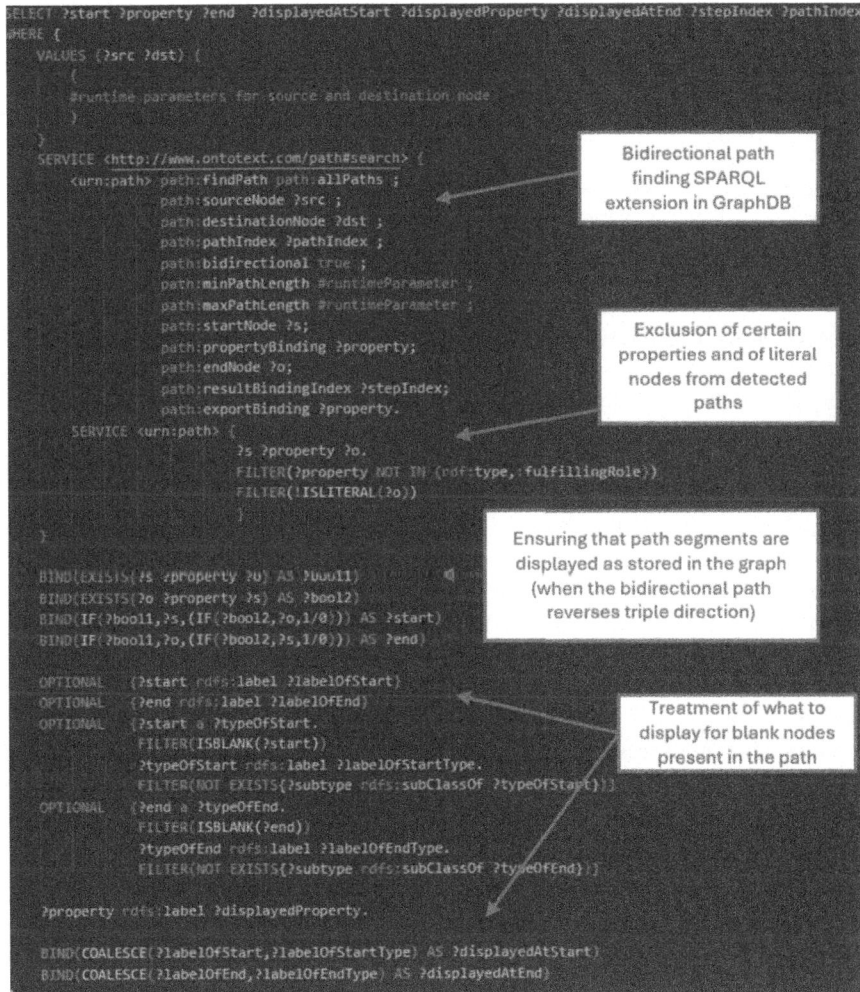

Fig. 9. Path finding SPARQL and path visualization preparation in GraphDB

---

[20] See a discussion on RDF4J: https://github.com/eclipse-rdf4j/rdf4j/issues/2078.
[21] https://graphdb.ontotext.com/documentation/10.7/graph-path-search.html.

employees). Selected samples of how these treatments were applied can be seen in the custom SPARQL example shown in Fig. 9.

The resulting graph database hosted by the Ontotext GraphDB 16 core version, currently stores over 3 million instance-level relations (i.e. ABox) – derived from graph transformations and inference from a total of 9 million raw relations from the institution's relational databases and other 4 million raw relations from external sources. The SPARQL queries and transformations have been parameterized in such a way that the wealth of navigable and accessible information can evolve in time both by accumulating data and expanding the graph schema without changing the source code. That is, the ontology properties are characterized by description hints guiding their handling and rendering at the level of front-end components – which properties to be navigated instance-to-instance, which should be navigated instance-to-aggregates, which should be excluded by path finding etc. This will allow the Information Systems Center from the university to continuously enrich the system by simply feeding data and annotating any new properties found relevant for the diverse visualization patterns.

5 Conclusions

The paper presented a Data Fabric solution to the integration of legacy data silos in a university. The solution is based on RDF knowledge graphs populated with legacy data to establish relationships that were not explicit between multiple relational DB servers leading to a need for dedicated systems for synchronization and cross-functional aggregation of reporting. To expose the knowledge graph to laypersons, a visual navigator was developed, implementing a user experience of gradual relationship discovery through path finding and a contextual sliding window that implements dedicated visualization semantics through graph transformations.

The paper advocates a notion of visualization semantics where visualization hints are semantically annotated to knowledge graph fragments in order to guide front-end components with rendering them, influenced by the OWL typology of RDF properties as well as specific features of the knowledge graph deployment platform, Ontotext GraphDB.

Future work on the resulting knowledge graphs focuses on enriching the semantics layer of the data fabric, with on-going research [23] employing the Work Systems Theory conceptualization as an enterprise architecting lens and an additional schema layer to facilitate richer semantic queries than basic navigation of the data fabric.

Acknowledgments. This research used infrastructure acquired as part of the project POC/398/1/1/124155 - co-financed by the European Regional Development Fund (ERDF) through the Competitiveness Operational Programme for Romania 2014-2020. This work was supported by a mobility project of the Romanian Ministry of Research, Innovation and Digitization, CNCS - UEFISCDI, project number PN-IV-P2-2.2-MC-2024-0821, within PNCDI IV.

Disclosure of Interests. The authors have no competing interests to declare that are relevant to the content of this article.

References

1. Patnaik, A.: Demystifying data fabric architecture: a comprehensive overview (2023). https://dzone.com/articles/demystifying-data-fabric-architecture-a-comprehens
2. Buchmann, R.A., Dragoș, R., Ghiran, A.M.: From the application-centric to the knowledge-centric university: a design science proof-of-concept. In: Proceedings of ISD 2021. AIS (2021). https://aisel.aisnet.org/isd2014/proceedings2021/currenttopics/14/
3. Microsoft Documentation: Linked Servers. https://docs.microsoft.com/en-us/sql/relational-databases/linked-servers/linked-servers-database-engine?view=sql-server-ver15. Accessed 25 Sept 2024
4. Bonatti, P.A., Decker, S., Polleres, A., Presutti, V.: Knowledge graphs: new directions for knowledge representation on the semantic web. Dagstuhl Rep. **8**(9) (2019)
5. Nonthakarn, C., Wuwongse, V.: Linked OpenScholar: a researcher network using linked open data. In: Chen, H.-H., Chowdhury, G. (eds.) ICADL 2012. LNCS, vol. 7634, pp. 325–328. Springer, Heidelberg (2012). https://doi.org/10.1007/978-3-642-34752-8_41
6. Färber, M.: The Microsoft academic knowledge graph: a linked data source with 8 billion triples of scholarly data. In: Ghidini, C., et al. (eds.) ISWC 2019. LNCS, vol. 11779, pp. 113–129. Springer, Cham (2019). https://doi.org/10.1007/978-3-030-30796-7_8
7. Angioni, S., Salatino, A.A., Osborne, F., Recupero, D.R., Motta, E.: Integrating knowledge graphs for analysing academia and industry dynamics. In: Bellatreche, L., et al. (eds.) TPDL/ADBIS/EDA -2020. CCIS, vol. 1260, pp. 219–225. Springer, Cham (2020). https://doi.org/10.1007/978-3-030-55814-7_18
8. Cambridge Semantics, Data Fabric. https://cambridgesemantics.com/data-fabric/. Accessed 25 Sept 2024
9. Elsevier, Pure Community Module. https://www.elsevier.com/solutions/pure/features/pure-community-module. Accessed 25 Sept 2024
10. Monash University Research Portal. https://research.monash.edu/en/. Accessed 25 Sept 2024
11. Börner, K., Conlon, M., Corson-Rikert, J., Ding, Y.: VIVO: A Semantic Approach to Scholarly Networking and Discovery. Synthesis Lectures on the Semantic Web: Theory and Technology, vol. 7, no. 1. Morgan & Clapyool (2012)
12. VIVO, Ontology for Representing Scholarship. https://github.com/vivo-ontologies. Accessed 25 Sept 2024
13. Springer Nature Linked Data Platform: SciGraph. https://github.com/springernature/scigraph. Accessed 25 Sept 2024
14. Semantic Scholar. https://www.semanticscholar.org/. Accessed 25 Sept 2024
15. VOSviewer. https://www.vosviewer.com/. Accessed 25 Sept 2024
16. Chen, C.: CiteSpace: visualizing patterns and trends in scientific literature (2010). http://cluster.ischool.drexel.edu/~cchen/citespace/download/
17. ConnectedPapers. https://www.connectedpapers.com/. Accessed 25 Sept 2024
18. Uifălean, Ș, Ghiran, A.-M., Buchmann, R.A.: Employing graph databases for business process management and representation. In: Silaghi, G.C., et al. (eds.) ISD 2022. LNISO, vol. 63, pp. 73–92. Springer, Cham (2023). https://doi.org/10.1007/978-3-031-32418-5_5
19. Cinpoeru, M.: Dereferencing service for navigating enterprise knowledge structures from diagrammatic representations. In: Abramowicz, W. (ed.) BIS 2017. LNBIP, vol. 303, pp. 85–96. Springer, Cham (2017). https://doi.org/10.1007/978-3-319-69023-0_9
20. Firey, L.: Quick visual analysis using carts in stardog studio (2021). https://www.stardog.com/blog/quick-visual-analysis-using-charts-in-stardog-studio/. Accessed 25 Sept 2024
21. GraphDB Documentation, Visualize and Explore. https://graphdb.ontotext.com/documentation/10.7/visualize-and-explore.html. Accessed 25 Sept 2024

22. Metaphacts, Ontology Visualization and Editing. https://help.metaphacts.com/resource/Help:VisualOntologyEditing. Accessed 25 Sept 2024
23. Chis, A., Ghiran, A.M., Alter, S.: Informing enterprise knowledge graphs with a work system perspective. Enterp. Model. Inf. Syst. Archit. EMISAJ **19** (2024). https://doi.org/10.18417/emisa.19.7

Process Mining and Business Process Analysis

Enriching Business Process Event Logs with Multimodal Evidence

Aleksandar Gavric[✉], Dominik Bork, and Henderik A. Proper

Business Informatics Group, TU Wien, Vienna, Austria
{aleksandar.gavric,dominik.bork,henderik.proper}@tuwien.ac.at

Abstract. Process mining uses data from event logs to understand which activities were undertaken, their timing, and the involved entities, providing a data trail for process analysis and improvement. However, a significant challenge involves ensuring that these logs accurately reflect the actual processes. Some processes leave few digital traces, and their event logs often lack details about manual and physical work that does not involve computers or simple sensors. We introduce the **B**usiness-knowledge **I**ntegration **C**ycles (BICycle) method and *mm_proc_miner* tool to convert raw and unstructured data from various modalities, such as video, audio, and sensor data, into a structured and unified event log, while keeping human-in-the-loop. Our method analyzes the semantic distance between visible, audible, and textual evidence within a self-hosted joint embedding space. Our approach is designed to consider (1) preserving the privacy of evidence data, (2) achieving real-time performance and scalability, and (3) preventing AI hallucinations. We also publish a dataset consisting of over $2K$ processes with $16K$ steps to facilitate domain inference-related tasks. For the evaluation, we created a novel test dataset in the domain of DNA home kit testing, for which we can guarantee that it was not encountered during the training of the employed AI foundational models. We show positive insights in both event log enrichment with multimodal evidence and human-in-the-loop contribution.

Keywords: Event Log Creation · Event Log Completion · Event Log Quality Improvement · Artificial Intelligence · Multimodal data

1 Introduction

Consider an entertainment park, where the pre-designed pathways represent the official, mapped-out processes of an "idealized" visit to the park. These paths are laid out by planners with a specific flow in mind, directing the visitors (the participants of an entertainment process) on how they should navigate the space (or the entertainment business process). However, over time, the park's visitors may create a shortcut through the grass, a path not originally designed but formed out of convenience and efficiency. This real-life scenario serves as a perfect metaphor for process discovery in the sense of process mining. This paper aims to explore the ways how processes are executed in practice and not blindly trusting the designed process, but rather by making the evidence data about process execution more complete.

Support for the design and improvement of business processes and realizing the benefits of information systems have been proposed by a broad spectrum of methods since the 1990s [18]. Pegoraro et al. [21] study process mining from uncertain event data and the result of automatically discovering process models and checking if event data conform to a certain model. Importantly, numerous authors [3] showed that tension between human involvement and task automation in work process management underscores the critical impact solutions to these identified problems will have on knowledge-intensive work processes with a conclusion that a better representation of the real-world context is crucial for process mining. To address the question of representing real-world contexts, this paper defines, implements, and evaluates the automatic creation of event logs for process mining from multiple modalities of data sources. In support of our motivation, the global video surveillance market, valued at USD 53.7 billion in 2023, is projected to reach USD 83.3 billion by 2028[1]. This growth is fueled by smart city initiatives and advancements in AI-driven video technology combined with the Internet of Things (IoT) across various sectors.

The research question addressed in this paper is: *How can multimodal evidence be effectively utilized to create or complete event logs?* This inquiry aims to explore the potential of combining different types of data sources, such as audio, video, text, and sensor data, to enhance the completeness and precision of event logs. The findings are expected to provide insights into improving event log generation and completion processes, ultimately contributing to more robust and dependable event documentation for the purposes of process mining. Consequently, this paper aims to contribute first techniques and a method toward realizing the vision of multimodal process mining [8].

The remainder of this paper is structured as follows. First, in Sect. 2, we introduce our general perspective on multimodal process evidence. This is followed, in Sect. 3, by an outline of related work. In Sect. 4, we then discuss the implementation of a tool for improving event log completeness with multimodal evidence, as well as the associated designed **B**usiness-knowledge **I**ntegration **C**ycles (BICycle) method. Finally, before concluding, Sect. 5 reports on the evaluation of our solution. All the data of this research and the developed tool are available via: https://github.com/aleksandargavric/mm_proc_miner.

2 Perspective on Multimodal Process Evidence

Relying on a single modality (such as text) for event log creation is comparable to navigating a complex environment with only one sense. While valuable insights can be obtained, significant aspects of the process may remain obscured, leaving blind spots in our understanding and traceability of the process.

---

[1] https://www.marketsandmarkets.com/Market-Reports/video-surveillance-market-645.html.

Consider the scenario of assembling a piece of furniture; a process that involves various steps and interactions with multiple components. If we were to rely solely on written instructions (a single modality), we might miss out on the details of how different parts fit together, the angle of assembly, and the duration of each step that signals a correct assembly. These details might be better captured through video demonstrations (another modality), which provide a visual and auditory understanding of the assembly process. Similarly, sensor data from tools used in the assembly (yet another modality) could provide insights into the amount of force required for certain steps or the tactile feedback, offering a more complete picture of the process.

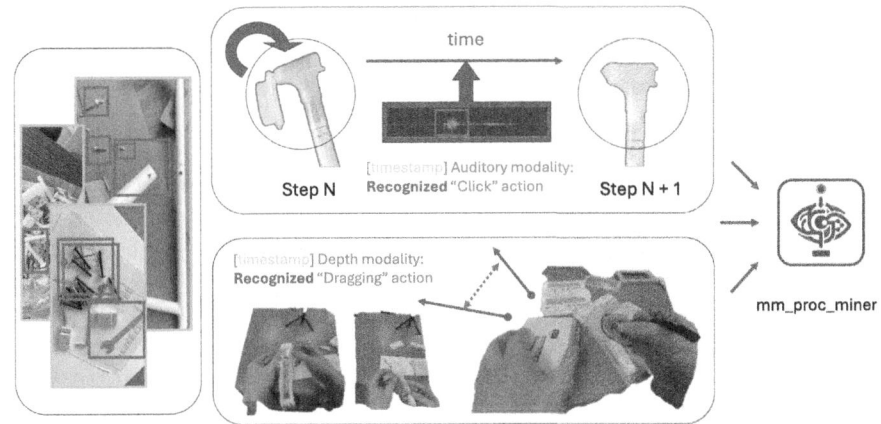

Fig. 1. An illustration of an effect from various modalities.

The integration of multiple modalities – textual, visual, auditory, and general sensor data – thus becomes crucial in uncovering the full spectrum of activities and interactions within a process. Each modality essentially offers a lens through which to view the process, revealing different aspects that may not be visible through other means. Just as a video can capture what written instructions cannot, sensor data can reveal details about the physical execution of a process that neither text nor video can capture.

In this paper, we show that by integrating diverse modalities, blind spots left by single-modal event log creation methods can be uncovered, ensuring a (1) privacy of evidence data, (2) performance and scalability, and (3) preventing AI hallucinations in the representation of processes in event logs. Our solution is illustrated in Fig. 1.

To define the research objective of this paper, we first formulate the research gap which we aim to contribute to.

Given a process P, let there be a set of N modalities $M = \{m_1, m_2, \ldots, m_N\}$, where each modality m_i provides a unique perspective of the process. Let, for $1 \leq i \leq N$, the set D_i represent the dataset of raw data (typically comprising unstructured data such as depth sensing maps, audio, and raw pixels of video frames) associated with modality m_i, reporting on a sequence of events $E_i = \{e_{i,1}, e_{i,2}, \ldots, e_{i,O_i}\}$ observed through modality m_i. Each event $e_{i,j}$ in E_i is characterized by a tuple $(a_{i,j}, t_{i,j}, v_{i,j})$, where $a_{i,j}$ is the activity, $t_{i,j}$ is the timestamp, and $v_{i,j}$ is a vector of modality-specific attributes observed for the event.

Our objective is to construct a comprehensive event log EL that accurately represents the sequence and characteristics of activities in the process as observed across all modalities in M. Formally, we seek to optimize the following objective function:

$$\max_{EL} \sum_{i=1}^{N} \lambda_i \cdot \Phi(PM, D_i)$$

where $\Phi(EL, D_i)$ is a function that measures the fidelity of the event log EL with respect to the dataset D_i of modality m_i, and λ_i is a weighting factor that denotes the importance or reliability of modality m_i in the overall process understanding.

The challenge lies in accurately integrating the disparate and possibly conflicting information from different modalities to construct a process model that is both comprehensive and faithful to the observed data. This involves not only aligning events across modalities but also reconciling differences in the granularity, scale, and interpretation of the data.

To solve this optimization problem, we employ a multi-stage approach that first involves the alignment and fusion of multimodal datasets into a unified event log. Consequently, process discovery algorithms could be applied to this integrated dataset to construct the initial process model, which can be refined iteratively by evaluating its conformance against each modality-specific dataset and adjusting the model accordingly.

This paper proposes a novel method, termed **B**usiness-knowledge **I**ntegration **C**ycles (BICycle), for addressing the challenges associated with digital traceability in manually-intensive business processes with limited digital footprints or those processes completely invisible to IT systems. The proposed approach aims to create process mining-ready event logs from videos and other unstructured data forms, with the goal of enhancing process monitoring and optimization. This research takes a domain-agnostic stance and involves human-in-the-loop design. It emphasizes the versatility and applicability of its findings across various fields. Integrating human-in-the-loop design ensures that human insights and feedback are integral to the iterative process, fostering a symbiotic relationship between technology and its users. This aims to not only enhance the relevance and usability of the solution but also align the solution with human (business-relevant) values and needs, incorporate diverse human perspectives, and make the solution user-centered.

To meet the above challenges, we have designed the BICycle method and developed a BICycle-enabled tool for the creation of event logs, which employs joint embedding space for different modalities, and shows a capability of identifying moments in video, audio, and unstructured sensor data representing activities for an event log.

3 Related Work

Process mining from multimodal data represents an emerging domain within process analytics, aiming at extracting meaningful process-related information from video data. This paper is positioned as a continuation of our earlier implementation described in [8], and described in [7].

We investigate work on improving the completeness of event logs is a critical area of research in process mining, as it ensures the reliability and accuracy of the insights derived from these logs. In particular, this involves addressing issues related to preventing "AI hallucinations" [14] that could lead to erroneous conclusions. The core challenge to improve the completeness of event logs is to enable automation in understanding conventionally unstructured (raw) multimodal data.

3.1 Event Logs From Multimodal Data

Knoch et al. [12] introduced an unsupervised method for process discovery from video recordings of manual assembly tasks, leveraging overhead cameras to track workers' hands and associate movement patterns with specific work steps, illustrating the potential for practical applications in industrial settings. Kratsch et al. [13] proposed a reference architecture *ViProMiRA* for leveraging video data in process mining, offering a structured approach to transform raw video data into event logs for process analysis, thus expanding the toolkit available for exploring more complex and less structured processes. Lepsien et al. [15] applied process mining to surveillance videos in pigpens, highlighting the importance of further implementation and domain-specific knowledge. They designed an abstract pipeline for process mining on video data, which includes steps from dataset preparation to event log construction and subsequent process mining applications, highlighting the growing stage of this research area. Lepsien et al. [16] used a combination of object tracking, spatio-temporal action detection, and techniques for raising the abstraction level of events and showed the translation of video data into higher-level, discrete event data. Furthermore, Chen et al. [4] concentrated on comparing processes with Petri-net models obtained from videos. The exploration of process mining extends into the realm of sensor data, demonstrating the versatility of process mining techniques in diverse data environments. A significant contribution to this field includes the work by Rebmann et al. [22], who presented a multimodal approach to activity recognition and process discovery, utilizing both motion sensor and video data to enhance the accuracy of captured process activities. Janssen et al. [11] introduced an approach to process model discovery from smart home and IoT sensor event data, showcasing the potential of using sensor activations to map human daily routines through process mining. This methodology divides sensor activation logs into sequential sections, clusters them into patterns of similar sequences, and maps these clusters to activities, which are then grouped into cases based on specific sensor events. Results from a literature review conducted by Telli et al. [24] show that the term multimodal process mining has been used for multimodal models created by including different perspectives of data in the analysis. In our approach, we use multimodal embedding spaces created by encoder-only architectures, and we compare multimodal data by similarity function (such as cosine similarity).

3.2 Preventing AI Hallucinations

Preventing AI hallucinations in process mining involves ensuring the accuracy and reliability of the extracted process models. Tax et al. [23] suggested using supervised learning for event abstraction, which enhances the quality of process models by reducing noise and improving interpretability. Additionally, semantic-based frameworks like SPMaAF by Okoye et al. [19] have been shown to improve accuracy and conceptual reasoning capabilities in process mining. Folino and Pontieri [6] emphasized the importance of using AI-based strategies to handle low-quality logs, leveraging domain knowledge and auxiliary AI tasks to enhance process mining outcomes. Furthermore, Dixit et al. [5] developed methods for detecting and repairing event ordering imperfections in logs, which is crucial for maintaining high-quality process mining results. These efforts collectively contribute to improving the accuracy and reliability of process mining applications by addressing the challenges associated with AI hallucinations. Our approach deals with AI hallucinations through the human-in-the-loop BICycle method. Figure 2 shows an overview of our solution.

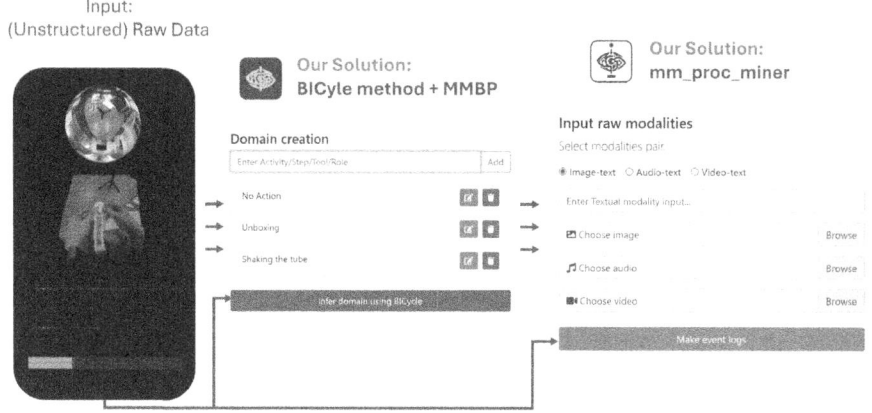

Fig. 2. Overview of our solution. Collected multiple modalities are sent to domain inferring and event log creation (completion).

4 Solution: mm_proc_miner

We have developed an event logs creation tool termed *mm_proc_miner* designed and implemented to enhance the way processes are documented and analyzed with multimodal awareness. We will begin by introducing essential theoretical foundations, followed by a description of multimodal event logs, and finally, we will discuss the human-in-the-loop method that is used for business-knowledge-aware entity extraction.

4.1 Multimodal Event Logs

To develop multimodal event logs that extend beyond the reach of traditional process mining tools, we explore different data modalities rich in process information yet largely untapped by conventional methods. Video datasets bring the potential for capturing the complexity of human actions in a way that textual data cannot. Videos, with their visual and temporal dimensions, offer a detailed chronicle of processes through the lens of human interactions, both with objects and with one another. Adding depth and realizing relative distances within these interactions becomes possible, further enhancing the comprehension of spatial dynamics critical for understanding complex scenarios.

The auditory modality emerges as another layer of understanding, enriching the insights gained from visual data. The power of sound to convey context, action, and interaction complements the visual narrative, offering a fuller, more nuanced portrayal of events. The significance of integrating auditory data lies in its ability to capture moments and interactions that visual cues alone might not fully reveal. For instance, the sound of a *click* serves as an audible confirmation of actions completed, which can be pivotal in processes requiring precise outcomes. This auditory cue is particularly important in scenarios where visual confirmation may be obstructed or ambiguous.

Consider the example of a home kit for sampling DNA, a process steeped in the need for accuracy and reliability. As users engage with the kit, they follow a sequence of steps, one of which involves closing a funnel lid to secure a sample. The visual action of closing the lid may seem straightforward, yet the auditory *click* sound is what conclusively indicates the lid has been securely fastened as illustrated in Fig. 1. This sound not only assures the user of the successful completion of this step but also serves as an auditory event log, marking a crucial point in the process.

Capturing such auditory cues extends the capability of process mining tools, allowing them to analyze and understand processes that rely on sound as a marker of successful interactions or steps. By integrating auditory data alongside visual recordings, we can develop more comprehensive event logs that capture the full spectrum of human interaction with objects and with one another. This multimodal approach opens up new avenues for analyzing complex processes, enabling the creation of systems that are more responsive and attuned to the details of human behavior.

Building upon the integration of visual, depth, and auditory modalities, the incorporation of sensor data introduces a new dimension to our multimodal event logs, significantly enhancing the traceability and reproducibility of processes such as DNA sampling. Sensors measuring humidity, temperature, and pressure become vital in environments where precise conditions are crucial for the accuracy and reliability of outcomes. This additional layer of data in our tool can be imported through textual modality to enrich the context around human interactions and actions but also ensure that these processes adhere to the necessary environmental standards.

To evaluate the business-related application of multimodal conformance checking, we have recorded new videos for testing purposes, and we have made the entire dataset publicly available. The videos are out-of-internet wild samples that we guarantee are not used in training any of our base LLM models. We recorded evidence data in two domains. The first domain is DNA sampling in home settings. We recorded two instances of processes in the domain of DNA sample collection using Ancestry DNA [2] test kits and 23andMe [1] DNA test kits (two instances). We show the opportunities of guided and supervised medical applications in home kits that are unlocked with efficient real-time process monitoring from multimodal data. For recording the evaluation video samples, we used the Ray-Ban Meta smart glasses with ultra-wide 12-megapixel cameras for capturing 1080p videos and the Insta360 X3 camera with a 72MP photo resolution, 5.7K 360° video at 30 fps. An overview of the collected dataset is given in Fig. 3.

Fig. 3. An overview of the dataset in the domain of DNA home kit collecting that we recorded, processed, and used for testing.

We implemented the integration of multimodal data for the purpose of conversion of raw data into structured insights, employing a pre-trained model, *Imagebind* [9] for joint embedding of diverse data modalities.

4.2 Turning Modalities Into Event Logs

To transform modalities into an event log, we compute the matching scores between the querying modality and keys of collected modalities. Both keys are queries that are simply values of their embeddings, over which we perform similarity matching.

For querying modality, we choose text to keep it compatible with conventional event logs and their textual labels (numeric or characters). We obtain the embedding vector for the querying text using a pre-trained space [9], denoted as E_q, and the embedding vector for the key modality, denoted as E_k. The matching score is calculated by performing a dot product between these embeddings, given

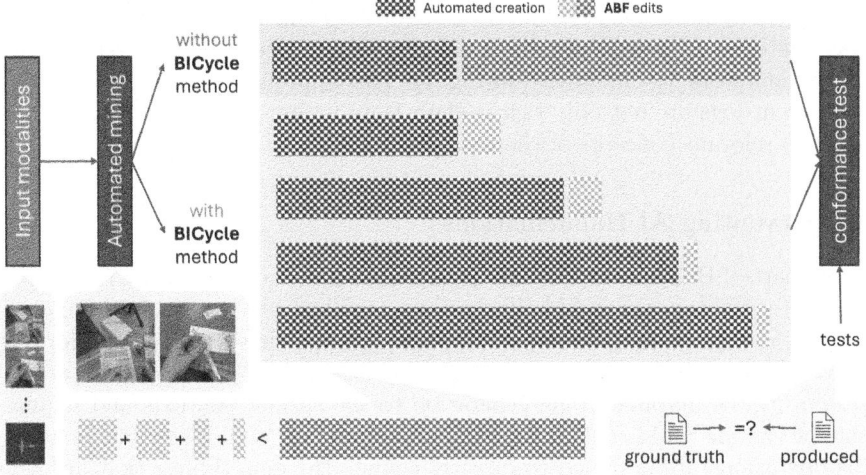

Fig. 4. The BICycle method. ABF - Atomic Business Feedback operations.

by $S = E_q \cdot E_k$. This dot product serves as a similarity measure between the two embeddings. To normalize these similarity scores across multiple key modalities and convert them into a probability distribution, we apply the softmax function. Given multiple key embeddings $\{E_k^1, E_k^2, \ldots, E_k^n\}$, we compute the dot product for each pair, resulting in similarity scores $\{S_1, S_2, \ldots, S_n\}$, where $S_i = E_q \cdot E_k^i$. The softmax function is then applied to these similarity scores to obtain the normalized probabilities P_i for each key modality. This is computed as:

$$P_i = \frac{\exp(S_i)}{\sum_{j=1}^{n} \exp(S_j)}$$

where $\exp(S_i)$ is the exponential of the similarity score S_i, and the denominator is the sum of the exponentials of all similarity scores. This process ensures that the resulting probabilities $\{P_1, P_2, \ldots, P_n\}$ sum to one, providing a robust measure of the likelihood that each key modality matches the querying text. Higher values of P_i indicate a better match between the querying text and the corresponding key modality. Thus, by using the dot product of embeddings and the softmax function, we compute and normalize the matching scores across different modalities, and pick the best match. For instance, if our query is an image modality and the key is text, we can calculate the matching probabilities in PyTorch[2] using:

Softmax(emb[Modality.VISION] · emb[Modality.TEXT]^T, dim = -1)

4.3 Business-Knowledge Integration Cycles Method (BICycle)

To facilitate the importance of incorporating domain-specific knowledge into our system, we developed a human-in-the-loop method named the Business-

---
[2] https://pytorch.org/.

knowledge **I**ntegration **Cycle**s method (BICycle), which is designed to systematically integrate human (usually a domain expert) feedback into our process mining framework (as illustrated in Fig. 4). This approach ensures that the generated event logs are not only rich in data from various modalities but are also related to relevant concepts of the business domain of the process.

4.4 Preventing AI Hallucinations

At the heart of BICycle are **A**tomic **B**usiness-knowledge **F**eedback (ABF) operations, designed to prevent AI hallucinations (as illustrated in Fig. 5). ABF operations are designed as a granular set of edits that domain experts can perform to refine and enhance the accuracy of the event logs. These operations are crucial for tailoring the automated log generation to the specific contexts and requirements of various fields, making the data more relevant and actionable for users. ABF operations are designed to directly change the embeddings that are keys for the matching described in Sect. 4.2, and include three actions:

- *Instancing.* ABF operation involves specifying a general tool or action mentioned in the event log to a particular named instance. For example, if the automated system identifies a "cutting" action, a domain expert can instance this action to a more specific "cutting with a surgical scalpel" in a medical context. This operation increases the specificity and contextual relevance of the event logs.
- *Renaming.* ABF operation is to fix when terms or labels used by the automated system do not align perfectly with the domain-specific terminology. The renaming operation allows experts to replace these with the correct terminology, enhancing the clarity and usability of the event logs. For example, if the automated system labels an action as "data input," a domain expert might rename this to "patient information entry" in a healthcare setting.
- *Removing.* When certain actions or events captured might be irrelevant or noisy in the context of the specific process being analyzed we can use the *Removing* ABF operation. The removing operation enables experts to delete these entries, ensuring that the event logs remain focused and pertinent. For example, if the event log contains entries for "background noise detection" in an audio processing task, these can be removed to focus solely on relevant audio events.

The BICycle method incorporates these ABF operations into iterative cycles of feedback and refinement. After an initial set of event logs is generated by the system, domain experts review the logs and apply ABF operations where necessary. The system then integrates this feedback, refining its algorithms and improving the accuracy and relevance of the generated logs. This process is not a one-time effort but rather a continuous cycle of improvement. As more feedback is integrated, the system's understanding of domain-specific processes deepens, leading to progressively more accurate and actionable event logs.

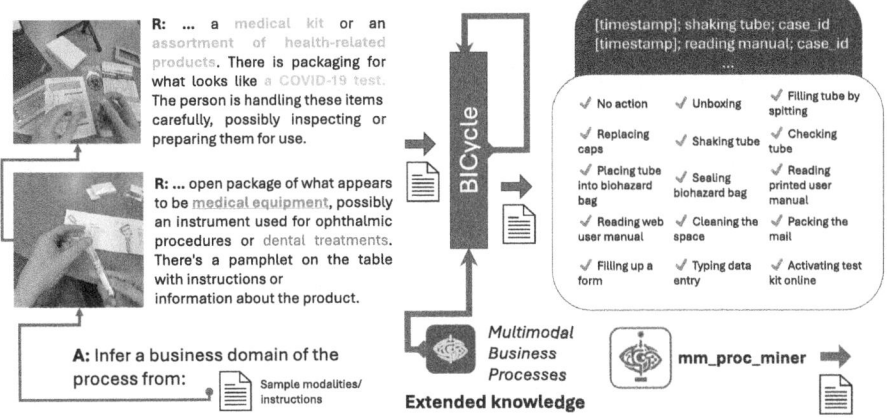

Fig. 5. Preventing AI hallucinations using BICycle.

4.5 Privacy of Evidence Data

Addressing the critical intersection of data privacy and business process management, we propose an **auto-completion** approach to suggest evidence of data missing values within the knowledge about business processes from datasets extracted from natural language processing machine learning models. We introduce the *Multimodal Business Processes dataset*, a comprehensive compilation derived from the concerted efforts of leveraging the state-of-the-art in large language models (LLMs) including Google's Gemini 1.5 [10], and both, OpenAI's GPT4 and GPT3.5 [20].

Our primary objective was to mine and distill extensive business knowledge from vast corpora of multimodal data, predominantly texts and images, across a wide range of business domains. By adopting the teacher-student model, we significantly expanded the knowledge base of a smaller, locally hosted LLaVa 2 [17] multimodal language model.

This approach ensures that sensitive and private data are processed locally, without the need to transmit any information to external cloud servers. This local processing capability is crucial for businesses concerned with data sovereignty and privacy, as it supports secure conformance checking and other data-sensitive operations without requiring an internet connection. An aspect of our solution, particularly relevant to domain inference tasks, involves the selection of a small number of samples from our input domain as initial business knowledge clues. This initial set serves as a foundation upon which we build and refine our understanding of the business domain by employing the BICycle method iteratively. We do this through two steps. The first step is to embed elements of our Multimodal Business Processes dataset into the latent embedding space described in Sect. 4.2. The second step is to include the top K nearest neighboring embeddings in their decoded version (value) as the input to our locally hosted language model.

Table 1. Preview of the Multimodal Business Processes dataset.

Process	Activities
Building a Modular Wine Rack System	Design system, Select wood or metal, Cut and assemble modules, Finish wood or coat metal, Stack and secure modules
Creating Hand-Carved Soap Bars with Custom Scents	Choose soap base, Melt and pour into molds, Carve designs once semi-set, Add essential oils
Making Hand-Tied Bouquets with Dried Flowers	Select dried flowers, Arrange in bouquet, Tie with twine or ribbon, Wrap stems in hessian
Building a Handmade Leather Sling Chair	Design chair, Cut leather for seat, Cut and shape wood for frame, Assemble, Attach leather to frame
Creating Hand-Dipped Beeswax Taper Candles	Melt beeswax, Dip wicks repeatedly until desired thickness, Cool, Trim wicks

4.6 Data Availability

The outcome of our multimodal process auto-completion data is a publicly available dataset comprising 2,644 business processes with a detailed breakdown into 16,180 steps, aimed at enhancing domain inference tasks, as previewed in Table 1.

5 Evaluation

In this section, we evaluate the effectiveness and efficiency of the process model generated from the event logs, which have been enhanced to improve completeness. Our evaluation focuses on three main aspects: *alignment with the official user manual, performance and scalability metrics*, and *manual validation of connected modalities*.

5.1 Alignment with User Manual

The process model was meticulously compared with the user manual provided by the DNA test kit company to ensure that it accurately represents the intended operations. This comparison was crucial as the user manual serves as the definitive guide for the process. Through systematic alignment techniques, we confirmed that the model mirrors the step-by-step instructions and sequences described in the manual. This validation ensures that our model not only captures all necessary components of the process but also adheres to the company's operational standards, thereby improving the reliability of the model in practical scenarios.

Using Disco[3] for Process Mining, we analyzed DIY home kits in the domain of DNA collection (Fig. 6). We designed our ground truth in accordance with the provided user manuals by selected AncestryDNA and 23andMe official instructions provided with the kit.

---

[3] https://fluxicon.com/disco/.

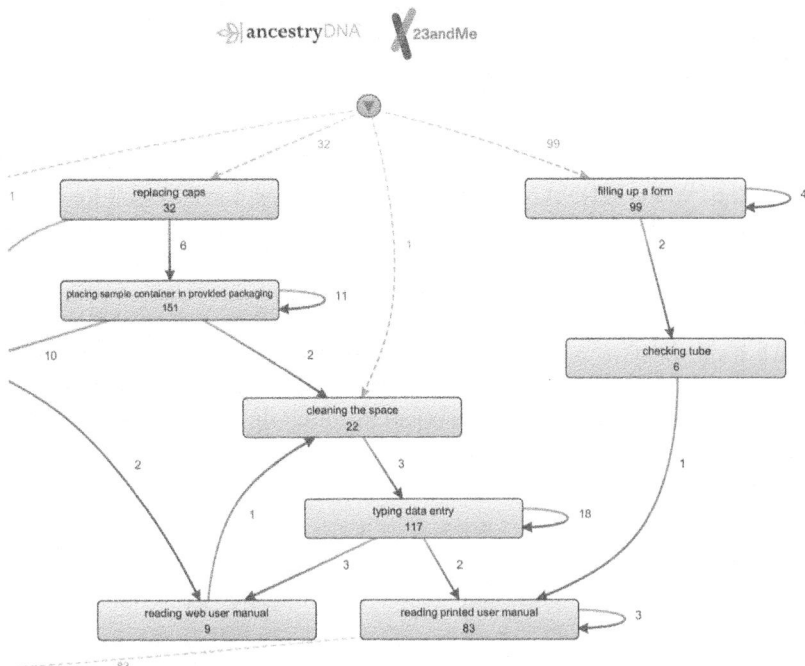

Fig. 6. Process model from our extracted event logs.

5.2 Performance and Scalability

To assess the practical applicability of the enriching of the event logs, we evaluated its performance and scalability on a single A40 GPU with 48GB RAM. Results are given in Fig. 7. The metrics used included process execution time, resource utilization, and scalability under varying loads. The results demonstrate that the model performs efficiently, with low latency, supporting real-time execution. The scalability tests indicate that our model can handle increases in workload without significant degradation in performance, making it suitable for both small-scale and large-scale operations.

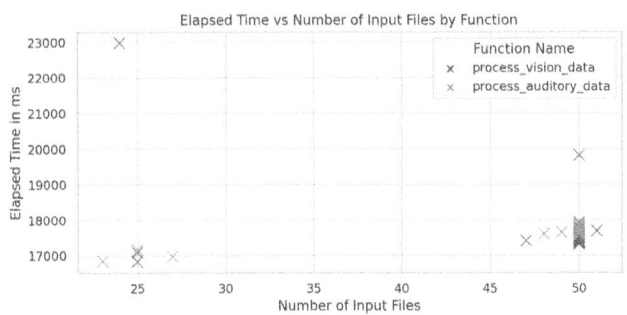

Fig. 7. Evaluation metrics for performance and scalability tests.

5.3 Assessment of the Created Event Logs

Further validation of the event log creation was conducted through manual observations to ensure that all modalities linked to specific steps in the process were accurately represented. Figure 8 provides the results of a manual observation study evaluating the accuracy of event log creation for the DNA testing kits 23andMe and AncestryDNA. Each step of the process was assessed for accuracy in image and audio modalities. These findings confirm the practical accuracy of the model in representing real-life execution, with generally higher accuracy in visual logs compared to audio. This manual check involved scrutinizing the log against observed operations to confirm that each step was correctly associated with its respective modalities. The value of accuracy is calculated over the average of five independent assessments, on the scale from 1.00 to 100.00. This observation confirms the model's practical accuracy in representing the real-life execution of the DNA testing process.

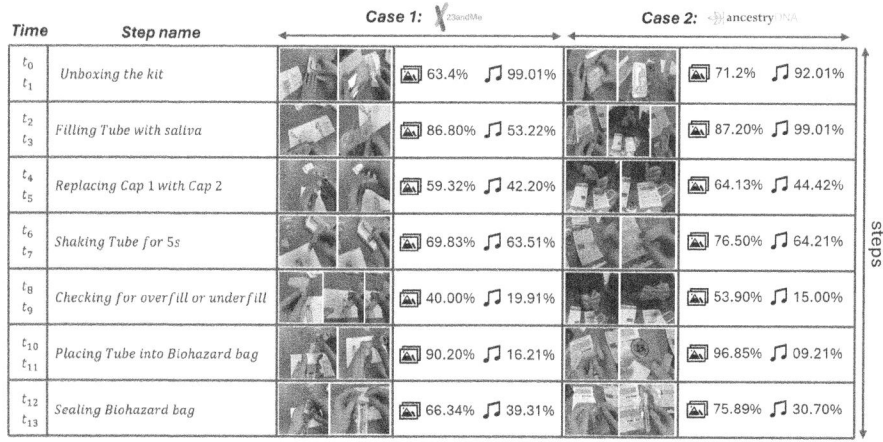

Fig. 8. Validation of created multimodal event log for the test process.

The evaluation of the created event log shows that it is not only a faithful representation of the prescribed process according to the official user manual but also excels in performance and scalability. Additionally, the manual verification of modalities connected to specific process steps further confirms the model's accuracy and utility in real-world applications. This comprehensive evaluation underscores the model's potential to enhance the operational efficiency and reliability of DNA testing processes.

5.4 Evaluating the Human-in-the-Loop Aspect

Table 2 presents the results of evaluating the Human-in-the-loop aspect through ABF operations across ten independent assessments. Without BICycle intervention, the average number of ABFs is 41.2, with individual assessments ranging

Table 2. Evaluating Human-in-the-loop aspect. ABFs over ten independent assessments.

Test		Avg # of ABFs	Assessment No. / Count(ABFs)									
			01	02	03	04	05	06	07	08	09	10
No-BICycle		41.2	30	26	54	40	48	40	50	46	34	44
BICycle	Iteration 1	3.2	3	1	2	4	1	5	5	5	4	2
	Iteration 2	3	3	3	4	3	5	2	4	2	2	2
	Iteration 3	2.9	1	3	4	2	3	2	5	4	2	3
	Iteration 4	3.2	2	1	5	4	4	4	1	3	3	5
	Iteration 5	2.2	3	1	3	1	4	1	4	2	1	2
	∑	14.5	12	09	18	14	17	14	19	16	12	14

from 26 to 54. When BICycle is used, iterative improvements are evident. In Iteration 1, the average number of ABFs drops significantly to 3.2, with assessments ranging from 1 to 5. By Iteration 5, the average further decreases to 2.2, showcasing a reduction in unnecessary or inaccurate entries, with assessments ranging from 1 to 4. The cumulative total of ABFs across all iterations (Iterations 1 to 5) is 14.5, indicating a consistent decrease in ABFs and reflecting the effectiveness of the Human-in-the-loop design in refining and enhancing the event logs.

6 Conclusion

This paper introduced a method for enhancing the fidelity and truthfulness of event log creation through the integration of multiple data modalities and the implementation of a human-in-the-loop business-knowledge integration method. Our method leverages video, audio, text, and sensor data to transform diverse actions, conversations, and interactions into detailed, semantically rich event logs. This multimodal perspective provides a nuanced understanding of business processes, capturing everything from spoken dialogues to physical interactions with unprecedented depth and clarity.

Through the development of the **B**usiness-knowledge **I**ntegration **C**ycles method (BICycle) and the application of the base set of **A**tomic **B**usiness-knowledge **F**eedback (ABF) operations, we have facilitated a dynamic, iterative process of improvement and refinement. This human-in-the-loop approach ensures that our generative models are continuously informed by domain expertise, enhancing the accuracy and relevance of the generated event logs. Our rigorous formal analyses and testing with out-of-internet samples underscores the effectiveness of our methodology. Data and tools related to our methodology, as well as a test dataset in the domain of DNA collecting home kits, are openly available on our GitHub page, https://github.com/aleksandargavric/mm_proc_miner, ensuring accessibility for further research and application.

References

1. 23andMe (2020). https://www.23andme.com/
2. Ancestry.com: Ancestrydna. Ancestry.com (2020). https://www.ancestry.com/dna/
3. Beerepoot, I., et al.: The biggest business process management problems to solve before we die. Comput. Ind. **146**, 103837 (2023). https://doi.org/10.1016/j.compind.2022.103837
4. Chen, S., Zou, M., Cao, R., Zhao, Z., Zeng, Q.: Video process mining and model matching for intelligent development: conformance checking. Sensors **23**(8), 3812 (2023)
5. Dixit, P.M., et al.: Detection and interactive repair of event ordering imperfection in process logs. In: Krogstie, J., Reijers, H.A. (eds.) CAiSE 2018. LNCS, vol. 10816, pp. 274–290. Springer, Cham (2018). https://doi.org/10.1007/978-3-319-91563-0_17
6. Folino, F., Pontieri, L.: Pushing more AI capabilities into process mining to better deal with low-quality logs. In: Di Francescomarino, C., Dijkman, R., Zdun, U. (eds.) BPM 2019. LNBIP, vol. 362, pp. 5–11. Springer, Cham (2019). https://doi.org/10.1007/978-3-030-37453-2_1
7. Gavric, A.: Enhancing process understanding through multimodal data analysis and extended reality. In: Companion Proceedings of the 16th IFIP WG 8.1 Working Conference on the Practice of Enterprise Modeling and the 13th Enterprise Design and Engineering Working Conference (2023)
8. Gavric, A., Bork, D., Proper, H.: Multimodal process mining. In: CBI 2024: 26th International Conference on Business Informatics (2024)
9. Girdhar, R., et al.: ImageBind: one embedding space to bind them all. In: CVPR (2023)
10. Google: Google gemini. Website (2024). https://gemini.google.com. Accessed 2 June 2024
11. Janssen, D., Mannhardt, F., Koschmider, A., van Zelst, S.J.: Process model discovery from sensor event data. In: Leemans, S., Leopold, H. (eds.) ICPM 2020. LNBIP, vol. 406, pp. 69–81. Springer, Cham (2021). https://doi.org/10.1007/978-3-030-72693-5_6
12. Knoch, S., Ponpathirkoottam, S., Schwartz, T.: Video-to-model: unsupervised trace extraction from videos for process discovery and conformance checking in manual assembly. In: Fahland, D., Ghidini, C., Becker, J., Dumas, M. (eds.) BPM 2020. LNCS, vol. 12168, pp. 291–308. Springer, Cham (2020). https://doi.org/10.1007/978-3-030-58666-9_17
13. Kratsch, W., König, F., Röglinger, M.: Shedding light on blind spots - developing a reference architecture to leverage video data for process mining. Decis. Support Syst. **158**, 113794 (2022). https://doi.org/10.1016/j.dss.2022.113794
14. Körber, N., Wehrli, S., Irrgang, C.: How to measure the intelligence of large language models? (2024). https://arxiv.org/abs/2407.20828
15. Lepsien, A., Bosselmann, J., Melfsen, A., Koschmider, A.: Process mining on video data. In: ZEUS 2022, CEUR Workshop Proceedings, vol. 3113, pp. 56–62. CEUR-WS.org (2022). https://ceur-ws.org/Vol-3113/paper9.pdf
16. Lepsien, A., Koschmider, A., Kratsch, W.: Analytics pipeline for process mining on video data. In: Di Francescomarino, C., Burattin, A., Janiesch, C., Sadiq, S. (eds.) BPM 2023. LNBIP, vol. 490, pp. 196–213. Springer, Cham (2023). https://doi.org/10.1007/978-3-031-41623-1_12

17. Liu, H., Li, C., Li, Y., Lee, Y.J.: Improved baselines with visual instruction tuning (2023)
18. Malinova, M., Gross, S., Mendling, J.: A study into the contingencies of process improvement methods. Inf. Syst. **104**, 101880 (2022). https://doi.org/10.1016/j.is.2021.101880. https://www.sciencedirect.com/science/article/pii/S0306437921001022
19. Okoye, K., Islam, S., Naeem, U., Sharif, M.S., Azam, M.A., Karami, A.: The application of a semantic-based process mining framework on a learning process domain. In: Arai, K., Kapoor, S., Bhatia, R. (eds.) IntelliSys 2018. AISC, vol. 868, pp. 1381–1403. Springer, Cham (2019). https://doi.org/10.1007/978-3-030-01054-6_96
20. OpenAI: ChatGPT (2024). https://chat.openai.com. Accessed 01 Aug 2024
21. Pegoraro, M., van der Aalst, W.M.: Mining uncertain event data in process mining. In: 2019 International Conference on Process Mining (ICPM), pp. 89–96 (2019). https://doi.org/10.1109/ICPM.2019.00023
22. Rebmann, A., Emrich, A., Fettke, P.: Enabling the discovery of manual processes using a multi-modal activity recognition approach. In: Di Francescomarino, C., Dijkman, R., Zdun, U. (eds.) BPM 2019. LNBIP, vol. 362, pp. 130–141. Springer, Cham (2019). https://doi.org/10.1007/978-3-030-37453-2_12
23. Tax, N., Sidorova, N., Haakma, R., van der Aalst, W.M.P.: Event abstraction for process mining using supervised learning techniques. In: Bi, Y., Kapoor, S., Bhatia, R. (eds.) IntelliSys 2016. LNNS, vol. 15, pp. 251–269. Springer, Cham (2018). https://doi.org/10.1007/978-3-319-56994-9_18
24. Telli, A., Erdogan, T.G., Kolukısa, A.: Detecting novel behavior and process enhancement with multimodal process mining. In: 2023 4th International Informatics and Software Engineering Conference (IISEC), pp. 1–6 (2023). https://doi.org/10.1109/IISEC59749.2023.10391012

Towards Timeline-Based Layout for Process Mining

Harleen Kaur[1], Jan Mendling[1,2,3(✉)], Timotheus Kampik[4], and Christoffer Rubensson[1,2]

[1] Humboldt-Universität zu Berlin, Berlin, Germany
{jan.mendling,christoffer.rubensson}@hu-berlin.de
[2] Weizenbaum Institute for the Networked Society, Berlin, Germany
[3] Wirtschaftsuniversität Wien, Vienna, Austria
[4] SAP Signavio, Berlin, Germany
timotheus.kampik@sap.com

Abstract. Process mining techniques have been developed in order to help process analysts to obtain better insights into the performance of business processes. A key dimension of such analysis is time, as it is closely connected with performance problems such as waiting times or bottlenecks. So far, process mining techniques have mostly focused on behavioral patterns such as directly-follows relationships, missing the opportunity to show time explicitly in generated process models. In this paper, we argue that representing time in process models is essentially a layout problem. We present a technique for aligning a process model with the time axis and exemplify it for directly-follows graphs. We use an illustrative evaluation using BPIC event logs to investigate the plausible benefits of a timeline-based layout.

Keywords: Process Mining · Automatic Process Discovery · Visual Analytics · Timelines · Directly-Follows Graphs

1 Introduction

Process mining is a research area that focuses on automatic analysis techniques that provide insights into the operational performance of business processes. Larger corporations use process mining tools for analyzing bottlenecks, waiting times, and operational costs. Various algorithms have been developed in process mining research, mostly for automatic process discovery [32], often with the ambition to improve quality measures of the generated process models such as precision and recall [22].

The research of the authors was supported by the Einstein Foundation Berlin under grant EPP-2019-524, by the German Federal Ministry of Education and Research under grant 16DII133, and by Deutsche Forschungsgemeinschaft under grant 496119880.
The original version of the chapter has been revised. The DFG grant number has been corrected as well as a few typing errors. A correction to this chapter can be found at https://doi.org/10.1007/978-3-031-77908-4_18

© IFIP International Federation for Information Processing 2025, corrected publication 2025
Published by Springer Nature Switzerland AG 2025
E. Paja et al. (Eds.): PoEM 2024, LNBIP 538, pp. 192–206, 2025.
https://doi.org/10.1007/978-3-031-77908-4_12

Arguably, a more practically pressing concern than providing an accurate representation of the control flow order of activities is the accurate representation of temporal distance. Process analysts are generally interested in understanding where and why waiting times occur and to which extent they contribute to overall cycle times [9, Ch.7]. So far, temporal distances between activities have not gained much attention in process mining research. There are a few exceptions, though. These include color highlighting of long durations [9, p.445], performance spectra [7], or dotted charts [26]. However, there are no techniques that integrate the strengths of a time-proportional visualization as used in timelines with automatically generated process models.

This paper presents an approach for automatically constructing process models that explicitly align with the time axis. We address this research challenge at the level of graph layout and position activities according to their relative temporal distance to the start of the process. We exemplify this idea for directly-follows graphs, though it can be equally adopted for process mining algorithms that construct other types of graphs like Petri nets or BPMN. We demonstrate the effectiveness of our approach based on a comparison of the standard layout with our timeline-based layout.

The remainder of the paper is structured as follows. Section 2 summarizes prior research on timelines in visual analytics. Section 3 presents the concepts of our approach to layout graphs using a timeline. Section 4 evaluates the effectiveness of our approach and discusses its implications. Section 5 concludes with a summary and outlook on future research.

2 Background

The time perspective has been investigated for event sequences, however with little integration of process mining concepts. In this section, we summarize related work that considers time as an explicit analysis dimension. First, we focus on timeline-based techniques from visual analytics. Then, we cover the few timeline-related contributions from process mining. Finally, we identify requirements based on a reflection of the related work.

2.1 Timelines in Visual Analytics

Timelines play an important role in analyzing events and temporal phenomena in visual analytics [2]. A timeline defines a horizontal or vertical axis and represents a set of discrete time points or a scale of time units. Events can then be presented as glyphs or shapes on the canvas aligned to the timeline, optionally extended with edges connecting related events [11, p. 4]. A plethora of visualizations have been developed in visual analytics research. Here, we refer to a recent taxonomy of visualizations for event sequence data developed and extended in [11,35]. This taxonomy distinguishes five categories: fixed, duration, converging-diverging, evolution, and combinations of these techniques (Fig. 1).

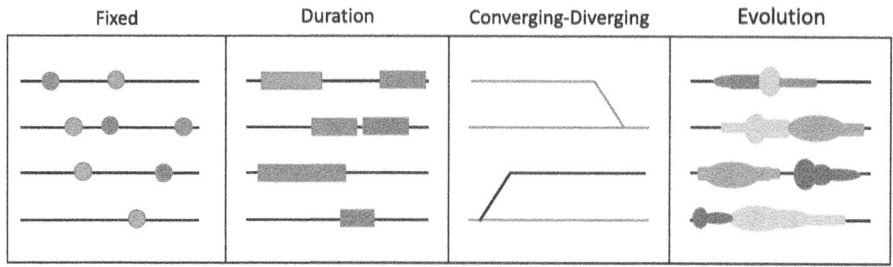

Fig. 1. Timeline-based Visualizations.

Fixed timeline-based visualization techniques map each event to a specific point in time on the timeline [35]. These events are then represented as different types of glyphs in order to distinguish event types. Examples of contributions to this category are [6,8,14,15,20]. The second axis is typically used to distinguish types of event sequences [6,14]. *Duration timeline-based* visualization techniques explicitly represent event durations. Such durations can be shown using rectangular glyphs on the canvas aligned with the time axis. Examples of works in this category are [12,21,25,30,31]. Often, color highlighting is used to further emphasize domain-specific information about the importance of certain events. *Converging-diverging timeline-based* visualization techniques use different horizontal lines that converge and diverge at different stages. These represent the change of affiliation of sequences of events. Often, lines represent the lifeline of an entity and the events that are associated with it. For example, Liu et al. [17] use lines to represent a character in a story, or a similar story-related object, with bundled lines indicating relational interactions. Several examples of this visualization type are found in the literature, a.o. [3,17,17,23,34]. *Evolution timeline-based* visualization techniques represent event sequences as density charts or evolution line graphs. In this way, they visualize the concentration of quantitative properties over time. Examples of such visualizations are Wu et al. [33] who represent the propagation of opinions on social media, and Sung et al. [27] who visualize online lecture satisfaction. The category of *combination* techniques refers to solutions that combine features of other types. Some works group elements and position them according to average times [10,20,27]. Other works enhance Gantt charts to visualize complex events in a compact way [13].

All these works from visual analytics typically show instances of event sequences and map them to timelines in one or the other way. Some combination techniques highlight the potential of aggregating events and position them according to average times [10,20,27]

2.2 Process Mining with Time Axis

Research on process mining typically focuses on a compact aggregation of a group of event sequences as a process model that is able to generate these sequences. These models describe the control flow but hardly the temporal distances between different types of events. Only a few works on process mining integrate a time axis into their approaches.

Some process mining contributions relate to the category of *fixed timeline-based* visualizations. Bose et al. [5] describe a scatter plot similar to a Gantt chart that they call Dotted Chart. This visualization uses a horizontal time axis and positions separate cases as rows from top to bottom. Events are positioned according to their timestamp and colored according to their respective event type. Also in this category is the work by Leoni et al. [16]. Their visualization shows work tasks as dots in a timeline map with colors indicating the geographical distance between a resource and a task. Other works relate to the category of *duration timeline-based* techniques similar to Gantt charts. Low et al. [18] provide a view for comparing various process-related characteristics of two event logs simultaneously. Richter et al. [24] use bar lengths to encode transition times between activities. There are also works in the category of *evolution timeline-based* visualizations. Suriadi et al. present visualization tools showing event properties as line graphs aligned with a horizontal time axis with a focus on analyzing durations and resource behaviour [28,29].

2.3 Requirements for Timeline-Based Process Mining

We observe that contributions on timelines largely abstract from replay semantics as provided by process models. Most process mining techniques do not explicitly map to a time axis, and if they do, they abstract from model semantics. Timeline visualizations have essentially two characteristics in common: the timeline defines the reading direction, and elements are positioned according to temporal order.

Based on these observations, we define the research objective of our work as developing an approach for automatically constructing process models that explicitly align with a time axis. This translates into the following two requirements:

REQ1. A process model must define a reading direction.
REQ2. Edges from preceding to succeeding events must follow the reading direction.
REQ3. The length of edges must be proportional to temporal distance.

3 Timeline-Based Layout of Process Models

This section presents the concepts of generating a timeline-based layout for a process model generated from an event log addressing requirements REQ1-3. To this end, we make use of the calculation of average times per activity type. Using these times, we construct a layout of a directly-follows graph (DFG).

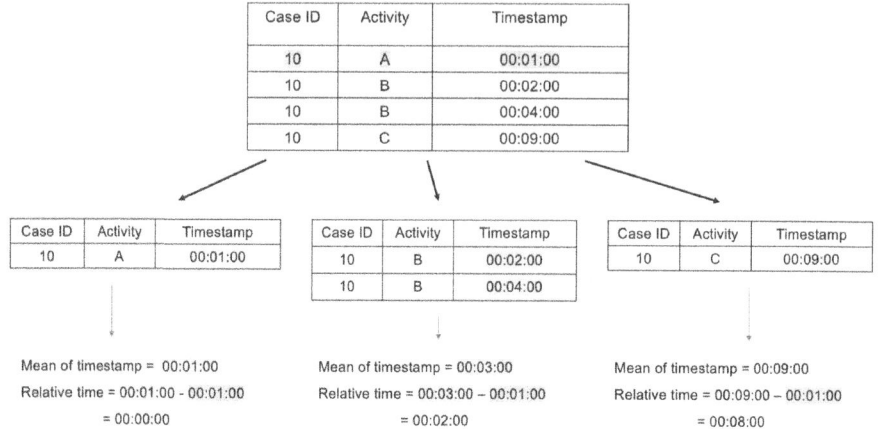

Fig. 2. Diagram showing how relative time is calculated for each case in event log. For each case, the earliest activity is taken to be the start activity, here activity A. Case ID 10 has activity B repeated. Each case is then split into a sub-table for each activity to deal with loops. A mean value is calculated for each sub-table's timestamp column.

3.1 Average Time Calculation

To address our requirements, we consider the average time difference between event types that are in directly-follows relationships. This means that we give priority to REQ3. Mind that REQ3 does not necessarily lead to the satisfaction of REQ2. Both are in conflict e.g. when a directly-follows relationship exists between two activities and through a path from the second, there is eventually a loop back to the first one. We will look at the extent of this conflict in our evaluation.

As a starting point, we assume an event log L as a finite set of traces. Every trace $C \in L$ is a sequence of activities such that for every $(a,t) \in C$ it holds that $a \in A$. Here, A is a finite background set of activity identifiers and $t \in \mathbb{N}_0$[1]. To visualize the event log from the perspective of relative physical time, we need to adjust the timestamps in the event log so that they are relative to the start time of the case and not logged in global time (see Fig. 2).

First, we determine the case start time. This is the minimal time for which any event of a case is logged. We define $t_{min}(C) := avg(\{t | (a,t) \in C, \forall (a',t') \in C : t \leq t'\})$ (avg is used as an aggregation function for merely technical purposes). Second, we determine for each case and for each event the relative timestamp (relative to the start time of the case) by subtracting the case start time from the timestamp of the event. We can introduce a function f that makes the time adjustment according to relative time, i.e., $f(C) := \{(a, t - t_{min}(C)) | (a,t) \in C\}$.

---

[1] Here, we use $\mathbb{N}_0$ as an approximate domain for Unix time. Note that a uniqueness assumption for timestamps can typically be made (or enforced); hence, assuming a multiset of traces or event tuples is not necessary.

This transformation of the event log allows us to compute the average (and roughly analogously: median and mode) times at which an event occurs relative to the start time of the process. We define a function $g_L : A \to \mathbb{R}$, i.e., for $a \in A$, $g(a) := avg(\{t|(a',t) \in \bigcup_{C \in L} C, a' = a\})$. Given the average occurrence time, we can then construct the timeline. Note that the transformation is executed on a copy of the event log, i.e., we retain the initial log.

3.2 Construction of the Layout

The construction of the layout has to reflect REQ1. In this paper, we exemplify our concepts by using a reading direction from top to bottom. This reading direction follows the timeline that we use for aligning process model elements. To this end, we proceed as follows.

After calculating the average relative time points, we automatically discover the DFG using a standard process mining algorithm [1] and align it with the timeline. This involves creating a time axis representing the temporal distance between each node. By assuming a software-supported implementation using a graphical rendering and layout engine, we can proceed along the following steps. We consider Graphviz and its DOT framework, since it is able to render digraph objects.

First, we initialize the graph by creating a digraph object. This ensures that the graph's vertices are drawn in horizontal rows and the layout is optimized to create edges pointing downwards where possible. Second, different elements of the graph have to be generated. This includes the generation of time and activity labels. To this end, each timestamp is rounded to the nearest second, minute, month, and year and formatted in a human-readable way. Two examples of this are the time values *0 days 00:44:12.1234* and *66 days 14:32:55.4321*, which are converted to *44 m* and *2MO*, respectively. Each unique rounded-off time value will be utilized as a label for a node of the time axis and for edge length calculation. Then, we generate the nodes of the time axis and assign each one a unique identifier. This unique identifier is used to align the nodes of the DFG with the nodes of the time axis. We determine the edge length of each subsequent node in the time axis by subtracting the rounded-off numerical value according to the temporal distance. Third, we generate the DFG based on the initial event log using a process discovery technique. Nodes are created for each activity and assigned a unique identifier. The edges are assigned a frequency label. Then, we map each activity of the DFG to a node of the time axis according to its timestamps. A node of the time axis can have more than one associated activity if its rounded timestamps are identical. Finally, the mapping is used to align the DFG nodes with the time axis according to their respective heights on the canvas. This is achieved by creating subgraphs that are equal to the number of nodes on the time axis. Each subgraph includes the unique identifier of the time axis node. Additionally, it includes the identifiers referencing those activities that are supposed to be aligned with the current time axis node.

3.3 Prototypical Implementation

Our layout technique has been implemented as a fork[2]. In the implementation, we used *Graphviz*[3] to generate a script in the DOT language, Graphviz's abstract graph grammar. The DOT script specifies what to include and where to position the nodes and edges of the graph. An example of the resulting DOT script is shown in Fig. 3. Assume we have an event log with four activities a, b, and c, and the directly-follows relations are (a, b) and (b, c)}. a is the start activity. The relative time taken for each of the activities to execute is as follows: a: 0s, b: 3m, c: 4m. Following the steps mentioned above will result in the graph shown in Fig. 3. The DOT script from which the graph is rendered is shown next to the graph.

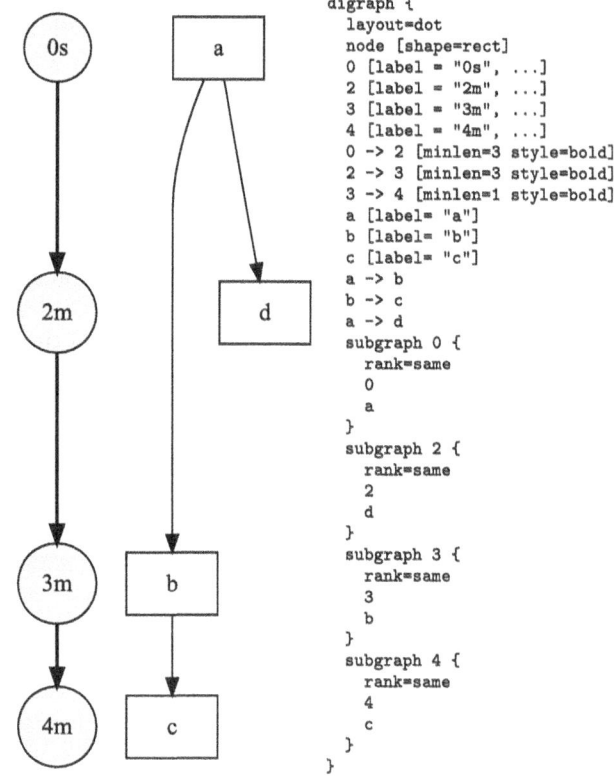

Fig. 3. A simple example of a visualization result (right) after generating the DOT script (left) from directly-follows and time relations of three activities.

---

[2] The code is available at https://github.com/Har-leen-kaur/pm4py-timeline-axis of the PM4Py library [4]. An example notebook can be found at https://github.com/Har-leen-kaur/pm4py-timeline-axis/blob/release/6_timeline_axis_dfg.ipynb.
[3] https://graphviz.org/.

4 Evaluation

In this section, we present an evaluation of the effectiveness of our approach. To this end, we compare the output of a classic DFG representation (in our case, rendered by PM4Py) with the one from our novel approach. Our comparison focuses on the following questions. First, we count how many pairs of activities in the standard layout are positioned in a way that contradicts their temporal order. Second, we discuss to which extent the temporal ordering provides a graph segmentation that is not visible with a standard layout. Finally, we investigate to what extent the distances along the time axis provide meaningful cues to the process analyst.

4.1 Datasets Used for Comparison

For this evaluation, we apply our implementation to two different event logs. First, we use the event logs from the BPI Challenge 2017[4], which is based on real-life data of a loan application processes from a Dutch financial institute. The event log from the BPI Challenge 2017 comprises 1,202,267 events and 31,509 cases and contains all applications filed through the institute's online system in 2016 and their subsequent events until February 1st, 2017, 15:11.[5] We have a total order imposed by time.

Furthermore, we use a proprietary event log of a sales process. The process instances were executed as part of a business-to-business software sales process of a medium-sized European company. In this process, a *lead* (customer contact) is generated and eventually converted into an *opportunity* (lead with specific purchase scenario) that is then either lost/closed or turned into a paying customer. The data cannot be shared for privacy and compliance reasons; thus, only the resulting graphs are illustrated. Furthermore, because of the complexity of the data, only a small sample (0.5% of the event data) was considered.

4.2 Comparison for the BPIC Dataset 2017

Figure 4 depicts the resulting DFGs after applying our approach to the BPI Challenge 2017 event log.

In the standard DFG, none of the 26 activities are consistent with the temporal order as depicted in the timeline-based DFG. We observe that the position of the starting activity "A_Create Application" is in the bottom left corner of the diagram. The following activities are accurately ordered visually after the starting event, which is a contradiction to the time axis (cf., Fig. 4a). "A_Accepted" is the event at the top left corner. It receives four edges pointing upwards contradicting temporal order and two outgoing edges correctly pointing downwards. The next top-most event, "O_Create Offer," in the middle is worse: 13 of its

---

[4] https://doi.org/10.4121/uuid:5f3067df-f10b-45da-b98b-86ae4c7a310b.
[5] https://ais.win.tue.nl/bpi/2017/challenge.html.

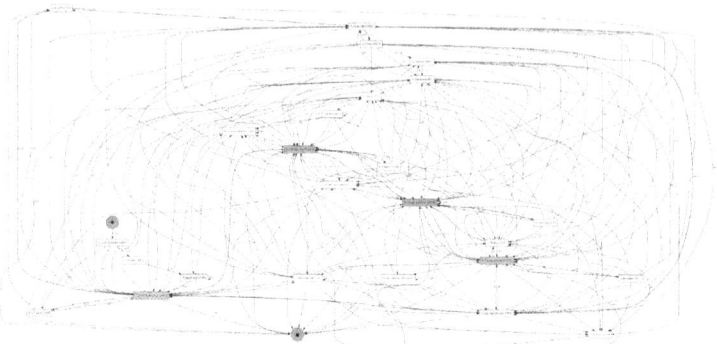

(a) DFG with PM4Py standard layout

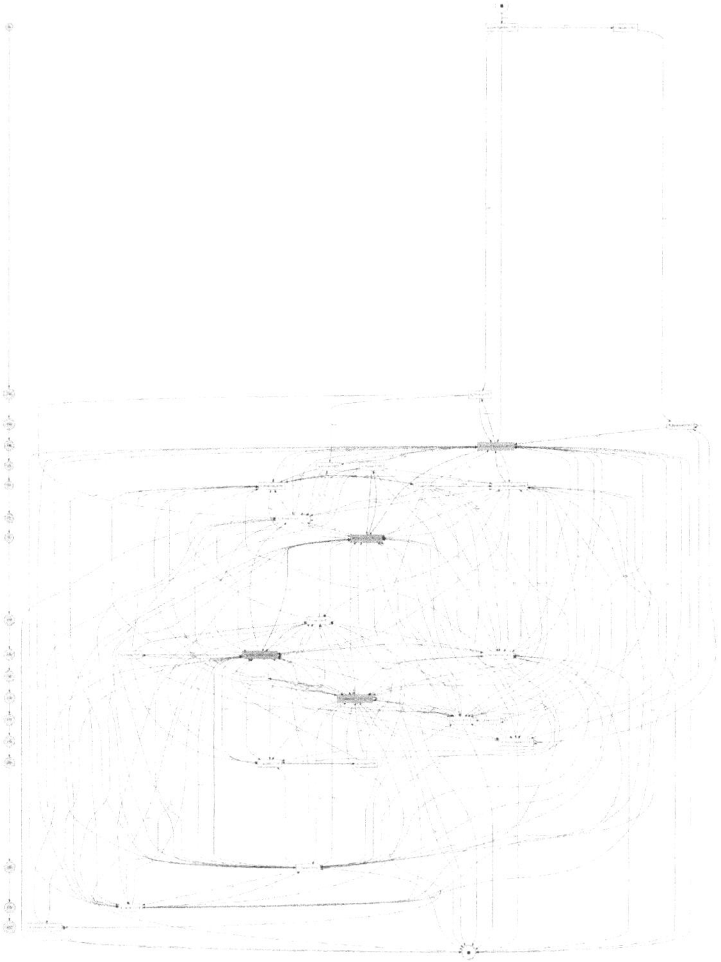

(b) Timeline-based DFG

Fig. 4. BPI Challenge '17 event log: a simple DFG and DFG based on a timeline showing frequencies.

incoming edges point upwards against the reading direction. Similar observations can be made for many other events.

The timeline-based DFG changes the positioning of the process graph elements. This creates some apparent temporal segmentation of activities, but not for all parts of the model (see Fig. 4b). We observe that the start activity "A_Create Application" including the "A_Submitted" are positioned at the top right corner of the timeline-based DFG. Most other activities follow a spaghetti-like pattern at the bottom half of the canvas. The previously mentioned event "O_Create Offer" now has nine upwards pointing incoming edges, four less than in the standard layout. Still, the end activities are now located toward the end of the process rather than visually dispersed. Moreover, due to the reading direction of the timeline-based graph, activities with similar approximate time points are vertically aligned, providing a sense of temporal concurrency.

The timeline-based approach apparently provides process analysts with additional temporal cues unavailable in the classical DFG layout. A noticeable improvement is the inclusion of the timeline itself, which allows for a holistic view of performance for the entire process, rather than for single process segments. As this results in a hierarchical process model with activities grouped into temporal segments, the timeline-based graph also eases the finding of concurrent events or possible decision points. This cue is not visible in the standard DFG. For example, roughly four phases are visible: an application phase, a submission phase, a validation phase, and a cancellation phase. In addition, the timeline can be used to study the differences in process duration for different cases depending on their outcome. For example, a loan application that is later denied takes approximately 16 days, whereas a loan application (offer) later accepted takes approximately 18 days. An outlier activity is also apparent: "W_Personal Loan collection" extends the process duration by an estimated additional three months. None of these visual cues is evident in the standard DFG.

However, the simplified view of time also leads to further challenges. Accurate time analysis is still difficult because the activities align on an approximative logarithmic scale based on their average execution time. Also, some control flow cannot be adequately interpreted according to the temporal orientation. Such as the edges that appear to go "backward" in time. While this is less of a problem than with the classical layout, it cannot be fully resolved using the layout strategy developed here. Challenges stem from loops and from some constellations of splits and joins.

4.3 Comparison for Private Sales Dataset

Figure 5 illustrates the resulting DFGs after applying our approach to the proprietary sales process data.

In the standard DFG, only six of the 24 activities ("Create Lead", "Activity logged: Task (Call)", "Team Member added: BDR", "Opportunity net new ARR updated", "Opportunity Campaign_Code_2__c updated" and "Customer contact role added: Billing Contact") are consistent with the temporal order displayed in the timeline-based DFG. Additionally, the starting and ending symbols of

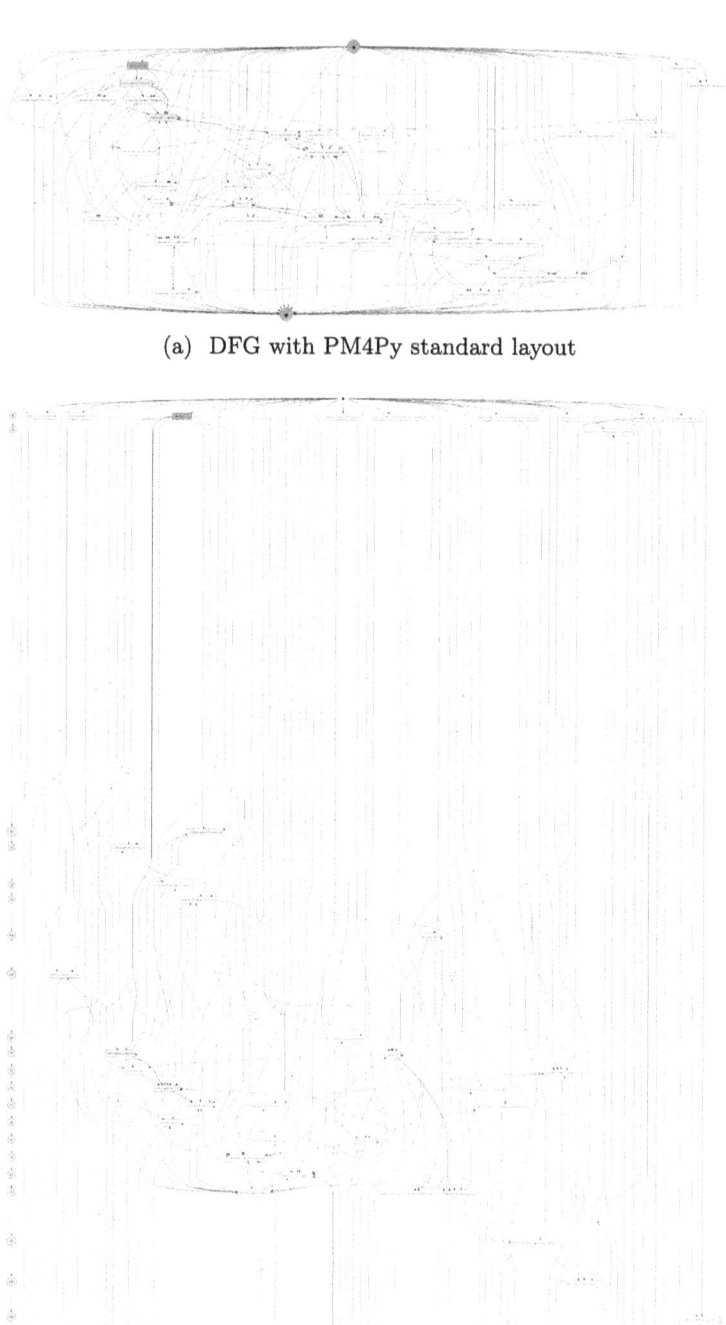

(a) DFG with PM4Py standard layout

(b) Timeline-based DFG

Fig. 5. Proprietary sales process dataset: a simple DFG and a DFG based on a timeline showing frequencies.

the standard DFG are positioned respectively at the top and the end of the canvas, giving the false illusion of a temporally ordered graph. In the center of the diagram is the event "Opportunity close date updated". It has four incoming edges from below and one outgoing edge pointing upwards.

The timeline-based counterpart generates a more accurate depiction of the temporal order. As an example, the event "Opportunity close date updated" is positioned much further downwards in the diagram. It is the lowest element on the left-hand side of the diagram. All its incoming edges run in the reading direction, coming from the top. It still has three outgoing edges pointing upwards as part of cycles.

Similar to the previous comparison (4.2), the timeline-based approach, in this case, visually reflects a notion of phases in the process model. In this process, a *lead* (customer contact) is generated and eventually converted into an *opportunity* (lead with specific purchase scenario) that is then either lost/closed or turned into a paying customer. Four phases are visually noticeable, such as a lead creation phase (first seconds), a lead setup phase (first hours), an opportunity nurturing phase (first week), and a closing phase (last two to three weeks). In this regard, the timeline does not only provide temporal cues but can reveal important details about the sales process and its critical stages.

Because the sales event log is highly complex, with many trace variations, the layout is not fully ordered in both DFGs. However, the timeline-based DFG captures some of these variations indirectly through the vertical alignments of activities at their respective time points. This is especially evident for the different start activities.

4.4 Discussion

Based on the two comparisons, we can summarize the effectiveness of our approach according to the three requirements we identified in the beginning.

The first requirement (REQ1) highlights the importance of the reading direction. The timeline-based DFG layout displays the process model in a hierarchical structure, thus providing a more intuitive visualization of processes. Starting activities are visualized at the top, whereas ending activities are positioned toward the bottom of the canvas. This is only sometimes the case in a standard DFG layout.

The second requirement (REQ2) stresses temporal order. Our timeline-based approach effectively aligns a process model along a time axis, ordering the activities according to their respective estimated temporal occurrence. The standard DFG layout, at least as provided by PM4Py, is not a viable alternative in this regard because it produces many edges that contradict the temporal order of the preceding and succeeding events. We also observed limitations of our approach. Not all edges can be easily aligned with the timeline. Loops in process models necessarily result in at least one edge that points upwards. Also, uneven temporal distributions of splits and joins can lead to edges pointing upwards. In these matters, requirements REQ2 and REQ3 can be in conflict.

The third requirement (REQ3) refers to temporal distances. We have observed that our layout can untangle some parts of the process model in a way that temporal segments can be easily identified. Furthermore, activities that are approximately executed simultaneously are vertically aligned on the same row, forming temporal groups. These groups result in an additional depth of a process model, as they may indicate phases. In this way, the timeline-based approach provides critical visual cues on process performance for analysts, cues that are not prominent or unavailable in the standard layout. The integrated time axis in the timeline-based DFG allows for a holistic view of performance, as it can be analyzed for the entire process rather than just on fragments. This supports the finding of bottlenecks and delays but also temporal outliers.

5 Conclusion

In this paper, we addressed the challenge of providing insights into the temporal distances of activities of a process model generated by process mining techniques. We identified three requirements for aligning a process model with a timeline: a process model must define a reading direction, edges from preceding to succeeding events must follow the reading direction, and the length of edges must be proportional to temporal distance. To address these requirements, we developed a time axis proportional to the occurrences of events in a process. Our evaluation using two different event log datasets demonstrates that implementing a timeline in a process model provides apparent benefits for the visual analysis of the temporal dimension of a process. However, we also observe that there are conflicts addressing the requirements. A temporal alignment is not possible for loops and for uneven temporal distributions of splits and joins.

In future research, we plan to address the conflict between requirements, potentially with preprocessing techniques. Furthermore, the apparent benefits of a timeline-based visualization of process models need further substantiation. To this end, we plan user studies to test the cognitive effectiveness [19] of the layout in a real-world setting, considering the trade-offs of the layout options.

References

1. van der Aalst, W.M.P.: Process mining - data science in action, Second Edition. Springer (2016). https://doi.org/10.1007/978-3-662-49851-4
2. Aigner, W., Miksch, S., Schumann, H., Tominski, C.: Visualization of Time-Oriented Data. Springer, 2nd edn, Human-Computer Interaction Series (2023)
3. Baumgartl, T., et al.: In search of patient zero: visual analytics of pathogen transmission pathways in hospitals. IEEE Trans. Visual Comput. Graphics **27**(2), 711–721 (2021). https://doi.org/10.1109/TVCG.2020.3030437
4. Berti, A., van Zelst, S.J., van der Aalst, W.M.P.: Process mining for python (pm4py): bridging the gap between process- and data science. CoRR **abs/1905.06169** (2019), http://arxiv.org/abs/1905.06169
5. Bose, R.P.J.C., van der Aalst, W.M.P.: Process diagnostics using trace alignment: opportunities, issues, and challenges. Inf. Syst. **37**(2), 117–141 (2012)

6. Chen, Y., Xu, P., Ren, L.: Sequence synopsis: optimize visual summary of temporal event data. IEEE Trans. Vis. Comput. Graph. **24**(1), 45–55 (2018)
7. Denisov, V., Fahland, D., van der Aalst, W.M.: Predictive performance monitoring of material handling systems using the performance spectrum. In: 2019 International Conference on Process Mining (ICPM), pp. 137–144. IEEE (2019)
8. van Dortmont, M.A.M.M., van den Elzen, S., van Wijk, J.J.: Chronocorrelator: enriching events with time series. Comput. Graph. Forum **38**(3), 387–399 (2019)
9. Dumas, M., Rosa, M.L., Mendling, J., Reijers, H.A.: Fundamentals of Business Process Management, 2nd Edn. Springer (2018)
10. Fulda, J., Brehmer, M., Munzner, T.: Timelinecurator: interactive authoring of visual timelines from unstructured text. IEEE Trans. Vis. Comput. Graph. **22**(1), 300–309 (2016)
11. Guo, Y., Guo, S., Jin, Z., Kaul, S., Gotz, D., Cao, N.: A survey on visual analysis of event sequence data. IEEE Trans. Vis. Comput. Graph. 1–20 (2021). https://doi.org/10.1109/TVCG.2021.3100413
12. Han, Y., Rozga, A., Dimitrova, N., Abowd, G.D., Stasko, J.T.: Visual analysis of proximal temporal relationships of social and communicative behaviors. Comput. Graph. Forum **34**(3), 51–60 (2015)
13. Jo, J., Huh, J., Park, J., Kim, B.H., Seo, J.: Livegantt: interactively visualizing a large manufacturing schedule. IEEE Trans. Vis. Comput. Graph. **20**(12), 2329–2338 (2014)
14. Kwon, B.C., et al.: Dpvis: visual analytics with hidden markov models for disease progression pathways. IEEE Trans. Vis. Comput. Graph. (2020)
15. Leite, R.A., Gschwandtner, T., Miksch, S., Gstrein, E., Kuntner, J.: NEVA: visual analytics to identify fraudulent networks. Comput. Graph. Forum **39**(6), 344–359 (2020)
16. de Leoni, M., Adams, M., van der Aalst, W.M.P., ter Hofstede, A.H.M.: Visual support for work assignment in process-aware information systems: framework formalisation and implementation. Decis. Support Syst. **54**(1), 345–361 (2012)
17. Liu, S., Wu, Y., Wei, E., Liu, M., Liu, Y.: Storyflow: tracking the evolution of stories. IEEE Trans. Vis. Comput. Graph. **19**(12), 2436–2445 (2013)
18. Low, W.Z., van der Aalst, W.M.P., ter Hofstede, A.H.M., Wynn, M.T., Weerdt, J.D.: Change visualisation: analysing the resource and timing differences between two event logs. Inf. Syst. **65**, 106–123 (2017)
19. Malinova Mandelburger, M., Mendling, J.: Cognitive diagram understanding and task performance in systems analysis and design. MIS Q. **45**(4), 2101–2157 (2021)
20. Monroe, M., Lan, R., Lee, H., Plaisant, C., Shneiderman, B.: Temporal event sequence simplification. IEEE Trans. Vis. Comput. Graph. **19**(12), 2227–2236 (2013)
21. Nguyen, P.H., Turkay, C., Andrienko, G.L., Andrienko, N.V., Thonnard, O., Zouaoui, J.: Understanding user behaviour through action sequences: From the usual to the unusual. IEEE Trans. Vis. Comput. Graph. **25**(9), 2838–2852 (2019)
22. Polyvyanyy, A., Solti, A., Weidlich, M., Ciccio, C.D., Mendling, J.: Monotone precision and recall measures for comparing executions and specifications of dynamic systems. ACM Trans. Softw. Eng. Methodol. (TOSEM) **29**(3), 1–41 (2020)
23. Reda, K., Tantipathananandh, C., Johnson, A.E., Leigh, J., Berger-Wolf, T.Y.: Visualizing the evolution of community structures in dynamic social networks. Comput. Graph. Forum **30**(3), 1061–1070 (2011)
24. Richter, F., Seidl, T.: Looking into the TESSERACT: time-drifts in event streams using series of evolving rolling averages of completion times. Inf. Syst. **84**, 265–282 (2019)

25. Rosenthal, P., Pfeiffer, L., Müller, N.H., Ohler, P.: Visruption: intuitive and efficient visualization of temporal airline disruption data. Comput. Graph. Forum **32**(3), 81–90 (2013)
26. Song, M., van der Aalst, W.M.: Supporting process mining by showing events at a glance. In: Proceedings of the 17th Annual Workshop on Information Technologies and Systems (WITS), pp. 139–145 (2007)
27. Sung, C., Huang, X., Shen, Y., Cherng, F., Lin, W., Wang, H.: Exploring online learners' interactive dynamics by visually analyzing their time-anchored comments. Comput. Graph. Forum **36**(7), 145–155 (2017)
28. Suriadi, S., Ouyang, C., van der Aalst, W.M.P., ter Hofstede, A.H.M.: Event interval analysis: why do processes take time? Decis. Support Syst. **79**, 77–98 (2015)
29. Suriadi, S., Wynn, M.T., Xu, J., van der Aalst, W.M.P., ter Hofstede, A.H.M.: Discovering work prioritisation patterns from event logs. Decis. Support Syst. **100**, 77–92 (2017)
30. Vrotsou, K., Johansson, J., Cooper, M.: Activitree: interactive visual exploration of sequences in event-based data using graph similarity. IEEE Trans. Vis. Comput. Graph. **15**(6), 945–952 (2009)
31. Vrotsou, K., Ynnerman, A., Cooper, M.: Are we what we do? exploring group behaviour through user-defined event-sequence similarity. Inf. Vis. **13**(3), 232–247 (2014)
32. Weerdt, J.D., Backer, M.D., Vanthienen, J., Baesens, B.: A multi-dimensional quality assessment of state-of-the-art process discovery algorithms using real-life event logs. Inf. Syst. **37**(7), 654–676 (2012). https://doi.org/10.1016/j.is.2012.02.004
33. Wu, Y., Liu, S., Yan, K., Liu, M., Wu, F.: Opinionflow: visual analysis of opinion diffusion on social media. IEEE Trans. Vis. Comput. Graph. **20**(12), 1763–1772 (2014)
34. Xu, P., Mei, H., Ren, L., Chen, W.: Vidx: visual diagnostics of assembly line performance in smart factories. IEEE Trans. Vis. Comput. Graph. **23**(1), 291–300 (2017)
35. Yeshchenko, A., Mendling, J.: A survey of approaches for event sequence analysis and visualization. Inf. Syst. **120**, 102283 (2024). https://doi.org/10.1016/J.IS.2023.102283

Conceptualisation and (Meta)modelling of Problem-Solution Chains in Early Business-IT Alignment and System Design

Stijn Hoppenbrouwers[1,2](✉), Mark A. T. Mulder[3], and Joris Sunnotel[2,4]

[1] HAN University of Applied Sciences, Arnhem, The Netherlands
stijn.hoppenbrouwers@han.nl
[2] Radboud University, Nijmegen, The Netherlands
[3] TEEC2, Leusden, The Netherlands
markmulder@teec2.nl
[4] Capgemini, Utrecht, The Netherlands
j.c.sunnotel@gmail.com

Abstract. The Problem-Solution Chain (PSC) models proposed in this exploratory paper are conceived as describing chains of problem-solution links, thereby modelling specific multi-link 'problem-solving' paths, typically (but not exclusively) from a high-level business problem to lower-level functional solution components. The main elements are 'Problems' and 'Solutions'. These may be selected from purpose-made, domain-specific collections of elements. Single 'Problem-Solution links' are comparable to compact, high-level descriptions of *design patterns* and can be directly related to *design problem templates* as used in Design Science. Coherent collections of such links would resemble boiled-down representations of *pattern languages*.

Instantiations of PSCs for specific situations aim to help conceptualise and discuss pre-architectural, high-level overviews, for example, of (options for) functionalities or applications representing 'solutions' for 'solving' some business need or capability 'problem'. A useful metaphor is that PSCs help describe and discuss basic ingredients (related problems and solutions) for some specific situation, which can later (out of scope here) be developed into a recipe (e.g. an enterprise or process architecture and roadmap) and eventually into an actual dish (realisation of the architecture/solution). Thus, PSCs can, for example, be conceptualisations and conversation aids in the early stages of business-IT alignment efforts and system design.

This explorative, practice-oriented paper presents our initial conceptualisation of PSCs. We also present a syntax and notation for problem-solution chains as specified for the Simplified Modelling Platform (SMP), and we briefly discuss the possibility of supporting PSC modelling with guided conversations for PSC modelling. We demonstrate and evaluate our proposed concepts by applying them in a single real case. Much work lies ahead.

Keywords: problem-solution chains · Business-IT Alignment · design patterns · modelling platforms

1 Introduction

The practical focus of this explorative paper is on communication about and analysis of IT-and informatics-related combinations of functionalities, typically (but not exclusively) as an answer to requirements from 'the business' (as in business-IT Alignment [17,21]). We are aware of the vast body of knowledge in this field; we also realise that our idea currently represents only a limited, not fully developed contribution. Yet, we believe in its potential value for early, exploratory phases of design projects in IT and beyond (particularly for use in professional training and education) and are curious about its reception in the community and ensuing feedback. We expect that our proposed approach can also be useful in domains and practices beyond business-IT alignment; our real-life example (see Sect. 3.5) stems from an ongoing research project concerning visualisation and human factors in process modelling.

The basic idea of Problem-Solution Chains (PSCs) was conceived against a background of several decades of academic teaching, thesis supervision, and practice-oriented research in information systems and related disciplines, often using the design science research paradigm. More concretely, this paper is roughly based on a 2021 Master's Thesis written for a Master Information Sciences graduate project of Radboud University, Nijmegen, the Netherlands [34]. The initial ideas were augmented by some further years of ideation and discussion, and recently, the modelling concepts have been experimentally included in the Simplified Modelling Platform (SMP) [26], requiring applied-formal specification and coding of syntax and notation.

The core idea behind PSCs is that basic but solid 'problem-solution thinking' is key in the early stages of problem-solving, which, for example, includes business-IT alignment efforts linking business needs and IT functionalities. Conceptualisation and language patterns related to 'problem-solution communication and conversation' are fairly commonplace in many interrelated disciplines, including requirements engineering, functional systems design, enterprise architecture, and the description and use of design patterns. We also observe that despite a huge effort by academia and practice to lessen the gap between 'business thinking/talking' and different levels of 'IT thinking/talking', the gap (which is largely communicational in nature) still persists, in particular if resources are limited and stakeholders involved operate in the not-so-sophisticated but common context of Small and Medium Enterprises (SMEs). This suggests that PSCs as a communication and 'thought structuring' aid can function as effective *boundary objects* [3].

[21] proposes a six-step approach to enhance business-IT Alignment. The approach starts with setting the goals and establishing a team. In the second step, 'understand the business-IT linkage', individuals of each relevant team in an organisation discuss the problems and opportunities in the business and IT environment. This enhances the mutual understanding between stakeholders. The third step is to analyse and prioritise gaps between the 'as-is' state and the desired 'to-be' state of alignment. The fourth step aims to identify what must be done and who is responsible. In the fifth step, criteria are set to evaluate

the strategy's actions. Finally, 'sustained alignment' emphasises the importance of continuous improvement to increase the potential of business-IT Alignment. According to [13,20,21], clear communication via strong partnerships between IT personnel and line managers is vital for successful alignment. Professionals from various backgrounds experience noise in conversations, resulting in differing perceptions between groups. At the same time, collaboration asks for a mutual understanding between subjects to achieve a certain goal or task [22].

The use of Problem-Solution Chains (PSCs) mainly aims to support steps 2–4 in the six-step approach of [21]. Regarding the second step, the business-IT linkage is made explicit through related problem-solution patterns at and between the 'business level' and 'IT level'. However, a PSC may then extend further 'down' into the realm of IT design, typically from higher to lower levels of abstraction. Related to the third step in [21], alignment gaps should become easier to identify because the current state (as-is) can be compared with the desired state (to-be). In the fourth step in the alignment process, PSCs can also be a tool to help communication about singled-out deliverables and ownership thereof: assigning ownership of problem-solution combinations to actors.

Thus, PSCs are meant to aid communication and exploration in view of bridging the gap between business needs/capabilities and IT functionalities at the application level and also across different levels in application/solution design. Note that we emphatically focus on *exploratory* design activities in such a context. We are fully aware that actual fleshing out and realising IT 'solutions' for business-and-IT 'problems' requires much more detailed and intricate systems design and development, usually combined with some form of digital architecture. We suggest PCSs merely for use in the stages *leading up to* architectural modelling and/or software engineering: "just conceptualising the main ingredients of the dish; not writing the full recipe for cooking it, nor doing the actual cooking".

We are very much aware that the PSC approach could *in theory* be applied in any situation requiring 'solutions' for 'problems' in the form of created artefacts or interventions, just as the design science paradigm and design patterns can *in principle* be applied to all such situations. However, our current ambition does not extend far beyond the context of 'digitization' and 'business-IT alignment', particularly for/with SMEs.

The basic paradigm in which this research took place is Design Science Research [36], but the current paper cannot claim to be a very rigorous instance thereof. Although the work is explorative, it includes some initial yet well-described conceptual results; it presents a promising, already usable idea and technique that calls for further work.

The structure of the remainder of this paper is as follows. We present some key literature that inspired and informed our conceptualisation of PSCs. Next, we present a specification of our modelling technique in terms of the comprehensive set of specifications required to include PSC in the Simplified Modelling Platform and briefly discuss how guided dialogues can augment such modelling. Evaluation of the results was limited to first trying out the conceptualisations through some fictional cases (as reported in [34]); in the current paper, we present one real-life case (presented in Sect. 3.5), which serves as a limited but realistic proof of concept. We end with conclusions and suggestions for further research.

2 Building Blocks for PSC Conceptualisation

In this section, we present some main ideas/sources from the literature that inspired our conceptualisation of PSCs.

2.1 Design Patterns and Pattern Languages

A design pattern is "the re-usable form of a solution to a design problem" [1]. A pattern describes a common problem and the solution's core, such that the solution can be used repeatedly, producing a distinct solution every time. Patterns can be useful to a certain extent as a generic solution for a class of problems.

Patterns can also be *linked* by a relationship [4]. For instance, multiple solutions are offered to enable a designer to compare them and select the best option for a problem. In this way, patterns offering alternative solutions can constitute an overview of possible solutions to a particular problem. Furthermore, patterns can complement each other more strictly when a combination of solutions is required, and several patterns are to be realized together to solve a problem.

Another relationship between patterns is seen when using a pattern invokes the consecutive use of another pattern. This type of relationship is that of a *pattern sequence* [6,29]. The context of each pattern is explained by its predecessors. Pattern sequences are specific development paths and, in fact, are a direct inspiration for PSCs. However, how these sequences are used in pattern-driven software development is much more complex than our PSC approach, intended to support ideation and conceptualisation in pre-design, not head-on software systems engineering.

The core idea for 'Problem-Solution Chains' thus is that they are a way of representing logical sequences of interrelated design patterns. Each pattern essentially combines an abstract description of a (class of) problem with a (class of) solution. While this is a gross oversimplification that does little justice to the careful crafting of full-fledged design patterns (as commonly represented in pretty elaborate, templated texts, often complemented with models), the notion of combining problems and solutions *is* the core here, reflected in our core concept of a 'problem-solution link'.

Another key idea in the world of design patterns is that of *pattern languages* [4]: collections of patterns that somehow belong together and can be potentially combined, matching related patterns (in our conceptualisation: problem-solution links) into a series of combined patterns. The next step is to view a 'solution' represented in a link as a 'problem' in the link below it, and so on. Quoting ontologist Giancarlo Guizzardi: it's "patterns all the way down".

A boiled-down visualisation of a *chain* of combined 'problem-solution links', putting the most abstract pattern on top and the least abstract one at the bottom, is what we conceived as a 'Problem-Solution Chain' or PSC.

2.2 Patterns and Capabilities

The Capability Driven Development (CDD) process, as proposed in the CaaS project [9], consists of three cycles: Capability Design, Capability Delivery, and Capability Refinement. The main deliverable of the CDD process is reusable design patterns. Such 'capability delivery patterns' are "reusable solutions for reaching business goals under specific contexts" [9]. For each capability, one or more goals exist. The context is 'measured' through context indicators represented in a context set. A capability delivery pattern is delivered when its context set is equal to the context set of the capability [18].

A link between a business capability (as a 'problem') and (one or more) high-level IT functionalities (as 'solutions') can thus be modeled in a PSC as a 'problem-solution link', typically at the upper end of a PSC.

A Capability Pattern Repository enables the storage and retrieval of delivery patterns [8]. The repository is a tool to help reuse best practices as represented by patterns: each pattern represents a solution to a problem. The patterns can be represented in text or models [7].

Though Context is vital to the CDD approach, in our simpler PSC approach, and in view of our objective to use PSCs primarily a 'stakeholder conversation piece', we choose for now to work with boiled-down problem-solution patterns/links only, without the explicit 'context' concept. Nevertheless, the similarity in spirit between the CDD and the PSC approaches is quite clear. Indeed it seems quite worthwhile to study possibilities for a combination of the the CDD process (and related ideas) with our similar but much simpler, stakeholder communication-oriented PSC approach; this would clearly classify as future research.

2.3 Design Science: The Design Problem Template

Within the research paradigm of Design Science [10,36], some approaches include the use of a 'design problem template' [36] or 'design assertion' [35]. We resort to the Wieringa version [36, p15-16]:

"Design problems assume a context and stakeholder goals and call for an artefact such that the interaction of (artefact X context) helps stakeholders to achieve their goals. We specify requirements for the artefact that are motivated by the stakeholder goals. This gives us the [following] schema for expressing design problems:

- Improve <a problem context>
- by <(re)designing an artifact [or intervention]>
- that satisfies <some requirements>
- in order to <help stakeholders achieve some goals>"

The two upper bullets directly represent a paired 'problem' and 'solution' and can be seen as a 'problem-solution link'. This implies that a PSC can represent (partly explicitly, partly implicitly) a top-down chain of design problem assertions (possibly, yet to be realized, i.e. to be designed in detail), which complements an underlying chain of design patterns.

Interestingly, Wieringa notes that the first and last items of the design problem template are typically phrased in the language of the 'commissioning stakeholder'. In contrast, the middle two (including the requirements description, which is not included explicitly in the PSC approach) are formulated using the (usually more technical) language of the designers.

We are aware that we are not the first in a long way to come up with the idea to actively combine Design Science Research with design patterns; a case in point is the work of Curley et al. [5]. However, we believe a lot of work is needed to make such an approach really 'fly' in practice. In the long run, we strive to combine a number of existing ideas in this vein (also including the Capabilities and patterns ideas) into a viable practice oriented knowledge-based system for the support of Learning Communities and Innovation Teams, and have it actually *adopted*. For now, we start at the beginning, which for us is the conversation-oriented modelling of PSCs.

2.4 Goal-Oriented Requirements Engineering (KAOS)

Somewhat further removed from the core ideas of PSCs, but still a clear inspiration for the approach, is the KAOS method for Goal-Oriented Requirements Engineering [19]. The method includes a 'top-down' goal hierarchy roughly comparable to the idea of a PSC, and it also uses a visualisation that inspired our own (much simpler) version thereof.

[30] define the KAOS Goal Model as: "the set of interrelated goal diagrams that have been put together for tackling a particular problem." Goals are expressed in the stakeholders' vocabulary of whom it concerns: higher goals in business language and lower goals in more technical terms. Identification of goals takes place either via a top-down approach, from business goals to technical goals, or a bottom-up approach.

A KAOS goal model is a directed graph indicating that a goal can be a subgoal of multiple higher-level goals and be in multiple goal diagrams [30]. Goals refer to system states and not state transitions. For instance, 'elevator called' and not 'call elevator'. This is done by naming the subject, then a past tense verb, and finally, a further description if needed (Fig. 1).

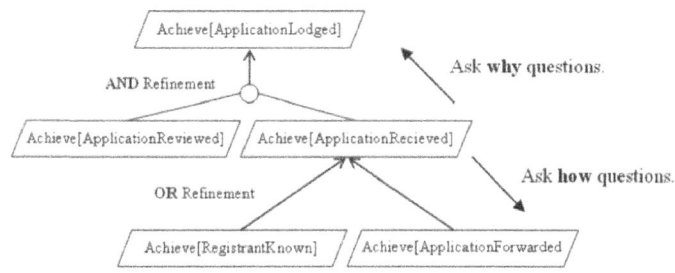

Fig. 1. Goal model example from [30]

2.5 Some Similar Modelling Techniques

Reviewers of this paper kindly pointed out that various existing modelling techniques include features somewhat similar to the PSC modelling approach (IBIS/*Arg&Dec* [2], BMM [28], and 4EM [32]). Admittedly, PSC modelling was conceived based solely on the ideas presented in this section, and though we knew of the existence of the three approaches mentioned (at least their general outline), comparison with them was not carried out simply because we focused on laying down a first, solid basis for our own ideas. Clearly, such comparison should be part of further work and might, in hindsight, have improved our initial conception of PSC modelling.

3 Modelling

In this section, we will explain how, in the context of our PSC project, we approached meta-modelling in general and how we built and used the specific tool-oriented metamodel for PSCs.

```
1   ScriptVersion01
2   Notation for PROBSOL version 1.0
3   //***************************** Type *****************************
4   typedef "ProblemType" ENUM (None, Business, User, Developer)
5   //***************************** Element *****************************
6   element "Solution" Solution
7       notation folder Elements
8       comment ""
9   (
10      "Description" TEXT ,
11      "Type" ProblemType ,
12      "DomainTags" TEXT ,
13      "Problem Owner" TEXT
14  )
15  ...
16  //***************************** Connection *****************************
17  connection "SolutionProblem" SolutionProblem
18      notation folder Connections
19      from Solution
20      to Problem
21  ...
22  //***************************** Diagram *****************************
23  diagram "Problem Solution Diagram" ProblemSolutionDiagram
24      notation folder Elements
25  contains (
26      Solution,
27      Problem,
28      Links
29  )
30  //***************************** Visual Element *****************************
31  visual "Solution" of Solution
32  on (*)
33  {
34      initialSize(150,100)
35      group (0,0) scale {
36          penWidth(2)
37          penColor(0,0,0)
38          fillcolor(0,127,0)
39          rectangle(0,0,150,100,10,0)
40      }
41      group (0,0) noscale {
42          printalign(centre, middle)
43          print(0, 5, "{visual.width}"*"{visual.scalex}", "{visual.height}"*"{visual.scaley}"/2, "{element.
                    identification}", 0)
44      }
45  }
46  ...
47  //***************************** Visual Connection *****************************
48  visual "SolutionProblem" of SolutionProblem
49  on (*)
50  line {
51      penwidth(2)
52      pencolor(0,0,0)
53      linestyle(solid)
54  }
55  end {
56      initialsize(5,5)
57      fillcolor(255,255,255)
58      polygon(-9, 0, 3, 15, 90)
59  }
60  ...
```

Fig. 2. Partial PSC Notation Script on the SMP

3.1 SMP and Metamodelling

The Simplified Modelling Platform (SMP), a generic platform for modelling, has been explained in [25–27]. In summary, the SMP is a cloud-based open environment which can administrate metamodels (called notations) and models (blocks and arrows, or graphs) restricted by those metamodels.

The platform can interact graphically, programmatically, and textually with the user (automated or not). The server extensions allow the user to expand SMP functionality to allow for new functionality, e.g. new transformations [31].

Metamodels and models are represented as graphs, using elements (or vertices or nodes) and connections (or edges or arcs) accompanied by meaningful attributes (or labels). The platform supports the diagram-specific graphical visualisation of elements and connections, which can use the attributes to enhance the visual information. The metamodel reflects the model for all three objects. The platform additionally orders these objects hierarchically in folders, models, and repositories within a company context at the highest level.

For a complete analysis of the script in Fig. 2, we recommend reading [25].

3.2 PSC Specification in the Simplified Modelling Platform

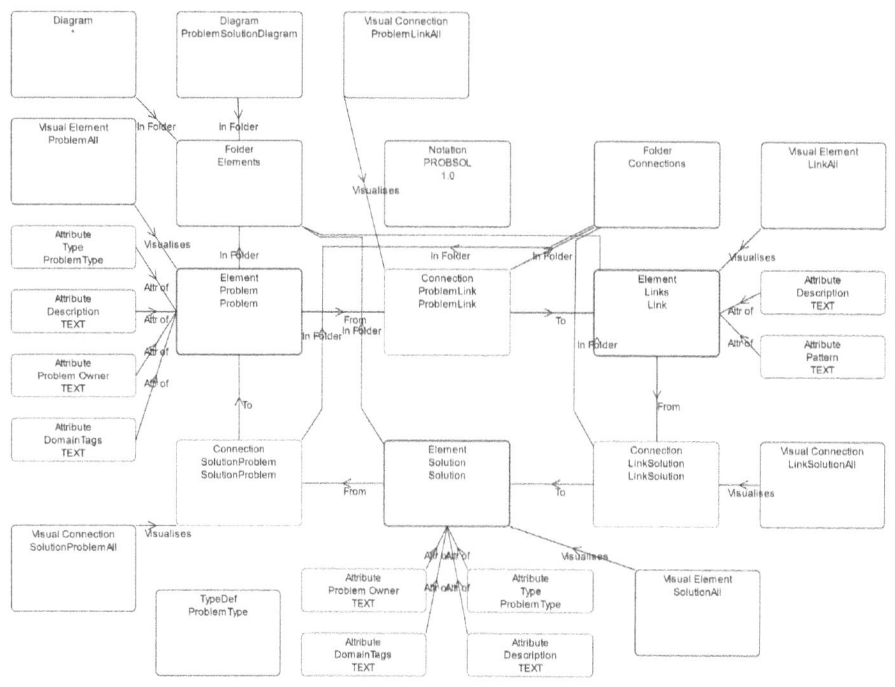

Fig. 3. PSC Meta Model in SMP

Note that in Fig. 3, the generic metamodel is combined with PSC-specific elements. We refrain from naming the generic concepts as being part of a 'meta-meta model' to avoid unnecessary complexity, but technically this classification would hold.

In Fig. 3, the following elements stand out: The *Notation* element is name-giving and is now set to 'PROBSOL' with the version number '1.0'. Next, to both sides, we see the *Folder* elements that have the name 'Elements' and 'Connections', which refer to the Folders in the toolbox of Simplified, e.g. Fig. 6. All other elements and connections must have a connection '*In Folder*' to these elements, but they may be hidden in diagrams to prevent cluttering of the diagram. Another element is the *TypeDef* element that defines usable types in the attributes. We have defined the 'ProblemType' type, which is used in almost all connections using a textual reference. TypeDef is the first section in the notation script in Fig. 2. The next element is the *Diagram* element. Every notation has to have a '*' (star) diagram and a custom diagram, in this case, the 'Problem Solution Diagram'. All visualisation elements will refer to the diagram that supports their visualisation. When no specific diagram is connected to a visualisation element, it is, by default, supported for all diagrams. Furthermore, we have the *Element* element (red border) that is used to create the elements in a model (the 'blocks'). An *Element* has a visual counterpart, the *Visual Element*, that holds the visual script drawing the 'block' in the diagram. Next in the model is the *Connection* element (green border) that is used to connect the elements in the model (the 'arrows'). The *Connection* has its visual counterpart, the *Visual Connection*, that holds its visual script, e.g. Fig. 4. Last, we have the *Attribute* element that can be connected to a Folder, Element or Connection (Begin, Middle, or End) to hold extra information on that level, e.g. Fig. 5. Connections run from an element to an element, shown in the image as lines with the from and to keywords. Attributes are connected to the appropriate connections or elements with the connections with 'Attr of' labels.

The PSC-specific concepts in the metamodel are further specialisations of the generic concepts. The PSC-specific metamodel includes the following main elements:

- **Problem**, with attributes 'Problem type' (for example, Business or Software), 'Description' (short textual description), 'Problem owner' (self explanatory), and 'Domain tags' (set of tags signifying domain(s) the problem belongs to)
- **Solution**, the counterpart of Problem, with similar attributes
- **Link**, combining one or more Solutions to one or more Problems, and with attributes 'Description' (short textual description) and 'Pattern' (an optional reference to a design pattern matching the problem-solution link)

The model described above and in Fig. 3 represents the notation, as does Fig. 2 (but in a different format). Both can be compiled to the generic notation representation in the core of the Simplified Modelling Platform. This compilation occurs in either the meta-modeller for the script version or the modeller for the model version. Public or private notations can be assigned to users and are visualised in the toolbox area of the modelling environment, e.g. Fig. 6.

Now that the notation is available to the user, we can create a model with the appropriate notation by selecting the elements and connections for the diagram, using any of the interface options available on the SMP.

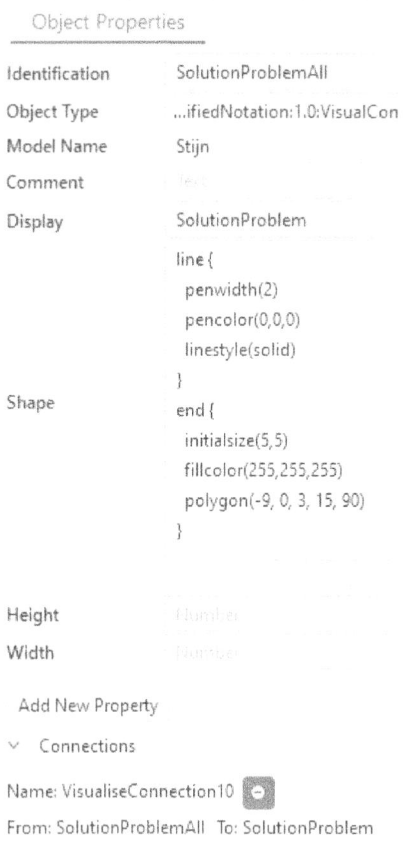

Object Properties

Identification	SolutionProblemAll
Object Type	...ifiedNotation:1.0:VisualCon
Model Name	Stijn
Comment	Text
Display	SolutionProblem

Shape	line {
	  penwidth(2)
	  pencolor(0,0,0)
	  linestyle(solid)
	}
	end {
	  initialsize(5,5)
	  fillcolor(255,255,255)
	  polygon(-9, 0, 3, 15, 90)
	}

Height	Number
Width	Number

Add New Property
∨ Connections
Name: VisualiseConnection10
From: SolutionProblemAll To: SolutionProblem

Fig. 4. Object properties Visual Connection ProblemType

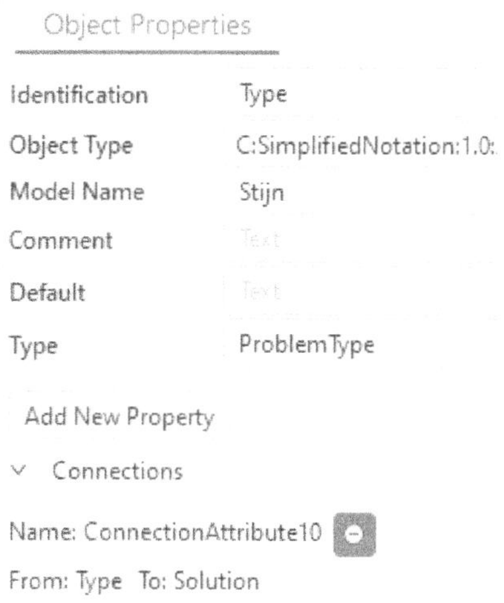

Object Properties

Identification	Type
Object Type	C:SimplifiedNotation:1.0:
Model Name	Stijn
Comment	Text
Default	Text
Type	ProblemType

Add New Property
∨ Connections
Name: ConnectionAttribute10
From: Type To: Solution

Fig. 5. Object properties Attribute Type

Fig. 6. PSC Notation Toolbox

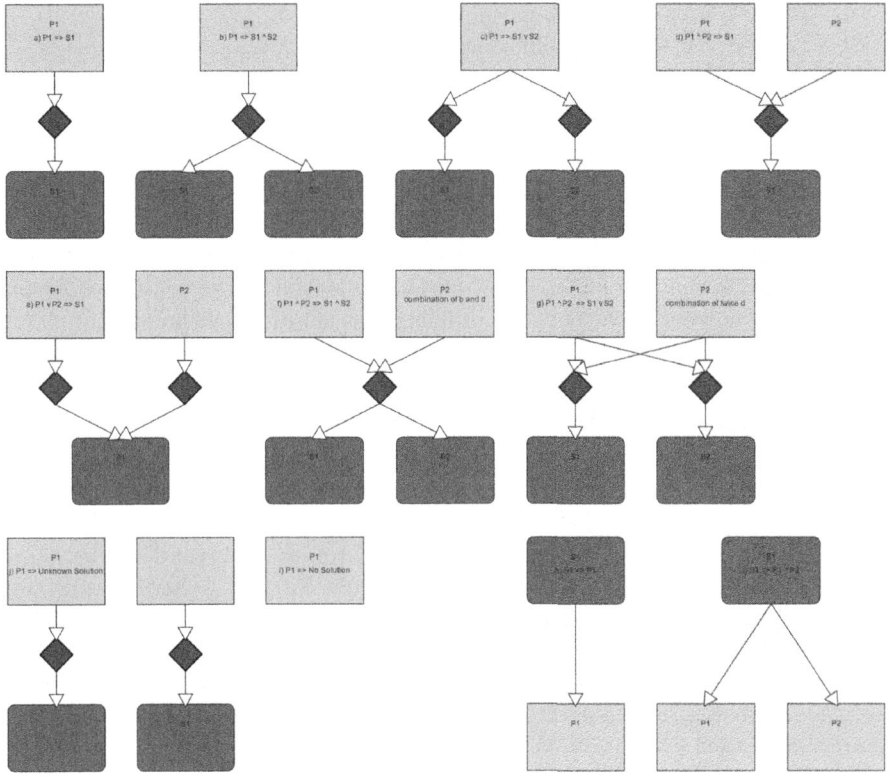

Fig. 7. Basic PSC patterns

3.3 Some Basic Examples of Allowed Structures in PSCs

In Fig. 7, we present the full set of basic structure examples, which expands to all PSCs. We describe these examples individually.

a) $P1 \implies S1$: A single problem leads to a single solution and is solved, e.g. when I get hungry, I eat some food.

b) $P1 \implies S1 \wedge S2$: A single problem leads to a solution that consists of two partial solutions, e.g. when I have to go from A to B, I need a bus and a train to get there.

c) $P1 \implies S1 \vee S2$: A single problem leads to two possible solutions, e.g. when I am thirsty, I can get water or a beer.

d) $P1 \wedge P2 \implies S1$: when two problems occur simultaneously, there is a solution for those problems. One can find this structure in requirement management, e.g. when I want to work together and need to model this paper, there is the opportunity to use SMP.

e) $P1 \vee P2 \implies S1$: two problems can lead to the same solution, e.g. when it is sunny or raining, an umbrella will give some cover.

f) $P1 \wedge P2 \implies S1 \wedge S2$: (combination of b and d)
g) $P1 \wedge P2 \implies S1 \vee S2$: (combination of twice d)
h) $S1 \implies P1$: The solution gives a more detailed problem.
i) $S1 \implies P1 \wedge P2$: The solution gives a set of new problems.

3.4 Known Limitations of the Notation

For the current notation, we still have to create the verification rules. Also, the practical evaluation of the visualisation has to be verified in a larger group of stakeholders. The notation has a limited notion of solution to problem connection. Practical evaluation has to show whether this AND interpretation holds in all cases. The current 'link' between problem and solution can handle the AND and OR logic, but we might see a case where the XOR or NOT logic could be applicable.

3.5 A Real-Life Example of a PSC Diagram and the Session that Produced It

We carried out a first real-life test and evaluation of the PSC approach at a proof of concept level by selecting and taking on an appropriately complex case: a PhD project in its initial stages, for which a top-down breakdown in interconnected problem-solution links could contribute directly to structuring and understanding of the problem and solution spaces. We used the input from the papers [23,24] and a live session with their author. We further reflect on the approach underlying this 'guided dialogue for collaborative modelling' in Sect. 3.6. The evaluation was only superficial and should be augmented in future by more rigorous emperical evaluation.

The PhD student involved in our PSC modelling session was the main (and only) stakeholder. One of the authors of the current paper acted as session facilitator, initially using a whiteboard to elicit, first, the 'main problem' addressed in the PhD project, then, through a stepwise dialogue, a list of elements (problems, solutions, links) and also, progressively, a roughly drawn sketch of the larger model. Next, another author entered the model in the SMP using the whiteboard sketch combined with direct verbal input from stakeholders and facilitators. The resulting model in the SMP was then checked and corrected once more by the stakeholder, leading to the final diagram (Fig. 8).

The stakeholder reported that the session and the diagram were helpful and enjoyable and provided good structure and new insights for her ongoing work. Findings include that the conversational approach is key in eliciting the models, and that the model concepts and structure actively help elicit conceptualisation by explicitly prompting the description of at least one problem for every solution, and vice versa. The concepts proved clear and helpful in the conversation (its results sketched on a whiteboard), which afterwards informed a modeller in entering the information in a model. Hence, the domain expert did not do actual modelling using the SMP, which probably would have yet been somewhat of a challenge.

The resulting 5-level model includes 9 problems and 17 solutions, combined in 14 problem-solution links. From top (P1) to bottom ('finals' of the hierarchy: S2, S12, S13, S14, S15, S17), 6 distinct Problem-Solution Chains were described.

3.6 Perspective on Conversations for Modelling

Apart from the (meta-)model-oriented perspective we took so far in this paper, a complementary perspective on PSC (and other) modelling can be taken: that of the conversations that embody the (typically collaborative) creation of (conceptual) models, including PSCs [11,12,37]. In [14,16,33], this idea was further developed into a framework aiming to provide active and operational guidelines for 'conversations for modelling', in the form of structured *dialogue games*, consisting of *focused conceptualisations*. For an example of the application of this framework, see [15].

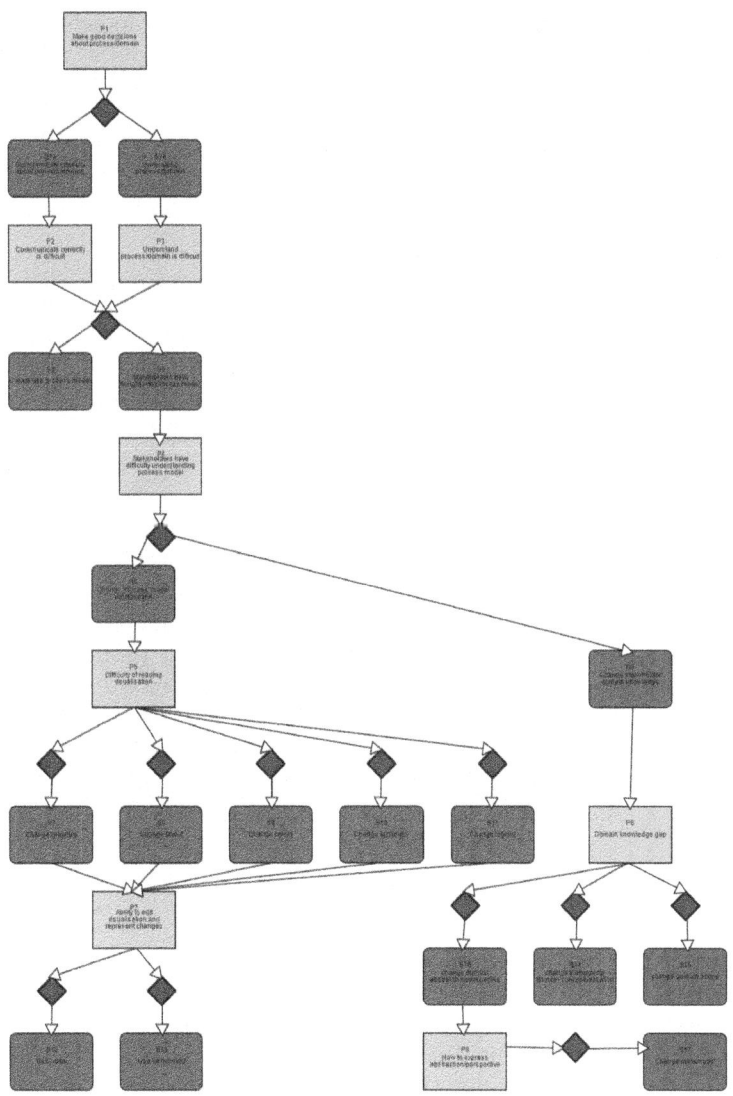

Fig. 8. Real-life example of several combined PSCs

The core idea is that models are created through *propositions* being made as part of a goal-driven conversation in which questions can be asked, propositions and counter-propositions made and discussed, and acceptance and rejection thereof stated by participants in the session [11,16]. The underlying communicational patterns resemble that of a *negotiation*. The basic goals of such conversations revolve around the main meta-concepts of the type of modelling performed, as represented in its notation and syntax. For example, a PSC creation session will typically and straightforwardly start with the question:

- "What is the main *problem* that drives the project under consideration?"

Once this initial question has been answered through a proposition of a short phrase stating the 'main problem', accepted by the participants in the session, a 'conversational to-do list' presents itself, as it were, in the form of more questions:

- "What are possible *solutions* to this *problem*?"
- "Is a particular *combination of solutions* required"?

But also:

- "What is the 'higher' *problem* of which the main problem is meant to be a *solution*?"

... and so on. In principle, every answer (i.e. every proposition) triggers new questions. As a whole, the PSC approach helps a great deal in systematically talking (and thinking) through an exploratory problem-and-solution landscape, mainly in terms of required and provided functionality of a design (possibly, a *design science*) project.

Though a full-fledged dialogue game for PSCs and some examples were presented in [34], we refrain from presenting it here for reasons of scope and space. In the 70-minute session resulting in the example PSC diagram in Sect. 3.5, such guidelines were purposeful, if informally, used by the session facilitator, leading to an efficient and satisfactory session. The point we want to make here is not that the questions mentioned above are beyond straightforward (they are not), but rather that PSCs, just like any other form of modelling, can benefit from goal-driven and deliberate structuring of a modelling session with respect to preset questions and formatted answers [14]: the possible 'moves' in a dialogue game.

4 Conclusion and Future Research

To conclude, let us recap the contribution of the paper.

We propose a modelling approach and notation for the support of exploratory conversations in the early stages of business-IT alignment or system design. In particular, we aim for our notation and its concepts to help stakeholders of various backgrounds to collaboratively 'sketch' combinations and patterns of 'problems' linked to 'solutions', leading to 'chains' of 'problem-solution links'.

PSC modelling is helpful for stakeholders to gain an overview of some main problem and of what sub-problems they need to solve once they have selected a partial solution: of the interrelated 'ingredients' of a desired but unknown recipe for solving the main problem with a combination of solutions.

After explaining how various sources from the literature inspired our core idea, we presented how our modelling language and notation was specified in the Simplified Modelling Platform. We provided examples of basic (syntactic) patterns possible in the notation, and we also gave and discussed a real-life example, providing a first and limited evaluation of our approach. We then briefly discussed the session in which this example was created, and, referring to existing work, we reflected on how this relates to a perspective on the process of collaborative modelling as a focused dialogue.

Despite its worked-out detail, the PSC modelling language and notation is still in its early stages of development; the current paper is the very first time we present it. The PSC idea is part of a wider effort to create a knowledge-based toolbox or platform for the support of Design Science style projects (though it could also be useful for 'Design' projects without much emphasis on the 'Science' aspect), mostly for education or training settings.

Much further work is anticipated. The link with the extensive world of design pattern creation and (re)-use seems obvious, though we are aware that it is a huge challenge to make work on and with design patterns usable and accessible for a relatively non-specialist public. Another important direction of study concerns the field of Business Capability description and design (in particular, the Capability Driven Development process). It seems possible and worthwhile to study a combination of the CDD process and our PSC approach. Integrating the model and tool with a graph database query language seems useful in analysing the patterns.

Other work required is further and more rigorous emperical evaluation of the approach in (collaborative) modelling sessions, including assessment of how user friendly PSC modelling is and how it can be improved to achieve optimal accesibility and usefulness for non-expert stakeholders. This can also help identify and remedy possible barriers for adoption. Finally, systematic comparison is required of PSC modelling with some other existing, similar techniques (see Sect. 2.5), and could lead to improvement of our approach.

References

1. Alexander, C.: A Pattern Language: Towns, Buildings. Construction. Oxford University Press, New York, NY, USA (1977)
2. Aurisicchio, M., Baroni, P., Pellegrini, D., Toni, F.: Comparing and integrating argumentation-based with matrix-based decision support in arg&dec. In: Black, E., Modgil, S., Oren, N. (eds.) Theory and Applications of Formal Argumentation, pp. 1–20. Springer International Publishing, Cham (2015)
3. Bergman, M., Lyytinen, K., Mark, G.: Boundary objects in design: an ecological view of design artifacts. J. Assoc. Inf. Syst. Special Issue Syst. Anal. Des. 8(11), article 34 (2007)

4. Buschmann, F., Henney, K., Schmidt, D.C.: Pattern-Oriented Software Architecture, On Patterns and Pattern Languages, vol. 5. John Wiley & Sons, Chichester, England (2007)
5. Curley, M., Kenneally, J., Ashurst, C.: Design science and design patterns: a rationale for the application of design-patterns within design science research to accelerate knowledge discovery and innovation adoption. In: Communications in Computer and Information Science, vol. 388, pp. 29–37, January 2013. https://doi.org/10.1007/978-3-319-04090-5_4
6. Doble, J., Meszaros, G.: A pattern language for pattern writing. In: Proceedings of the International Conference on Pattern Languages of Program Design, vol. 131, p. 164 (1997)
7. Grabis, J., Kampars, J.: Capability management in the cloud. In: Capability Management in Digital Enterprises, pp. 175–188. Springer, Cham, Switzerland (2018)
8. Grabis, J., Zdravkovic, J., Stirna, J.: Overview of capability-driven development methodology. In: Capability Management in Digital Enterprises, pp. 59–84. Springer, Cham, Switzerland (2018)
9. Henkel, M., Zdravkovic, J., Valverde, F., Pastor, O.: Capability design with CDD. In: Capability Management in Digital Enterprises, pp. 101–116. Springer, Cham, Switzerland (2018)
10. Hevner, A.R., March, S.T., Park, J., Ram, S.: Design science in information systems research. MIS Q. **28**(1), 75–105 (2004)
11. Hoppenbrouwers, S., Proper, H., van der Weide, T.: Formal modelling as a grounded conversation. In: Goldkuhl, G., Lind, M., Haraldson, S. (eds.) Proceedings of the 10th International Working Conference on the Language Action Perspective on Communication Modelling (LAP 2005), p. 139-155. Linköpings Universitet and Hogskolan I Boras, Linköping, Sweden, EU, Kiruna, Sweden, EU (2005)
12. Hoppenbrouwers, S., Proper, H., van der Weide, T.: Fundamental understanding of the act of modelling. Technical Report, ICIS-R05006, Radboud University Nijmegen, January 2005
13. Hoppenbrouwers, S., van Stokkum, W., Iacob, M.E., Wilmont, I., van der Linden, D.J.T., Amrit, C.: Stakeholder communication. In: Lankhorst, M. (ed.) Agile Service Development - Combining Adaptive Methods and Flexible Solutions, chap. 7. Springer Verlag, Berlin Heidelberg London New York Johannesburg Mumbai Punta Arenas Wladiwostok (2012)
14. Hoppenbrouwers, S.: Asking questions about asking questions in collaborative enterprise modelling. In: IFIP Working Conference on The Practice of Enterprise Modeling, pp. 16–30. Springer (2012)
15. Hoppenbrouwers, S., Rouwette, E.: A dialogue game for analysing group model building: framing collaborative modelling and its facilitation. Int. J. Organ. Des. Eng. **2**(1), 19–40 (2012)
16. Hoppenbrouwers, S., Wilmont, I.: Focused conceptualisation: Framing questioning and answering in model-oriented dialogue games. In: IFIP Working Conference on The Practice of Enterprise Modeling, pp. 190–204. Springer (2010)
17. Jonathan, G.M., Rusu, L., Perjons, E.: Business-it alignment in the era of digital transformation: Quo vadis? In: Hawaii International Conference on System Sciences (HICSS), Maui, Hawaii, USA, 7–10 January 2020, pp. 5563–5572, January 2020. https://doi.org/10.24251/HICSS.2020.685
18. Koç, H., Sandkuhl, K.: Context modelling in capability management. In: Capability Management in Digital Enterprises, pp. 117–138. Springer, Cham, Switzerland (2018)

19. Lamsweerde, A.V.: Requirements Engineering: From System Goals to UML Models to Software Specifications. Wiley, Chichester, West Sussex, UK (2009)
20. Lee, S., Kim, K., Paulson, P., Park, H.: Developing a socio-technical framework for business-it alignment. Ind. Manage. Data Syst. **108**, 1167–1181 (2008). https://doi.org/10.1108/02635570810914874
21. Luftman, J., Brier, T.: Achieving and sustaining business-it alignment. California Management Review **42**, October 1999. https://doi.org/10.2307/41166021
22. Martinez-Moyano, I.: Exploring the dynamics of collaboration in interorganizational settings. The International Association of Facilitators Handbook (2006)
23. Mulder, I.: Towards enhancing process model visualisation and reducing stakeholder-designer static. In: Prince Sales, T., Aveiro, D., Mandelburger, M.M., Proper, H., Koschmider, A. (eds.) PoEM & EDEWC - Companion 2023, vol. 3645. CEUR-WS.org, November 2023. https://ceur-ws.org/Vol-3645/dc2.pdf
24. Mulder, I.: Enhancing process model visualisation to facilitatie the understanding of stakeholders. In: 37th Bled eConference - Resilience Through Digital Innovation: Enabling the Twin Transition: June 9 - 12, 2024, Bled, Slovenia, Conference Proceedings. Bled eConference (2024). https://doi.org/10.18690/um.fov.4.2024, https://press.um.si/index.php/ump/catalog/view/880/1284/4181
25. Mulder, M.A.T., Mulder, R., Bodnar, F.: Towards a demo description in simplified notation script. In: Advances in Enterprise Engineering XVI: 12th Enterprise Engineering Working Conference, EEWC 2022, Leusden, The Netherlands, 2–3 November 2022, Revised Selected Papers, pp. 53–70. Springer (2023)
26. Mulder, M.A.T., Mulder, R., Bodnar, F., van Kessel, M., Gomez Vicente, J., et al.: The simplified platform, an overview. Modellierung 2022 Satellite Events (2022)
27. Mulder, M.A.T., Proper, H.A., Bodnar, F., Mulder, R.: Simplified enterprise modelling platform architecture. In: PoEM (Forum), pp. 16–30 (2022)
28. OMG: Business motivation model (bmm) specification, version 1.0 (2007). www.omg.org
29. Porter, R., Coplien, J., Winn, T.: Sequences as a basis for pattern language composition. Science of Computer Programming (2004)
30. Respect-IT: A kaos tutorial. http://www.objectiver.com/fileadmin/download/documents/KaosTutorial.pdf (2007)
31. Ruci, E.: Transforming Business Process Models into System Dynamics Models-Developing a Transformation Tool. Ph.D. thesis, Technische Universität Wien (2024)
32. Sandkuhl, K., Stirna, J., Persson, A., Wißotzki, M.: Enterprise Modeling-Tackling Business Challenges with the 4EM Method. The Enterprise Engineering Series, Springer, Heidelberg (2014)
33. Ssebuggwawo, D., Hoppenbrouwers, S., Proper, E.: Interactions, goals and rules in a collaborative modelling session. In: Persson, A., Stirna, J. (eds.) The Practice of Enterprise Modeling, 2nd IFIP WG8.1 Working Conference, PoEM 2009. LNBIP, vol. 3. Springer (2009)
34. Sunnotel, J.: Conceptualisation of Problem-Solution Patterns: Knowledge Sharing Across Professional Boundaries. Master's thesis, Radboud University (2021)
35. van Turnhout, K., Andriessen, D., Cremers, P. (eds.): Handboek ontwerpgericht wetenschappelijk onderzoek. Boom, Amsterdam, Netherlands (2019)
36. Wieringa, R.J.: Design Science Methodology for Information Systems and Software Engineering. Springer, Germany (2014). https://doi.org/10.1007/978-3-662-43839-8, 10.1007/978-3-662-43839-8
37. Veldhuijzen van Zanten, G., Hoppenbrouwers, S., Proper, H.: System development as a rational communicative process. J. Syst. Cybern. Inf. **2**(4), 47–51 (2004)

Security, Compliance, and Configuration in Enterprise Modeling

SYMBOLEOAC: An Access Control Model for Legal Contracts

Sofana Alfuhaid[1,2](✉), Amal Ahmed Anda[1], Daniel Amyot[1], Marco Roveri[3], and John Mylopoulos[1]

[1] School of EECS, University of Ottawa, Ottawa K1N 6N5, Canada
{salfu014,aanda027,damyot,jmylopou}@uottawa.ca
[2] Faculty of Computing and Information Technology, King AbdulAziz University, Jeddah 21589, Kingdom of Saudi Arabia
[3] Department of IECS, University of Trento, Trento, Italy
marco.roveri@unitn.it

Abstract. Legal contracts have served as the bedrock of business transactions for millennia. Many are now automated through the use of smart contracts, supported by blockchain and IoT technologies. However, automation poses security challenges as to who should have access to operate on contract elements. This paper proposes a role-based access control model, treating all contract elements as resources and ensuring regulated access by designated parties. The access control model extends the SYMBOLEO specification language for legal contracts with new modeling concepts inspired by Role-Based Access Control (RBAC), tailored for the legal contract domain, resulting in SYMBOLEOAC. Specifically, we: (i) model a set of access control concepts, including resource, access rule, and access policy, thereby extending the SYMBOLEO ontology, (ii) define controller rules that specify who can authorize access to each resource, and (iii) present pre-authorization rules that specify who has access to what. Our contributions include an access control model for legal contracts, an extension of the SYMBOLEO language with pre-authorization access rules, as well as a tool that generates smart contract code for Hyperledger Fabric (in JavaScript, from SYMBOLEOAC) that is compliant with access policies and access rules.

Keywords: Access control · Legal contracts · Model-driven engineering · Ontology · RBAC · Smart contracts · SYMBOLEO

1 Introduction

Legal contracts have served as the bedrock of business transactions for millennia. A legal contract consists of obligations and powers that define the terms and conditions of the contract. Smart contracts are software systems that monitor, automate, and control the execution of legal contracts, often through the use of IoT and blockchain technologies. There is great interest in such systems to support the operation of supply chains, financial transactions, and enterprise/government deeds, among many others.

An example of a smart contract involves a sale transaction between a meat supplier (the seller) and a supermarket chain (the buyer). Such a contract may include an obligation by which the seller delivers to the buyer meat of a certain quantity and quality and a second one by which the buyer is obliged to pay a certain amount for the meat before the meat is shipped. Monitoring the execution of such a transaction by a smart contract involves receiving messages from different parties and IoT devices that indicate when payment was made, when the meat container was loaded on a truck for its trip to the buyer's warehouse, the report of an assessor about the quality and quantity of the meat, measuring the temperature in and location of the container throughout the trip to ensure compliance with regulations, and delivery time and location. Based on such information, the smart contract can determine whether the execution complies with the terms and conditions of the meat sale contract.

We are interested in making legal contract executions secure by including safeguards against physical and social attacks. For the meat sale contract, such attacks include stealing some of the meat during its transportation or damaging its quality, both physical attacks concerning unauthorized access to the meat. They also include having an intruder who poses as an assessor and sends a report that misrepresents the quality of the meat, a social attack. In addition, we consider privacy concerns, such as what information is available to each participant in a contract execution. For the meat sale contract, this information may involve the happening of events (When was the meat delivered?) and data generated by IoT devices (What was the temperature in the container throughout the trip?). However, the scope of our interests does not include cyber attacks that exploit vulnerabilities of blockchain technology or IoT devices.

Our proposed solution consists of an access control model for legal contracts that views all things that participate in a contract execution as *resources*: contracting parties, assets, the contract itself, obligations and powers, as well as all information generated during contract execution (events, state transitions for legal concepts, other data, such as meat container temperature). Every resource has associated operations through which the state of the resource can be changed during contract execution. Moreover, every resource has one or more parties as *controller* who collectively decide who else has access to the operations and information of the resource. For example, an obligation has as controller its debtor, the party who is responsible for fulfilling the obligation. On the other hand, the creditor of an obligation, the party who stands to benefit from its fulfillment, has access to the current state of the obligation. In other words, the creditor's right to see the obligation satisfied includes the right to know what is the current state of the obligation. Access rules such as the above are derived from the semantics of the legal concepts of a contract, obligation, and power [7].

The contributions of this work include: (1) an *access control model* for legal contracts that integrates the RBAC and SYMBOLEO ontologies; (2) *controller rules* for each resource derived from the semantics of legal concepts;

(3) *pre-authorization rules* that give access to resources for different roles of a legal contract, also derived from the semantics of legal concepts; and (4) *a tool (SYMBOLEOAC2SC)* that generates JavaScript code from an access control model that complies with all the access rules of the model.

The rest of the paper is structured as follows. Section 2 presents the baseline for this research. Section 3 presents the SYMBOLEOAC access control model as an ontology, while Sect. 4 illustrates the SYMBOLEOAC language using a meat sale example. Section 5 presents controller and pre-authorization access rules. Section 6 presents the implementation of SYMBOLEOAC's ontology as a reusable library, while Sect. 7 presents the code generator that generates JavaScript code with access control safeguards. Section 8 presents an evaluation of our proposal. Section 9 discusses related work, and Sect. 10 concludes.

2 Research Baseline

SYMBOLEO [14] is a formal specification language for legal contracts. Its ontology core includes three legal concepts: contract, obligation, and power. These are supplemented by the concepts of role, asset, event, and situation, as well as time instance, and interval to define the constituents of obligations and powers. Many of these concepts can be found in other legal/contractual ontologies [7].

A contract is a collection of obligations and powers, as well as a domain model (e.g., for sales, rental, and transportation). An obligation consists of:

- a trigger, a logical expression that instantiates the obligation when true.
- a debtor, a role who is responsible for fulfilling the obligation;
- a creditor, a role who is the beneficiary of the obligation having been fulfilled.
- an antecedent, also a logical expression that enables the obligation.
- a consequent, an expression that a debtor must satisfy to fulfill the obligation.

The meat sale contract may include an obligation that the seller is obliged to deliver meat to the buyer within 3 days of payment (consequent) every time she receives a purchase order (trigger), provided payment is made before delivery (antecedent). This obligation is represented in SYMBOLEO as:

Odelivery: **Happens**(receivedPurchaseOrder)) —> **Obligation**(seller, buyer, **Happens**(paid),
HappensWithin(delivered, **Date**.add(paid.date , 3, days)))

The logical expressions that capture the meaning of triggers, antecedents, and consequents use events that happen and situations that occur. For example, receivedPurchaseOrder is an event that must happen to trigger the obligation.

Inspired by Alexy's definition [8], a power is a 5-tuple (trigger, creditor, debtor, antecedent, consequent). For example, the meat sale contract may contain a clause that gives the buyer the option (antecedent) to get back 10% of the payment (consequent) if delivery does not happen within 3 days (trigger):

PgetBack: **Happens(Violated(Obligations**.Odelivery))—>
Power(buyer, seller, **Happens**(decidedToExerciseP), **Activated(Obligations**.Opayback))

where (Opayback) is another obligation for which the seller has to pay back 10% of the price of the meat. Note that triggers are optional for obligations and powers. These concepts, as well as contracts, have semantics defined as state machines, and **Activated** is one of their states [18].

Now, both obligations and powers need three players in order to be enacted: a *performer* who acts to fulfil the obligation or exercises the power; a responsible party who is legally *liable* for the consequences of the obligation or power; and a *rightholder* who benefits from the fulfillment of the obligation. When an obligation is initiated, the debtor is its performer and also liable for it, while the creditor is its rightholder. For powers, the creditor is performer and liable, while its debtor is rightholder. These players may change while an obligation or power is being enacted or delegated (e.g., to a transportation company) [13].

Other important concepts of the SYMBOLEO ontology include Role (that participants in a contract execution play, e.g., buyer and assessor), Asset (something of value, e.g., meat), Event (an instantaneous happening that changes the state of an obligation or power, e.g., delivery), and Situation (that occurs over a period of time, e.g., meat temperature).

Our proposed access control model is based on the Role-Based Access Control (RBAC) security mechanism [17,19] designed to regulate and manage access to resources within a software system, ensuring that only authorized parties can interact with resources. The RBAC ontology consists of **Permissions** to **Subjects** (aka Roles), i.e., system users, enabling them to execute **Actions** (aka Operations in SYMBOLEOAC), such as read, write, etc. on **Resources** (also Resources), such as classes, files, etc. A role can only apply operations on a resource if it has permission assigned by an access rule. An **Access control policy** (aka Policy) contains Rules that must hold in priority over other rules). For example, a policy by a Food Industry regulator may be that the buyer has full access to all relevant information about the transportation of the meat, whereas only the assessor of the transaction has access to meat quality/quantity attributes. Policies define constraints on what is (dis-)allowed for access rules. Accordingly, they need to be checked against the initial set of access rules (aka *preauthorized access rules*) as well as after every incremental access rule insertion/deletion. This access control framework ensures that only authorized roles can perform operations on a resource, safeguarding the system's integrity and security. By delineating access rights, the flow of information and activities within systems can be managed and regulated, reducing the risk of unauthorized access or misuse.

In traditional RBAC proposals, the assigned permissions are maintained by the security engineer/administrator or anyone in a similar position. In our case, access rules are embedded in smart contract code to only recognize as legitimate permissible access to operations and information about a contract execution.

3 SYMBOLEOAC: Access-Control Model for SYMBOLEO

In this section, we integrate the SYMBOLEO ontology [14,18] with the RBAC ontology of five concepts (Policy, Rule, Resource, Operation, and Role) discussed in the previous section, resulting in SYMBOLEOAC as depicted in Fig. 1.

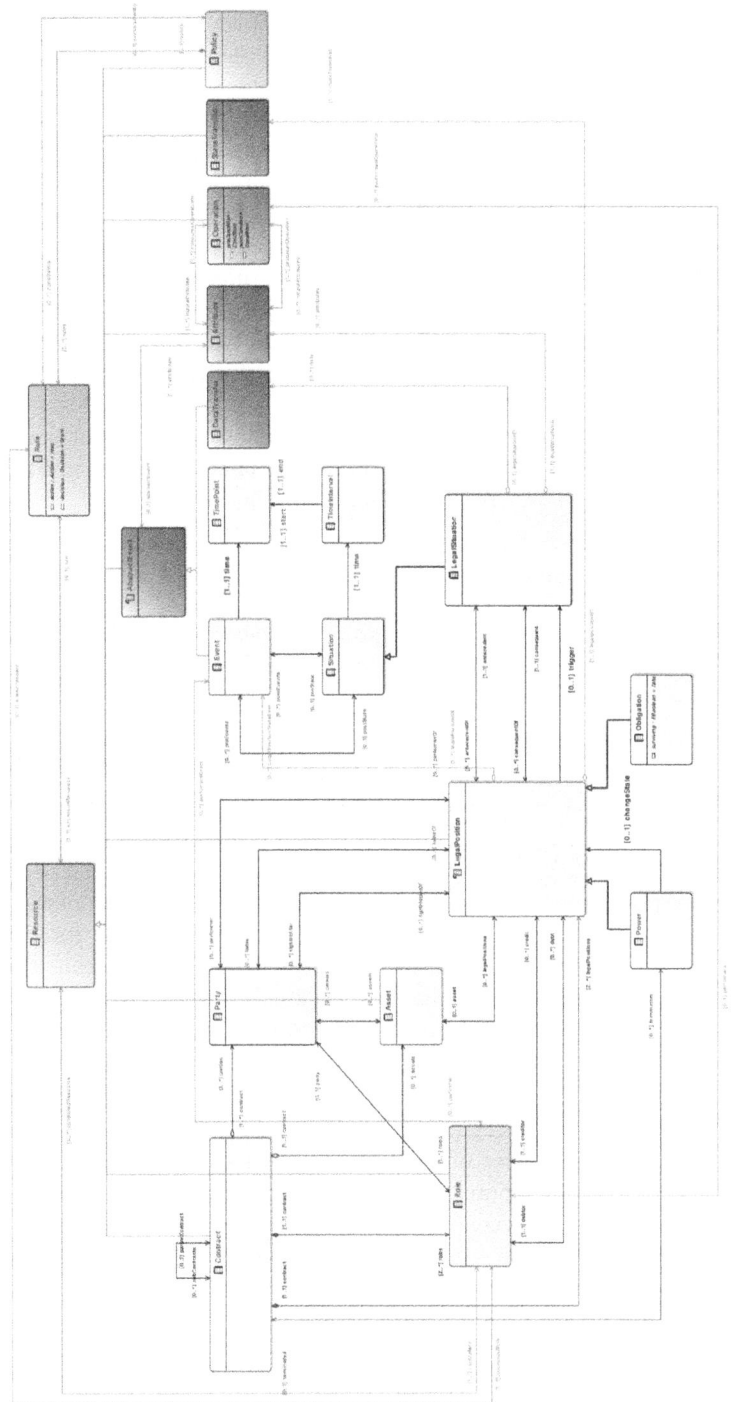

Fig. 1. SYMBOLEOAC ontology, with the original SYMBOLEO ontology (in yellow), access control ontology (in blue), merged classes from both ontologies (in green and purple), and newly added classes as resources (in red). (Color figure online)

The integration is founded on a simple principle: The concepts in the core SYMBOLEO ontology (except Party, Situation, TimePoint and TimeInterval) – shaded in yellow in Fig. 1 – are resources and can have associated access rules. This means that an Obligation is a Resource and Operations on it, such as enacting it, can be performed only by a Role who has access to enact Operation. In other words, if the smart contract receives notice of meat delivery, it checks that the sender is the seller. If not, that delivery is invalid. A Role is a Resource too; e.g., for a TransportCo role, the seller needs access to the profile and reviews of TransportCo candidates. So is the Asset meat, since the Assessor who checks the quantity and quality of the meat must have physical access to it for inspection. The Assessor also needs Write access to the two Attributes qualityFound and quantityFound, which no one else should have. All these access Rules help make a contract execution meaningful and valid.

In order to be able to talk about access to information about some of the SYMBOLEOAC resources, we also need two more classes, in addition to the class Event that is already part of the SYMBOLEO core ontology:

- Class StateTransition, whose instances are collections of tuples (fromState, toState, timePoint) and can be specialized to a particular obligation or power, e.g., Odelivery.
- Class DataTransfer, whose instances are data generated by IoT devices, and can be specialized, for example, to TempLocTime (temperature, location, time) for the data generated during the enactment of Odelivery.

The RBAC ontology class Policy has particular policies as instances, such as "Buyer has read access to all data about food delivery" (assigned by, e.g., a *regulator* role), which can be represented with SYMBOLEOAC's syntax as:

> Grant read To buyer On temploctime by regulator

The above policy means: if temploctime is a **DataTransfer** (e.g., part of the Odelivery resource), then the buyer is authorized to access temploctime and its attributes, including the temperature of the meat, its location, etc. It also means that there cannot be a new or existing rule that revokes read access to the buyer.

Another example: "Only the assessor has write access to the inspection quality attributes of the meat". In SYMBOLEOAC, this is equivalent to:

> Grant write To assessor On inspectedQuality by regulator

The assessor is the performer of resource event inspectedQuality and, by default, has write access to its attributes, i.e., qualityFound and quantityFound. If this rule is defined as a policy, other access rules have to conform to that policy. In other words, other roles such as the seller (controller of the asset meat) or transportCo, will have their write access to these attributes revoked as shown below.

> Revoke write To seller On inspectedQuality by regulator
> Revoke write To transportCo On inspectedQuality by regulator

Finally, for uniformity purposes, we also treat **Attribute** as a resource class with two associated operations Read and Write. This addition allows us to deal with

Assessor access needs, as discussed earlier. In addition, we treat Operation as a resource class as well with precondition and postcondition, along with two associations: inputAttributes (parameters) and outputAttributes (return values).

Figure 1 presents the SYMBOLEOAC ontology. For simplicity, it only shows some of the attributes. The root ontological element is Resource, with access-protected classes as subclasses. The merger between the SYMBOLEO ontology (shaded in yellow) and the RBAC ontology (in blue) has resulted in the merging of two classes, Role (in green) and Operation (in purple). Additionally, new classes (in red) have been added as resources, as explained earlier. New associations (colored in blue in Fig. 1) have also been added to classes AbstractEvent, Event, LegalPosition, LegalSituation, Operation, StateTransition, and DataTransfer.

In SYMBOLEOAC, our goal is to manage access to instances of particular resources and attributes. Therefore, we assume that access to instances of all resources and attribute values is denied by default, aiming to prevent unintended security breaches. To this end, roles must explicitly be granted access to resources, including their respective operations and attributes. However, there are some exceptions: the *controller* of a resource, by default, has full access to that resource and is allowed to change its policy as well as authorize other roles to use it. Additionally, if a role is *pre-authorized*, then it has access without the need to request permission. Details on the controller of each resource and pre-authorization rules are found in Sect. 5.

The main elements of the SYMBOLEOAC ontology and the additional steps carried out to secure SYMBOLEO are explained below. From RBAC, we integrate:

- **Policy**: Is a collection of access Rules. Each policy is a constraint on access rules. Policies are enforced automatically both at resource instantiation time (i.e., pre-authorization rules) and incrementally at run time after each addition/deletion of access rules. Policy, as a resource, has operations such as *isValid(accessRules)*, *updatePolicy(accessRules)* and *updateRule(accessRules)*.
- **Rule**: Represents the authorization of a Role to execute a particular Operation on a Resource (e.g., deliver meat, addPerformer for meat delivery, or read/write for an attribute). Each rule specifies that a role has access to a resource, one or more operations associated with that resource, and read/write permissions for certain attributes of the resource. A rule can either Grant to allow access or Revoke to deny/remove access. The possible actions that can performed by a role are READ, WRITE, and ALL. SYMBOLEOAC includes CRUD operations (create, update, and delete) on the WRITE operation.
- **Resource**: Represents objects that must be protected and to which the Rules apply. Inheritance is used to connect the class Resource from the RBAC ontology and original SYMBOLEO classes that require restriction and protection. Each resource will be assigned a *controller* role consisting of one or more users, which may change over time.
- **Role**: Represents an active party that interacts with protected Resources for which controllers can grant/revoke access permission.

Other extensions made to the SYMBOLEO ontology, in addition to those mentioned earlier for the purpose of protecting access to resources, include:

- SYMBOLEO includes associations between the classes Party and LegalPosition (performer, rightHolder, and liable), depending on the role a party plays in the legal position [13]. The performer is the party that performs legal positions, which is akin to execution in conventional access control. We have added performer relationships to the Event and Operation classes, as we must also restrict who can generate events and perform operations.
- New associations: composite resources, such as obligations and powers, comprise informational components sourced from other resources – specifically, events generated during the fulfillment of legal positions, data, attributes, and state transitions. In SYMBOLEOAC, we capture this aspect of LegalPosition by aggregating Event, DataTransfer, Attribute, and StateTransition.

4 SYMBOLEOAC Contract Specification Example

An extended version of the meat sale contract initially proposed in [14,18] and specified in Listing 1 will serve as a running SYMBOLEOAC example for illustrating access rules and generating smart contract with access control aspects.

```
1   Domain meatSaleDomain
2       // Controller by default is the role itself
3       Seller isA Role with returnAddress: String, name: String;
4       Buyer isA Role with name: String, warehouse: String;
5       // thirdParty added to differentiate third party role from contracting parties
6       TransportCo isA Role thirdParty with name:String;
7       Assessor isA Role thirdParty with name: String;
8       Regulator isA Role thirdParty with name: String;
9       MeatQuality isAn Enumeration(PRIME, AAA, AA, A);
10      // Controller by default is the owner
11      PerishableGood isAn Asset with quantity: Number, quality: MeatQuality, barcode:String, owner: Seller;
12      Meat isA PerishableGood;
13      // For delivered event, the controller is its performer
14      Delivered isAn Event with deliveryAddress: String, delDueDate: Date, performer: TransportCo,
            controller: Seller;
15      InspectedQuality isAn Event with Env quantityFound: Number, Env qualityFound:MeatQuality, Env
            barFound: String, performer:Assessor;
16      TempLocTime isA DataTransfer with Env temp:Number, Env locLatitude:String, Env locLongitude:String,
            Env dataTime:String; // Other events exist but are skipped here.
17  endDomain
18      // ... Omitted code describing the contract signature and local definitions
19  Obligations
20      // Controller by default is the debtor (seller) of obligation delivery
21      delivery: Obligation(seller, buyer, true, WhappensBefore(delivered, delivered.delDueDate) and Happens
            (temploctime) and temploctime.temp <= 18 and delivered.deliveryAddress == buyer.warehouse);
22      // Controller by default is the debtor (assessor) of obligation delivery
23      inspectMeat: Happens(delivered) -> Obligation(assessor, buyer, Happens(passwordNotification), Happens
            (inspectedQuality) and inspectedQuality.barFound == goods.barcode and inspectedQuality.
            qualityFound == goods.quality and inspectedQuality.quantityFound == goods.quantity);
24
25  Powers
26      // Controller by default is the creditor of power terminateContract, i.e.,buyer
27      terminateContract: Happens(Violated(obligations.delivery)) -> P(buyer, seller, true, Terminated(
            self));
28
29  ACPolicy with Controller regulator // Controller of policy is the regulator who can override rules and
            pre-authorization rules
30      Rule1: Grant read To buyer On goods.quantity by seller; // Access to specific asset attribute
31      Rule2: Grant read To assessor On obligations.delivery by seller; // Access to obligation
32      Rule3: Grant read To transportCo On inspectedQuality by assessor;
33      Rule4: Grant read To seller On inspectedQuality by assessor;
34      Rule5: Grant read To buyer On temploctime.temp by regulator;
35      Rule6: Grant write To assessor On inspectedQuality by regulator;
36      Rule7: Grant write To transportCo On powers.suspendDelivery by seller;
37      Rule8: Grant write To transportCo On powers.resumeDelivery by seller;
38  endContract
```

Listing 1. Meat sale contract specification in SYMBOLEOAC, adapted from [14,18]. Note that objects (specific events, roles, or assets) instantiating the domain classes start with a lowercase letter; see full specification online for details see footnote 1).

This contract specification has multiple roles for contractual parties (seller and buyer) and third parties (a transportation company – TransportCo, an assessor, and a regulator). The contract also includes an obligation for the seller to deliver meat (asset) of a specified quantity, quality, and temperature to the buyer, and another obligation requiring the buyer to pay a specified amount for the meat before it is shipped. Additionally, there is an obligation for the assessor to inspect the quality and quantity of the delivered meat. The occurrence of delivery, payment, and meat inspection is indicated by the delivered, paid, and inspectedQuality events, respectively. Moreover, the seller has the right to suspend their delivery obligation in case of a violation of the payment obligation.

Each of the resources (roles, assets, events, data, obligations, and powers) has information that should not be available to all roles. For example, we do not want anyone to modify the meat quality and quantity during the meat inspection. In the inspectedQuality event, the assessor is the performer (Listing 1, line 15) and the only role with write access to its attributes (quantityFound, qualityFound). Therefore, proper access control is added to SYMBOLEO to manage who is entitled to do what on which resource and protect others. To this end, each of the roles (lines 3–8) can interact with different resources according to the permissions detailed in the policy (lines 29–37). A complete example is accessible online[1].

5 SYMBOLEOAC Rules

As SYMBOLEOAC is tailored for contract execution, it differs from other access control approaches (i.e., centralized) designed for other software. We aim to protect contract execution through a distributed access control mechanism. In this context, there are two sets of SYMBOLEOAC rules: (1) rules that determine a controller for every resource, and (2) pre-authorization rules that determine who has access to what, on the basis of the role they play in contract execution.

5.1 Controller Rules

A controller is a role that sets access rules to its controlled resource for other roles. The controller can access all operations and attributes of that resource, and can authorize and deauthorize other roles to use that resource or part thereof. Controller rules determine who is the controller of every resource and they are founded on two principles: *responsibility* and *informational composition*. The controller of a legal position is the role legally responsible/liable for that legal position. The informational composition principle defines the informational parts of each obligation/power, i.e., the different kinds of information that are generated during the enactment of an obligation/power, and assigns as a controller for all of these the controller of the legal position. Applying these principles, we arrive at the following default rules for controllers, which are core to SYMBOLEOAC and do not need to be specified explicitly in a contract:

---
[1] https://bit.ly/POEM2024MeatSaleSymboleo.

- **Contract:** The controller of a contract is the set of contracting parties who jointly authorize permissions to contract operations and state. For example, the meat sale contract involves five roles. The seller and the buyer are the contracting parties (see Listing 1, lines 3–4), and the others third parties.
- **Role:** The controller of a role is the role itself (lines 3–8). In the meat sale example, for the seller role, the seller grants access to its activities such as personal profile information.
- **Asset:** Its controller is its owner. For the meat sale contract, the seller is the owner of the meat and can access its operations and attributes, and determine access permission to that asset (line 12).
- **Obligation:** The role responsible for an obligation serves as its controller. When an obligation is instantiated, the debtor is both performer and responsible (i.e., liable) for it and, therefore, is its controller. For the delivery obligation (line 21), the seller is responsible and therefore the controller.
- **Power:** The creditor, being a power's rightholder and performer, is its controller. For terminateContract (line 27), the buyer is the controller.
- **Policy:** Its controller is one of the contracting or third parties (line 29). The policy controller has more authority than the controllers of other resources and can override any access permission established by other controllers.
- **Event:** The controller of an event is its performer (line 15).
- **Attribute:** Its controller is the one of the containing resource.
- **Operation:** Its controller is the one of the containing resource.
- **StateTransition:** Its controller is the one of the containing obligation, power, or contract (along the partOf relationship in the ontology).
- **DataTransfer:** Its controller is the containing obligation/power (line 21).

5.2 Pre-authorization Rules

Pre-authorization refers to automated authorizations that take place when a resource is instantiated, serving as the initialization of access rules for the resource instance. The controller of a policy can however override these pre-authorization rules with a newly added policy. This ensures that the pre-authorizations align with broader governance, which is always there during the execution of a legal contract. Pre-authorization rules in SYMBOLEOAC (with examples) cover:

- **Contract**: The contracting parties that jointly control a contract have access to the contract execute operation and state transition information during each execution. For the meat sale contract (Listing 1), this is the case for the seller and the buyer.
- **Obligation**: The debtor (i.e., performer and liable) is pre-authorized and has access to the obligation's operations and informational parts (i.e., antecedent, consequent, and events that determine the status of the trigger). The creditor (i.e., rightHolder), on the other hand, is pre-authorized and has access to state transitions only. For example, in the meat sale contract (Listing 1, line 21), the seller, as the debtor and performer of the obligation, has access to all

information generated during the fulfillment process, including temperature data and related events, and all state transitions. Conversely, the buyer, as the creditor and rightholder of the delivery obligation, is pre-authorized to access state transitions like when was delivery initiated.
- **Power**: The creditor (i.e., performer and rightHolder) is pre-authorized and has access to the power's operations and all its informational parts (i.e., antecedent, consequent, and events that determine the status of the trigger). The debtor (i.e., liable) of a power has access to state transitions only. For example, as the performer of the terminate contract power shown in Listing 1 (line 27), the buyer has access to state transitions and trigger events, and can execute the antecedent and consequent's events, whereas the seller has only access to the state transition information.

6 SYMBOLEOAC Ontology Implementation

To generate a robust and secure smart contract, we extended the JavaScript library implementation of the original ontology (SYMBOLEOJS [16]) to cover the new SYMBOLEOAC concepts introduced in Sect. 3, leading to a reusable and secure library called SYMBOLEOACJS. This library can then be used by JavaScript code generated from a SYMBOLEOAC specification, which can then be run on the Hyperledger Fabric[2] smart contract platform.

Following the approach taken by Rasti [16], we first added/updated the classes, attributes, and associations of the SYMBOLEOAC ontology in a Umple model [5], from which we automatically generated Ecore files (visualized in Fig. 1) and Java files[3]. Since Umple does not directly generate JavaScript code, we manually transformed the Java code into its corresponding JavaScript form.

Here, we are illustrating the JavaScript equivalent of some of the ontology classes (Fig. 1), while the rest is accessible online[4]. Each ontology class has its equivalent JavaScript class. In particular, the `Resource` class has a list of controller roles (see Fig.1), and all access-controlled classes in the ontology extend `Resource`. This class also contains the necessary methods to manipulate controllers (`add/removeController()`); such methods are generated automatically from Umple for all attributes and associations.

```
1 class Obligation extends LegalPosition {
2   constructor(name, creditor, debtor, contract, surviving) {
3     super(name, creditor, debtor, contract, debtor);
4   }
5   // ... omitted code
6 }
7
8 class LegalPosition extends Resource {
9   constructor(name, creditor, debtor, contract, controller) {
10    super(controller)
11  }
12  // ... omitted code
13 }
```

Listing 2. Snippets of the `Obligation` and `LegalPosition` JavaScript classes, where the debtor is passed as the default controller in the superclass constructor calls.

---

[2] https://www.hyperledger.org/projects.
[3] https://bit.ly/POEM2024-SymboleoAC-Ontology-Java.
[4] https://bit.ly/POEM2024-SymboleoAC-Ontology-Core.

Class constructors also handle the default access control rules discussed previously. For example, Listing 2 shows the `Obligation` class, where the debtor is assigned as the controller by default in the constructor of its superclass (`LegalPosition`), which then sets it properly in its own superclass (`Resource`).

The `Policy` class contains rules that determine access permissions based on roles (Fig. 1), as well as the necessary methods to `add/removeRule()`. Additionally, a set of utility functions was added to the class. Listing 3 shows a utility function `hasPermission()` that assesses whether the role holds controller privileges, or is pre-authorized. If any of these conditions is met, we do not need to grant specific permissions to that role.

```
1  function hasPermission(aDecision, aAction, aAccessedResource, aAccessedRole, aByRole) {
2      let aRule = new Rule(aDecision, aAction, aAccessedResource, aAccessedRole, aByRole, this);
3      if (this.findRule(aRule)) {
4          return true;
5      } else {
6          if (aRule.accessedResource.findController(aRule.accessedRole)) {
7              if (!(aRule.accessedResource instanceof Event) &&
8                  !(aRule.accessedResource instanceof Asset) &&
9                  !(aRule.accessedResource instanceof Role)) {
10                 return true;
11             } // ... omitted code
12         }
13         if (aRule.accessedResource instanceof Asset) {
14             if (aRule.accessedResource._owners._value === aRule.accessedRole) {
15                 return true;
16             }
17         }
18         // ... omitted code
19 }
```

Listing 3. Snippet of a JavaScript utility function (`hasPermission()`) in `Policy`.

Other utility functions collectively form a robust access control management library for SYMBOLEOAC that ensures policies and rules remain consistent, secure, and up to date: `isValid()` checks if a new rule is compatible with existing policy constraints, and `updatePolicy()` modifies the current set of constraints to align them with changes made by the policy controller. Function `updatePolicy()` is not limited to merely changing decisions from **Grant** to **Revoke** or vice versa; it also dynamically manages access rules by adding, removing, or updating parameters of constraints. Similarly, `updateRule()` modifies the rules to reflect changes made by controllers of the resources.

7 IDE and SYMBOLEOAC2SC Code Generator

This section describes the Eclipse-based tools developed to support the SYMBOLEOAC language, demonstrating the feasibility of our approach.

We used Eclipse's Xtext [4] to formally define the grammar and concrete syntax of SYMBOLEOAC[5] by extending the definition of the original SYMBOLEO grammar [18]. Additionally, we built the new SYMBOLEOAC Eclipse IDE by updating the original SYMBOLEO IDE [14]. In addition to new domain concepts (**DataTransfer**) and attribute qualifiers (e.g., **thirdParty**), a SYMBOLEOAC contract specification can now declare policies and rules. Listing 1 (lines 29–37) shows a policy with rules for our meat sale example.

---
[5] https://bit.ly/POEM2024-SymboleoAC-Grammar-Xtext.

An existing code generator, named SYMBOLEO2SC and written in Xtend [4], generates executable smart contracts for the HyperLedger Fabric platform from SYMBOLEO specifications [16]. We have also extended this tool to support the new access control concepts found in SYMBOLEOAC, resulting in a new SYMBOLEOAC2SC code generator. This new tool exploits the extended SYMBOLEOACJS library developed in Sect. 6. There are two important considerations for the conversion here: default security settings (i.e., controller and pre-authorization rules, discussed in Sect. 5) and the access control rules and policies specified explicitly at design time using the IDE.

The rules defined in a SYMBOLEOAC specification (e.g., Listing 1, lines 29–37) are extracted, and corresponding instances of the Rule class are created using the getSpecifiedRulesUncond(rule) method, as shown in Listing 4 (lines 3–5). This method extracts the role, the provided permission, and the accessed resource from the rule specification, and then passes them to the addRulee() method. This method (Listing 5) ensures the validity of the rule before adding it to the policy's rules list. It checks whether the role already has this permission on the specified resource (i.e., has pre-authorization rights or the rule already exists). If the rule is new, it is created and added to the policy.

```
1  class <<model.contractName>> extends SymboleoContract {
2      // ... omitted code
3      <<FOR rule : model.rules>>
4          <<getSpecifiedRulesUnCond(rule)>>
5      <<ENDFOR>>
```

Listing 4. Xtend source code of part of the improved compileContract() method.

```
1   def String getSpecifiedRulesUnCond(Rule rule){
2       var String addRule=""
3       var Permission contr = rule.getPermission()
4       var Ref rl=rule.getAccessedRole()
5       var String rName=""
6       if (rule.accessedResource instanceof ResourceObligation) {
7           val obr = rule.accessedResource as ResourceObligation
8           val obl = obr.resourceOp as Obligation
9           rName = "obligations."+obl.name
10          if (obl.trigger === null){
11              addRule=addRule+"this.aCPolicy.addRulee("+contr.name+", "+rName+", this."
12                  +(rl as VariableRef).variable+")\n"
13          }
14      }
15      if (rule.accessedResource instanceof ResourceDot) {
16          val resourceDot = rule.accessedResource as ResourceDot
17          val r = resourceDot.resourceDot
18          rName =generateDotExpressionString(r, "this")
19          addRule=addRule+"this.aCPolicy.addRulee("+contr.name+", "+rName+", this."
20              +(rl as VariableRef).variable+")\n"
21      }
22      return addRule
23  }
```

Listing 5. New Xtend function getSpecifiedRulesUnCond().

8 Evaluation

Our evaluation focuses on the feasibility of the conversion from SYMBOLEOAC to executable smart contracts with access control, using the meat sale contract shown in Sect. 4. The contract class (MeatSale, Listing 6) is generated correctly by SYMBOLEOAC2SC, specifying the controller of each resource , along with a list of specified rules. Due to space limitation, the instance variables, controllers, and other rules are omitted. The other classes were also generated successfully.

```
1  class MeatSale extends SymboleoContract {
2      // ... omitted code
3      //Rules
4      this.aCPolicy.addRulee('rant','read', this.goods.quantity, this.buyer, this.seller)
5      this.aCPolicy.addRulee('Grant','read', obligations.delivery, this.assessor,this.seller)
6      this.aCPolicy.addRulee('Grant','read', inspectedQuality, this.transportCo, this.assessor)
7      this.aCPolicy.addRulee('Grant','read', temploctime.temp, this.buyer, this.regulator)
8      // ... omitted code
9  }
10 module.exports.MeatSale = MeatSale
```

Listing 6. Snippet of the MeatSale class in JavaScript, with access control rules.

The meat sale smart contract was deployed on Hyperledger Fabric to test its validity. In addition to testing the generated code from various specifications that assigned controllers and performers through both explicit and implicit means, we also successfully evaluated multiple combinations of specified rules and constraints. This included comprehensive assessments of pre-authorization processes, granting and revoking permissions, and resolving conflicts.

At runtime, for policy evaluation and enforcement within smart contract transactions, SYMBOLEO AC2SC embeds security checks (i.e., access control) as part of every transaction to prevent unauthorized access. Listing 7 (lines 10–15) shows the transaction method that triggers the delivered event, with access control. This event can only be generated by its performer (`hasPermission()`) or by a role that has write access (`isValid()`). The example from Listing 7 was successfully tested with unit tests to ensure its validity and compliance with the access control policy. Two scenarios for the delivered event are considered: i) the event must be triggered/generated by an authorized role only, and ii) an unauthorized role or attacker is trying to generate that event.

```
1  async trigger_delivered(ctx, args) {
2      const inputs = JSON.parse(args);
3      const contractId = inputs.contractId;
4      const event = inputs.event;
5      const contractState = await ctx.stub.getState(contractId);
6      // ... omitted code
7      this.initialize(contract);
8
9      if (contract.isInEffect()) {
10         if (
11             !contract.accessPolicy.hasPermission('grant', 'write', contract.delivered, contract.seller)
               ||
12             !contract.accessPolicy.isValid(new Rule('grant', 'write', contract.delivered, contract.seller))
13         ) {
14             throw new Error('Access denied...');
15         }
16         contract.delivered.happen(event);
17         // ... omitted code
18         return { successful: true };
19     } else {
20         return { successful: false };
21     }
22 }
```

Listing 7. Delivered event transaction with access control (JavaScript)

As shown in Fig. 2 (top), the test results indicate that the delivered event (and others) can only be triggered by an authorized role, such as the seller in the case of delivered. If an unauthorized role attempts to generate delivered, access will be denied (bottom), which aligns with the access policy of the contract.

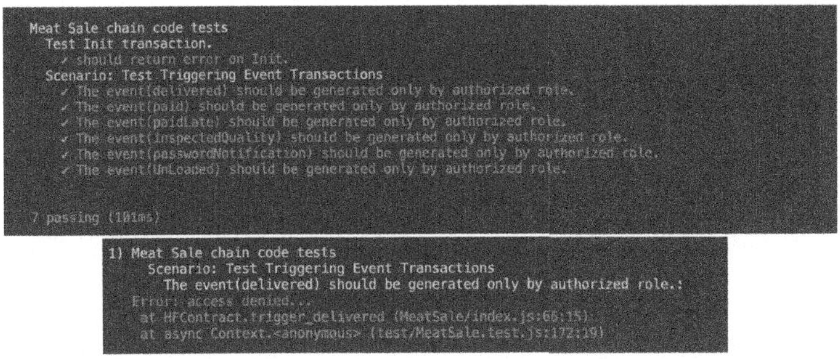

Fig. 2. Test results for successful event triggering and an unauthorized attempt.

9 Related Work

Security concerns, including RBAC, have been a significant focus in conceptual modeling. Planas et al. [15] integrate RBAC protocols into the Conversational User Interface (CUI) of chatbot resources. Similar to our work, their approach focuses on restricting access to resources such as events and states. However, it neither provides a fine-grained control that includes attributes of events, nor covers a broad range of resources, such as assets. Al-Azzoni et al. [1] propose an access contact model that extends the metamodel of iContractML [9], with similar access control concepts to ours. However, that model only restricts access to assets and does not provide fine-grained control over those assets.

Other domain-specific languages (DSLs) focusing on access control modeling, such as [2,3,10–12], employ RBAC primitives similar to ours. However, these approaches remain at the modeling stage and do not extend to code generation for implementing access control policies. None of the legal contract DSLs, such as those in [6,20], provides access control modeling. While these works highlight the need to integrate security aspects, they do not propose primitives to define access control policies. To our knowledge, our work is the first approach to integrate access-control primitives into a legal contract language, with code generation.

10 Conclusions and Future Work

In this paper, we extended a contract specification language and its underlying ontology with an RBAC-based access control model that enables defining rules and restricting access to contract resources (including assets, events, and their attributes and operations). The semantics of SYMBOLEOAC also includes rules that determine the controller of each resource, and default pre-authorization rules that come into effect when a resource is instantiated. Also, we introduced a tool (SYMBOLEOACJS) capable of generating JavaScript-based smart contract code for Hyperledger Fabric from SYMBOLEOAC specifications. This code is compliant with the implicit and specified access rules, ensuring robust security and seamless integration. For future work, we plan to improve the validation and the code generation tool (functionality and usability), and will work towards extending current SYMBOLEO model checking tools [14] to support SYMBOLEOAC.

Acknowledgments. The authors are thankful to Luigi Logrippo for useful discussions on access control. This work was partially funded by an NSERC Discovery Grant titled *From Legal Contracts to Smart Contract*, and by the ORF-RE project *CyPreSS: Software Techniques for the Engineering of Cyber-Physical Systems*. S. Alfuhaid is supported by the KSA King AbdulAziz University. M. Roveri is partially supported by the PNRR project *FAIR - Future AI Research* (PE00000013).

Disclosure of Interests. The authors have no competing interests to declare that are relevant to the content of this article.

References

1. Al-Azzoni, I., Iqbal, S.: Model-driven approach for generating smart contracts for access control. In: 2023 Fifth International Conference on Blockchain Computing and Applications (BCCA), pp. 112–115 (2023). https://doi.org/10.1109/BCCA58897.2023.10338863
2. Basin, D., Doser, J., Lodderstedt, T.: Model driven security: from UML models to access control infrastructures. ACM Trans. Softw. Eng. Methodol. **15**(1), 39–91 (2006). https://doi.org/10.1145/1125808.1125810
3. Ben Fadhel, A., Bianculli, D., Briand, L.: GemRBAC-DSL: a high-level specification language for role-based access control policies. In: Proceedings of the 21st ACM on Symposium on Access Control Models and Technologies, pp. 179–190. SACMAT 2016, ACM (2016). https://doi.org/10.1145/2914642.2914656
4. Bettini, L.: Implementing Domain Specific Languages with Xtext and Xtend, 2nd edn. Packt Publishing, Birmingham (2016)
5. Forward, A., Badreddin, O., Lethbridge, T.C., Solano, J.: Model-driven rapid prototyping with Umple. Softw.: Pract. Exp. **42**(7), 781–797 (2012). https://doi.org/10.1002/spe.1155
6. Frantz, C.K., Nowostawski, M.: From institutions to code: towards automated generation of smart contracts. In: 2016 IEEE 1st International Workshops on Foundations and Applications of Self* Systems (FAS*W), pp. 210–215 (2016). https://doi.org/10.1109/FAS-W.2016.53
7. Griffo, C., Almeida, J.P.A., Guizzardi, G., Nardi, J.C.: Service contract modeling in enterprise architecture: an ontology-based approach. Inf. Syst. **101**, 101454 (2021). https://doi.org/10.1016/j.is.2019.101454
8. Griffo, C., Almeida, J.P.A., Lima, J.A., Prince Sales, T., Guizzardi, G.: Legal powers, subjections, disabilities, and immunities: ontological analysis and modeling patterns. Data Knowl. Eng. **148**, 102219 (2023). https://doi.org/10.1016/j.datak.2023.102219
9. Hamdaqa, M., Met, L.A.P., Qasse, I.: iContractML 2.0: a domain-specific language for modeling and deploying smart contracts onto multiple blockchain platforms. Inf. Softw. Technol. **144**, 106762 (2022). https://doi.org/10.1016/j.infsof.2021.106762
10. Kashmar, N., Adda, M., Atieh, M., Ibrahim, H.: Access control metamodel for policy specification and enforcement: from conception to formalization. Proc. Comput. Sci. **184**, 887–892 (2021). https://doi.org/10.1016/j.procs.2021.03.111. the 12th International Conference on Ambient Systems, Networks and Technologies (ANT) Affiliated Workshops

11. Kim, D.-K., Ray, I., France, R., Li, N.: Modeling role-based access control using parameterized UML models. In: Wermelinger, M., Margaria-Steffen, T. (eds.) FASE 2004. LNCS, vol. 2984, pp. 180–193. Springer, Heidelberg (2004). https://doi.org/10.1007/978-3-540-24721-0_13
12. Kuhlmann, M., Sohr, K., Gogolla, M.: Employing UML and OCL for designing and analysing role-based access control. Math. Struct. Comput. Sci. **23**(4), 796–833 (2013). https://doi.org/10.1017/S0960129512000266
13. Parvizimosaed, A., Sharifi, S., Amyot, D., Logrippo, L., Mylopoulos, J.: Subcontracting, assignment, and substitution for legal contracts in Symboleo. In: Dobbie, G., Frank, U., Kappel, G., Liddle, S.W., Mayr, H.C. (eds.) ER 2020. LNCS, vol. 12400, pp. 271–285. Springer, Cham (2020). https://doi.org/10.1007/978-3-030-62522-1_20
14. Parvizimosaed, A., et al.: Specification and analysis of legal contracts with Symboleo. Softw. Syst. Model. **21**(6), 2395–2427 (2022). https://doi.org/10.1007/s10270-022-01053-6
15. Planas, E., Pérez, S., Brambilla, M., Cabot, J.: Modeling and enforcing access control policies in conversational user interfaces. Softw. Syst. Model. **22**, 1–20 (2023). https://doi.org/10.1007/s10270-023-01131-3
16. Rasti, A., et al.: Automated generation of smart contract code from legal contract specifications with Symboleo2SC. Softw. Syst. Model. (2024). https://doi.org/10.1007/s10270-024-01187-9
17. Sandhu, R., Samarati, P.: Access control: principle and practice. IEEE Commun. Mag. **32**(9), 40–48 (1994). https://doi.org/10.1109/35.312842
18. Sharifi, S., Parvizimosaed, A., Amyot, D., Logrippo, L., Mylopoulos, J.: Symboleo: towards a specification language for legal contracts. In: 2020 IEEE 28th International Requirements Engineering Conference (RE), pp. 364–369 (2020). https://doi.org/10.1109/RE48521.2020.00049
19. De Capitani di Vimercati, S., Paraboschi, S., Samarati, P.: Access control: principles and solutions. Softw. Pract. Exp. **33**(5), 397–421 (2003). https://doi.org/10.1002/spe.513
20. Wöhrer, M., Zdun, U.: Domain specific language for smart contract development. In: 2020 IEEE International Conference on Blockchain and Cryptocurrency (ICBC), pp. 1–9 (2020). https://doi.org/10.1109/ICBC48266.2020.9169399

Functional Security in Automation: The FAST Approach

Vjatšeslav Antipenko[✉] and Raimundas Matulevičius

University of Tartu, Ülikooli 18, 50090 Tartu, Estonia
{vjatseslav.antipenko,rma}@ut.ee

Abstract. Automated systems and technologies, integral to Industry 5.0, combine interconnected actuators, such as industrial robots and computational devices, forming a network spanning various manufacturing stages, including design, logistics, and sales. These systems, which automate tasks traditionally performed by humans, vary from manual to fully automated and depend on vendor support for maintenance and troubleshooting, often requiring remote access for optimal operation. As digitalisation grows, alongside the demand for on-demand production and rising labour costs, securing these systems becomes crucial, not merely optional. Despite their importance, awareness of the security risks associated with automated systems still needs to be improved. Companies need to recognise and adhere to security standards and regulations. This paper outlines a systematic literature review introducing the Functions, Assets, Security Threats, and Mitigation Techniques (FAST) approach, a structured framework for managing security risks in automated systems. It explores using a domain model for security risk management to assess threats and their impacts on data confidentiality, integrity, and availability. Additionally, it proposes risk treatment strategies and countermeasures to mitigate these risks.

Keywords: STRIDE · ISSRM · RAMI 4.0 · Automated systems and technology · Security Risk Management · Industry 5.0

1 Introduction

In the era of Industry 5.0, digitalisation and intelligent infrastructure are transforming human activities and industrial systems. Disruptive technologies such as cloud computing, blockchain, artificial intelligence/machine learning (AI/ML), and various automated solutions have found widespread applications across different manufacturing domains [18,31,32]. The intensive deployment of these technologies facilitates generating and managing substantial volumes of data and information. It necessitates their proper use, availability as needed, and integration into decision-making processes. As institutions explore the potential of Industry 5.0 [33], it has become clear that security must be prioritised as a fundamental component within digitalised processes and automated systems [2,3,24].

The urgency of this prioritisation is highlighted by the annual Cyber Security report in Estonia [9] and ENISA Threat Landscape 2024 [6], which indicates a rising trend in security threats and risks. These threats particularly target institutional and service sectors, with numerous cases involving automated systems and technologies. Organisations must fortify their security frameworks with the ongoing emphasis on digitalisation within the business sector. This entails preparing for potential threats and proactively developing strategies to mitigate risks, thus safeguarding against adverse outcomes in severe scenarios.

Given such a state of affairs, our paper analyses the context, assets, risks, and countermeasures in automated manufacturing systems, with particular attention to Small and Medium-sized Enterprises (SMEs). Although SMEs play an important role in the economy [30], they often lack robust security infrastructures due to limited resources, expertise, and reliance on external vendors [15]. These limitations make them particularly vulnerable as they integrate automation [26]. This emphasis on SMEs highlights the importance of understanding how they manage security while balancing cost-efficiency. It is necessary developing tailored solutions that address their specific challenges in Industry 5.0.

To address the management of security risks in automated systems and technology, this study is guided by a set of research questions formulated to explore the scope, challenges, protected assets, risks, and necessary security measures within these systems. These questions include exploring the context and challenges of automated systems, identifying protected assets, assessing security risks, and determining appropriate security requirements and controls. A systematic literature analysis, underpinned by applying the Information Systems Security Risk Management (ISSRM) process and domain model [5,19] provides the methodological foundation for addressing these queries, offering strategic insights into effective security management practices. Based on the literature review, we introduce the Functions, Assets, Security Threats, and Mitigation Techniques (FAST) approach, a structured framework for identifying and managing security risks in automated manufacturing systems through targeted mitigation techniques.

2 Background

2.1 Automated Systems and Technologies

There exist various related terms for automated systems and technology. For instance, industrial robots [24] are utilised in intelligent and automated manufacturing environments or automated manufacturing systems [10] comprising interconnected stations. Embedded computing systems [3] blend hardware and software components and mechanical elements. Cyber-physical systems [25] encompass a range of hardware and software components, including mechanical actuators, controllers, sensors, devices for human interaction, control logic, firmware, and operating systems. Cyber-infrastructure elements (in cyber-physical systems) [16], such as computational processes, control algorithms, decision systems, databases, and physical infrastructure components, are interconnected through sensors and actuators. In automated manufacturing systems, the control mechanisms coordinate the functions of the various stations within the manufacturing chain via a communication network [10].

2.2 Reference Architectural Model Industrie 4.0

We utilise the Reference Architectural Model Industrie 4.0 (RAMI 4.0) to advance digital transformation in manufacturing [4]. RAMI 4.0 categorises layers and dimensions of industrial systems, from physical components to business models [23]. This ensures the framework's resilience and adaptability for integration at any manufacturing level [11,20,32] (Fig. 1).

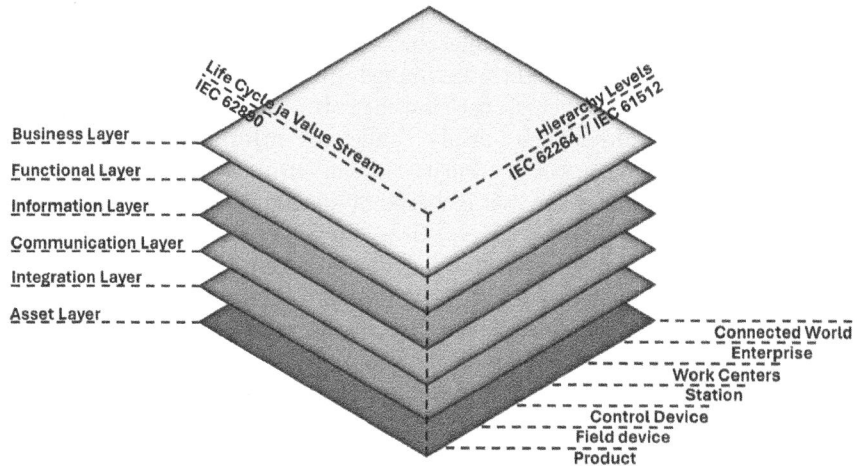

Fig. 1. Reference Architectural Model Industrie 4.0 (RAMI 4.0), figure adapted from [4]

The **Asset Layer** forms the foundational level, concerned with physical components like machinery and tools, and is critical for data collection and initial processing. Each level interacts with the **Asset Layer**, playing a pivotal role in digital transformation by:

- Collecting real-time data from field devices.
- Implementing control strategies based on data insights.
- Providing interfaces for human-machine interactions.
- Feeding operational data into enterprise systems for strategic planning.
- Ensuring global connectivity for integrated supply chains.

The **Hierarchy Levels Axis** of RAMI 4.0, organises processes into seven levels:

- **Product:** Focuses on manufacturing output, including all stages from design to prototype testing.

- **Field Device:** Involves hardware like sensors and actuators for data capture and action.
- **Control Device:** Includes Programmable Logic Controllers (PLC) and Distributed Controls (DC) for processing inputs and sending commands.
- **Station:** Represents the monitoring and control hub, typically involving SCADA systems.
- **Work Centers:** Data storage and analysis occur here, supported by Manufacturing Execution Systems (MES).
- **Enterprise:** Enterprise Resource Planning (ERP) systems integrate production, inventory, and financial data for decision-making.
- **Connected World:** Integrates the system with global networks, linking to suppliers and customers.

This framework aids in digitalising traditional industrial setups, ensuring each component's role is clearly defined and integrated. Our focus on the **Asset Layer** and its hierarchical interactions enhances operational visibility and drives strategic improvements.

2.3 Security Risk Management

Security engineering involves reducing the risk of unauthorised harm to assets to acceptable levels through prevention and response strategies [7]. This process encompasses the ISSRM domain model, which includes asset-related, risk-related, and risk treatment-related concepts, particularly aligning with ISO/IEC 27001 standards [5,8,19].

Assets, vital for achieving organisational goals, are classified into business and organisational types. Business assets, typically intangible, include information, processes, capabilities, and skills critical to the organisation's mission [5,19]. Security criteria or properties on business assets define security needs—confidentiality, integrity, and availability—ensuring restricted access, data reliability, and timely data access respectively [5,19]. System assets support business assets, including tangible components (e.g., hardware) and intangible elements (e.g., software, people). System assets are identified as assets that facilitate the functioning of business assets [19]. In [1], information processing functions are derived. These are *capturing* (e.g. using keyboard, bar code reader, etc.), *transmitting* (e.g., wired or wireless means, etc.), *storing* (e.g., hard disk, databases, etc.), *retrieving* (e.g., from any device), *manipulating* (e.g., calculations, statistics, etc.), and *displaying* (e.g., monitor, printer, etc.) information. All functions contribute to supporting business assets, which may be represented as data, information, or operations and processes.

Risk involves a threat exploiting vulnerabilities to impact assets negatively. Risk events combine these elements, with impacts ranging from data loss to loss of system integrity and confidentiality [5,19]. Risk treatment decisions involve avoiding, reducing, transferring, or retaining risks. These decisions define security requirements to address identified risks appropriately [5,19]. In the context of this work, we focus on risk reduction strategies.

Security risk analysis includes consideration of security threats. This work uses the STRIDE approach for security risk analysis to categorise identified threats by their types [29]. STRIDE, an acronym, stands for *Spoofing, Tampering, Repudiation, Information disclosure, Denial of service, and Elevation of privilege*, each describing different threat types and corresponding security violations. The selection of STRIDE is driven by its structured approach and suitability for addressing security risks in automated systems [13]. Its ability to systematically map security threats aligns well with the modular nature of such systems, where functions and assets must be protected at various layers. In our approach, STRIDE aids in identifying potential software attacks, with each category offering detailed insights into specific threats and their impacts on security requirements.

2.4 Related Work

The FAST approach differentiates itself from established methodologies like the SecBPMN, STS method, and Secure Tropos, which share similar elements regarding assets, threats, and mitigations. However, each method serves different contexts. For example, SecBPMN focuses on integrating security into business process models, targeting process-level security rather than system automation [27]. Similarly, the STS method [22] addresses security requirements from a sociotechnical perspective, whereas FAST is explicitly designed for industrial automation. Secure Tropos extends goal-oriented requirements engineering to integrate security into software systems [21], but unlike FAST, its primary focus is on software. FAST addresses security for automated systems across multiple functional layers, including physical assets like sensors and actuators, making it particularly suited to Industry 5.0 environments. FAST's use of the STRIDE threat model further allows for systematic categorisation and mitigation of threats within the functional architecture of automated systems.

While these approaches aim to enhance security, FAST distinguishes itself by focusing on automated manufacturing, integrating with RAMI 4.0, and offering a comprehensive framework for securing both business and system assets.

3 Research Method

To ground and guide our work, we formulate a primary research question: *How can security risks in automated systems and technologies be effectively managed?*

3.1 Literature Review

Following [14], we performed a systematic literature, which was structured around the ISSRM application. The goal is to survey literature covering security risks in automated systems and technology. We explore the context of automated manufacturing systems and define the nature and components of automated manufacturing systems, their security needs, systems' security risks, strategies and methods (requirements and controls) employed to mitigate these risks.

Search Process: We used SCOPUS[1] and Web of Science[2] digital libraries. The search queries include "automated manufacturing system, cyber security, cybersecurity". Table 1 shows the results of the search results from the sources. We identified 125 results, from which we selected 10 for analysis based on the inclusion/ exclusion criteria (see Table 2).

Table 1. Selected sources and corresponding results for literature review

Sources	SCOPUS	Web of Science	Total
Returned	70	55	125
Filter 1	29	23	52
Filter 2	6	4	10

Paper Selection: We subjected the identified papers to an initial screening, which covered the title, keywords, abstract, results, and conclusion. To select relevant papers, we applied the two filters based on our research questions:

1. Filter 1: Applying inclusion/exclusion criteria in Table 2 on the selected papers. Table 1 presents the results of applying the inclusion/exclusion criteria, resulting in 52 results.
2. Filter 2: Quality assessment of the papers that passed Filter 1 following the quality guidelines [14] (e.g., Does the study cover the scope of work? Does the study describe security risks in automated manufacturing systems? Does the study provide countermeasures to mitigate security risks?)

Table 2. Inclusion/exclusion criteria on the selected papers

Inclusion criteria	Exclusion criteria
Papers in the area of industrial automation	Focus on security in limited aspects of automated manufacturing systems
Explicit security risk assessment or analysis	Focus on safety features (unintentional harm to stakeholders)
Present security risk solutions	Non-English papers
Accessible academic papers	Duplicate works

3.2 Threats to Validity

Several potential threats to the study's validity were identified. First, the selected keywords may not fully capture the research scope, potentially limiting the depth of the literature review. Second, some relevant studies might have been excluded

---

[1] https://www.scopus.com/home.uri.
[2] https://www.webofscience.com/wos/woscc/basic-search.

due to keyword issues, affecting completeness. Third, included studies might lack academic rigour, potentially weakening conclusions. To mitigate these concerns, a quality assessment using specific inclusion and exclusion criteria ensured the scientific merit of the selected articles. Lastly, the adaptation of the RAMI 4.0 framework, while widely recognised, may introduce biases or limitations that require careful consideration to avoid compromising the study's validity.

4 Findings

In this section, we consolidate key findings from the literature review. Subsequently, we elaborate on a new technique designed to allocate mitigation techniques tailored to a specific combination of asset, function, and security threat.

Recognising modern industrial systems' complexity, we must first clarify the system context. System context is derived from the combination of business and system assets. Hence, addressing RAMI 4.0, we target **Asset Layer** as it consolidates only physical components. Table 3 represents extracted system asset levels based on our literature review findings. Table 4 expands the findings by summarising system assets and describing the business assets they support.

Table 3. Extracted RAMI 4.0 Asset layer levels from literature review.

Public.	FD[a]	CD[a]	S[a]	CC[a]	E[a]	CW[a]
[12]	✓	✓	✓	–	–	–
[31]	✓	✓	✓	✓	–	✓
[18]	✓	–	–	✓	✓	–
[3]	✓	–	✓	–	–	–
[16]	✓	–	✓	✓	–	–
[25]	✓	✓	✓	–	✓	✓
[10]	✓	–	✓	–	–	–
[2]	✓	–	–	–	✓	–
[28]	✓	✓	✓	✓	✓	–
[24]	✓	✓	✓	–	–	–

[a] For ease of reference, we have abbreviated the dimensions of the RAMI 4.0 Asset layer as follows: Field Device - FD; Control Device - CD; Station - S; Control Center - C; Enterprise - E; Connected World - CW
✓ refers to mentioning assets

This alignment provides a structured way to assess these assets' business value and relevance to organisational objectives. Surprisingly, reviewed publications focus on the *Field Device* and *Station* dimensions of RAMI 4.0, highlighting a shortcoming in addressing security risks across the Asset Layer of RAMI 4.0. Additionally, the surveyed literature overlooks business assets' security requirements *(confidentiality, integrity, and availability)*. Our approach assumes these criteria are universally critical, though their significance may vary according to specific organisational policies.

Once the foundation for system context is established, we can enrich it with specific functions that manipulate business assets. In Chap. 2.3, we described six information processing functions. We expanded our literature review by extracting specific functions and data types covered in each publication, which are combined in Table 5. Most studies focus on information transmission, with only one examining information retrieval. This gap suggests an oversight in covering all functional areas, potentially impacting the robustness of system security implementations.

Table 4. RAMI 4.0 Asset layer assets

Hierarchy levels	System assets	Business assets
Product	Manufactured goods	Revenue from sales, Customer satisfaction
Field devices	Robots, Actuators, Sensors, Motors, Transmitters, Embedded devices, Physical manufacturing machines, Cameras, 3D Printers	Production data, operational conditions data, environmental factor data, quality control data, operational data, visual data
Control device	Programmable Logic Controller (PLC), Remote Terminal Unit (RTU), Distributed Control System (DCS), Gateways	Production data, operational conditions data, quality control data, automated decision-making process
Station	Workstation (Digital Control Unit), SCADA/SCADA Masters, Operators, Operator Stations	Operational data, operational processes, operational services
Work Centers	Office Products, Collaboration software, IT Hosts, Computers, Servers, Data centres, Mail and Web services	Application data, the application process, application services
Enterprise	Enterprise resource planning systems (ERP), Total productive maintenance systems (TPM), Vendors, Partners, Business applications, Data analytics, Cloud computing	Business process, operational resource planning, supply chain process, business application data
Connected world	Internal network, Robot Network, Industrial demilitarised zone (DMZ), public internet	Business application data, operational data, services and processes

Table 5. Extracted Functions and Business Assets from Literature Review

Function	Publication	Asset	Publication
To Capture	[2, 12, 18, 28]	Sensor data	[2, 12, 16, 28, 31]
To Transmit	[10, 12, 16, 18, 24, 25, 28, 31]	Robot data	[12, 24]
To Store	[16, 24, 25, 28, 31]	Device data	[25, 28, 31]
To Retrieve	[25]	Operational data	[18, 24, 25, 28]
To Manipulate	[16, 18, 28, 31]	Business data	[3, 18, 24, 28]
To Display	[3, 18, 25]	Production data	[10, 25, 28]
		Configuration data	[24, 25]
		Error messages data	[25]
		Personal data	[28]

Having established the system context, we can analyse it for both extracted security threats and mitigation techniques. Table 6 represents security threats, while Table 7 outlines mitigation techniques. We selected the STRIDE method to categorise and classify both threats and mitigations. Notably, the *Repudiation* threat category is absent from our findings, suggesting potential areas for further investigation or unconsidered vulnerabilities in the current literature.

Our literature review identified several gaps. Most studies focus on the *Field Device* and *Station* dimensions of RAMI 4.0, neglecting other levels. Additionally, the *Retrieval* function is underrepresented, leaving gaps in the coverage of information processing functions. Finally, not all STRIDE categories are addressed, particularly *Repudiation*, which remains unexplored.

Table 6. Extracted and categorised by STRIDE security threats

Spoofing	Tampering	Information Disclosure	Denial of Service	Elevation of Privilege
IP Address Spoofing [28]	Code Manipulation [2,3,12]	Network Sniffing [28]	Flooding [12,24,28]	Physical destruction of IT Infrastructure [10,12,25]
	Malware infection [3,12,24,28]	Eavesdropping [3,12,28]	SYN Flooding [2]	Micro Defects Injection [25]
	Network Worm Infiltration [12]	Man-in-the-Middle Attack [2,28]	Barrage attack [2]	Disabling or Altering Safety Devices [25]
	Virus Infection [3,12]	Side Channel attack [28]	Ransomware infection [24]	Unauthorized access to Systems and Data [25]
	Life-cycle Implants of Backdoors [3,12]			Exploitation of Remote Network Vulnerabilities [25]
	Eavesdropping [3,12,28]			Insider-Enabled Network Attack(Local access) [25]
	Hardware Backdoor Implementation [3,12]			Theft and Cloning of Access Badges [10]
	Fault Injection [3,25]			Command Injection [10]
	Unauthorized Hardware Modification [3]			Sleep deprivation [2]
	Buffer Overflow Exploit [3]			Reverse Engineering of Software or Hardware [28]
	Physical Tampering with Sensors [10]			Brute force attack [28]
	Unauthorized Configuration Alteration [10]			Replay attack [28]
	Unauthorized Access to Human Machine Interfaces(HMI) [10]			Phishing [28]
	Physical and Digital Tampering [2]			Password attack [28]
	Data Manipulation [24,28]			
	SQL Injection [28]			
	DNS Poisoning [28]			
	Operation manipulation [24]			

We propose a new approach to addressing security threats by considering both the data at hand and the functions through which this data is manipulated. In Fig. 2, we illustrate the *Information Disclosure* category of threats, showing how business assets are linked to their respective functions and enriched with appropriate security threats and countermeasures. Figure 2 illustrates how business data is transmitted across an organisation's network using the RAMI 4.0 Communication Layer logic and Asset Layer devices, such as routers and end-user devices. This scenario presents a potential vulnerability to *Eavesdropping attacks*, where an unauthorised party could access confidential information, compromising data confidentiality. This security risk can be mitigated by implementing encrypted communication protocols within the organisation's messaging systems, ensuring the protection of sensitive data.

Table 7. Extracted and categorised by STRIDE security treatments

Authenticity (S)	Integrity (T)	Confidentiality (I)	Availability (D)	Authorisation (E)
Multi-factor authentication [28]	Encrypted communication protocols [3,28]	Payload Detection Solutions [3]	Intrusion detection system [2]	User screening [2]
	Hardware Inspection [3]	Anomaly detection alarm [31]	Number of data packets over short time scale [2]	User access management [2]
	Command whitelisting [31]	Protocol health monitoring [31]	Regular updates/patching [2,28,31]	
	Utilisation of virtual private networks [28]		Compare initiated and established TCP connection [2]	
	Secure coding practices [3]		Traffic Management & Limitation [2,31]	
			IT Security training [2]	
			Regular backups generation [28]	

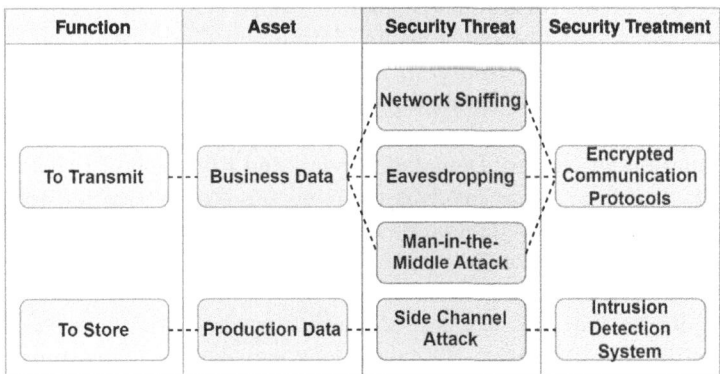

Fig. 2. Information Disclosure - FAST

Let's consider another example, this time focusing on the *Denial of Service* category of threats. Figure 3 illustrates how business assets, such as data, interact with a new set of functions, including data capture and manipulation, while being enriched with appropriate security threats and countermeasures. For instance, *Configuration data* is susceptible to manipulation, making it vulnerable to *Ransomware Infection* threats. This threat can be mitigated by implementing *Regular Backup generation*, ensuring data recovery and continuity in case of an attack.

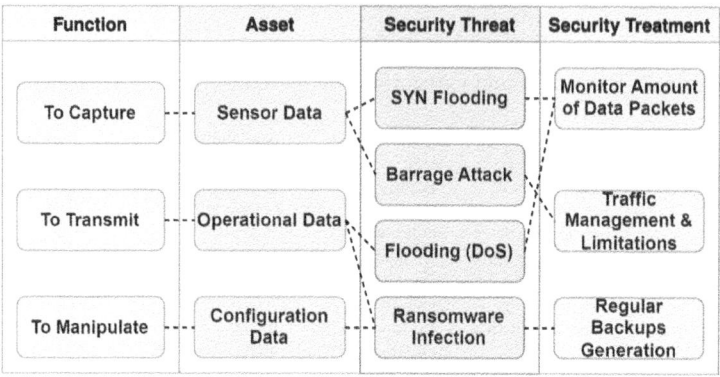

Fig. 3. Denial of Service - FAST

Considering the integration of functions, assets, security threats, and mitigation techniques, we have developed and named this approach **FAST**. By aligning assets and functions with identified threats and tailored mitigation techniques, FAST provides a framework for automated manufacturing environments. In the first phase, system functions and assets are identified across the RAMI 4.0 framework layers, covering digital components (data processing systems) and physical components (sensors and actuators). In the second phase, security threats are categorised using the STRIDE threat model. Each function and asset is evaluated to determine which of the six threat categories—Spoofing, Tampering, Repudiation, Information Disclosure, Denial of Service, and Elevation of Privilege—may be relevant. The final phase involves applying targeted mitigation techniques. These techniques are selected based on the STRIDE classification and tailored to the unique vulnerabilities of the identified functions and assets, ensuring robust protection across the system's architecture.

We emphasise that this categorisation and representation are experimental and require further validation. Organisations can develop more targeted and effective security strategies by addressing security threats based on the types of functions to which data is exposed. This approach could be particularly beneficial for organisations experiencing rapid growth, those understaffed, or those dealing with complex variables within specific function types. Moreover, it is essential to test the compliance of this strategy with established security frameworks and standards. Such validation will ensure that the proposed approach aligns with best practices and regulatory requirements, ultimately enhancing its credibility and reliability in real-world applications.

5 Feasibility Study

To demonstrate the proposed technique, we apply the FAST method to Company Baltic WoodCo, a wood manufacturing enterprise in Estonia [17]. Baltic WoodCo operates under a B2B model, offering a range of products and services, including design and manufacturing, and follows an order-driven production model without prior inventory accumulation. Key influences on Baltic WoodCo include the EU's Green Growth Objectives, geopolitical challenges, technological advancements, digital transformation, and a labour shortage.

Given the competitive market in which Baltic WoodCo operates, the company aims to maintain competitive pricing, high product quality, timely deliveries, short lead times, and rapid product development. Any disruptions in these processes can have significant impacts. Therefore, robust security measures must be implemented to protect operations without hindering the manufacturing processes.

System Context: Company Baltic WoodCo uses an ERP system, SolidWorks, and internal software alongside MS Office to manage operations. These systems streamline key processes:

- **Sales and Product Drafting:** Involves evaluating customer requests, negotiating prices, and planning manufacturing after prepayment.
- **Product Design:** Starts with sales request analysis, followed by project setup and development of new components as needed. Costs are calculated and communicated to sales.
- **Manufacturing:** Includes planning and execution phases, from metadata setup to final dispatch, potentially involving product assembly.

Based on the Baltic WoodCo profile, we can apply the FAST method in three distinct phases:

- **Phase 1:** Identify system functions and assets across the RAMI 4.0 framework, covering both digital (data processing systems) and physical components (sensors, actuators).
- **Phase 2:** Categorise security threats using the STRIDE threat model, evaluating each function and asset against six threat categories.
- **Phase 3:** Apply targeted mitigation techniques based on the STRIDE classifications, tailoring them to the specific vulnerabilities of the identified functions and assets.

Having outlined the system, business context and specific steps, we now explore two case studies.

5.1 Information Disclosure

As our first case, let's consider *Information Disclosure*, which involves unauthorised access to sensitive information. With Company Baltic WoodCo's increasing digitisation, the threat of Man-in-the-Middle (MitM) attacks increases. These attacks can occur across various data transmission channels, including email communication, file transfers, and web-based interactions. For instance, during data exchange with its supply chain and retail partners, an attacker could intercept and potentially alter communications between two parties, as depicted in Fig. 4.

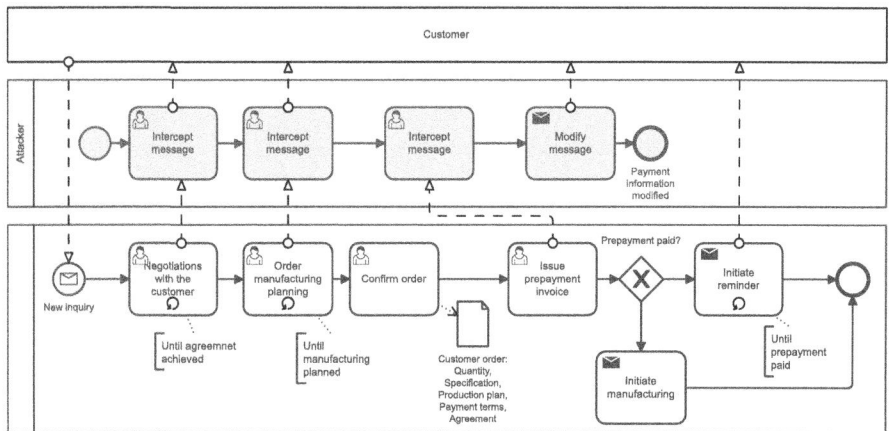

Fig. 4. Man-in-the-Middle attack scenario

In this scenario, the ***function*** under threat is the transmission of sensitive data (***asset***) between internal and external systems. The ***assets*** at risk include business-critical information such as contract negotiations, proprietary designs, and payment instructions. According to the FAST method, the ***security threat*** is categorised under *Information Disclosure* in the STRIDE model, where the risk stems from unauthorised access and data alteration during transmission.

Baltic WoodCo could implement a strategy addressing aspects of data transmission to mitigate these risks. Based on the FAST approach's ***mitigation techniques***, this strategy should incorporate countermeasures such as encrypting data, using secure file transfer protocols, and monitoring network activity for unauthorised connections. Table 8 contextualises this example, illustrating specific measures and their applications.

Functional Security in Automation: The FAST Approach 257

Table 8. Instance of Man-in-the-middle attack

Aspect	Details
Business Asset	Data in transit
IS Asset	Communication Network
Risk	An attacker intercepts and potentially alters communications between two parties without their knowledge
Impact	Corruption of data confidentiality and integrity
Vulnerability	Unsecured and/or unencrypted communication channels
Threat Agent	An attacker with corresponding means
Attack Method	Interception of communication channels
Security Requirement	All digital data transmissions must be encrypted
Controls	Ensure communication in transit is secure and encrypted, preventing unauthorised access and data breaches

5.2 Denial of Service

As our second case, let's examine *Denial of Service (DoS)* attacks, which deplete the resources necessary to provide services. A typical example is a Flooding attack, where excessive traffic overwhelms the company's network or systems, making them unable to handle legitimate requests. Such disruptions can significantly impede Company Baltic WoodCo's supply chain, delay production, and disrupt business operations. The threat might originate from an internally compromised manufacturing machine, IoT device, or any other sensor involved in capturing information.

In this scenario, the *function* under threat is the to capture function, which collects operational data from sensors and devices throughout the manufacturing process. The *assets* at risk include system infrastructure, such as IoT devices and sensors, that enable real-time data collection crucial to maintaining operations. According to the FAST method, the *security threat* is categorised under *Denial of Service (DoS)* in the STRIDE model, where an attacker can generate excessive traffic to overload system capacity and disrupt normal operations.

Baltic WoodCo could implement a comprehensive strategy to mitigate these risks. Based on the FAST approach's *mitigation techniques*, this strategy could include monitoring data packet volumes, identifying unusual spikes that may indicate a DoS attack, and applying traffic management solutions to prioritise critical data while limiting non-essential traffic. This ensures that the system remains resilient against DoS attacks targeting data capture.

Similar to the first example, Table 9 contextualises this case.

Table 9. Instance of Flooding (Denial of Service) attack

Aspect	Details
Business Asset	Availability of operational services
IS Asset	Network infrastructure
Risk	An attacker overwhelms the organisation's network resources or services with excessive traffic
Impact	Loss of service availability
Vulnerability	Insufficient network bandwidth; Lack of filtering mechanisms
Threat Agent	An attacker with corresponding means
Attack Method	Overwhelming the organisation's resources with excessive traffic
Security Requirement	Implement real-time intrusion detection for monitoring data flow
Controls	Use rate limiting and request filtering; monitor data packets to identify and respond to potential DDoS attacks

6 Concluding Remarks

As industrial manufacturing becomes digitised, frameworks like RAMI 4.0 play a fundamental role in establishing efficient processes and workflows. However, these frameworks overlook the security aspects of digital services. In this paper, we conducted a literature review of security threats in automated systems, applying the ISSRM model to identify and analyse system and business assets requiring protection. The STRIDE method was applied to categorize threats and mitigation techniques and to explain vulnerabilities.

Our analysis revealed gaps in the literature, with threat scenarios focusing on the Field Device and Station levels of RAMI 4.0, see Table 3, leaving other levels underexplored despite their susceptibility to exploitation. A similar trend was observed in the literature on protectable assets, see Table 5, which often focuses on specific functions while neglecting a comprehensive approach to asset protection.

The STRIDE method categorises threats and mitigations, offering actionable strategies. However, the study also raises questions about the unique security challenges of automated systems compared to traditional information technologies, indicating the need for further exploration. To address these gaps, we propose a framework that integrates functions, assets, security threats, and mitigation techniques The feasibility study highlights additional research, validation, and refinement.

The FAST approach, while systematic and useful, has its limitations. It assumes that companies have their assets well-documented and mapped, which is vital for its effectiveness. It remains to be validated whether companies, especially SMEs, consistently maintain complete and up-to-date documentation of their assets, which may affect the applicability of FAST. Additionally, its success depends on skilled personnel identifying and categorising assets and threats, which some organisations may lack. FAST also relies on predefined threat models like STRIDE. While effective, STRIDE may not account for emerging or industry-specific threats. Companies using FAST must regularly update their threat models and mitigation strategies to keep pace with the evolving cybersecurity landscape.

Future research should delve into the lesser-explored layers of RAMI 4.0, ensuring that all functions are included. Moreover, empirical studies are needed to validate the FAST approach through real-world testing, such as simulations, pilot tests, and statistical analyses. These evaluations will demonstrate the framework's value, scalability, and adaptability across various industrial sectors.

References

1. Alter, S.: The Work System Method: Connecting People, Processes, and IT for Business Results. Work System Method (2006)
2. Chundhoo, V., Chattopadhyay, G., Karmakar, G., Appuhamillage, G.K.: Cybersecurity risks in meat processing plant and impacts on total productive maintenance. In: 2021 International Conference on Maintenance and Intelligent Asset Management (ICMIAM), pp. 1–5. IEEE, Ballarat (2021)
3. Clark, G.W., Doran, M.V., Andel, T.R.: Cybersecurity issues in robotics. In: 2017 IEEE Conference on Cognitive and Computational Aspects of Situation Management (CogSIMA), pp. 1–5. IEEE, Savannah (2017)
4. Schweichhart, K.: Reference architectural model industrie 4.0 (RAMI 4.0) (2016). https://ec.europa.eu/futurium/en/system/files/ged/a2-schweichhart-reference_architectural_model_industrie_4.0_rami_4.0.pdf
5. Dubois, É., Heymans, P., Mayer, N., Matulevičius, R.: A systematic approach to define the domain of information system security risk management. In: Nurcan, S., Salinesi, C., Souveyet, C., Ralyté, J. (eds.) Intentional Perspectives on Information Systems Engineering, pp. 289–306. Springer, Heidelberg (2010)
6. European Union Agency for Cybersecurity (ENISA): ENISA Threat Landscape (2024). https://www.enisa.europa.eu/publications/enisa-threat-landscape-2024. Accessed 07 Oct 2024
7. Firesmith, D.: Engineering safety and security related requirements for software intensive systems. In: ICSE Companion, p. 169 (2007)
8. Ganji, D., Mouratidis, H., Gheytassi, S.M.: Towards a modelling language for managing the requirements of ISO/IEC 27001 standard. In: In Proceedings of the 5th International Conference on Advances and Trends in Software Engineering (SOFTENG 2019), pp. 17–23 (2019)
9. Information System Authority: Cyber Security in Estonia 2023 (2023). https://www.ria.ee/en/media/2702/download. Accessed 15 Apr 2024
10. Jablonski, M., Yu, B., Ciocarlie, G.F., Costa, P.: A case study in the formal modeling of safe and secure manufacturing automation. Computer **54**(9), 59–71 (2021)
11. Kaiser, J., McFarlane, D., Hawkridge, G., André, P., Leitão, P.: A review of reference architectures for digital manufacturing: classification, applicability and open issues. Comput. Ind. **149**, 103923 (2023)

12. Khalid, A., et al.: Understanding vulnerabilities in cyber physical production systems. Int. J. Comput. Integr. Manuf. **35**(6), 569–582 (2022)
13. Khan, R., McLaughlin, K., Laverty, D., Sezer, S.: STRIDE-based threat modeling for cyber-physical systems. In: 2017 IEEE PES Innovative Smart Grid Technologies Conference Europe (ISGT-Europe), pp. 1–6 (2017). https://doi.org/10.1109/ISGTEurope.2017.8260283
14. Kitchenham, B., Pearl Brereton, O., Budgen, D., Turner, M., Bailey, J., Linkman, S.: Systematic literature reviews in software engineering - a systematic literature review. Inf. Softw. Technol. **51**(1), 7–15 (2009)
15. Kutsekoda, S.: Tulevikuvaade töötleva tööstuse ametialagruppide tööjõu- ja oskuste vajadusele
16. Kutzler, T., Wolter, A., Kenner, A., Dassow, S.: Boosting cyber-physical system security. IFAC-PapersOnLine **54**(1), 976–981 (2021)
17. Laanemets, Hendrik: Normeerimise ja marsruudi loomise kontseptsioon ettevõtte x näitel (2023). https://dspace.tktk.ee/items/b58f0577-e0f8-443d-b2d1-ac19fd076d46
18. Lane Thames, J.: Distributed, collaborative and automated cybersecurity infrastructures for cloud-based design and manufacturing systems. In: Schaefer, D. (ed.) Cloud-Based Design and Manufacturing (CBDM), pp. 207–229. Springer, Cham (2014). https://doi.org/10.1007/978-3-319-07398-9_8
19. Matulevičius, R.: Fundamentals of Secure System Modelling. Springer, Heidelberg (2017). https://doi.org/10.1007/978-3-319-61717-6
20. Mirani, A.A., Velasco-Hernandez, G., Awasthi, A., Walsh, J.: Key challenges and emerging technologies in industrial IoT architectures: a review. Sensors **22**(15), 5836 (2022)
21. Mouratidis, H., Giorgini, P.: Secure tropos: a security-oriented extension of the tropos methodology. Int. J. Softw. Eng. Knowl. Eng. **17** (2007). https://doi.org/10.1142/S0218194007003240
22. Paja, E., Dalpiaz, F., Giorgini, P.: Modelling and reasoning about security requirements in socio-technical systems. Data Knowl. Eng. **98**, 123–143 (2015). https://doi.org/10.1016/j.datak.2015.07.007, https://www.sciencedirect.com/science/article/pii/S0169023X1500052X
23. Plattform Industrie 4.0: The background to Plattform Industrie 4.0 (2022). https://www.plattform-i40.de/IP/Navigation/EN/ThePlatform/Background/background.html. Accessed 15 Apr 2024
24. Pu, H., He, L., Cheng, P., Sun, M., Chen, J.: Security of industrial robots: vulnerabilities, attacks, and mitigations. IEEE Netw. **37**(1), 111–117 (2023)
25. Quarta, D., Pogliani, M., Polino, M., Maggi, F., Zanchettin, A.M., Zanero, S.: An experimental security analysis of an industrial robot controller. In: 2017 IEEE Symposium on Security and Privacy (SP), pp. 268–286. IEEE, San Jose (2017)
26. Riigi Infosüsteemi Amet: Cyber Security in Estonia (2024). https://www.ria.ee/kuberturvalisus/kuberruumi-analuus-ja-ennetus/olukord-kuberruumis. Accessed 15 Apr 2024
27. Salnitri, M., Dalpiaz, F., Giorgini, P.: Designing secure business processes with SecBPMN. Softw. Syst. Model. **16**, 737–757 (2015). https://doi.org/10.1007/s10270-015-0499-4
28. Shah, Y., Sengupta, S.: A survey on classification of cyber-attacks on IoT and IIoT devices. In: 2020 11th IEEE Annual Ubiquitous Computing, Electronics & Mobile Communication Conference (UEMCON), pp. 0406–0413. IEEE, New York (2020)
29. Shostack, A.: Threat Modeling: Designing for Security. Wiley, Hoboken (2014)

30. Statistikaamet: Eesti Tööstus (2023). https://www.stat.ee/et/avasta-statistikat/valdkonnad/majandus/toostus. Accessed 15 Apr 2024
31. Urooj, B., Ullah, U., Shah, M.A., Sikandar, H.S., Stanikzai, A.Q.: Risk assessment of SCADA cyber attack methods: a technical review on securing automated real-time SCADA systems. In: 2022 27th International Conference on Automation and Computing (ICAC), pp. 1–6. IEEE, Bristol (2022)
32. Wang, B., Tao, F., Fang, X., Liu, C., Liu, Y., Freiheit, T.: Smart manufacturing and intelligent manufacturing: a comparative review. Engineering **7**(6), 738–757 (2021)
33. Xu, X., Lu, Y., Vogel-Heuser, B., Wang, L.: Industry 4.0 and industry 5.0-inception, conception and perception. J. Manuf. Syst. **61**, 530–535 (2021)

Configuration of Software Product Lines Driven by the Softgoals: The TEAEM Approach

Eddy Kiomba Kambilo[✉], Nicolas Herbaut, Irina Rychkova, and Carine Souveyet

University Paris 1 Pantheon-Sorbonne, Paris, France
{eddy.kiomba-kambilo,nicolas.herbaut,
irina.rychkova,carine.souveyet}@univ-paris1.fr

Abstract. The Model-Driven Architecture (MDA) serves as an essential framework for designing enterprise information systems, emphasizing the alignment and traceability of goals across different modeling layers. However, MDA typically overlooks the integration of qualitative attributes, or softgoals, which are critical for enhancing user satisfaction. Our previous work introduced the Technology-Aware Enterprise Modeling (TEAEM) approach, which enhances MDA by integrating model checking, validation, and impact analysis.

This paper extends TEAEM to more effectively incorporate softgoals. We achieve this by integrating SysML component modeling for low-level, and softgoals into the high-level of the MDA. These advancements facilitate bottom-up constraint propagation and ensure that technological decisions are reflected consistently at all levels of abstraction, thereby optimizing the system to meet strategic business goals.

Additionally, we propose generating configurations in software product lines, driven by the fulfillment of softgoals, to apply the TEAEM approach.

Keywords: MDA · Enterprise Modeling · Softgoals · Software Product Lines

1 Introduction

The Model-Driven Architecture (MDA) provides a foundational framework for the design and development of enterprise information systems, emphasizing a top-down design approach with three levels of model abstraction: the Computational Independent Model (CIM) for capturing business goals, the Platform Independent Model (PIM) for representing system functionality independent of specific technologies, and the Platform Specific Model (PSM) for detailing the technological choices made [13]. This structured approach allows for deferred technological decisions, assuming that such choices primarily have localized impacts.

However, the MDA approach often overlooks the integration of softgoals due to their subjective and qualitative nature. Softgoals, unlike hardgoals, lack clear-cut achievement criteria and encompass aspects such as cost, security, response time, and performance. These qualitative attributes are crucial for successful software production as they influence user satisfaction, feature prioritization, and development trade-offs.

Motivated by the need to better incorporate qualitative attributes and analyzing technological impacts into enterprise modeling, we previously introduced Technology Aware for Enterprise Modeling (TEAEM) [17] which extends MDA by integrating model checking, validation and impact analysis of technological choices before product generation. This approach enables the unification of CIM-PIM within a "Unified Model", allowing the identification and resolution of inconsistencies across different MDA levels. If inconsistencies are detected, TEAEM reports constraint violations to the business user and assists in decision-making. TEAEM had some limitations. Firstly, it focused on the unification of CIM and PIM without extending support to the PSM. Additionally, the approach was centered on the use of hardgoals, with little attention given to softgoals.

This paper aims extends TEAEM with two major contributions: First, we integrate the MDA low-level PSM using SysML component modeling, achieving a unified CIM-PIM-PSM model that enables bottom-up constraint propagation and analysis. This integration ensures that technological choices made at the PSM level are consistently reflected across all abstraction levels, enhancing the overall coherence and bottom-up traceability within the enterprise modeling process. Second, we extend TEAEM by integrating softgoals into the CIM. By including softgoals in the early stages of modeling, we can better address qualitative attributes throughout the system development life-cycle. This approach allows for the generation of code (configuration) guided by the satisfaction of these softgoals, thereby optimizing the system for user satisfaction and strategic business goals.

The remainder of this paper is organized as follows: Sect. 2 provides a brief overview of key concepts such as MDA, Software Product Lines, and Softgoals. Section 3 details the TEAEM approach and its extension to integrate softgoals. Section 4 discusses the implementation, mapping details, and an illustrative example used to validate our approach. Finally, Sect. 5 presents the discussion and conclusions of this work.

2 Background

2.1 MDA, Top-Down Design and Enterprise Architecture

The architecture of a system constitutes what is essential about that system considered in relation to its environment [8]. There are different frameworks used in enterprise architecture and software engineering.

Model Driven Architecture is a software design approach that provides a set of guidelines for structuring specifications, which are expressed as models. The core of MDA is its focus on three primary types of models; *Computation Independent*

Model represents the system's requirements and business context, without detailing the structure or processing. *Platform Independent Model* specifies the system's structure and functionality but abstracts away the details of any specific platform. *Platform Specific Model* combines the specifications in the PIM with the details of how the system uses a particular type of platform.

Many works exist in the literature that exploit the MDA concept to make goal alignment and traceability of goal. In [14], authors presents a strategy-to-code (S2C) methodological approach integrating organizational, business process, and information system modeling to support strategic alignment in software development. It emphasizes model-driven development and conceptual modeling for semi-automatic software generation and traceability across different modeling levels. By using a working example, it illustrates how strategic definitions can be transformed into specific software components through the integration of Lite*, Communication Analysis, and the OO-Method, demonstrating the feasibility of achieving strategic requirements, traceability, and automatic software generation.

Recent Enterprise Architecture frameworks exist that give advice on the processes and practices of Enterprise Architecture, and one of these, that the ArchiMate Specification is fully aligned with, is the TOGAF standard [8]. ArchiMate is focus on the problem of aligning strategic business plans with the plans and goals for the development of Information Systems based on Information Technology (IS/IT).

2.2 Software Product Lines

MDA and SPL are complementary approaches that greatly benefit from the integration of softgoals. Software Product Line Engineering (SPLE) serves as a methodological framework for developing software families, characterized by significant overlap in functional and non-functional attributes [3].

A primary focus of SPLE is to identify and codify the common features of a cluster of software-intensive applications within a specific domain [1]. An SPL is generally composed of three main types of artifacts: *Problem Space*: this describes the features and functionalities desired by users across all potential products in the family. *Solution Space:* This includes the design and implementation specifics for all components across different products within the SPL and *The Mappings:* These establish the connections between features in the problem space and their respective components in the solution space. In this work, we choose SPL like application domain of TEAEM.

2.3 Softgoals and Utility Functions for Evaluating Softgoals

Softgoals serve as quality criteria that software systems or their components must meet during development. Softgoals are subjective, relative, diverse, and interactive, making them crucial yet challenging to model due to their qualitative nature [7].

The literature highlights the significance of softgoals in determining the success of software projects. For instance, consider the softgoals for a software system such as *performance* ("The system should respond quickly to user inputs") and *security* ("The system should protect user data from unauthorized access"). These qualitative goals pose the question: how can we effectively evaluate them?

Significant research has been conducted on identifying softgoals within Information Systems (IS). For example, one study presented a comprehensive list of 114 softgoals identified in information systems [12], while another proposed a taxonomy categorizing these softgoals into four groups: Real and Web-based Systems, Web-based Systems, Real-time Systems, and Information Systems [5]. We aim to adapt some of these identified softgoals and quantify them.

To quantify softgoals, we propose writing a utility function for each softgoal, facilitating the evaluation of how well a system meets these goals. Softgoals like usability, reliability, and performance are inherently qualitative. By converting these into quantifiable metrics through a utility function, we enable more objective assessments and comparisons.

The following section will introduce our extended approach and explain how to generate configurations that meet these softgoals.

3 TEAEM Approach Guiding Configuration by Softgoals

TEAEM is a holistic approach that extends the top-down MDA design paradigm with bottom-up traceability and constraint propagation analysis.

3.1 TEAEM Extension

We propose extending TEAEM with the following contributions: (1) Integration of PSM to illustrate technological choices using component modeling (SysML). (2) Integration of softgoals to guide business users in generating configurations within the SPL.

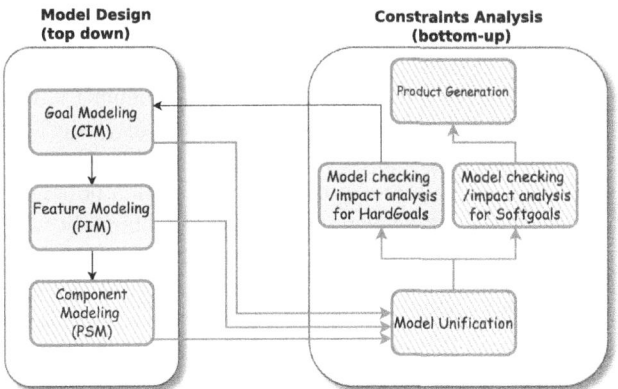

Fig. 1. TEAEM approach to meet Softgoals. Hashed blocks show TEAEM extension proposed in this paper

Figure 1 illustrates the extension of the TEAEM approach. The model is subdivided into two parts:

On the left hand side represents the top-down MDA design approach with three abstraction levels: CIM, PIM, and PSM.

- *CIM Layer:* We start by creating the goal model using the i* framework [4] with the PiStar tool [15]. This model includes both hardgoals (functional requirements) and softgoals (non-functional requirements).
- PIM Layer: We design the Feature Model using the FeatureIDE tool [10].
- PSM Layer: We create component models with SysML, which include technical metadata about alternative implementations of the designed solution.

On the right-hand side, we extend TEAEM by unifying the PIM, CIM, and PSM layers of MDA into a single model called the "Unified Feature Model (UFM)". This unification is crucial for several reasons:

- Model checking and validation help validate the UFM to confirm it meets requirements, identify inconsistencies in the specification, and show conflicts between elements of the unified feature models.
- Impact Analysis: Helps identify how changes in one part of the model affect others by reporting constraint violations from low-level to high-level.
- Configuration Generation in SPL: Facilitates the generation of configurations that satisfy softgoals.

To achieve this unification, we define the following mapping:

- *Goal to Feature Mapping* (TEAEM): This mapping associates business goals with the technical features that fulfill those goals. It reflects the technical assumptions made by system engineers.
- *Feature to Goal Mapping* (TEAEM): This mapping associates technical features with the goals that could potentially be compromised or hindered by their implementation.
- *Feature to Component Mapping* (this paper): This new mapping associates features with the specific technological components that implement them.

The mappings are formalized using a symbolic mathematics library to structure the logical expressions. This library also develops utility functions to optimize the softgoals. Further details are provided in Sect. 4.

After unifying the model, we use model-checking with a boolean solver to validate the UFM and identify inconsistencies causing conflicts between goals, features, and components.

If model checking returns false, indicating no feasible configuration, we provide a domain-specific interpretation of these conflicts and recommend solutions. If model checking returns true, indicating multiple feasible configurations, we integrate softgoals into the decision-making process. We use a utility function to quantify each softgoal and apply a Multiple-Criteria Decision Making (MCDM) algorithm to optimize softgoal satisfaction, determining the best configuration for the business user.

The main distinction between TEAEM and other frameworks like MDA or ArchiMate is its integration and analysis of inconsistencies across different abstract level (goal, feature, component) within the MDA. While ArchiMate offers a holistic view of enterprise architectures, it does not specifically focus on detecting and managing inconsistencies between different model types or guiding product generation by softgoals.

3.2 Modeling Softgoals with the Utility Function

As mentioned in Sect. 2.3, we reuse some of the softgoals defined by [12].

In this context, Key Performance Indicators (KPIs) are commonly used to measure the performance of various aspects of a system. However, we use a utility function instead of KPIs because the utility function allows for a more comprehensive and integrative approach. While KPIs provide valuable insights into specific performance metrics, they often fail to account for the trade-offs between conflicting goals. The utility function, on the other hand, can encapsulate multiple softgoals into a single measure, allowing for the optimization of overall user satisfaction and system performance in a balanced manner.

The utility function quantifies values derived from component modeling (value of each component) and serves as input for the MCDM algorithm to generate configurations that maximize user satisfaction. We focus on the following softgoals for the implementation and test phases in Sects. 4 and 5 (Table 1).

Table 1. Description of Softgoals with Blockchain Components

Softgoals	Description	Refined-into	Notation
Cost	System should be cost-efficient	Operates with minimal expenses and reduces the overall cost of ownership	C
Response_Time	System should be fast	Processes requests quickly and efficiently, providing timely feedback to users	R
Throughput	System should have high throughput	Processes incoming data quickly and sends new data without delay	T

The overall goal is to minimize the total cost of the components, which is the sum of individual cost functions $C_i(x_i)$ for each component i. C is the total cost, and x_i are the decision variables adjusted to optimize the cost. R is the total response time, $R_i(x_i)$ is the response time function for each component i, and T is the total throughput that we aim to minimize, $\min_{0 \leq i \leq n} T_i$, the throughput function for each component i.

We define this objective function by integrating the different softgoals to optimize:

$$\text{Min } F = w_1 C + w_2 R - w_3 T$$

where F is the combined objective function, C is the total cost, R is the total response time, and T is the total throughput. w_1, w_2, w_3 are the weights assigned to cost, response time, and throughput, respectively, reflecting their relative importance for the business users.

The next section presents the different modules we developed.

4 Implementation

We implemented TEAEM, an automated process for model unification across different MDA abstraction levels, detecting constraint violations, performing impact analysis, and generating software product line configurations driven by softgoals. We developed the following modules[1]:

1. *Generation of the Unified Feature Model (UFM)*: The unified model includes the goal model, feature model, component models, and constraints. For top-down model design, we use the i* modeling language [4] and the PiStar tool for Goal Modeling, FeatureIDE for feature modeling, and SysML for component models. Mapping for CIM-PIM-PSM is achieved using SymPy with logical expressions. This module automates the generation of the unified feature model.
2. *Extraction of Constraints from the UFM*: This module performs model checking/validation. We use FeatureIDE and its bundled Sat4j solver [11] to retrieve constraints from the UFM, generating an output in JSON for constraint analysis when inconsistencies arise between the three MDA levels.
3. *Interpretation of Constraint Violations and Their Implications*: We developed a module that takes the outcomes.json list of constraint violations from FeatureIDE and produces domain-specific interpretations of these violations to guide business users in their decision-making.
4. *Generation of Configurations that Meet Softgoals*: This module calculates utility functions using SymPy, based on parameter values from SysML component models. The utility function's Min/Max values help identify the best configuration that matches the specified requirements.
5. *Optimization Using the Topsis Algorithm*: We implement the Topsis algorithm for Multiple-Criteria Decision Making, ensuring the optimization and evaluation of our Unified Model to achieve highly optimized solutions.

We make three types of mapping as specified on the Sect. 3.1. For The mapping of Goal to Feature and Feature to goal, We use the mathematical logical expressions rules that we passed with Sympy in order to execute automatically the logic.

For the mapping PIM-PSM, We have two cases:

---

[1] https://github.com/Eddykams/TEAEM_develop.

(1) Mapping One Feature - One Component:
The following bijection function modeling the mapping between PIM-PSM :

$$H_1 = F \implies C \text{ (A)}$$

with, F: Features and C: Components.

(2) Mapping One Feature With Multiple Components: We use TOPSIS (Technique for Order of Preference by Similarity to Ideal Solution) is a multi-criteria decision analysis method that ranks alternatives based on their distance to an ideal solution and a negative-ideal solution. It helps in selecting the best option by comparing the relative closeness of each alternative to the ideal solution.

In the next section, we present an illustrative example where we apply TEAEM to configure products to meet soft goals.

5 Illustrative Example: Counterfeiting Drugs in Supply Chain

5.1 Motivation

The market of counterfeit drugs has become a 200-billion-dollar business annually, according to the World Health Organization (WHO). According to a WHO report, up to 10% of all sold drugs globally are fake, with significantly higher rates in parts of Africa and Asia. This business is very dangerous because of life-and-death implications for patients (thousands of deaths every year) and also for the pharmaceutical industry's reputation, which can lose a lot of money. The complexity of pharmaceutical supply chain operations is the primary reason for this issue. With a large number of handovers to different supply chain partners before drugs reach hospitals and pharmacies, there is a significant lack of traceability. Manufacturing is vulnerable to counterfeit raw materials or ingredients from unknown sources. Moreover, illicit producers can relabel fake products to infiltrate legitimate distribution channels. For the pharmaceutical sector, the European Union (EU) and the Drug Supply Chain Security Act (DSCSA) in the United States provide a deadline of 2023 for the industry to implement a traceability system.

Based on the work [6,9], we present the following illustrative example. Company X, based in Europe and Africa, must enter the pharmaceutical market in compliance with EU regulations and operate in Africa. The organization has many branches in different countries that require a system to manage transactions recorded across multiple locations. Additionally, there is a need for a system that enhances trust among various stakeholders.

The system must address the following needs: *Reduce drug counterfeiting (fraud detection)* by ensuring traceability and transparency at every step of the product transfer. Ensure *secure data management* by enhancing privacy through access controls and encryption, and by maintaining the integrity and immutability of data. *Manage recalls of defective products*; conditions of transporting drugs must be verified through real-time audits using IoT, sensors, or RFID tags. The authenticity of products must be checked by log-audit.

5.2 TEAEM for Configuration in SPL to Meet Softgoals

The main goal of Enterprise X is to determine if, with their goals, features, and components, they can generate a product or if there are any inconsistencies between them before generating the product. The organization proposes to integrate the following softgoals: maximal performance, minimal cost for blockchain components, better response time, and minimal cost for the electronic solutions (RFIDs, IoT sensors, or NFC tags).

Step1: We present a partial goal model of the enterprise, depicting different softgoals and the links between goals and softgoals in the Fig. 2.

Step 2: To build the feature model, we made a literature review to identify different solutions proposed for combating drug counterfeiting in the supply chain illustrated in Table 2. According to some findings in the literature, [2,16] assert, for example, that the ideal anti-counterfeit technology in an enterprise system should have a high level of safety, faster product application, established standards, simple to check, have automatic authentication, be accessible to consumers, and comply with industry regulations.

Table 2. Requirements and Technologies Identified

Goals - Requirements	References	Blockchain	Cloud	ML
Transparent	[16]	✓	-	-
Traceability	[2, 16, 19]	✓	-	✓
Reliable	[2, 16, 18, 19]	✓	✓	✓
High Level of Safety	[16]	✓	-	-
faster product application	[18]	-	✓	-
Simple to audit	[16]	✓	-	-
Automatic Process	[2, 16, 18]	✓	✓	-
Compliant with industry Regulations	[18, 19]	-	✓	✓
Accountability	[18]	-	✓	-
Trust	[16]	✓	-	-
Decentralized	[2, 16]	✓	-	-
High Security	[2]	✓	-	-
Flexibility	[18]	-	✓	-

We built the feature model based on the technologies identified in Table 2. Three prominent technologies were proposed: blockchain technology, for its features such as traceability, trust, and immutability; Cloud Computing [18], known for its flexibility and faster application production; and Machine Learning, which can identify counterfeit drugs through algorithmic data analysis. Additionally, associated electronic equipment for traceability is proposed, such as RFID tags, IoT sensors (pressure, geolocation), and NFC tags (Figs. 3 and 4).

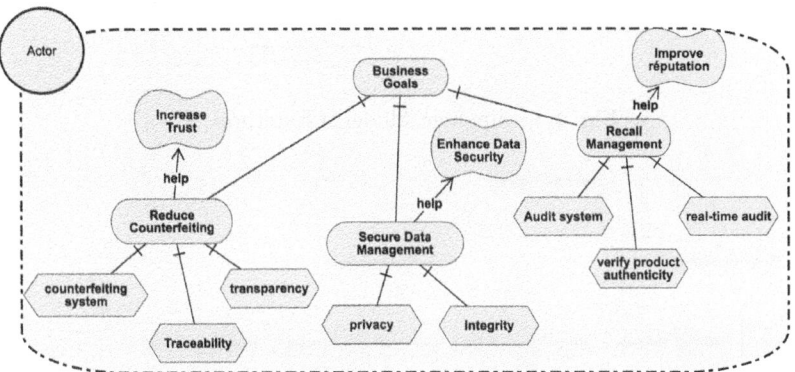

Fig. 2. Goal Modeling of Enterprise X

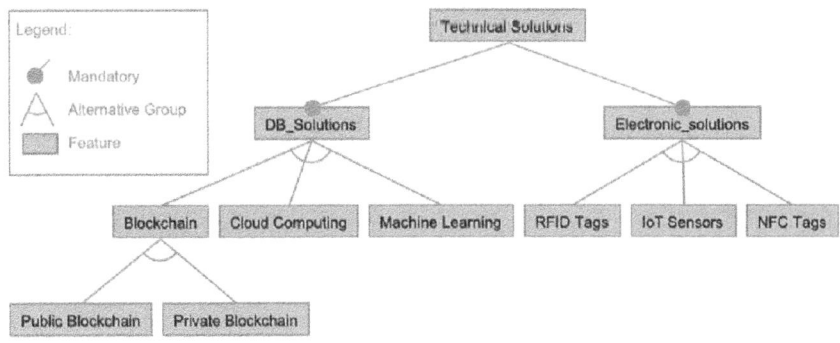

Fig. 3. Feature Model of Enterprise X

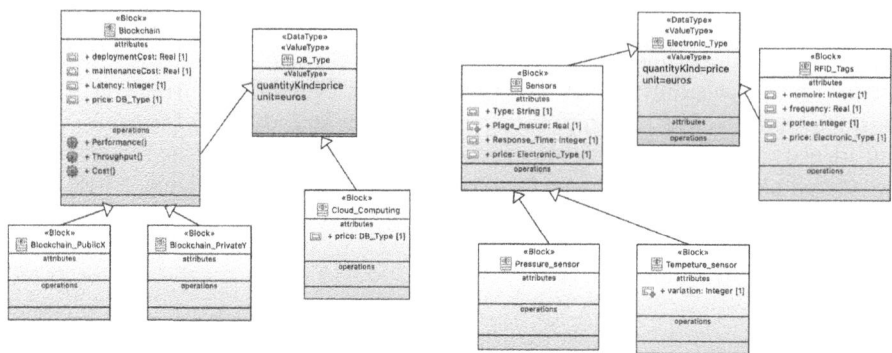

Fig. 4. Component Model of Enterprise X

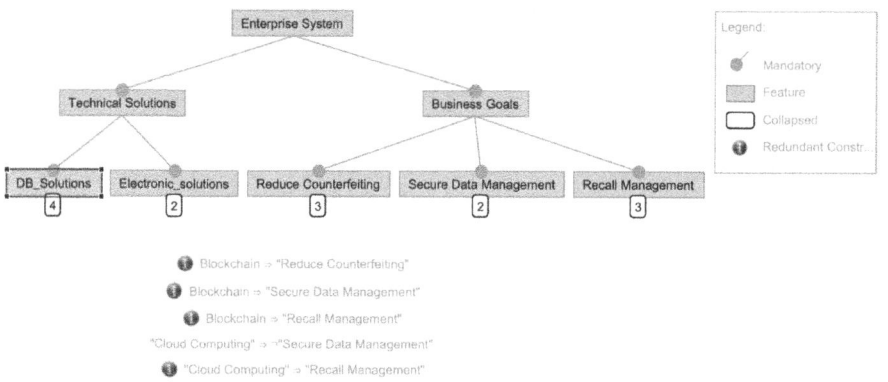

Fig. 5. Model Unification

Step 3: Based on the analysis presented in Table 2, we decided to use blockchain technology as a component to illustrate our example. Blockchain is a novel technology that has not yet been widely adopted by enterprises due to the lack of standardization and scarcity of engineers skilled in its implementation. The literature identifies two principal types of blockchains: public blockchain and private blockchain. Using SysML, we illustrate the component model for blockchain technology and other technologies. However, for the evaluation phase, we focus on the value of the blockchain component.

Step4: TEAEM - The unified model, as depicted in Fig. 5, put within a single model the three abstract level of the MDA. In our study, the model checking results were positive, indicating that the unified model is valid. However, the next step involves generating configurations that satisfy the softgoals defined in the previous section.

Step 5: After model unification, we use model checking/validation to determine if a valid configuration exists for this unified model or if there are any inconsistencies. *The unified feature model generates 4 possible configurations*, indicating that there are no inconsistencies or constraint violations. Therefore, refining the model is unnecessary. In [17], we presented an example where constraint violations were detected. The question then arises: how do business users choose the "best" configuration that meets their softgoals?

Step 6: As outlined in the previous section, to generate configurations guided by the satisfaction of softgoals, we detail the softgoals discussed in Sect. 3.2, including their associated utility functions and the blockchain components employed. The values of component properties are inputted as parameters into the utility functions to select the optimal configuration. We use blockchain configurations and utilize the TOPSIS method for multi-objective optimization.

In the absence of a generalizable throughput/response time formula for all possible cases, we have chosen to formulate the following assumptions: Response Time is the minimal time for the detection of counterfeiting drugs and depends on the component properties: Transaction Processing Time, Block Creation Time, and Smart Contract Execution Time. The throughput is a function of block size, block execution time, and network bandwidth for the blockchain (Table 3).

Table 3. Utility functions and blockchain component properties of softgoals

Softgoals	Utility function	Components properties
Blockchain Cost	$C = (\min \sum_{i=1}^{n} C_i(D_c, M_c))$	Deployment cost, Maintenance cost
Throughput	$T = T(B_s, B_t, N_b)$	Block Size, Block Time, Network Bandwidth.
Response Time	$R = R(Tx_i, B_c, SC_e)$	Tx Processing Time, Block Creation Time, SC Execution Time
Electronic_Cost	$EC = (\min \sum_{i=1}^{n} C_i(D_c, E_c, M_c))$	Deployment cost, Execution cost, Maintenance cost

5.3 Results

After integrating the blockchain component values as parameters in the utility function to generate products, we made the following tests:

(1) We help to choose configurations that meet one softgoal. For example, when the organization needs to minimize blockchain costs (Fig. 6):
To minimize blockchain costs, the implemented module maps the value of the component across different configurations, calculates the value using the utility function implemented by SymPy, and returns this value for comparison with other con-

```
*********** Components Mapping Completed. ***************
Analyze of configuration: conf1.xml
Selected Feature: PublicBC_X
PublicBC_X - Ethereum: Price = 40.0
###
Analyze of configuration: conf0.xml
Selected Feature: PrivateBC_Y
PrivateBC_Y - Hyperledger: Price = 35.0
*********** DECISION GUIDING CHOICE *********************
The utility function: 35.0
To reduce Cost, The best Configuration is: conf0.xml
******** *************** ***********************
```

Fig. 6. Configuration guiding by the Minimal Blockchain Cost

figurations. The configuration with the lowest cost is considered the winner. For one component, it is easy to generate a product that matches this softgoal.

(2) Help to choose configurations that meet multiple criteria: In this case, we have a multi-objective optimization. We need to choose the best configuration guided by multiple softgoal criteria.

Table 4. Softgoals Criteria with Heigh

Attributes	Blockchain Cost	Response_Time	Throughput	Electronic Cost
Conf0	300	15 s/bloc	18 Tx/seconds	140
Conf1	350	15 s/bloc	16 Tx/seconds	120
Conf2	200	2 s/bloc	100 Tx/seconds	200
Conf3	250	3 s/bloc	200 Tx/seconds	180

For the test phase, it is important to clarify that the values presented in Table 4 are provided for illustrative purposes only and do not represent calculations from a utility function. Instead, these values are intended to demonstrate the application of MCDM with TOPSIS.

The Table 4 illustrates the four configurations found after the model checking/validation. Different values (Blockchain Cost, Response Time, Throughput, and Electronic Cost) were passed as inputs to our component model. In this case, we have a multi-objective optimization where we need to choose the best configuration guided by multiple softgoal criteria. Many optimization algorithms exist in the literature, and we implemented the TOPSIS method for Multiple-Criteria Decision Making.

For the evaluation phase, for example, if we have input data illustrated in Table 4, we have the following outcomes (Table 5):

Scenario 1: We defined the same weight for all parameters [0.25, 0.25, 0.25, 0.25] and identified Response Time, Blockchain Cost, and Electronic Cost as non-benefit

Table 5. Scenario 1 Outcomes Overview

Attributes	BC_Cost	R_Time	Throughput	E_Cost	S_POS	S_NEG	Score	Rank
Conf0	300	15	18	140	0.2215	0.0862	0.2801	3
Conf1	350	15	16	120	0.2349	0.0613	0.2069	4
Conf2	200	2	100	200	0.0689	0.2139	0.7561	2
Conf3	250	3	200	180	0.0532	0.2215	0.8061	1

parameters (functions to minimize) and Throughput as a benefit parameter (function to maximize). We have the following outcomes:

To reduce the blockchain cost, the cost of the electronic equipment, and the response time, while increasing performance with throughput, the best configuration is Configuration 3 (Conf3), which achieves 80% satisfaction among business users. The worst configuration is Configuration 1 (Conf1), with only 20% satisfaction among business users. This is clearly specified with different constraints and the values of blockchain components as parameters. The configuration that meets the specified softgoals is Configuration 3.

Scenario 2: Business users place significant emphasis on Response_Time compared to other criteria. We adjust the weight according to preferences, for example, 0.6 for Response Time and 0.13 Blockchain Cost, 0.13 Throughput and 0.13 Electronic Cost.([0.13, 0.61, 0.13, 0.13]) (Table 6).

Table 6. outcomes for Scenario 2

Attributes	BC_Cost	R_Time	Throughput	E_Cost	S_POS	S_NEG	Score	Rank
Conf0	300	15	18	140	0.3682	0.0344	0.0856	3
Conf1	350	15	16	120	0.3695	0.0245	0.0622	4
Conf2	200	2	100	200	0.0275	0.3675	0.9301	1
Conf3	250	3	200	180	0.0347	0.3416	0.9075	2

The best configuration has changed and is now Configuration 2 (Conf2), with 92% satisfaction among business users. The worst configuration is still Configuration 1 (Conf1), with only 6% satisfaction among business users. We can clearly see that a different softgoal weight will lead to different configurations.

6 Lesson Discussion, and Research Challenges

The TEAEM approach by integrating softgoals ensures that qualitative attributes such as user satisfaction, security, and performance are prioritized, resulting in configurations that align more closely with business goals. The unified CIM-PIM-PSM model enhances coherence and traceability across abstraction levels, leading to fewer errors and more complete configurations. This integration ensures that technological choices made at the PSM level are consistently reflected across all levels, reducing the risk of inconsistencies. TEAEM-generated configurations exhibit fewer errors and higher completeness, as validated by model checking.

The use of the TOPSIS method for MCDM in TEAEM facilitates the selection of optimal configurations based on multiple softgoal criteria. This approach allows business users to make informed decisions quickly, balancing trade-offs between competing goals. Empirical data show that TEAEM reduces the time required for configuration generation and decision-making compared to manual methods and other SPL approaches.

Compared to other approaches, TEAEM adds value in model-checking validation and constraints analysis propagation for bottom-up traceability. MDA focuses on top-down design, traceability, and alignment of goals from business goals to code generation. ArchiMate is designed to provide a comprehensive, integrated view of enterprise architecture, focusing on the relationships between different domains (such as business, application, and technology). However, it does not inherently include specific mechanisms for detecting and managing inconsistencies between different model types. Additionally, while ArchiMate can represent various goals and requirements, it does not explicitly focus on guiding product generation through softgoals.

The implementation of TEAEM and the various evaluations carried out have allowed us to learn the following lesson:

– *Business users have the ability to express their preferences on the different softgoals, and expressing these preferences will have a technical impact. The weight or importance that a business user assigns to a softgoal during the configuration of a product in a Software Product Line (SPL) significantly influences the best configuration that can be proposed to them.*

TEAEM presents certain limitations, such as the complexity involved in formalizing utility functions for systems with non-linear attributes. This complexity can challenge the accurate quantification and optimization of softgoals. Also, managing the explosion of the feature model in large-scale projects remains a significant challenge, potentially complicating the optimization of solutions for specific product derivations.

Future work on the TEAEM approach should focus on developing formal guidelines for defining and applying utility functions, which will improve accuracy and make the approach more adaptable across various scenario. Exploring advanced modularity techniques will be crucial for managing the complexity of feature models and addressing the feature model explosion problem, simplifying the process of configuration generation. Evaluating the methodology's practical impact through real-world applications is also critical to ensure its effectiveness. By tackling these areas, the TEAEM approach can be further enhanced to offer greater value in enterprise modeling.

7 Conclusion

In this paper, we extend the Technology-Aware Enterprise Modeling approach by incorporating softgoals to generate configurations within Software Product Lines. Our enhancement addresses the limitations of MDA methods in managing non-functional requirements, which are essential for user satisfaction.

Our primary contribution is the unification of the CIM-PIM-PSM into a single model, ensuring a traceable design process that connects business goals with technical implementations. We also integrate model checking and impact analysis to detect inconsistencies early, aiding decision-making and minimizing errors. The second contribution integrates softgoals into the TEAEM process, enabling SPL configurations to meet both goals and softgoals, ensuring the final products align with both user needs and business goals.

We demonstrate our approach using a counterfeit drug detection example in the supply chain, leveraging blockchain technology as a component. Future work will focus on managing feature models to address the challenge of feature model explosion.

References

1. Bagheri, E., Ensan, F., Gasevic, D., Boskovic, M.: Modular feature models: representation and configuration. J. Res. Pract. Inf. Technol. **43**(2), 109–140 (2011)
2. Bapatla, A.K., Mohanty, S.P., Kougianos, E., Puthal, D., Bapatla, A.: Pharmachain: a blockchain to ensure counterfeit-free pharmaceutical supply chain. IET Netw. **12**(2), 53–76 (2023)
3. Bošković, M., Mussbacher, G., Bagheri, E., Amyot, D., Gašević, D., Hatala, M.: Aspect-oriented feature models. In: Dingel, J., Solberg, A. (eds.) MODELS 2010. LNCS, vol. 6627, pp. 110–124. Springer, Heidelberg (2011). https://doi.org/10.1007/978-3-642-21210-9_11
4. Franch, X., López, L., Cares, C., Colomer, D.: The i^* framework for goal-oriented modeling. In: Karagiannis, D., Mayr, H., Mylopoulos, J. (eds.) Domain-Specific Conceptual Modeling, pp. 485–506. Springer, Cham (2016). https://doi.org/10.1007/978-3-319-39417-6_22
5. Gazi, Y., Umar, M.S., Sadiq, M.: Classification of NFRs for information system. Int. J. Comput. Appl. **115**(22) (2015)
6. Hastig, G.M., Sodhi, M.S.: Blockchain for supply chain traceability: business requirements and critical success factors. Prod. Oper. Manag. **29**(4), 935–954 (2020)
7. Hu, H., et al.: Semantic modelling and automated reasoning of non-functional requirement conflicts in the context of softgoal interdependencies. IET Softw. **9**(6), 145–156 (2015)
8. Josey, A.: ArchiMate® 3.0. 1-A pocket guide. Van Haren (2017)
9. Kambilo, E.K., Zghal, H.B., Guegan, C.G., Stankovski, V., Kochovski, P., Vodislav, D.: A blockchain-based framework for drug traceability: Chaindrugtrac. In: Proceedings of the 37th ACM/SIGAPP Symposium on Applied Computing, pp. 1900–1907 (2022)
10. Kastner, C., et al.: FeatureIDE: a tool framework for feature-oriented software development. In: 2009 IEEE 31st International Conference on Software Engineering, pp. 611–614. IEEE (2009)

11. Le Berre, D., Parrain, A.: The sat4j library, release 2.2. J. Satisf. Boolean Model. Comput. **7**(2–3), 59–64 (2010)
12. Mairiza, D., Zowghi, D., Nurmuliani, N.: An investigation into the notion of non-functional requirements. In: Proceedings of the 2010 ACM Symposium on Applied Computing, pp. 311–317 (2010)
13. Mellor, S.J.: MDA Distilled: Principles of Model-Driven Architecture. Addison-Wesley Professional (2004)
14. Pastor, O., Noel, R., Panach, I.: From strategy to code: achieving strategical alignment in software development projects through conceptual modelling, pp. 145–164 (2021)
15. Pimentel, J., Castro, J.: piStar tool–a pluggable online tool for goal modeling. In: 2018 IEEE 26th International Requirements Engineering Conference (RE), pp. 498–499. IEEE (2018)
16. Rajora, N.: Pharmaceutical drug traceability by blockchain and IoT in enterprise systems. Univ. J. Pharm. Pharmacol. 11–18 (2023)
17. Rychkova, I., Kiomba Kambilo, E., Herbaut, N., Pastor, O., Noel, R., Souveyet, C.: Technology-aware enterprise modeling: challenging the model-driven architecture paradigm. In: van der Aa, H., Bork, D., Schmidt, R., Sturm, A. (eds.) BPMDS EMMSAD 2024. LNBIP, vol. 511, pp. 388–396. Springer, Cham (2024). https://doi.org/10.1007/978-3-031-61007-3_28
18. Vijayaraj, N., Rajalakshmi, D., Immaculate, P., Sathianarayani, B., Rajeswari, S., Gomathi, S.: An innovative approach to improve the quality of pharmaceuticals approach using cloud computing. EAI Endors. Trans. Pervasive Health Technol. **10** (2024)
19. Zhou, R., et al.: Traceable machine learning real-time quality control based on patient data. Clin. Chem. Lab. Med. (CCLM) **60**(12), 1998–2004 (2022)

The Dual Nature of Organizational Policies

Hans Weigand[1]([✉]) [ID], Paul Johannesson[2] [ID], and Giancarlo Guizzardi[3] [ID]

[1] Tilburg University, P.O. Box 90153, 5000 LE Tilburg, The Netherlands
h.weigand@tilburguniversity.edu
[2] Department of Computer and Systems Sciences, Stockholm University, Stockholm, Sweden
[3] Semantics, Cybersecurity and Services, University of Twente, Enschede, The Netherlands

Abstract. Organizational decisions are usually constrained by policies and rules, sometimes up to the point of completely automated decision making. Policies exist on multiple levels within the organization and require organizational power to be created. They are typically expressed in a policy document that has multiple practical functions. Drawing on and extending the UFO-L ontology on legal positions, we offer a critical analysis of the relationship between policy and policy document and make an argument for the dual nature of policies. We present four ontological patterns that we claim to be fundamental for organizations as social and economic phenomena. These patterns address: (1) organizational coordination and policy, (2) policy documents, (3) delegation, (4) community ruling. For an initial evaluation, the patterns are exemplified in the university domain.

Keywords: UFO-L · ontology of organizations · policies

1 Introduction

Many organizational decisions are constrained by policies and rules – sometimes more open, sometimes closed up to the point of completely automated decision making. Policy making and implementation are essential elements of organizing. But what exactly is a policy? This is a question of ontology.

One widespread foundational ontology is UFO [14]. In earlier UFO papers [12], a policy has been conceptualized as a normative description, a term originally developed in DOLCE [4]. Informally, a description is the content of a book or document. Some descriptions are normative, in the sense that they prescribe what to do or not to do. A norm is identified with its description [3]. Whatever the merits of this approach are, it is incompatible with the UFO-L view in which legal positions (such as duties, rights and powers) are modes of agents and dependent on a relator between these agents. We made this argument in an earlier workshop paper [24] from which the current paper is derived. Here we not only distinguish the two views, but also propose a reconciliation through a "dual nature" view on policies.

We briefly recall some terminology. An often-applied definition is that a policy is a set of rules based on an organizational decision that addresses an important issue concerning the achievement of the overall purpose of the organization. A procedure details the steps to comply with the policy, whereas a guideline provides general guidance, and additional advice and support. These distinctions are also found in OMG standards (BMM, SBVR)[1]. Here a business rule is a "rule [element of guidance] - that is practicable and that is under business jurisdiction" whereas a business policy is "an element of governance that is not directly enforceable whose purpose is to guide an enterprise". A business rule implements or is derived from a business policy. Furthermore, OMG distinguishes a business policy from an advice (or guideline). The OMG standards provide useful definitions of a broad range of concepts in the policy domain, but still do not solve all questions. The impression is that a policy is just less precise than a rule, because of intentional or unintentional ambiguity. OMG tries to create clear distinct realms, by saying that rules are practicable and under business jurisdiction and policies are guiding the organization. However, why would business policies not be under business jurisdiction, and why would rules (classified as elements of guidance) not guide organizations? There is a need for more ontological analysis.

Research on business rules and their representation and implementation has been pursued for decades. In one stream, business rules are formalized in *deontic logic*. In the *Multi-Agent System* area, norms and obligations are typically described in the tradition of Speech Act theory, with a focus on the notion of *commitment*. Many representation languages and enterprise models have been proposed of which we already mentioned SBVR. Some of these languages are focused on economic contracts and their obligations. The goal of this paper is not to propose a new representation language, or to criticize the current ones, but to explore the ontological aspects of policies by means of argumentation and ontological modeling in UFO. We already mentioned the tension between norms as legal positions and norms as descriptions. Apart from that, the following ontological questions aim to guide our research:

- What does it mean for a policy to be grounded in a higher-level policy?
- Delegation – how is it possible that a duty is transferred to another agent? What are the necessary conditions?
- Anchoring [8]. Duties are embedded institutionally in some policy. Lower-level policies can be grounded in higher level policies, but what is the ultimate ground for deontic phenomena?
- A policy is not a policy document [24], but the two are also intrinsically related. What characterizes this relationship?

In [24], we discussed the UFO definition of policy as normative description and introduced two initial policy patterns for policy and policy document. In this paper, we briefly summarize the first point, and we describe how it leads to a "dual nature" view of policies. Furthermore, we improved and extended the policy patterns to address the ontological questions above.

The paper is structured as follows. Section 2 provides the background and introduces the dual nature view of policies. In Sect. 3, we describe a Policy Ontology, grounded in

---

[1] See www.omg.org. The BMM definition of policy is derived from the SBVR definition.

UFO, in the form of four OntoUML[2] models. By way of evaluation, we apply the policy ontology to the case of a university in Sect. 4. Section 5 is a brief conclusion.

2 Background

UFO-L is the UFO- based ontology of legal relations. Although it is not about organizational policies as such, the conceptualization of norms in UFO-L is of direct relevance. We point out the tension that exists in UFO on the ontological nature of norms and introduce the idea of "dual nature" of policies to address the tension.

2.1 UFO-L

The Legal Core Ontology termed UFO-L [10] was developed by extending the foundational ontology UFO and by incorporating the theory of constitutional rights proposed by Alexy and Hohfeld [1]. In this perspective, rights are defined in terms of legal relations, as correlative to obligations of the other party. A legal position is a mode (an existentially dependent entity) inhering in an agent that is part of the relator between them, so it disappears when the relationship ends (institutional embedding). For instance, the rights and duties of John as husband disappear when the marriage relator with Mary would be dissolved. UFO-L has been further extended with a relational notion of normative power. Rights and duties can be given for actions that the agent is capable of materially, such as speech or delivering a product. However, there are also actions that only exist in the legal reality, such as declaring John and Mary husband and wife or imposing a tax. These actions require not only a right but also a legal power.

Recent work on UFO-L [11] models a power-subjection relator between Power Holder and Subjection Holder, with power and subjection being modes inhering the first and the second relata, respectively. It also shows a creation event for this relator and how a *derived* legal relator can be created through an action that *manifests* the power-subjection relator. Between the creation event and the derived action, a historical dependence has been posited.

UFO-L has been designed specifically for the legal domain. Examples are tax collection and the right of free speech, as well as contractual service agreements. In this paper, we generalize this beyond the legal domain and apply the patterns to internal organizational policies as well, whether these policies have a legal force or not.

2.2 Policies as Normative Descriptions?

In the UFO tradition, a policy is classified as a "normative description", being a social object. DOLCE [3–5] identified norms with norm descriptions.

In a recent paper of Griffo [11] on contract dynamics in UFO-L, normative descriptions are mentioned alongside legal positions. The idea that norms are the content of a normative document seems to be maintained, but at the same time, a clear distinction is made between a document such as Service Agreement Description and a legal relation

---

[2] OntoUML is an ontology-driven conceptual modeling language grounded on UFO.

(with legal positions), such as a Service Agreement: "[T]here is a difference between the ontological nature of the Service Agreement and Service Agreement Description. The first one has an ontological nature of the relation and the second one has an ontological nature of object; a service agreement Description is a text while the Service Agreement is the relation itself described in the Service Agreement Description".

It has been argued in [24] that [11] does not always maintain the distinction rigorously, but also that the distinction is important. Simply said, the norm is not in the document. We can have a text describing Paris, but that does not mean that the object Paris is in the document. It is not in the physical text object (the text bearer). It is also not in the text content – the Information Content Entity (IAO [7]). The former contains ink patterns for the 5 characters, the latter contains the *term* 'Paris', that is, a reference to Paris.

2.3 The Dual Nature of Policies

Policies contain (typically complex) legal positions governing the behavior of agents in a community, as in UFO-L (taking legal in a broad sense of "regulatory" [14]). The *policy document* is a kind of *symbolic* artifact [20], and a *regulatory* artifact. An artifact is built based on a *design*. In the case of documents, the design specifies the document structure; it can be identified with what IAO calls the Information Content Entity [23]. The design is not an independently existing entity but is institutionally embedded in a design conversation [22] between designers and users. The primary users are decision makers, at all levels of the organization, but indirectly, every community member is a potential stakeholder. The design conversation may involve substantial work in policy preparation and drafting at the designer' side. The intended users may express requirements. The design conversation is most often not a one-shot project, but a continuous effort with many adaptations over time (deliberative history).

A policy document draft does not create a policy automatically. An organizational action is needed for a policy document to come into effect and that action requires normative power. Both policy documents and policies need to be accounted for in a policy ontology. The relationship between the two is that a policy document *is about* [7] or *refers to* [22] a policy.

What is the added value of a policy document with respect to a policy? The primary value is that it has at least a representation *capability* of representing a policy and hence a decision-support *capability* for users/decision makers, although for its effective use, the use condition is that the policy is generally accepted (similar to the use condition of money as an artifact). Policy documents, such as accounting standard documents, or medical decision guidelines, can be easily distributed within and between organizations. A policy document is an object, it can be read by all, discussed and criticized. On the other hand, policies inhere in specific organizations and are intangible. Hence, although the document "merely" represents, the policy cannot do without. We call this the *dual nature* of policies: both institutional and technical.

The dual nature of policies includes another duality, the artifactual duality between the make aspect of the policy document and its use aspect. A policy document in an organization, or a law in society, is an artifact with a deliberative history that gives it an identity beyond the original intentions of the designer and independent from how it is actually used. Law is law, as the saying goes. However, the effectiveness of the use plan depends on the use conditions, which in cases of social artifacts such as money and laws include trust and shared acceptance. According to Roversi's artifact view of law [18], both aspects of legal institutions are important: objectivity on the one hand, and empirical effectiveness on the other. The former aspect is typically stressed in legal positivism, the latter in anti-formalist approaches such as legal realism. The artifact view builds a bridge between these two opposed approaches.

The artifact view of law bears similarities to the cognitivist approaches in the line of Searle [19] in which a social realty is created by an agent A expressing an intention, e.g., that a kind of paper counts as money, and a recognition and acceptance of this intention in the group. Also in this approach, the acceptance is essential; a law, or any other social object, is not effective simply because someone states it to be effective. However, the two approaches differ in the nature of the acceptance. In the cognitivist approaches, acceptance means that the group, or a majority, recognizes the intention of the lawmaker and accepts (believes) that the law exists, perhaps willy-nilly. In the artifact view, the group does not need to be aware of the original intentions or how they have developed, as long as they see that the law effectively serves their interests and therefore accept it (trust and use it).

3 Ontological Patterns of Organizational Policies

In this section, we introduce ontological patterns for organizational policies. First, we must relate to the UFO analysis of organizations.

For the representation of organizations, UFO-C [16] takes its basis in delegation. Delegation is a material relation derived from a social relator delegatum. When an agent A (delegator) delegates a goal to an agent B (delegatee), a social claim of B towards A is created. By B assuming the achievement of the goal on behalf of A, a social commitment of B towards A is created. The commitment/claim pair composes the delegatum from which the delegation is derived. UFO-C makes a distinction between agent allocation and task allocation. According to [14], an agent is first added to a collective (agent allocation) before it can be given a role (appointment/ task allocation). Although UFO-L (Sect. 2.1) builds on UFO-C, it also deviates from it. First, it generalizes the notion of commitment to legal position. Not only commitments are created, but also rights, powers, subjections, liabilities, immunities, etc. Second, there cannot be a claim from one side without a correlative duty at the other side. Third, it focuses on the legal domain; it talks about *legal* positions and does not include agent goals. In Sect. 3.2, we will introduce an adapted delegation pattern that builds on UFO-C and UFO-L but with a focus on organizations.

3.1 The Organizational Policy Pattern

Organizations are first a way of *coordinating* the contributions of specialized agents towards a common goal (in the context of a division of work, e.g. [2]). Coordination implies the definition of complementary organizational roles. Secondly, most organizations own resources that are used by the agents, which implies a distinction between the abstract roles of Principal and Agent and a need for some kind of steering and monitoring (agency theory [9]) to ensure that the resources are indeed used to the benefit of the organization.

Figure 1 presents the policy pattern in the context of how the relationship between Organization and Agent evolves. From top to bottom, we start with an **Employing** action. Employing is a complex event with legal and economic aspects, but part of it is **Allocating** (as in UFO-C) the hired employee to the organizational community. To reduce space, we have omitted the employment relator that is created by the employing. Although we assume here an employment contract, the pattern can be generalized easily to other organizational forms such as clubs or agent networks. The organizational community may have a compositional structure (not in the model). The relation between Org member and Org Community is a material member-of relation grounded in the Allocating relator.

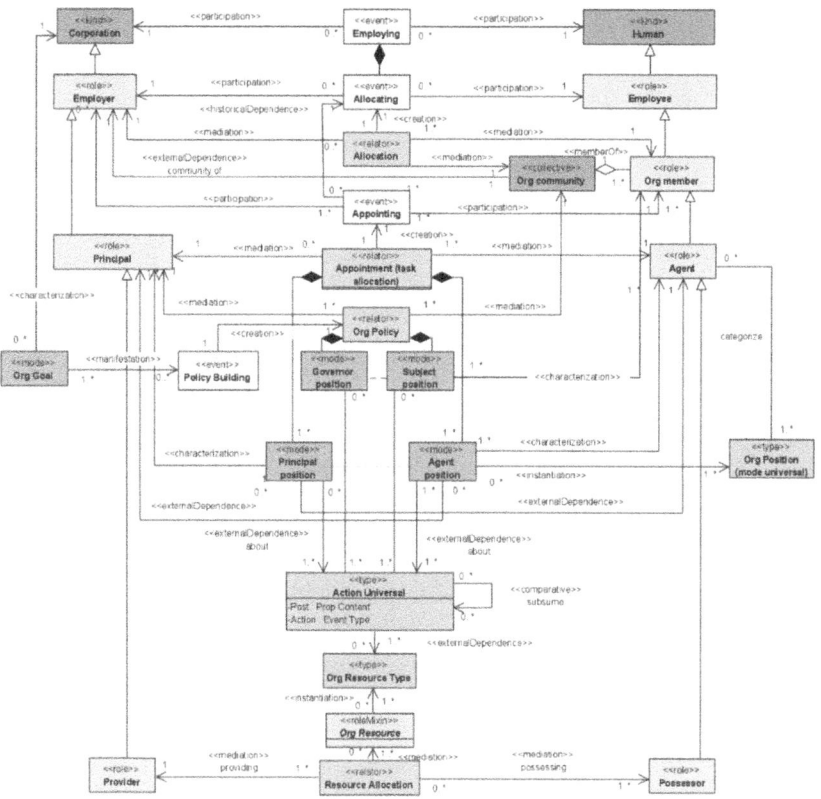

Fig. 1. Organizational policy pattern

Central to the organizing is the **Appointment** (task allocation in UFO-C) relator. This relator mediates the **Principal** and **Agent** role. The appointment is a relator, i.e., it is an Endurant that is existence-dependent on its relata playing these roles, but which can evolve over time. The appointment contains bundles of mutual rights and duties, or any other Hohfeldian primitive [1]. We avoid the term legal position (as the positions are typically not governed by law), but just talk about position, such as **Principal position** and **Agent Position**. The positions are correlative (as in UFO-L). Correlation does not mean that the relationship is symmetric. Typically, the Principal has certain powers not possessed by the Agent, based on the employment contract and the Principal's ownership of organizational resources.

The Agent position is a mode that inheres in the Agent role, so it is unique for each agent. The proper distribution of tasks in the organization is served by having it based on standardized roles that are subject-independent, such as Pizza Baker, Pizza Delivery Boy and Receptionist in a pizza shop. These roles have been modeled in UFO in different ways [6, 15, 21]. Here we model the **Org Position** as the types of agent positions, i.e., mode universals — what is common to all the Pizza Boys positions. The mode universals partition or *categorize* [6] the agents.

The duties of the agents are about what they should *do* or are forbidden to do in the first place. There is an *about* relationship between the agent position and an **Action Universal**, for instance "paying invoice" or "delivering a pizza". We assume that action universals can be general or more specific. On the most general level, the action type is identified by a postcondition only, for instance, "making sure that the room is clean", or "delivering orders at home". Action types can also be more specific, such as "sending goods to the home address by DHL within 48 h". When an agent performs an organizational action, for instance, paying the invoice of creditor X to the amount of $2000 on June 1, 2023, this event instantiates "paying invoice" but also "paying an international invoice above $500", for which specific rules may apply. Between action universals, there is a *subsumption* relation of generalization (and the relation of specialization/subtyping in the opposite direction)[3].

As most organizational actions involve resources being consumed or produced, there is an external dependence between Action Universal and Resource Type. When an agent performs the organizational action, it typically uses resources of the specified type. What is important here at organizational policy level is that the resources are also allocated to agents, that is, made available. Availability is not a matter of rights: it means that the agent is **Possessor** [20]. A core feature of organizations is that its agents are both *enabled* and *constrained*. Enabled means that their material job needs are fulfilled *and* that they have the required authority for the tasks (power and rights). Constrained means that they have duties and that there are also actions for which they do not have authority or that are explicitly forbidden. The Resource Allocation provides the *material* access and should be complemented with access or consumption *rights* in the Agent Position. The required alignment between these two kinds of access could be modeled with an additional anti-pattern.

Finally, an **Org Policy** is modeled as an institutional relator as well, consisting of rights and duties. As a relator, it can evolve over time. The policy does not depend on individual agents, but on the organizational community, or a subunit, in the role of **Policy Subject** and the Principal in the role of **Governor**. Note that this implies that

---

[3] Strictly speaking, the relation is a *formal* one, but OntoUML only recognizes comparative formal relations.

a community must exist first and that in some sense the Policy Building is historically dependent on the allocating.

A policy is not a goal. An **Org Goal** inheres in the Corporation and is typically derived from its relationship with external stakeholders (not included in the model). The policy is a means to achieve goals, therefore the action (and its decision) of **Policy Building** that creates the Policy is a manifestation of the Org Goal. The Policy Subject position is a mode inhering in each Organizational Member. For a given policy, there are as many subject positions as there are members, but all positions are part of the same Policy, a relator mediating the Governor and the Org Community that persists over time and varying community populations.

The **Policy Operationalization** event is very similar to Policy Building (and therefore not modeled separately, for reasons of space). The difference is that the event is not a manifestation of an Org Goal but of an already existing Principal position. With Operationalization, it is possible to create policies on multiple levels. Whether we reserve the term "policy" for the highest level only (cf. The discussions in Sect. 1), is a matter of terminology, but ontologically, a distinction can be made between policies directly and policies indirectly dependent on Org Goals.

Policy subject positions exist on the level of Community Members (allocation), whereas agent positions exist on the level of appointment/task allocation. In general, the task allocation says *what* the agent should do (its aim is division of work), while a policy states *how* the agent should do or not do it (in order to realize an Org Goal). The separation has some correspondence to functional vs non-functional requirements [14].

Example: John is hired as an employee and allocated the organizational role of *Treasurer* that has the duty to *pay invoices* (part of his Agent Position) and that has the right and power to pay invoices (also part of Agent Position), but in the case of amounts higher than $500, only after written consent of the department head. The latter rule is part of the (complex) *Financial governance* policy that implements the goal to *minimize financial risks*. John has been given access to the corporate bank account so that he *can* perform the payment.

3.2 Policy Document Pattern

We have argued that policy documents should be treated as artifacts. They are characterised by make plans (the composition) and use plans. Moreover, they are particular sorts of artifacts: abstract artifacts having contents that are repeatable across multiple individuals. In other words, their content (design) exemplifies a universal that can have many instances in multiple copies. In this paper, we represent this universal (type) dimension of policy documents, i.e., represent themas types that can multiply instantiated.

Using a symbolic artifact always implies reading, including interpretation but it can involve more. In the case of a normative document such as a manual to put together an IKEA bookcase, the use plan includes the actions undertaken, and basically says that, given the use conditions the use effect is a completed bookcase. In the case of an organizational policy, the use plan can include a deliberation action and/or the action decided upon.

Policy documents are symbolic artifacts, they can be more high-level or more operational and refer to organizational policies. There are also regulatory artifacts instrumental to the operationalization of policies (e.g. traffic signs or speed limitation devices). Here we limit ourselves to policy documents, such as bylaws, law texts, or imposed medical guidelines whose instances can be on paper but also in computer code.

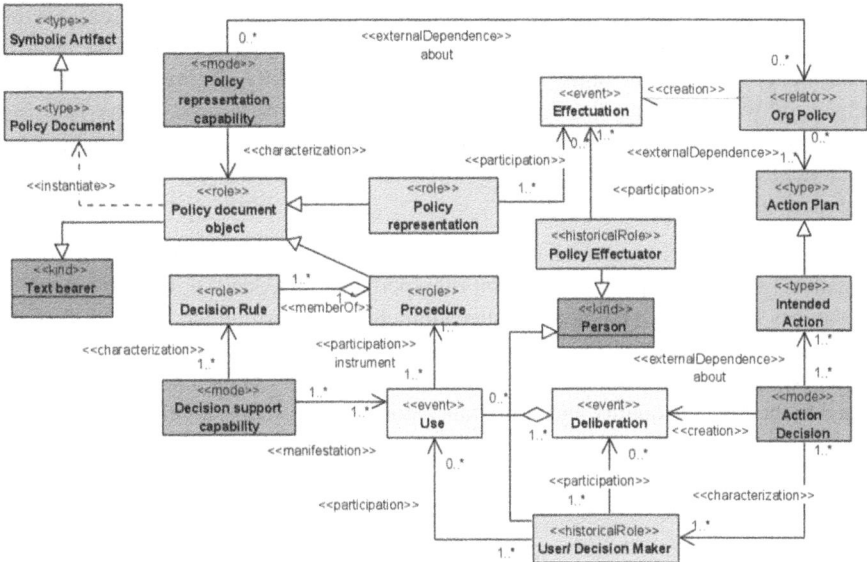

Fig. 2. Policy document pattern

Policy documents can be modeled with a life cycle (cf. [11]). They can be changed or deactivated, resulting in different policies or their removal. One essential step in the life cycle of a policy document is the *Activation* event – for instance, a decision of the board. We assume that the activation event is included in the design specification, therefore it is not modeled here. The activation is a *manifestation* of the normative power of the Activator and gives it the capability (a disposition) of law or policy document. This representational capacity that inheres in the policy document object is manifested in the creation of a Policy (see above) at a specified point in time or at an official publication event (**Effectuation**). In the case of a public standard, the document object has the policy making disposition when it is published by the standard organization and is effectuated when the organization adopts the standard. The Effectuation coincides with what we called Policy Building in Sect. 3.1. Note that this action is at the same time a manifestation of the policy making disposition, and of the power (Org Position) of the Governor and of the Org Goals of the Corporation.

Figure 2 models **Policy Document Object** (instantiating the **Policy Document** artifact as a role of some text bearer, e.g. of a piece of paper) in its **Policy representation** role and in its **Procedure** role in a **Deliberation** [13] process. The two different contexts are one reason for the document to exist in different variants, for instance, as text and as code. One practical challenge is to keep these variants consistent over time. This is where notations such as DMN[4] may help.

The **Use** event is the manifestation of a **Decision Support** capability offered by the decision rules in the Procedure. We use the term **Decision Rule** for the elements of the Procedure, aligning to some extent with the OMG definitions (Sect. 1).

Example: An organization has an ERP system in which invoices are processed according to internal controls. The system can be arranged in such a way that only the Treasurer role can order the payment, and, under certain conditions, only after consent of the Head of Department role and some other checks. In this case, the ERP software, with embedded decision rules, instantiates the Policy Document artifact that is used by the Treasurer in making the decision to pay the invoice. Strictly speaking, we should distinguish the IT application interpreting the rules from the rules themselves. They are used in combination.

Example: An oncology specialist uses a DMN table to check if there is a contra-indication to radiotherapy. The decision rule, perhaps embedded in a clinical decision service, has its basis in a Clinical Practice Guideline. We distinguish between the CPG policy *document* and the CPG *policy* adopted by the hospital (and the corresponding subject position of the specialists) which constrains the work of the oncology specialist, related to the medical quality and compliance goals. For instance, contra-indication and radiotherapy decisions (action universal) *must* be taken according to the rules (CPG policy). The DMN table *refers* to the hospital CPG policy.

3.3 Delegation Pattern

Our ontological pattern for Delegation is motivated by UFO-C [16, 17], but it deviates in some respects. We assume that the motivation for the Delegation is not a goal of the Delegatee that can be viewed in isolation, but that the Delegatee has some obligation towards a third party (in general, an internal or external customer), and that the accomplishment of the delegated action will act as partial fulfillment of this obligation. Secondly, the Delegation relator is not created out of the blue; it is historically dependent on a pre-existing institution –in the organizational setting, the agency. In other words, the starting point is that there are two relators, one between **Customer** and **Provider**, and one between **Principal** and **Agent** (the Appointment relator in Sect. 3.1). Both are defined by bundles of rights and duties (positions). We use the phrase **Authorize/Delegate,** the first part focusing on what the agent needs for his job and the second part on what the agent must do. That is why we base the **Delegation** relator on positions – to consider only goals or duties is too limited, but to consider only powers and rights as well.

The authorization/delegation action creates a new position, inhering (and unique to) the agent, but with the same action content (so there is no transfer of duties in the literal sense). By executing the Delegated Action, the agent *also* executes the service towards the Customer and his own agent duty towards the Provider/Principal. This is automatically the case when the Delegated Action is subsuming the Service Action and

---

[4] https://www.omg.org/dmn/.

the Agent action. We add this as a constraint that cannot be expressed in OntoUML itself. The constraint is a bit of a simplification, as the Delegated Action is usually a *partial* fulfillment only. For instance, the delegated action "baking the pizza" does not fulfill the pizza shop obligation to the customer fully if the pizza has to be delivered as well. The Positions are complex modes. For a further specification of the Authorization, we have modeled a historical dependency between Authorization and Appointment. Finally, the Authorization/Delegation is a manifestation of the power of the Provider/Principal in the Appointment relationship (Fig. 3).

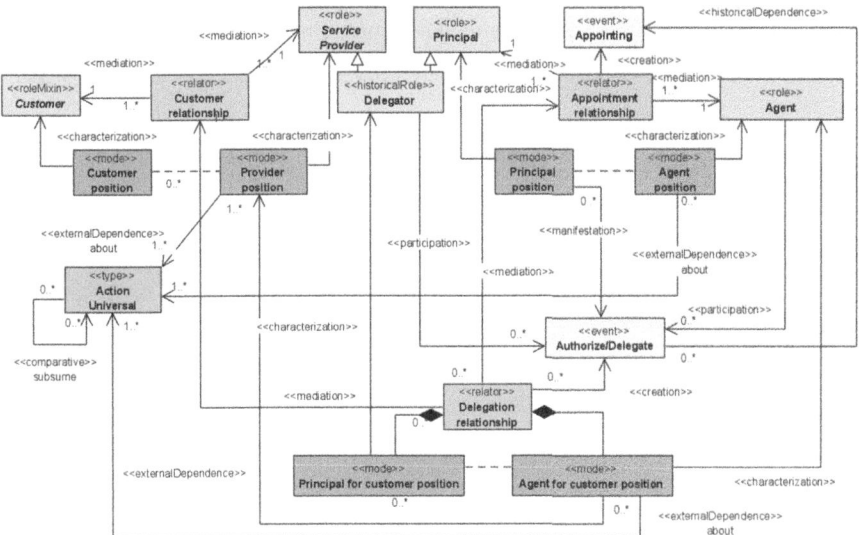

Fig. 3. Delegation/Authorization pattern

A question is whether the delegation leads to a duty of the Agent towards the Customer (and a corresponding claim from the Customer on the Agent). In general, there is no legal nor an organizational obligation between the two, but a social relationship may arise, including social commitments, as an effect of the combination of Customer and Appointment relationship.

3.4 Ruling Pattern

In any sustainable human community, there is not only coordination of tasks, but also management of social relationships which we call here roughly "ruling". The power of a Principal is based to a large extent on the resources that he owns (at least in organizations), but as Ruler of the community, his power is also based on power delegated to him. Community members choose to give away some of their privileges and powers to the Ruler in exchange for other privileges and immunities. The power delegated to the Ruler includes the power to impose sanctions on rule violators and the power to create new policies. Delegation/ authorization assumes that the Delegator has power. The power chain must start somewhere – what Donohue [8] calls the problem of anchoring. For national states, the anchoring is historically given, but there are several ways in which new Ruler/Community relationship can be set up. In the context of this paper, we do not go into the processes by which the relationship can be created but focus on the result, the relationship as an ontological pattern.

In Sect. 3.1, we made a distinction between Employing, Allocating and Appointing. Allocating is concerned with building a organizational community. Ruling is on the same level– it is aimed at maintaining the community.

Sanctions can be positive or negative. The former *put* a duty on the trespasser, such as paying a fine, the latter *take away* some of his immunities, for instance, in the case of imprisonment (Fig. 4).

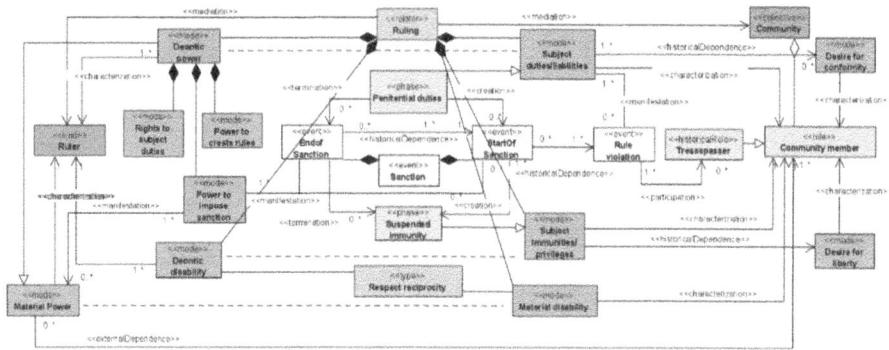

Fig. 4. The Ruler/Community pattern

We claim that the Ruling relationship is based on *reciprocity*, as most social relationships. In this case, the reciprocity is in the balance between the disabilities (in Hohfeld [1] terms) of the Ruler and of the community. Both parties restrain part of their power, in a relationship of mutual respect.

Donohue [8:151] who tried to provide an ontological account of deontic phenomena, concludes that they require two things: that there are agents invested with the authorized power to direct (directive actions), and that the directives have binding force because violation is met with sanction. Directing is a speech act done by words, but words alone are not enough. The two elements appear in our pattern in the Ruler's Power to create rules and the Power to impose sanction, respectively. In the Searlean approach followed by Donohue, these Powers are anchored in collective acceptance (cf. Sect. 2.3). In our view, the anchor is the **Respect** reciprocity in which Community Members receive certain immunities in exchange for giving away certain immunities and privileges. As long as there is a reasonable balance (as perceived by the subjects in the use context), the artifact policy/law is effective, and ruling is sustained.

The pattern is modeling the subject liabilities as historically dependent on the desire for conformity (non-conformers must be expelled), and the subject immunities as historically dependent on the desire for liberty. The dependence goes via explicit or implicit actions of acceptance not modeled here.

4 Application

As an application and an initial validation, we consider the following sentences from a university context.

1. Professor Mary has taught the Sept 11 class Databases.
2. The dean (makes a schedule and) has assigned Prof Mary to the Database class.
3. Mary is assigned by KTH as full professor on June 1, 2022.
4. KTH has issued a policy that professors are obliged to teach in Swedish only.
5. KTH has issued a general professor policy in 1832.
6. The Swedish Government has issued a professor policy for all universities in Sweden that, among others, grants professors the right/power to confer a doctorate degree.

The example sentences are analyzed one by one. Figure 5 shows the main elements of the model.

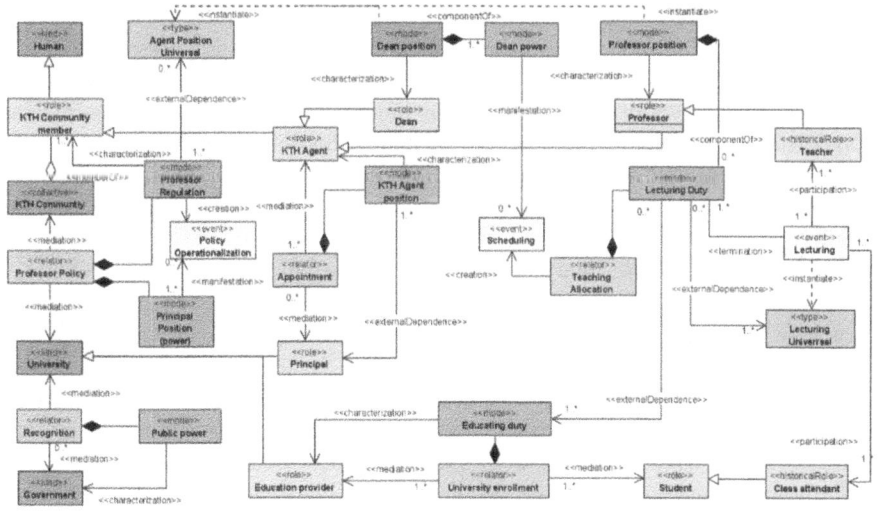

Fig. 5. University example

1. *Professor Mary has taught the sept 11 class Databases.*
   The teaching on Sept 11 is a *Lecturing* event. The event executes Mary's *Lecturing Duty.* At the same time, there is an *Enrollment* contract between University

and Student that contains a duty for the University to provide Lectures. This service obligation has been *delegated* to Mary. In other words, Mary's lecturing executes/terminates a twofold duty (instantiates the Action Plan of the duty): the duty that is in her *Employment* contract and a duty because the Dean allocates the specific course to her (sentence 2). Moreover, the duty is externally dependent on the educating duty that the University has towards the Students as well as. The teaching instantiates a Teaching universal, in this case, the Teaching Databases universal.

2. *The dean makes a schedule and has assigned Prof Mary to the Database class*

Creating or specializing an organizational duty, such as someone's duty to teach a class, requires (is a *manifestation* of) *Power*. The power is granted to the Dean, as part of the Dean's agent position (a complex mode), given a priori or by means of a later *delegation/authorization* action. With this power, the Dean delegates the duty to Prof Mary.

The sentence talks about a schedule. The schedule itself (not in the figure) is a *policy document* that refers to the policy containing the duties of Mary and the other professors. The schedule is used by Mary in her decisions on what to do next semester. The same document can be used for other purposes as well, e.g. by the financial office to allocate budget to Mary's department.

3. *Mary is assigned by KTH as full professor on June 1, 2022.*
4. *KTH has issued a general professor policy in 1827*

Mary's assignment is an *employment contract* that includes *allocation* – she becomes a member of the KTH community – and a *task allocation*. KTH as Principal has defined *organizational positions*, including full Professor in terms of rights and duties. The organizational agents, as community members, are subject (liability) to the normative power of the Principal. This implies that when KTH defines such an organizational position in 1827, as part of a policy, this definition holds for each organizational agent that is member of the KTH community, not in the sense that each organizational agent gets the role defined, but that if she is assigned this position, the rights and duties hold.

5. *KTH Has Issued a Policy that Professors Are Obliged to Teach in Swedish Only.*

This is a Policy duty part of the organization relator that comes on top of the general teaching policy and applies (external dependency) to the position Professor. The duty refers to an *Action Universal* (not included in Fig. 5) "teaching in Swedish". When Mary is lecturing in Swedish, she instantiates this Action Universal and executes the duty. The new policy is a high-level policy that implements a (new or old) *Org Goal*, or it is a *Policy Operationalization* of the general professor policy.

6. *The Swedish Government has issued a professor policy for all universities in Sweden that, among others, grants professors the right/power to confer a doctorate degree*

The left-bottom part Fig. 5 models the recognition relator that exists between the Swedish government and university institutions that follows the organizational policy pattern in the public domain. The government has the normative power to define positions, associate legal rights to them, and *delegate power*. The university is subject to this power. The power of the university as Principal, with respect to conferring legally recognized doctorate degrees, is grounded in the power delegated to it in the context of the recognition.

5 Conclusion

Although extensive research has been done on rule languages and enterprise modeling of policies, ontological analysis of organizational policies in general and based on the foundational ontology UFO in particular is limited so far. This paper fills the gap in several ways. (1) Earlier work in UFO conceptualized policies as normative descriptions. We have argued instead for a dual nature view of policies that acknowledges both their institutional embedding and their artifact aspect. The artifact aspect connects policies with the area of Decision Support Systems, but also provides a design perspective, with notions such as design objects, make plan, use plan, use conditions and use context (2) Our organizational policy ontology is compliant with UFO-L but transfers it to the organizational domain and adds the resource management dimension. (3) We have generalized the UFO-C Delegation pattern to authorization/delegation, with a key role given to positions rather than goals, embedded in relationships. (4) To address the anchoring challenge as described by Donohue [8], we have proposed a Ruling pattern grounded in reciprocity. Following Donohue, we have explicitly included sanctioning. Contra Donohue, we have suggested that the policy effectiveness requires an acceptance by use rather than an acceptance by belief.

We posit that this ontology can clarify conceptual distinctions around policy such as made in the OMG standards (Sect. 1). In the definitions of OMG and others, policies are distinguished from rules (or procedures) in being more abstract. In our ontology, the abstractness is only one dimension; ontologically, there are several relevant distinctions. One is between a policy as an institutional relator and the policy document with rules. The policy document is concrete in the sense that it has a material basis, and it has a role of guiding decisions – the procedure role. Another distinction becomes visible when we consider the chain that starts with Policy Building (creating a policy that manifests the Goal), and that continues via Policy Operationalization and Authorization/Delegation, to the allocation of specific tasks on agents (managerial level), up to the operational level of Decisions and the execution of concrete actions. For the Principal/head of the corporation, a policy is typically an output (something to create), for the Manager it is something to be operationalized (input and output) and for the work floor agent the policy is, what his decisions and actions should comply with (input). So, there are indeed levels of abstraction, albeit relative – in our ontology the levels show up in the subsumption relationship between Action Plans, up to their instantiation.

Future work: the policy ontology in this paper requires more empirical validation, for instance by applying it to an actual policy. Furthermore, we aim to connect it to other organizational ontologies, such as the decision-making ontology [13].

References

1. Alexy, R.: A Theory of Constitutional Rights. Oxford University Press, Oxford (2009). https://doi.org/10.1080/17521467.2009.11424683
2. Becker, G.S., Murphy, K.M.: The division of labor, coordination costs, and knowledge. Q. J. Econ. **107**(4), 1137–1160 (1992)
3. Boella, G., Lesmo, L., Damiano, R.: On the ontological status of norms. Law and the Semantic Web: Legal Ontologies, Methodologies, Legal Information Retrieval, and Applications, pp. 125–141 (2005)

4. Borgo, S., Ferrario, R., et al.: DOLCE: a descriptive ontology for linguistic and cognitive engineering. Appl. Ontol. **17**(1), 45–69 (2022)
5. Bottazzi, E., Ferrario, R.: Preliminaries to a DOLCE ontology of organisations. Int. J. Bus. Process Integr. Manage. **4**(4), 225–238 (2009)
6. Carvalho, V.A., Almeida, J.P.A., Fonseca, C.M., Guizzardi, G.: Multi-level ontology-based conceptual modeling. Data Knowl. Eng. **109**, 3–24 (2017)
7. Ceusters, W., Smith, B.: Aboutness: towards foundations for the information artifact ontology. In: Proceedings of the Sixth International Conference on Biomedical Ontology (ICBO) CEUR 1515 (2015)
8. Donohue, B.J.: Social ontology and social normativity. Doctoral dissertation, State University of New York at Buffalo (2020). https://philpapers.org/rec/DONSOA-3
9. Eisenhardt, K.M.: Agency theory: an assessment and review. Acad. Manag. Rev. **14**(1), 57–74 (1989)
10. Griffo, C., Almeida, J.P.A., Lima, J.A.O., et al: Legal powers, subjections, disabilities, and immunities: ontological analysis and modeling patterns. Data Knowl. Eng. (2023). https://doi.org/10.1016/j.datak.2023.102219
11. Griffo, C., Araujo, L.C., Brasil, M., et al.: Modeling the dynamics of contractual relations. Front. Artif. Intell. **6**, 1042319 (2023)
12. Guizzardi, G., de Almeida Falbo, R., Guizzardi, R.S.: Grounding software domain ontologies in the unified foundational ontology (UFO): the case of the ode software process ontology. In: CIbSE, pp. 127–140 (2008)
13. Guizzardi, R., Carneiro, B. G., Porello, D., Guizzardi, G.: A core ontology on decision making. In: Proceedings of the ONTOBRAS 2020 CEUR-WS, vol. 2728, pp. 9–21 (2020)
14. Guizzardi, G.: Ontological foundations for structural conceptual models. Ph.D. thesis, CTIT, Centre for Telematics and Information Technology, Enschede (2005)
15. Masolo, C., Vieu, L., Bottazzi, E., et al: Social roles and their descriptions. In: Proceedings of the KR2004, pp. 267–277 (2004)
16. de Oliveira Bringuente, A.C., de Almeida Falbo, R., Guizzardi, G.: Using a foundational ontology for reengineering a software process ontology. J. Inf. Data Manag. **2**(3), 511 (2011)
17. Poletaeva, T., Guizzardi, G., Almeida, J.P.A., Abdulrab, H.: Revisiting the DEMO transaction pattern with the unified foundational ontology (UFO). In: Advances in Enterprise Engineering XI: EEWC 2017, pp. 181–195 (2017)
18. Roversi, C.: On the artifactual - and natural - character of legal institutions. In: Burazin, L., Himma, K., Roversi, C. (eds.) Law as an Artifact, Oxford (2018)
19. Searle, J.R.: The Construction of Social Reality. Simon and Schuster (1995)
20. Scheller, C.V., Hruby, P.: Business process and value delivery modeling using possession, ownership, and availability (POA) in enterprises and business networks. J. Inf. Syst. **30**(2), 5–47 (2016)
21. Toyoshima, F.: Roles and their three facets: a foundational perspective. Appl. Ontol. **16**(2), 161–192 (2021)
22. Weigand, H., Johannesson, P., Andersson, B.: An artifact ontology for design science research. Data Knowl. Eng. **133**, 19 (2021). https://doi.org/10.1016/j.datak.2021.101878
23. Weigand, H., Johannesson, P.: Information entities and artifact ontology. In: Proceedings of the VMBO workshop co-located with CAiSE 2022, CEUR, vol. 3155 (2022)
24. Weigand, H., Johannesson P. Andersson, A.: Ontological analysis of policy-based decision making. In: Proceedings of the VMBO 2024. CEUR (2024)

Correction to: Towards Timeline-Based Layout for Process Mining

Harleen Kaur, Jan Mendling, Timotheus Kampik, and Christoffer Rubensson

Correction to:
Chapter 12 in: E. Paja et al. (Eds.): *The Practice of Enterprise Modeling*, **LNBIP 538,**
https://doi.org/10.1007/978-3-031-77908-4_12

In the originally published version of chapter 12, the wrong DFG grant number has been stated. In addition, footnote 5 stated a wrong URL and on page 3, ref. 3 was listed twice in the same multi-citation. This has been corrected.

The updated version of this chapter can be found at
https://doi.org/10.1007/978-3-031-77908-4_12

© IFIP International Federation for Information Processing 2025
Published by Springer Nature Switzerland AG 2025
E. Paja et al. (Eds.): PoEM 2024, LNBIP 538, p. C1, 2025.
https://doi.org/10.1007/978-3-031-77908-4_18

Author Index

A
Ahmadi, Zahra 67
Alfuhaid, Sofana 227
Amyot, Daniel 227
Anda, Amal Ahmed 227
Antipenko, Vjatšeslav 244

B
Bider, Ilia 52
Bork, Dominik 175
Buchmann, Robert Andrei 157

C
Cammaerts, Felix 140
Curty, Simon 87

F
Fill, Hans-Georg 87
Franch, Xavier 19

G
Gavric, Aleksandar 175
Ghiran, Ana-Maria 157
Guizzardi, Giancarlo 279
Gutschmidt, Anne 105

H
Henkel, Martin 52
Herbaut, Nicolas 262
Hoppenbrouwers, Stijn 207

J
Johannesson, Paul 279

K
Kampik, Timotheus 192
Kaur, Harleen 192
Kiomba Kambilo, Eddy 262
Kolev, Peter-Alexander 123

L
Lennartsson, Dan 3
Léonard, Michel 35

M
Matulevičius, Raimundas 244
Mekhryukova, Vlada 140
Mendling, Jan 192
Mulder, Mark A. T. 207
Mylopoulos, John 227

N
Nast, Benjamin 105

P
Pastor, Joan Antoni 19
Perjons, Erik 52
Portell, Xavier 19
Proper, Henderik A. 175
Pruss, Hauke Hansen 123

R
Ralyté, Jolita 35
Raudberget, Dag 3
Roveri, Marco 227
Rubensson, Christoffer 192
Rychkova, Irina 262

S
Sandkuhl, Kurt 3, 123
Seigerroth, Ulf 3
Serral, Estefanía 67
Snoeck, Monique 67, 140
Souveyet, Carine 262
Sunnotel, Joris 207

V
Vanderfeesten, Irene 67

W
Weigand, Hans 279
Wilken, Jim Robert 123
Wyffels, Mathis 67

The manufacturer's authorised representative in the EU is Springer Nature Customer Service Centre GmbH, Europaplatz 3, 69115 Heidelberg, Germany. If you have any concerns regarding our products, please contact ProductSafety@springernature.com

Printed and bound by CPI Group (UK) Ltd, Croydon, CR0 4YY

25/03/2026

02078191-0013